Engineering Real Time Systems

An object-oriented methodology using SDL

Rolv Bræk

SINTEF DELAB and
Department of Computer Systems and Telematics
The Norwegian Institute of Technology

Øystein Haugen

Norwegian Computing Center

D1316092

Prentice Hall
New York   London   Toronto   Sydney   Tokyo   Singapore

First published 1993 by
Prentice Hall International (UK) Ltd
Campus 400, Maylands Avenue
Hemel Hempstead
Hertfordshire, HP2 7EZ
A division of
Simon & Schuster International Group

Printed and bound in Great Britain at
Redwood Books Trowbridge

Library of Congress Cataloging-in-Publication Data

Braek, Rolv.
  Engineering real-time systems: an object-oriented
  methodology using SDL/Rolv Braek, Øystain
  Haugen.
    p. cm.—(BCS practitioner series)
  Includes bibliographical references and index.
  ISBN 0–13–034448–6
  1. Real-time data processing. 2. Object-oriented
  programming. 3. SDL (Computer program
  language)
  I. Haugen, Øystein. II. Title. III. Series.
QA76.54.B73 1993
005.1′2—dc20   93–7069
                                              CIP

British Library Cataloguing in Publication Data

A catalogue record for this book is available from
the British Library

ISBN 0-13-034448-6

---

2 3 4 5 97 96 95 94 93

–

Engineering Real Time Systems

BCS Practitioner Series

Series Editor: Ray Welland

BELINA ET AL   SDL: with applications from protocol specification
BRINKWORTH   Software quality management: a pro-active approach
FOLKES/STUBENVOLL   Accelerated systems development
GIBSON   Managing computer projects: avoiding the pitfalls
HIPPERSON   Practical systems analysis: for users, managers and analysts
HORROCKS/MOGG   Practical data administration
MONK ET AL   Improving your human–computer interface: a practical technique
THE RAISE LANGUAGE GROUP   The RAISE specification language
TANSLEY/HAYBALL   Knowledge based systems analysis and design: a KADS developer's handbook
VERYARD   Information modelling: practical guidance
WELLMAN   Software costing

Contents

Foreword   ix

Editorial Preface   xi

Preface   xiii
   1   Objective   xiii
   2   Background   xiv
   3   Intended audience and use   xv
   4   Outline of the book   xvi
   5   Acknowledgements   xvii

Part I Understanding Real Time Systems   **1**

1   **The Systems Engineering Context**   **3**
   1.1 The problem   3
   1.2 Major principles of systems engineering   9
   1.3 Managing the system evolution   17

2   **Basic Principles**   **23**
   2.1 Introduction to the system example   23
   2.2 Systems   26
   2.3 Techniques to manage complexity   32
   2.4 Approaches to behaviour description   39
   2.5 Some description approaches   44
   2.6 The methodology presented here   54
   2.7 The SOON notation   56

Part II Specification   61

3   Requirements Specifications   **63**
   3.1   The problem   63
   3.2   The *AccessControl* system   73

4   SDL – Structure and Behaviour   **94**
   4.1   SDL – CCITT Specification and Description Language 94
   4.2   Nested Blocks   97
   4.3   What is a process?   102
   4.4   Innermost block with processes   103
   4.5   Process behaviour   106
   4.6   Substructure   112
   4.7   Services   114
   4.8   SDL symbol summary   115

5   SDL – Data   **118**
   5.1   What is data?   118
   5.2   Simple data in SDL   119
   5.3   Advanced data in SDL   132
   5.4   Shared variables and enabling conditions   142
   5.5   Dynamic generation of process instances   145
   5.6   SDL symbol summary   148

6   SDL – Macros and Procedures   **150**
   6.1   Similarities   150
   6.2   Macro   151
   6.3   Procedure   153
   6.4   Differences between macro and procedure   157
   6.5   Value returning procedures   159
   6.6   Remote procedures   160
   6.7   SDL symbol summary   161

7   Object-oriented SDL   **163**
   7.1   Introduction   163
   7.2   Types and instances revisited   164
   7.3   Inheritance and modification   168
   7.4   Packages   177
   7.5   Context parameters   180

8   SDL Method   **184**
   8.1   Objectives   184
   8.2   System versus product   186
   8.3   Behaviour   187

8.4	Data types	205
8.5	Block structure	206
8.6	Signal routing	210
8.7	Types	212
8.8	Step-wise guidelines	213

Part III Design and Implementation   215

9 Implementation Design   217
9.1	What is implementation design?	217
9.2	Differences between real systems and SDL systems	225
9.3	Implementation descriptions	234
9.4	Design considerations	243

10 Software Design   256
10.1	The problem	256
10.2	Concurrency and time	260
10.3	Communication	265
10.4	Implementing the SDL processes	276
10.5	Overall software design	288
10.6	Hardware design	294
10.7	Step-wise guidelines to implementation design	295

11 Implementation in C++   298
11.1	Coding principles	298
11.2	Run-time support systems	302
11.3	Interfacing to foreign code	325
11.4	Configuring SDL systems	327
11.5	Debugging	329
11.6	Maintenance of the code	331

12 Verification and Validation   333
12.1	What is verification and validation?	333
12.2	Techniques	335
12.3	Reviews	335
12.4	Testing SDL systems	337
12.5	Validating interfaces	342

Part IV Evolution   353

13 Reuse Methodology   355
13.1	What is "reuse"?	355
13.2	What can be reused from *AccessControl* ?	357
13.3	Example: bank	359

13.4 Modes of reuse   375
13.5 Designing for reuse   376
13.6 Conclusion   378

14   Maintenance   379
14.1 What is maintenance?   379
14.2 Related activities   381
14.3 Organising maintenance   382
14.4 Using the methodology   383
14.5 Summary of the methodology   384

Bibliography   387

Index   393

Foreword

This book addresses a question of strategic importance for any company trying to make a living out of systems development: how to improve the company's ability to deliver the right quality on time at a competitive price. In other words: how can a company gain control over the development process, reduce its costs and lead times and improve the product quality, all at the same time?.

In 1989 a group of companies and research institutes in Norway initiated the SISU project having as its main goal to find and implement common answers to this question. As project leader it was my responsibility to build consensus around viable solutions that would produce the desired effect in the companies.

The participating companies make a diverse range of products, mostly sold on the international market-place: there are small data storage devices produced in large volumes, complex telecommunication products specifically tailored to each customer, military systems and signal processing systems. They have one thing in common: they are embedded, reactive systems facing real time and performance requirements.

To improve their practices, the companies asked for two things: better tools and better methods. They considered methods as a prerequisite for successful utilisation of the SDL language and its tools. The project therefore initiated an effort to provide methodology guidelines that would help the companies to make the most of their SDL usage. The result is what you are holding in your hands right now. It describes an object-oriented methodology taking you from requirements to implementation.

The companies have provided the authors with constant feedback from their applications. The authors are themselves experienced practitioners and have been able to give the methodology the practical bias needed for successful deployment on real projects. Once a company has started to use the methodology, it has so far continued to use it on new projects. The methodology also seems to form a sound base for using upcoming tools supporting formal analysis and automatic code generation.

Geir Melby

ix

Editorial Preface

The aim of the BCS Practitioner Series is to produce books which are relevant for practising computer professionals across the whole spectrum of information technology activities. We want to encourage practitioners to share their practical experience of methods and applications with fellow professionals. We also seek to disseminate information in a form which is suitable for the practitioner who often has only limited time to read widely within a new subject area or to assimilate research findings.

The role of the BCS is to provide advice on the suitability of books for the series, via the editorial panel and to provide a pool of potential authors upon which we can draw. Our objective is that this series will reinforce the drive within the BCS to increase professional standards in IT. The other partners in this venture, Prentice Hall, provide the publishing expertise and international marketing capabilities of a leading publisher in the computing field.

The response when we set up the series was extremely encouraging. However, the success of the series depends on there being practitioners who want to learn as well as those who feel they have something to offer! The series is under continual development and we are always looking for ideas for new topics and feedback on how to further improve the usefulness of the series. If you are interested in writing for the series then please contact us.

The complexity of modern real time systems makes their development a very challenging task. The authors of this book have used their wide experience of developing real time systems to produce an integrated set of methods for the production of such systems. The book brings together three key elements: communications and real time systems, software engineering methods and object-oriented techniques. The book uses SDL 92 as its implementation language, an up-to-date CCITT standard incorporating object-oriented principles.

Ray Welland
Computing Science Department, University of Glasgow

Editorial panel members
Frank Bott (UCW, Aberystwyth), Dermot Browne (KPMG Management Consulting),
Nic Holt (ICL), Trevor King (Praxis Systems Plc), Tom Lake (GLOSSA), Kathy Spurr
(Analysis and Design Consultants), Mario Wolczko (University of Manchester)

Preface

1   Objective

The objective of this book is to help the reader master the complexity of modern real time systems. As the application domain of these systems gradually extends into almost every part of modern life, their quality becomes more and more critical to individuals, companies and society as a whole. At the same time, steadily growing ambitions drive the complexity up and make the desired quality even harder to achieve. A methodology that helps companies and individuals to master the complexity and get quality under control is therefore in great demand.

Although the literature in software engineering in general is rich, few methods are devoted to the specific problems of real time systems. Those that do exist tend to address only some parts of the problem, whereas the developer needs an integrated and well-balanced approach to the whole problem. This book presents an integrated set of methods – a methodology – that gives a fairly broad coverage of the technical aspects. Managerial and organisational aspects are not specifically treated, although the methodology provides opportunities for improvement in those areas too.

What are the elements of this methodology? Since most quality problems stem from the complexity of system behaviour, the cornerstone is a formal definition of the functional behaviour expressed in a clear and concise way that can be understood, communicated and analysed independently from the implementation. Such a *functional design* is the basis for quality control, since it helps to understand and to validate the system behaviour at an early stage. It is also the starting point of *implementation design* where the functional design is mapped to a physical implementation. This process is eased by the fact that most concepts of the functional design are efficiently implementable and that workable guidelines for implementation design are provided in the methodology. As a result the functional design may be used both as input to the implementation design step and to document the functionality that is actually implemented. This means that a designer may trust the functional design to be valid for the implementation.

The specification and description language SDL (CCITT Z.100, 1993) defined by the CCITT, is used to express functional designs. This is an internationally standardised language, that has been successfully applied on numerous projects ranging from the development of small control units to highly complex communication systems.

This book does more than describe SDL, however, it offers a set of guidelines and extensions that helps using SDL to make functional designs that are clear and concise, providing an efficient vehicle for understanding and communication in a development team.

The book also describes how to design and document a hardware and software combination that faithfully and reliably implements the functional design. A number of guidelines are provided as well as notations for implementation design of hardware and software systems at the architectural level. The focus of implementation design is on additional information needed to map a functional design into a physical implementation satisfying requirements to non-functional properties. Thus, the implementation design complements the functional design of the system.

In addition to the design aspects, the methodology offers support for the initial requirement specification and for the later implementation. Aspects of reuse and evolution are also covered. An object-oriented perspective is applied all the way.

Using the methodology to its full potential is to work *design-oriented*. Being design-oriented means that systems are understood, validated and maintained primarily on the design level, while the implementations are derived more or less automatically. Design orientation requires a language for functional design that combines formality with readability and implementability. SDL provides that and even more; it has the object-oriented features needed to support composition and reuse on the design level.

Its potential for supporting design-oriented systems engineering sets this methodology apart from more pragmatic methodologies based on informal notations.

2   Background

There has been a substantial interaction with the users during the course of writing this book. A previous version has been used extensively on continuing education courses for the industry and, subsequently, on actual development projects. (Experiences are reported in Brechtbuehl, 1991). This has provided the authors with numerous comments and suggestions for improvements that have been included in this version. We are therefore confident that the methodology presented here works in real life.

The authors have long experience from applying the principles described in this book to real life applications in the fields of telematics, process control and software engineering tools.

Object orientation is a key principle that the methodology seeks to apply on all abstraction levels. One of the authors has a computer science background and much experience from the development and use of object-oriented languages such as SIMULA. The other author has a background in telematics and practical experience from the development of switching systems and similar real time applications.

One system may serve to illustrate the kind of background experience this book is based on: MAREIK – the first system in the world to provide fully automatic telephone and telex services to ships through satellites in the INMARSAT system. It was developed by EB, now ABB Nera, for the Norwegian Telecom Administration during 1979–1981. The project was faced by a number of challenges.

- The INMARSAT system was new and unproven.
- The system requirements were not stable.
- Requirements of reliability and error handling were severe. Fault-tolerance was needed to guarantee system availability.
- Performance and response times were critical.
- It was a new product line, where software and hardware were developed from scratch.

The project eventually involved a team of some 40 software people that developed software written in PL/M, running on hardware comprising some 30 microprocessors in a network. It was quite turbulent at times and suffered many of the problems so common to similar projects. However, the result was a system with such good quality that it earned EB a very good reputation and a big share of the world market for such systems. The MAREIK system has been consistently the most reliable INMARSAT shore station since its introduction in 1981.

This could not have been achieved without a methodology which helped the development team to communicate unambiguously and develop a thorough common understanding of the application and the system. Such systems are so complex and must be so reliable that *ad hoc* programming is completely inadequate. To succeed in the long run, a quality promoting methodology is essential on such large systems. But the methodology is also useful on smaller systems. The limitations lie more in the type of application than the size of the system.

3 Intended audience and use

The book is intended for a broad range of people interested in the specification, design and implementation of real time systems.

- Students and teachers can use the book both as a textbook and a practical guide to this exciting and complex field.
- Users and buyers of real time systems can use the book as a guide to their role in practical quality control.

- Specifiers can learn how to structure specifications so they become clear and unambiguous.
- Designers and implementors can learn how to derive implementation designs and then correctly and reliably implement the system.
- Managers can use the methodology to get a good practical grip on quality control and project management.

To understand the design and implementation part, it is necessary that the reader has some background in programming and has basic knowledge about real time software: interrupts, scheduling and synchronisation. Otherwise, the book is self-contained.

The book can be used for self-study, but simply reading the book will not be sufficient. It is essential to work with a practical example and to discuss it with other people. Even then, there may be problems in your first application that are better solved with a little assistance from people with more experience. We therefore recommend seeking the assistance of experienced people during the first project using this methodology. Following a project through implementation and test is a great eye-opener that has helped many people to see the purpose and value of a functional design.

4   Outline of the book

The book is organised into four parts.

Part I *Understanding real time systems.*
   This part provides context, motivation and underlying principles for the other parts. Chapter 1 introduces the systems engineering framework. Chapter 2 introduces the notion of a real time system and discusses some basic principles for describing and understanding such systems. It also introduces the system example used throughout the remaining book.
Part II *Specification.*
   Chapter 3, treats the requirements specifications or how to specify the essential external requirements to the system without going into unnecessary detail about internal operations or physical realisation. Notations for conceptual modelling and interface behaviours are introduced. Chapters 4–8 treat functional design, i.e. how to define the complete functional behaviour that can be observed at the system interfaces. First, the SDL language is described in Chapters 4–7, then methodology guidelines for using SDL to express functional designs in a clear and concise way are given in Chapter 8.
Part III *Design and implementation.*
   Chapter 9 introduces the implementation design problem. It discusses the common difficulties and the main design steps in going from an abstract functional design to an implementation satisfying requirements to non-functional properties such as performance, exception handling and modularity. A graphic notation used to describe hardware and software designs on the

architectural level is also introduced. Chapter 10 treats software design in more detail and Chapter 11 provides implementation examples in C++. Finally, in Chapter 12 the verification and validation issue is treated.

Part IV *Evolution.*

Chapter 13 deals with aspects of reuse and system evolution while Chapter 14 looks into maintenance.

The book is centred around a system example which is gradually developed through the chapters. This serves to illustrate the various aspects of a realistic, yet modest, system development. The system example is an access control system.

5   Acknowledgements

This book has been written as part of the SISU project, a Norwegian technology transfer program with the goal of improving the productivity and quality of companies that develop systems within the real time domain. The authors are very grateful for the confidence the project has shown by giving us the opportunity and continuous support needed to write this book. The enthusiastic and constructive criticism of numerous members of the project and others have contributed substantially to its quality. We will specifically mention Finn Arve Aagesen, Dag Belsnes, Harald Botnevik, Dag Brenna, Stein Erik Ellevseth, Jacqueline Floch, Luc Jadoul, Joe Gorman, Otto Grønningen, Arvid Strømme, Johan Fredrik Lindeberg, Geir Melby, Birger Møller-Pedersen, Ronny Nergård, Kristen Rekdal , Georg Ræder, Richard Sanders and Øystein Skogstad.

Eva Hedman helped a great deal by thoroughly checking all the SDL descriptions for syntactical and semantical errors.

The contributions of Geir Hasnes are especially acknowledged. Geir was our co-author during the initial draft of the book, but had to leave us after that due to other appointments. His ideas and comments are much appreciated.

We also wish to thank SINTEF DELAB and ABB Corporate Research Norway, for their support.

Rolv Bræk
Trondheim

Øystein Haugen
Oslo

Part I

Understanding Real Time Systems

This part provides context, motivation and underlying principles for the other parts. Chapter 1 introduces the systems engineering framework. Chapter 2 introduces the notion of a real time system and discusses some basic principles for describing and understanding such systems. It also introduces the system example used throughout the remainder of the book.

The Systems Engineering Context

This chapter starts by looking at the major reasons why quality systems are so hard to make. The notion of quality is defined and the major principles used to achieve quality are introduced. A reference model that covers the initial development of a system and its subsequent use as a product is outlined. No attempt is made to cover all aspects of systems engineering. The purpose is to outline a few key ideas that will place the following chapters in context.

1.1   The problem

1.1.1   Symptoms

The quality and cost of software has been a growing concern for many years. All too often software has been delivered long behind schedule at much higher cost than anticipated, without giving the desired benefits and user satisfaction. The symptoms are clear and well-known, but what is the cure?

The term *"software engineering"* was coined at a NATO conference in 1968 (Naur and Randell, 1969), to indicate that the solution would be to introduce systematic methods like those used in other engineering disciplines into the software field.

Have the years since 1968 brought any solutions then? In some respects yes, in others no. Substantial improvements have been made in both the productivity and quality of software development. At the same time the complexity of the systems has been steadily increasing making the problems more difficult to handle. Therefore, the typical symptoms of the software crisis can still be seen: unsatisfied customers, high cost, late projects and a shortage of qualified personnel. Many companies still experience the software development process as being unpredictable and uncontrollable, in spite of more than 20 years of effort spent on software engineering.

This lack of control is particularly unsatisfying since we are becoming more and more dependent on software. The consequences of faulty and unreliable systems are more severe now than ever.

Since 1968 the proportion of software content in systems has increased dramatically and so has the effort spent on maintenance of software. For every man-year spent on development many companies spend 2–3 man-years on maintenance. This is not necessarily bad, if it means that the product is popular and somebody is willing to pay for it. But in many cases valuable resources are tied up fixing quality defects that should not have been there in the first place.

1.1.2   Reasons

So what are the underlying reasons for these problems? Is the technology itself too hard to master? Quite the contrary; the technology itself is so simple that even children can use it! Not many high school children design VLSI circuits or suspension bridges, but quite a few of them make software and quite complex software too. So, up to a point, the technology itself is quite simple. But when the complexity of the software grows beyond a certain limit we seem to lose control and start making errors that are hard to correct.

The errors we make are roughly of three kinds.

- We plan a functionality that is not in harmony with the purpose of the system.
- We define the functionality in a way that is internally inconsistent.
- We implement a different functionality than the one we planned.

Unlike physical systems, software is not exposed to wear and tear. The errors are products of human failure and not of physical processes. Thus, the creation of software is constrained more by our mental capabilities than by physical processes. It is not the technology itself, but the conceptual complexity of its application domains that causes problems.

Although software does not wear out in the traditional sense, a piece of software will quickly get obsolete if it is not upgraded in step with the user expectations. Thus, to master software engineering it is not only necessary to master complexity, we have to cope with changing requirements as well.

All this sets software engineering apart from other engineering disciplines. It also makes alternative approaches to software engineering extremely hard to evaluate and to compare. Today there is no objective and generally accepted yardstick by which different approaches can be measured. They can only be measured more subjectively by the extent to which people find them useful in improving their performance.

There are a number of reasons why we make errors.

- It is hard to understand the purpose of a system well enough to plan its functionality in advance so that it really will satisfy the users needs.
- The complexity of systems and, in particular, their dynamic behaviour is too high. Even moderately complex behaviours tend to exceed our mental limits and thereby cause us to make errors both in functionality and implementation.
- The invisible nature of the product (behaviour), makes the development and maintenance process itself difficult to understand and control.
- There is a lack of proven components to use as high level building blocks. Too much is developed from scratch.

These reasons are not specific for software. But they are more profound in software because software is used to implement more complex behaviours than other technologies. Consequently, the solutions we seek will not be found by looking at the characteristics of the software itself. Rather, we must attack the core of the problem: functionality, complexity, visibility and reusability. To that end the emphasis has to be shifted away from the software itself towards "systemware". In consequence, the emphasis of this book is not on software engineering, but on systems engineering. In this perspective software can be seen as one implementation technology among several others such as electronics, pneumatics and "humanware".

1.1.3 Quality

"The test of the machine is the satisfaction it gives you. There isn't any other test. If the machine produces tranquillity, it´s right. If it disturbs you, it´s wrong until either the machine or your mind is changed." (Pirzig, 1976)

The methodology presented in this book focuses mainly on quality, but in a way that also promotes productivity. So, what is quality?

At the end of the day the quality of a system is determined by how well it fulfils its purpose. This will depend on the role it is supposed to play in its environment. In this respect system quality is not an absolute measure, but a relative one that depends on where and by whom, the system is used. Thus, a given system can have good quality in one context and poor quality in another. Quality can be seen as the systems ability to satisfy the needs and expectations of its environment.

Consequently, the first issue in quality control is to understand the needs and expectations of the environment.

In the environment there are people and there are other systems. Some will interact directly with the system in question, while others depend less directly on it. Users sitting at their terminals will interact directly with the system. A company manager, on the other hand, may not interact with the system directly, but will depend on its ability to provide cost-effective services to the users on his/her staff. Employees may not interact with a pay-roll system either, but they still depend on its services to get their salaries.

We may now identify three main roles that people and other systems play in relation to a given system.

- *Users.* This role is played by all those who interact directly with the system and use the system services to achieve some operative purpose. In addition to people, this role may be played by other technical systems, such as the process plant controlled by a process control system. Characteristic of this role is the direct dependency and communication between the system and the actors of the role.

- *Owners.* Owners are people that will either own or be responsible for the system during parts of its lifetime. Typical for this role is a preoccupation with economy and cost–benefit considerations. In a manufacturing company this role is played by the people responsible for the system as a product, i.e. the product owner. At a customer site it is played by the people responsible for an individual system's installation, i.e. the installation owner.

- *Subjects.* Subjects are known to the system, but do not directly interact with it. Typical examples are people and objects represented in a database, e.g. the customers of a company.

Of course, this is a very general classification, but it is sufficient for the purpose of this discussion. In addition to the roles above, a fourth role is essential in system development.

- *Developers.* These are the people that actually develop the system such as system designers, software designers, hardware designers and programmers.

None of these roles are mutually exclusive. One and the same person may play several roles and each role may be played by several people and/or other systems. In this picture the user may be the same person as the owner or may be a different person. The owner may be a manager and the user a staff member. Quite often the owner will act as a moderator of the users needs. Sometimes the users are not available for direct communication with the developer at all. During the system development the users may even be some imaginary people in the market the system is developed for. It is obviously quite a challenge to understand the needs and expectations of unknown persons. Nevertheless, the final test is how users actually feel about the system. This will depend on the functionality provided by the system and, in addition, on how dependable it is.

The quality of the system will depend mainly on how well it satisfies the needs of the users and the owners. It is the responsibility of the developer to build the right system and thereby achieve quality.

We now define quality in relation to the users and the owners.

Definition: system quality
System quality is the systems ability to satisfy the needs and expectations of the users and the owners, i.e. the system environment.

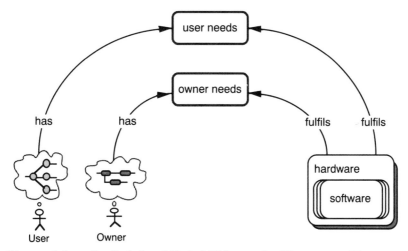

Figure 1.1   *Quality is the ability to fulfil the needs of the users and the owners*

Note that this definition is relative to a particular set of users and owners. For a different set of users and owners the same system may not have the right qualities.

Obviously it is essential that the user and owner have a clear picture of what they need and are able to communicate these needs to the developer. Unfortunately needs are nebulous matters that even the users and the owners themselves may find hard to understand, let alone communicate to others.

It is not sufficient that the users and owners have a clear picture of what they need. It can be seen from Figure 1.2 that the process of building a quality system also depends on user–owner communication, owner–developer communication, user–developer communication and the transformation from the developers conceptions into concrete hardware and software. It is evident that the quality of the system depends on each of these links. Consequently, it will be no better than the weakest link permits.

The essence of quality control is therefore to ensure that each communication link and transformation step works as intended. There are two aspects to this.

- The overall process. The organisation of the development process into major steps where specific documents are produced and certain quality assessment procedures performed.
- The technical content. The information content in the various documents produced, e.g. requirements specifications, system specifications and test plans.

The first aspect is the topic of this chapter. It is also the main concern of quality assurance standards such as (ISO 9000). The second aspect is the topic of the methodology presented in the remainder of this book.

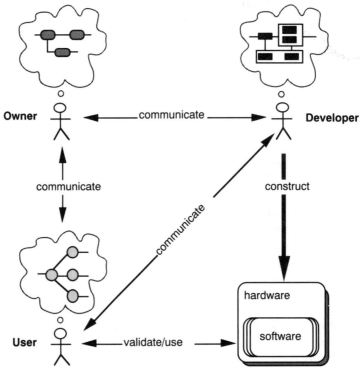

Figure 1.2   *The communication problem (Quality depends on clear and unambiguous communication among the actors involved in the system development)*

In order to improve software engineering practices and solve the software crisis, we must improve our ability to understand, analyse and communicate about systems. Only through improvement in those areas can the development process and the system quality be improved.

1.1.4   The traditional approach

In traditional software development the users and the owners needs were communicated to a software person who transformed the needs directly into a software solution. A programming language was used to express the functional requirements of the user and at the same time the technical solution. This illustrates one of the major advantages software has over other technologies: to describe the technical solution is almost the same as to realise it.

In this approach the software engineer has to do two things at the same time; to understand and structure the needs of the users and owners and to select and structure the technical solution. Frequently the complexity of this task exceeds the capacity of the human mind, which inevitably causes errors and shortcomings to be introduced into the system (Figure 1.3).

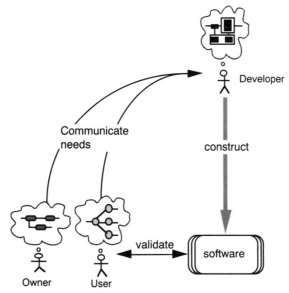

Figure 1.3   *The traditional software development approach*

Since there are no intermediate results, quality cannot be controlled until the software is up and running and the user is allowed to try it. Frequently the user will detect errors and shortcomings. The developer will then have to remedy the errors and shortcomings and let the user try again. In this way the process may continue until the user is satisfied or the process is stopped for other reasons. This feedback loop is normally quite expensive and more importantly, it often fails to give the desired results.

As long as the system complexity is limited, the traditional approach works well, but when the complexity grows an engineering approach is needed whereby the quality can be controlled during the development process. The traditional approach is not an engineering approach since the system is directly created more in the manner of traditional crafts or art than science.

Some kind of "software engineering" or "systems engineering" is needed whenever the complexity is non-trivial. This is the case for the majority of real time systems.

1.2   Major principles of systems engineering

1.2.1   Methodology

Systems engineering is performed by a system consisting of people and tools called the *project system* or the *engineering organisation*. The end results of systems engineering are *target systems* and their documentation, in the form of descriptions.

The role of a systems engineering methodology is to help the engineering organisation make target systems right the first time and every time, within budget and on time.

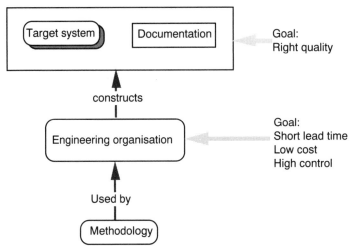

Figure 1.4   *The role of methodology*

A methodology, in general, is made up of a set of methods where each method is a systematic way of producing some result. In the context of systems engineering, most results take the form of descriptions expressed using some notation or language. A systems engineering methodology therefore prescribes a set of descriptions and associated methods to achieve the objectives above. Each method in turn provides guidelines for structuring and using descriptions in given notations.

A systems engineering methodology is a collection of methods that a systems engineering organisation uses in an attempt to achieve right quality, short lead times and low cost.

1.2.2   Descriptions

Clear and precise *descriptions*, i.e. symbolic representations of the subject matter, are essential for all our understanding, analysis and communication. Descriptions are the only means of representing and communicating about reality in a visible way. Descriptions are also instrumental in most human thinking and reasoning. Just consider doing arithmetics without the help of symbolic numbers or understanding how a radio works without a circuit diagram.

It is therefore fundamental to systems engineering, as well as to all other engineering disciplines, to make and analyse descriptions. To that end we need languages supported by rules for the structuring, analysis and transformation of descriptions. The languages we choose to use must provide the material we need to express descriptions. Their underlying concepts (semantics) must provide the material we need to build conceptual understanding. Syntax and semantics to a large extent determine the way we conceive a system and our ability to reason about it. Thus, the selection of languages is of prime importance.

But to select appropriate languages is not sufficient. It is necessary to use the languages properly too. To that end a method is needed that provides techniques and guidelines in addition to the language.

Communication may be performed by spoken words, but in systems engineering it is essential to have visible descriptions expressed in writing and/or drawing. Oral communication is well-suited for discussions and clarification, but for the formal work there should be written documents (see Figure 1.5).

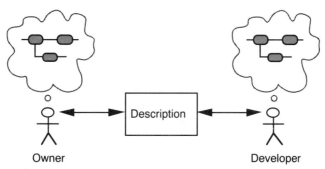

Figure 1.5   *Descriptions, the basis for exact communication, understanding and reasoning about systems*

Physically a description may be expressed on sheets of paper or on some electronic medium carrying text and drawings. Descriptions will be interpreted into concepts in the minds of the people involved. The quality of the system being developed very much depends on how well the concepts in the minds of users, owners and developers correspond to each other. An unambiguous description is the only way to ensure this correspondence.

But it is not sufficient that the descriptions are unambiguous, they must convey insight and understanding too. First of all, the concepts of the description language must fit the concepts one wants to describe. Secondly, the form (syntax) must be convenient with respect to:

- ease of making;
- ease of interpretation;
- ease of reasoning.

To illustrate this we may compare Roman and Arabic numerals. Both syntaxes describe the same numbers, but the Arabic form is vastly more convenient yo write and to do arithmetics with. Another example is a circuit diagram for, say, a radio. The same information can be described with linear text, but a service engineer would definitely prefer the diagram. Hence, the concrete form of descriptions is quite important.

Descriptions are needed as unambiguous and intelligible contracts between the people involved and, in particular, between the user/owner and the developer.

1.2.3   The main descriptions

Systems engineering is a highly intellectual operation usually performed by many people in cooperation. People cannot cooperate well unless they:

*   understand each other;
*   have the same goal.

This implies that the descriptions they use must be well-understood and commonly accepted.

The expressions in a programming language define the behaviour and the data of a computer and may be considered as a very detailed description intended for interpretation by the computer itself. It is, of course, essential that the programmer understands it as well. Otherwise it would be highly unlikely that the programs worked as intended. Modern high level languages have helped a great deal to make programs readable compared to assembly level languages, not to speak of the binary machine instructions.

High level languages can be considered as abstractions in relation to assembler level language and these again as abstractions in relation to binary code.

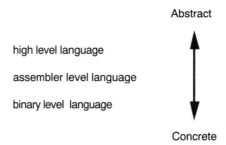

These are *abstractions* in the sense that they are removed from the details of the concrete machine and may be used and understood (by humans) independently of less abstract languages. The expressions in low level languages, on the other hand, are consequences of the high level language expressions (at least when generated by a compiler or a transformation system).

In the traditional approach, the source code was the main (and only formal) description. But even today, the high level languages are oriented more towards the needs of the machine, than towards the needs of the human readers. For most users and owners, program text is quite unintelligible. Hence, program text is not very useful for communication with them. In Chapter 2 we will argue that even for the software specialist it is hard to understand the functionality from program text alone. As we remarked previously, working with only the source code means mixing two aspects: the functionality and the implementation. Since the two aspects are quite independent it may help to keep them separate.

Going back to the kind of errors we make (see Section 1.1.2), it is clear that the functionality is a central quality issue. We need to understand better:

1.   *why* the system is needed;
2.   *what* its functionality should be;
3.   *how* it should be implemented.

To answer these questions we need abstract descriptions that are closer to the needs of human beings, first and foremost the needs of the user and the owner. We need to put their nebulous ideas down in descriptions that are as clear and unambiguous as possible. It is only when the needs are properly understood that it is possible to develop quality solutions.

The first step therefore should be to clarify the needs of the user and the owner and write them down as requirements that can be clearly understood by the user, the owner and the developer. This description is normally called a *requirements specification*. It serves as the first contract between the user, the owner and the developer.

The next step could be to write the software straight away, but normally the requirements will not prescribe all the functional details. They will express constraints that may be satisfied in many alternative ways.

Therefore, the next step should be to define the functionality of the system as clearly and completely as possible and then to define the architecture of the technical solution that will be used to realise the functionality. These descriptions are represented as *functional design* and *implementation design* in Figure 1.6. They can be considered as abstractions above the programming languages (and hardware description languages).

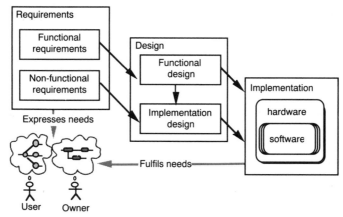

Figure 1.6   *The main descriptions*

The *requirements* should focus on the purpose and role of the system as seen from the environment (including the owners). It should concentrate on essential properties and avoid unnecessary detail. The underlying question is *why* the system is needed. Requirements are often split into two categories: *functional requirements* and *non-functional requirements* (or implementation requirements).

The *functional design* should primarily express the complete functionality that can be observed at external interfaces. It should tell *what* the system will do in a way that can be compared to the functional requirements. It should express the functionality clearly without bias towards the physical implementation. Thus, it provides a basis for selecting the implementation. It is therefore idealised with respect to the concrete system and will hold for a range of technical solutions. The language used for functional design should preferably be a formal language with well-defined semantics because that will enable us to understand, communicate and analyse the functionality precisely without knowing the implementation. Its semantics should be well-suited to the application domain and the syntax should be easy to write and understand.

Since the functional design is independent of technology, it is more appropriate to speak about systems engineering than software engineering at this level.

The *implementation design* should focus on the technical solution and its relation to the functional design. It forms the basis for the implementation of the concrete system consisting of hardware and software. Thus, it tells *how* the system is going to be realised. The implementation design is derived from the functional design and the non-functional requirements.

The idea is to develop the requirement specification first, then to use the functional requirements as the basis for a functional design, then to map the functional design and the non-functional requirements into an implementation design and finally to create a concrete system. In this manner descriptions are developed that serve as visible intermediate results between the user/owner needs and the concrete system. Moreover, the descriptions are developed in a sequence where the most important decisions are made first.

It is essential that the descriptions serve as the basis for precise communication between all the people involved in a project. The internal communication among developers is just as important as the external communication with the user/owner.

It is now possible, in principle, to consider quality as conforming with the requirement specification.

Definition: process quality
The process quality is the conformance between the requirement specification and the system.

This definition is much favoured by quality assurance people because it is more concrete and measurable than system quality, but one should be aware of the essential difference between system quality and process quality. The critical factor is the requirement specification. If it is a true representation of the user and owner needs, the process quality and the system quality are the same, but if there is a mismatch one will not achieve system quality even if the process quality is right.

Every effort should therefore be made to get the requirement specification right. But even the best of requirements will not remain unchanged for ever. Normally requirements change as time passes and more insight is gained. It is therefore essential to keep in contact with the users and the owners during the development process.

The descriptions may be used in step-wise quality assurance as illustrated in Figure 1.7. Initially the user and the owner may validate that the requirements correctly express their needs. Later they may validate that the design is correct. Both the user and the owner will be interested in the functional design, whereas the owner is more concerned with the implementation design than the user. The developers can verify that each step respects some sort of equivalence relation. Verification and validation is the topic of Chapter 12.

The final test of course, is the actual use of the concrete system. The methodology aims to ensure that there are no surprises at this stage. We intend to do it right the first time and every time!

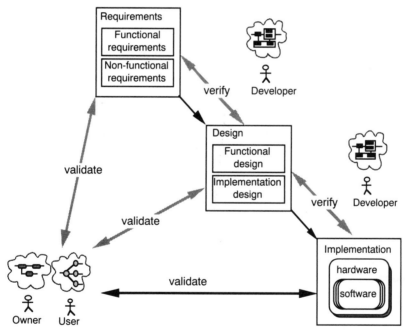

Figure 1.7   *Step-wise quality assurance*

This gives a number of benefits over the traditional approach:

- Step-wise quality assurance can be performed during the entire development.
- The user and owner needs are put into focus.

- The functionality can be validated at an early stage.
- The number of aspects to be considered at each step is reduced.
- The cost of error correction is reduced since errors can be detected earlier.
- Different descriptions correspond to different kinds of expert knowledge. Hence, experts can be utilised more effectively.
- Languages can be selected to fit the specific purpose of each description. Hence, the preciseness and comprehensibility of the descriptions can be enhanced.
- Descriptions can be modified without affecting each other (within bounds).
- The functional design documents the system as a whole independently of the implementation technology chosen for its various parts.
- Each step provides a firm foundation for the next step.

The main drawback is that several descriptions have to be developed and maintained instead of only one. This drawback is normally outweighed by the benefits and may in the future be reduced by automated transformation systems. When the functional design language has implementable semantics it is possible to develop automatic or semi-automatic transformations to implementations. This may improve efficiency and quality considerably. In fact it will allow a shift in paradigm from what we may call *implementation-oriented* to *design-oriented* development.

One aim of the methodology presented in this book is to avoid unnecessary redundancy between descriptions. A specific piece of information should be expressed only once in the description where it belongs. The descriptions are not intended to replace each other, but to complement each other in the system documentation. In that way efficiency can be achieved.

So far, the main descriptions have been illustrated, but practical systems engineering will often involve additional descriptions focusing on different properties such as performance and reliability.

The top down approach illustrated so far is a bit too simplistic. In reality one will not fully develop the descriptions step by step, but rather alternate between descriptions, sometimes working top down, other times bottom up. We will discuss this in more detail as we go along. Presently we limit ourselves to the most important principles.

High level languages are today automatically transformed into object code by compiling systems. Gradually, automated support will be introduced to the higher abstractions. But since the higher abstractions are oriented towards the user and not the machine it is necessary that the designer supplies some design information manually, before automatic transformation can be performed. The role of the implementation design is to represent this information.

1.3   Managing the system evolution

1.3.1   Reference model

The various descriptions are produced by *activities* that are ideally performed in a temporally ordered sequence. In the *waterfall model*, results in the form of descriptions appear to flow down a staircase of waterfalls, as in Figure 1.8.

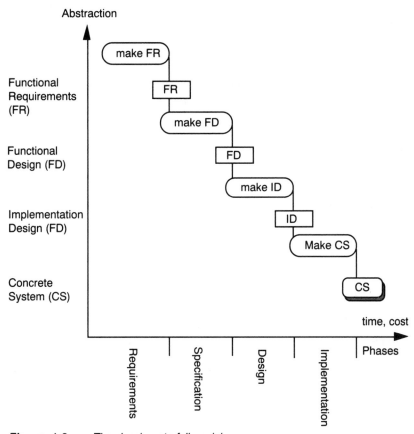

Figure 1.8   *The classic waterfall model*

In Figure 1.8 we have omitted the non-functional requirements in order to simplify the discussion. They may be seen as an abstraction somewhere between the functional design and the implementation design in Figure 1.8.

In many ways the waterfall model is too simplistic. It seems to exclude important and useful practices such as the following:

feedback and iterations between activities and results;

- the gradual evolution of results;
- incremental developments where operational system parts are built before everything is specified and then allowed to grow gradually towards the complete system;
- the use of early prototypes as a way to clarify requirements and define functionality;
- reuse of previously developed components.

Since we want to capture these practices the reference model we shall use in this book is not restricted to the waterfall model. Figure 1.8 is just an illustration of one possible way to execute the generic activity model depicted in Figure 1.11. We must distinguish between the generic model type in Figure 1.11 and its instantiation in temporally ordered activity executions during an actual project as illustrated in Figure 1.8.

Activities are the means of producing results. They consume resources and represent the expenses in a project, e.g. persons, time and money.

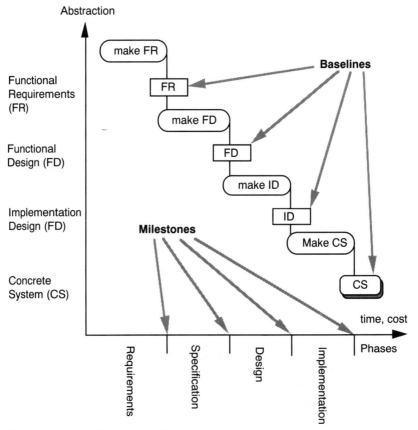

Figure 1.9   *Milestones and baselines*

In order to manage a development project, it is often split into *phases,* which are periods of time where specific activities are carried out and results produced. This is indicated along the time dimension in Figure 1.8. Note the difference between an abstraction, a phase and an activity! The notion of a phase is associated with the temporal instantiation of the model and should not be mixed up with the notion of an activity type.

The transition between two phases is normally made when one activity has produced a result that enables another activity to start. This should be some tangible result, such as a description, with a quality acceptable as input to succeeding activities. Since a phase result is the basis for further work it is frequently referred to as a *baseline* (see Figure 1.9). When a result becomes a baseline, more work will gradually be based on it and the consequences of a change will become more serious. In order to limit and control the changes, a formal *change control* procedure is often applied before baselined results may be changed.

A phase transition is often referred to as a *milestone,* to indicate that an important point in the development has been reached (see Figure 1.9). Milestones are control points where the obtained results are evaluated in relation to the resources and time spent and where future actions are decided on and planned.

In practice a result is developed by a sequence of smaller steps and not by a single monolithic activity. Each of these steps produces a *revision* of a previous result. This process continues even after a result has become a baseline and is sometimes referred to as *maintenance.* Consequently, maintenance may start early and continue throughout the lifetime of a system (see Figure 1.10).

Sometimes an activity produces results that call for revision of previous results. This is normal because more insight is gained and defects may be discovered as the work proceeds. Thus, feedback between the results and activities will occur in practice.

It is impractical to develop a system as a single unit. Rather, it is decomposed into subsystems, that may pass milestones at different times in order to obtain a flexible and efficient progress. The phases of the total development may therefore be decomposed into subphases corresponding to the subsystems and the milestones likewise.

To sum up: results are the goals of systems engineering. They are the deliverables and the control items. Activities are the means to achieve results; necessary evils that consume time and resources. Phases are major time intervals used to plan and control the progress of a project system. Transitions between phases are called milestones and their results, called baselines, are put under change control.

In a generic reference model we cannot prescribe a specific temporal sequence as in Figure 1.10. What we can do is to prescribe the main activities and descriptions and how they should be related. Figure 1.11 outlines the main activities and descriptions that are part of the methodology presented in this book. They will be gradually elaborated as we go along.

For each particular project this activity model must be instantiated and the temporal progression must be planned with respect to phases, milestones and baselines. It is up to each project to decide on how this should be done. One project might decide to use a classic waterfall approach. Another might decide to use a rapid prototyping approach where a prototype is developed early and used as a vehicle to settle the functional requirements. Still another project may choose an evolutionary approach, such as the spiral model (Boehm, 1988).

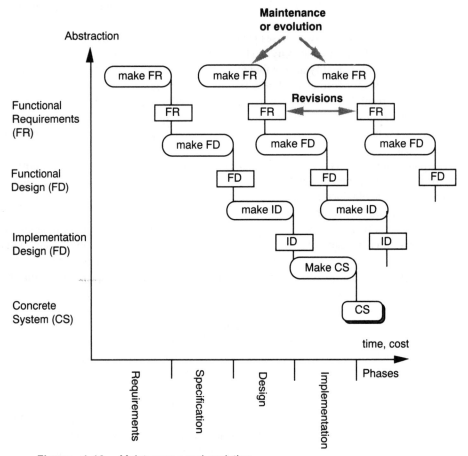

Figure 1.10   *Maintenance and evolution*

Numerous slightly different models may be found in the literature. We believe that the essential difference is not in the ordering of activities and phases, but in the descriptions. The key thing is to make the functional design before the implementation design and implementation. This does not mean that everything in the functional design must be complete before implementation design starts. A project may well start to design a critical subset of the functionality and then make an implementation design and perhaps even an implementation, before returning to make the functional design more complete. Figure 1.10 can be seen as an illustration of such an approach.

Although each phase normally focuses on one abstraction, it needs not be limited to that abstraction. Other activities may be carried out as well. In the specification phase, for instance, the main thing is functional design, but non-functional requirements and requirements to the project organisation may also be clarified. The corresponding results are logically separate descriptions, but for practical reasons they are sometimes presented in one document, such as the requirement specification.

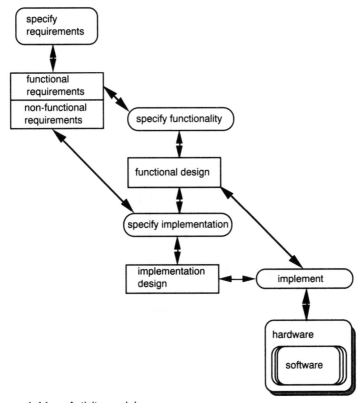

Figure 1.11   *Activity model*

1.3.2   Documents

Documents are the logical carriers of descriptions. Documents will have a structure of their own and may contain information in addition to the descriptions they carry. A typical document contains a structure of chapters, sections and paragraphs containing descriptions. In addition, the document may have a table of contents, an index and an identification.

A document may contain a single description, but frequently several descriptions are collected into one document to suit a particular purpose, such as a milestone review. Conversely, descriptions will be used in several different documents depending on circumstances and should therefore be maintained as separate units. The *deliverables* of a project are documents and concrete systems.

A system development is often planned and controlled in terms of documents, as illustrated in Figure 1.12. The main results are documents such as the requirements specification, the system documentation, the operator´s manual and the test-plan.

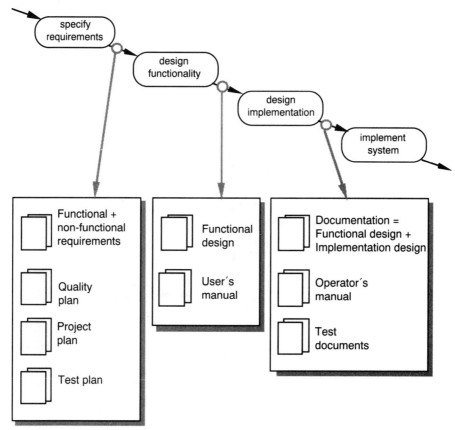

Figure 1.12   *A possible set of documents produced in a development project*

CHAPTER 2

Basic Principles

A system has many aspects that need to be understood, analysed and communicated by means of descriptions. A viable methodology must combine methods in a way that contributes effectively and efficiently towards low cost in the process and quality in the product. This chapter will introduce some basic principles we believe to be crucial to the success of a methodology. It will also introduce the system example we shall use throughout the rest of the book. Basic principles for complexity management and behaviour description will be presented and some popular description approaches will be outlined. The methodology we are going to present in the following chapters is also outlined.

2.1   Introduction to the system example

For the rest of this book an *Access Control system (AC-System)* will be used to illustrate aspects of the methodology. It has been chosen to shed light over different application areas: control of mechanical equipment, user dialogue, communication, databases etc. Although it has been constructed for the purpose of this book, it should not be viewed as a toy example, but as a realistically sized example from everyday life.

The purpose of the *AC-System* is to control the access to some service open only to trusted people with known identity. Ideally, users should be recognised by the system and granted or denied access depending on some unique physical attribute, such as a fingerprint. But the technology required to do that has not been developed yet, so the system is based on personal cards instead. The security rests on the user keeping their cards personal and, in addition, knowing a secret personal identification number (PIN).

Each card holds a unique *Card-code* that identifies the card. To grant access the system will read the *Card-code* and then check the corresponding access right. For additional authentication, the user may be asked to enter the secret personal number (PIN).

The initial service is simply to control the access to rooms, i.e. to open doors for authorised persons. Since the same kind of access control is needed in banking and shopping, it should be possible to accommodate services other than opening doors at a later stage.

The system provides its services at a number of *Access Points* controlled by *Local Stations* physically distributed to where the services are needed. The system keeps information about the users, their access rights, their cards and their secret PINs. Such information is kept and safeguarded in a *Central Station*, which also performs the authentication and authorisation. It is therefore necessary for *Local Stations* to communicate with the *Central Station*. The information in the *Central Station* may be entered and modified from operator terminals.

A *Local Station* consists of a control unit, a door lock mechanism and one or two panels, each containing a card reader, a display unit and a keyboard. The door itself is not that important to the system, only how the opening and closing is controlled (the door may be revolving, hinged or sliding). It is assumed that the door has a simple magnetic lock that will open and close on command. The open/closed status of the door lock is indicated by a signal which is monitored by the control unit.

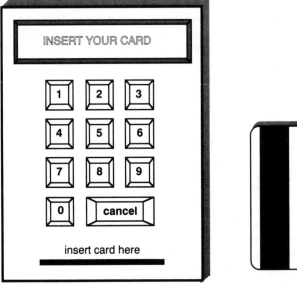

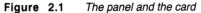

Figure 2.1   *The panel and the card*

The card is a plastic card with a magnetic strip holding a *card code* and possibly an encrypted PIN code. The encrypted PIN will not be used in our system initially. At a later stage it may be used for local authentication in the *Local Stations*. The physical appearance of the panel and the card is shown in Figure 2.1. Each panel represents an *Access Point*.

The main service demanded by the user is to gain access when the card is presented to the system. But access should only be given to authorised users. Hence, a user will be rejected if an attempt is made to enter at an access point where the user is not authorised to pass.

An instance of the system is depicted in Figure 2.2.

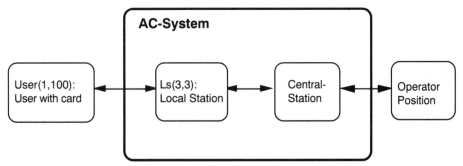

Figure 2.2   *The system structure*

The system itself is described inside the bold box called *AC-System* in Figure 2.2 while the environment is depicted outside. We have chosen to consider *Users* and *Operator Positions* as part of the environment, including only the *Local Stations* and the *Central Station* in the system itself. This particular system instance is configured with exactly three *Local Stations* to serve a minimum of one and a maximum of 100 *Users*.

Figure 2.2 uses a general box and arrow notation we call SOON (the SISU object-oriented notation) to describe the system structure. We shall use this notation to illustrate some basic principles and also to make conceptual models at the requirement stage (see Chapter 3). It will be informally introduced as we go along. A short description can be found at the end of this chapter.

Boxes represent entities; something having a real or distinct existence. The arrows represent connections that enable entities to communicate with each other. The arrows in Figure 2.2 tell us that the *Users* communicate with the *Local Stations* and that the *Local Stations* communicate with the *Central Station*. The notation also supports general relations (not shown in Figure 2.2). It is therefore related to the well-known entity relationship diagrams (see Section 2.5.2), but there are some differences that will be explained in Section 2.5.3.

The text inside a box consists of two parts that are separated by a colon. The first part consists of a local instance name and the number of instances. The second part consists of the type name. Everything except the type name is optional, so when there is only one name, such as in the *Central Station* box, this means exactly one instance of the entity type *Central Station*. The *Local Station* box represents three instances, called *Ls*, of the type *Local Station*. The types are defined elsewhere and are not shown in Figure 2.2. The number of instances in a set is specified by a low and a high limit placed inside parentheses. For example *(1,100)* which means at least one and a maximum of 100 or *(3,3)* which means exactly 3.

The number of connection instances follows, in most cases, from the number of connected entity instances. When the entity cardinalities are identical, one-to-one connections are normally assumed, giving just as many connections as there are instances on each side. When the cardinalities differ, each instance on one side may potentially connect to all instances on the other side. Following this rule, it can be seen from Figure 2.2 that the *Central Station* may connect to all the three *Local Stations* and that each *Local Station* may connect to all the *Users*.

Now there is a distinction to be made between static and dynamic connections. It is not clear from the figure whether the *Users* are permanently connected to the *Local Stations* or not. Of course, we expect the *Users* to move about, but this is not clear from the figure. What is clear is that each *Local Station* should be prepared to connect to any of the *Users*.

The boxes and arrows in Figure 2.2 may be understood in terms of physical things, but they may also be understood as having a more abstract nature. At this stage we leave the interpretation open.

2.2   Systems

2.2.1   What is a system?

Before we venture further into the realm of systems engineering methodology, we should try to clarify what we mean by a "system".

Throughout society the notion of a system is widely used to describe quite different phenomena. In its most general use it simply means order, ways of arranging or doing things. A methodology, for instance, may be described as a system of methods. Since our topic is system development methodology, we need a more precise definition whereby we may differentiate between the system being developed and the methodology being used to develop it.

Definition: system
A system is a part of the world that a person or group of persons during some time interval and for some purpose choose to regard as a whole, consisting of interrelated components, each component characterised by properties that are selected as being relevant to the purpose. (Adapted from (Nygaard, 1986).)

Why this elaborate definition? Because it implies a few important points well worth emphasising:

1. The system is part of the real world. It is not a description on the drawing board, but something actually existing as a phenomenon in the real world. This puts the system apart from the description of the system (on the drawing board). Figure 2.2 is a description of a system, printed on a page in this book. The system itself exists somewhere outside this book, where it actually provides access control services to real people.

2. What constitutes a system is a matter of definition. This means two things: firstly, that it is up to the observer to draw the borderline between the system and its environment and, secondly, that it is up to the observer to regard the system on an abstraction level that suits a given purpose. This means that even though a system is real, how it is described is a matter of choice. (But an important choice.) In Figure 2.2 we have chosen to exclude the *Operator Positions* from the system. For a different purpose we might choose to include them in the system.

3. Since the system boundary is a matter of definition, each component may also be regarded as a system. In general, a system is *aggregated from* subsystems and *partitioned into* subsystems. Figure 2.2 depicts the *AC-System* as an aggregate of several *Local Stations* and one *Central Station*. Each of these components may be regarded as a system by itself.

4. A system is not just any unordered collection of components. The components are related to each other to form a *structure*. In Figure 2.2, for instance, the *Local Stations* are connected to the *Central Station*. Such mutual relationships give the components purposes in relation to each other.

5. A system has *purposes*. The user inserting a card at a *Local Station,* for instance, has a purpose for doing so and hopefully the system will fulfil that purpose. Other users of the same system might have different purposes. The owner might have a different purpose still. Later we will associate the notion of a *role* with the purpose or the needs, of an individual user.

A system description also has a purpose. One important purpose is to describe the functional behaviour such that it can be fully understood, another is to describe the realisation such that the system may be produced. These different purposes usually require that the system is regarded in different ways, but both views are concerned with the same system existing in the real world.

The reader should be well aware of the distinction between a system and its corresponding system description. Without this distinction the essential difficulties of understanding and describing behaviour are hard to see. Behaviour is dynamically performed by the system. During system development we need behaviour descriptions that enable us to fully understand, analyse and predict the system behaviour. To do this we need a mapping from the (static) description of behaviour to the (dynamic) system behaviour. The nature of this mapping is instrumental to our ability to achieve quality.

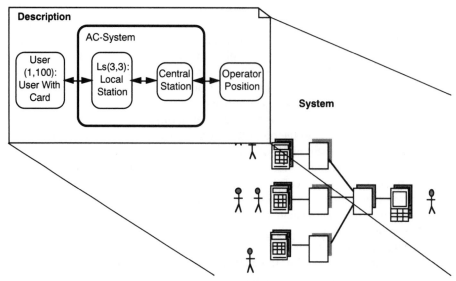

Figure 2.3   *The distinction between a system description and a system*

2.2.2   Behaviour

Just as the system exists in the real world, the behaviour is actually occurring in the real world as time goes by. It is not a static description on the drawing board, but a dynamic development taking place during the lifetime of the system. In contrast to the behaviour description, behaviour itself may only be observed once as it happens in real time.

In order to describe and understand behaviour we need to understand the basic nature of behaviour. As a first approximation we contend that behaviour basically consists of *actions* that change the *state* (*value*) of *variables*. In a discrete system each action results in a state that remains unchanged until the next action is performed. Consequently, behaviour is observable as states and state transitions generated by actions.

Definition: behaviour
The behaviour of a system is the development of states and state transitions generated by actions of the system during the time interval in which it is studied.

Of course, this is a very general definition where the notion of a state and a variable must be understood in a wide sense. The state of the *AC-System,* for instance, will be the composite state of all the *Local Stations*, the *Central Station* and the connections. Our general notion of a state has two aspects: communication and storage. Communication is a way to pass values between actions separated in space, whereas storage is a way to pass values between actions separated in time. We shall later use the word "signal" to denote communication values.

A system state may have many components where each component is generated by partly independent actions. Figure 2.4 illustrates a segment of behaviour where the user inputs a card to the card reader and the system responds by giving a message on the display. The user then keys in a PIN on the keyboard and the system responds by a message and perhaps by opening the door lock (not shown). Note that this behaviour has two ordered action sequences: the human behaviour and the machine behaviour.

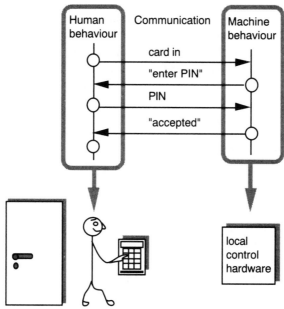

Figure 2.4   *A segment of behaviour*

The communication in Figure 2.4 serves to link the actions of the human to the actions of the machine, thereby giving each a purpose and meaning in relation to the other. It imposes a partial ordering among their actions and it conveys the information they need to select future actions.

Somehow behaviours must interact in order to do something meaningful for each other. Without communication there would be no information interchange and the system would be isolated from the rest of the world. Consequently, the system would not serve any purpose and would have no meaning for the rest of the world.

Figure 2.4 shows only one of several possible courses of behaviour that the system and the user might go through. On a different occasion they might go through a different sequence. The number of alternative behaviours may be very high, but in each instance of actual behaviour only one alternative is chosen. Which one depends on the communication that takes place.

In deterministic systems the behaviour is fully controlled by the external communication. Therefore, the communication is the key to understanding behaviour. If the system is seen as a black box, the communication taking place across its interfaces is the only directly observable aspect of behaviour.

A system and its environment may contain many independent subbehaviours. In the environment of the *AC-System*, for instance, the users at different *Local Stations* behave independently. We consider such independent behaviours as being concurrent or parallel. Each user behaves sequentially in relation to the system and expects the system to play a corresponding role. When a system has many users acting in parallel, it must play the corresponding roles concurrently. The system behaviour must somehow be composed from several independent/concurrent threads of sequential behaviour. This is a typical feature of a real time system.

In conclusion, a system behaviour may consist of many concurrent threads of sequential behaviour. These threads may be linked by communication and each thread consists of action sequences that generate sequences of state transitions in communication and storage variables.

2.2.3   Structure

It is useful to make a distinction between behaviour and structure. Behaviour is a dynamic development over time, whereas structure is the way things hold together for some time.

Definition: structure
The structure of a system is the aspects of the system which stay invariant during the time interval in which it is studied.

This is a very general definition that covers all kinds of structures. Some aspects of a system will remain static during its entire lifetime, while other aspects will change dynamically as part of behaviour. But even aspects that change, may be considered as structures for the time periods where they remain invariant, however short they are. Thus, a state may be considered as a structure of values.

Figure 2.2 shows a structure which will not change during normal system operation. It can be considered as the structure of substance in our *AC-System*. The substance itself is static, but it will carry values and perform behaviour.

In the real world of systems, all actions are performed by something and all values are represented by something. This something is what we, very generally, will call *substance*.

Substance is indispensable from any real system. In order to store values there must be some memory substance. In order to communicate values there must be some channel substance. In order to perform behaviour there must be some active substance. The notion of substance captures all the various physical or logical media that may be used to store and communicate values and to perform actions. The substance of a system is normally static for long periods of time, often for the entire lifetime. Therefore, the substance is sometimes considered as the structure of the system.

One of the big issues in methods for abstract system description is whether substance should be considered or not. On one hand it may be argued that substance is too physical; that too much implementation detail is introduced. On the other hand it may be argued that substance helps to structure and clarify even abstract descriptions; that they become more realistic and comprehensible. Object-oriented languages implicitly include the notion of substance in the notion of an object. Purely mathematical formalisms tend to exclude the notion of substance.

Since a single variable, such as an integer, is able to carry a sequence of values we may associate a sequential behaviour with it. In order to have concurrent behaviours we need separate variables, each carrying a sequence of values. In general, concurrent behaviours need separate substances. Therefore, the structure of the substance also provides the structure of concurrent behaviours.

In the following we shall refer to active substances as *objects*. Objects have the capability to store values, perform actions and communicate with other objects. In the pure object-oriented perspective, there is no storage outside objects. Consequently, the substance of a pure object-oriented system consists of objects and some form of communication channels only. This object structure also defines the decomposition of the system behaviour.

2.2.4   Real time systems

One should note that behaviour is always "real time", since it actually occurs in the real world. The term "real time" refers to how closely the (real time) behaviour of the system must follow the (real time) behaviour of the environment in order to fulfil its role. In other words; how closely must the behaviour of the system be synchronised with the environment? If there are well-defined and strict time constraints on the synchronisation in one or more of its roles, the system is a real time system. Unless the constraints are respected, the system will not function properly and, consequently, not play its role.

Definition: real time system
A system is a real time system if it has a role with time constraints.

Figure 2.2 is a fairly typical example of a distributed system. The users interact directly with the system, so it is what we call an *on-line system*. Human users will put some real time constraints on a system in the sense that response times should be in accordance with human expectations. Physical systems such as communication channels and process plants may put far stricter real time constraints on the system. In such systems the correct behaviour of the system depends strongly on real time constraints.

In order to be called real time the system has to be an on-line or embedded system, i.e. a system that directly interacts with its environment and plays a role essential to the continuous functioning of the environment. The term on-line is mostly used for business-oriented transaction systems such as the seat reservation systems used by airlines. Embedded is the term used in process control, e.g. a fly-by-wire system controlling the rudders and flaps of an aircraft. The latter category usually has the more severe real time constraints.

In most real time systems, correct and continuous service is of critical importance. One may tolerate that seat reservations are unavailable for a short period, but one cannot tolerate that the fly-by-wire system is inoperable during a flight.

Real time systems put heavy demands on the systems engineer. Firstly, because they have complex behaviour to perform. Secondly, because the real time constraints may call for careful optimisations of time-critical parts. Finally, because they have to function correctly and continuously. They have to be both robust and reliable. Sometimes fault tolerance is required, i.e. that the system continues to operate in the presence of errors. Sometimes operations have to be fail safe, i.e. that they will fail only in a way that prevents any damage being made to the environment.

All these requirements add up to a very complex engineering task where appropriate methodology is of the greatest importance. The methods used must promote the understanding and the analysis required to achieve success. They must enable the step-wise validation and verification necessary to achieve a controlled process towards a quality result.

The key issue in a systems engineering methodology is to manage complexity. To this end the problem domain must be decomposed into a set of subproblems that can be described and studied as independently as possible.

In the following section we shall look into some general principles that every methodology should apply in one form or another.

2.3   Techniques to manage complexity

2.3.1   Abstraction

Generally speaking, abstraction means to ignore some aspects of a phenomenon in order to describe (and understand) others more clearly. In a broad sense this definition also embodies two principles to be described in the following two sections; aggregation and generalisation.

In this book we use the term *abstraction* in a more restricted way, meaning the opposite of *concrete* or physical. This kind of abstraction is fundamental to all systems engineering approaches. They all share the basic idea that the system should be described on an abstract level, in order to fully understand its purpose and functionality, before it is realised.

We use abstraction primarily to make descriptions that are more suited to the needs of human understanding and analysis than those needed for physical realisation. To this end it is not sufficient to simply be abstract. The abstraction must be better suited to the problem at hand than a more implementation-oriented description is. (One does not gain much by replacing lots of implementation details by a similar amount of abstract detail.) Therefore, the abstraction must be based on concepts closely related to the problem domain in question.

As discussed in Chapter 1, we need abstractions to describe and understand at least the following aspects of a system:

1.   WHY the system is developed, its purpose and the requirements to functional and non-functional properties;
2.   WHAT the functionality is, the complete functional design or how the system will behave functionally;
3.   HOW the system is to be implemented, the implementation design, i.e. how the functional design shall be mapped to the concrete system.

Abstraction is not the same as being vague, incomplete or imprecise. It is a matter of using a formalism that can be understood without reference to a particular implementation. This formalism should allow conceptual systems to be built in our minds whereby we may analyse and simulate the real system.

We must maintain the distinction between a description and a system even on the abstract level. Even though the abstract system is different from the physical system, it gives us a way of regarding the physical system. Observe that the notion of abstraction applies to the system and not to the description.

Abstraction does not mean that the system can be viewed only from outside. One may just as well go into the system and describe its components, as long as they are abstract components belonging to the abstraction in question. It is a common misconception that partitioning a system into components means to reveal its implementation. We consider partitioning as being orthogonal to abstraction.

The choice of abstractions and methods for abstract descriptions is crucial for the success of a methodology. The different aspects of a system must be covered with maximum clarity and precision so that quality is well-controlled. But in order to reduce cost and lead times, each aspect should be described only once. What we need therefore is a well-balanced selection of descriptions that together cover all aspects that need to be described, without unnecessary redundancy and/or bureaucracy. In principle we need a set of descriptions that cover independent or orthogonal aspects.

The abstractions we use should also lead towards efficient implementation. It is not sufficient to gain insight if it cannot be transformed into an efficient implementation. We therefore need abstractions that are realistic and implementable. Finally, we need abstractions that support the continuing development and reuse required to be ahead of competition in todays market-place.

A good test of the usefulness of an abstract description is the degree to which it is maintained. Designers will tend to maintain descriptions they find really useful.

2.3.2   Projection

In abstractions we remove details of the implementation, but we still consider the whole system. In *projections* we look at the system from different angles. The idea of projections is well-known in geometrical modelling, but not so well-known in system descriptions. Instead of associating projections with geometrical views, we associate them with the observable interfaces of a system. A projection is a description of a system as it is observed at a subset of its interfaces. Only the observable interfaces are visible, while the other interfaces are hidden.

This allows us to study how the system appears at a particular interface, such as a user interface and to discard the other interfaces. This view corresponds to the subjective view of an individual user. A user of the *AC-System*, for instance, will interact with just one panel at a time and experience a projection of the total system behaviour on that panel. An operator will experience a different projection of the behaviour.

There may well be mutual dependencies between interfaces. The behaviour a user experiences on a given panel depends on the access rights the user has been granted through the operator terminal. Such dependencies will be visible as non-deterministic choices at the observed interface, but the exact nature of the influence will be hidden.

Projections are closely related to the notion of a role. A role specifies the required properties at a particular interface or set of interfaces (see Chapters 3 and 12 for examples).

Projections can be applied to abstract as well as to concrete system descriptions.

2.3.3   Aggregation and partitioning

All non-trivial systems are composed from components. The process of lumping components together to form a whole is called *aggregation*. The *AC-System* depicted in Figure 2.2, for instance, is an *aggregate* consisting of three *Local Stations*, one *Central Station* and a number of connections.

The opposite process of decomposing a whole into parts is called *partitioning* (or decomposition).

Aggregation enables us to associate a single concept and a name with a composite entity such as the *AC-System*. This helps to simplify matters considerably when we are dealing with the entity as a whole. But to build the entity and use it correctly we need to understand what it consists of. Partitioning allows us to go into the details when we need to.

Aggregation and partitioning are very basic principles in systems engineering. Not only do they help to structure and handle a physical system, they help to structure and handle the understanding of the system as well. If we are able to partition a system into independent parts, each part may be understood as a separate unit and the system may be understood as a straightforward composition of parts.

To achieve this, the word *independent* is important. The more independent the parts are, the easier they are to understand separately and to put together into a whole. In the *AC-System,* for instance, the *Local Stations* are totally independent of each other. We may therefore easily add more *Local Stations* to the system without affecting the existing *Local Stations*. The *Central Station*, however, interacts with the *Local Stations* and may therefore be affected. (To reduce this problem, the *Central Station* should be independent of the exact number of *Local Stations*.)

Aggregation and partitioning may apply not only to entities, i.e. something having a real or distinct existence, but also to the links between entities. This may be exemplified by decomposing a *Local Station* to show the different communication links between the user and the panel, as shown in Figure 2.5. A link on one level of partitioning may therefore be partitioned into several links on the next level. Note that this kind of *Local*

Station interacts with only one *User* at a time. The association between *Users* and *Local Stations* is therefore dynamic.

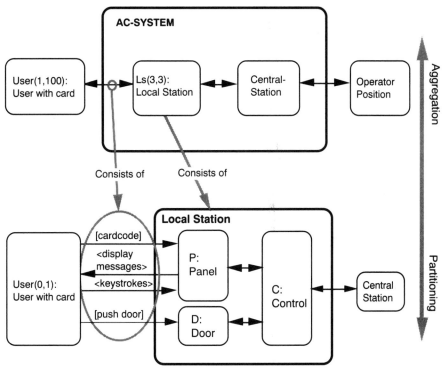

Figure 2.5   *Aggregation and partitioning*

Aggregation and partitioning are basic techniques we need in order to structure a description and, more importantly, to structure our conception of the described subject.

2.3.4   Generalisation and specialisation
In the real world there are huge amounts of similar subjects. All the users of the *AC-System,* for instance, are similar. All the panels are similar. There may even be many similar instances of the entire *AC-System* installed at various locations.

Similarity adds a new dimension to our complexity management techniques. Rather than describing and understanding all individuals in full detail (using aggregation and partitioning), we may describe and understand them in terms of similarity.

We use similarity all the time in everyday life. When somebody talks about "a cat", everybody knows (roughly) what kind of creature it is. From the similarity among cats most people have extracted a general pattern of properties that they consider to be common to all individual cats. They may then give meaning to the term "a cat" by associating to an instance of this pattern.

We will refer to such general patterns as *types* in the following. Types are conceptual entities that we use to structure our descriptions and thoughts. The type "cat", for instance, is a conceptual entity having the properties that we consider common to all individual cats.

Finding a repetitive pattern always helps to understand things more easily. The notion of a type allows us to describe a general pattern separately from where it is used and to give it a name. It allows us to study and understand the pattern as an entity and then apply this knowledge repeatedly wherever the pattern occurs. Not only does this help to simplify and structure our descriptions, it is the basis for understanding and reasoning.

Knowledge about a type gives meaning to its type name wherever it occurs in a description. Moreover, it enables us to reason about the individual instances of the type. From our general knowledge of cats, we know what individual cats like "Garfield" and "Felix" are likely to do and not to do.

Without any general concepts we would be unable to reason and draw conclusions. We could not predict anything and, consequently, could not build systems with planned and predictable behaviour. Types are therefore important for our ability to understand and reason about systems.

In fact, developing and applying types is what system development is all about. We do not intend to produce just one instance of the *AC-System*. We intend to sell and produce as many similar systems as we can. To this end we consciously or unconsciously treat the *AC-System* as a system type. We may also treat the *Local Station* and the *Central Station* as types. This will enable us to reuse these in systems other than the *AC-System*.

Figure 2.6 illustrates how the *AC-System* and the *Local Station* may be explicitly defined as types.

From Figure 2.6 two things are evident:

1.   a type is an aggregate of components;
2.   the components of a type may be instances of (other) types.

By comparing Figures 2.5 and 2.6, the close correspondence between aggregates and types is evident. Figure 2.5 shows that each *Local Station* is an aggregate whereas Figure 2.6 shows how the aggregate is defined separately as a type. The advantage of a separate definition is that the type, here the *Local Station*, becomes reusable. It is not particular to a given instance, but a general concept that may be used (and reused) in many places.

The notion of a type formalises the notion of a re-usable component. Types are made in two ways:

1.   *By composition*, as illustrated in Figure 2.6, where a type, the *AC-System*, is composed from three instances of *Local Stations* and one instance of *Central Station*;
2.   *By inheritance* and specialisation, where a new type is defined by inheriting and specializing the properties of an existing type.

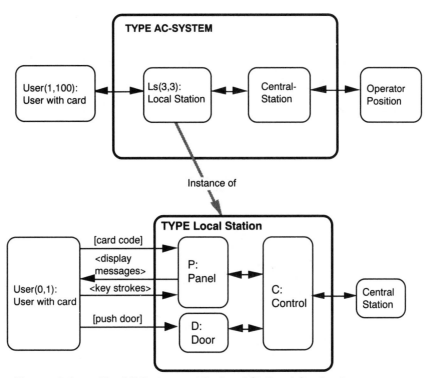

Figure 2.6   *The AC-System and the Local Station defined as types*

Frequently there are similarities among types. Tigers for instance have many traits in common with domestic cats. If we define the common traits as a supertype, tigers and domestic cats may be defined as subtypes. To derive a subtype, the common traits are inherited. New traits may then be added and existing ones may be changed. "A tricycle, is a cycle with three wheels" is an example from daily life.

More specialised subtypes of the *Local Station* may be derived by adding new components and/or modifying the existing components of the type as illustrated in Figure 2.7. Here we have defined a *Double Station* by adding an extra *Panel* and modifying the *Control* to handle two panels. The parts inherited from *Local Station* are dashed. We only need to represent components that are added or modified.

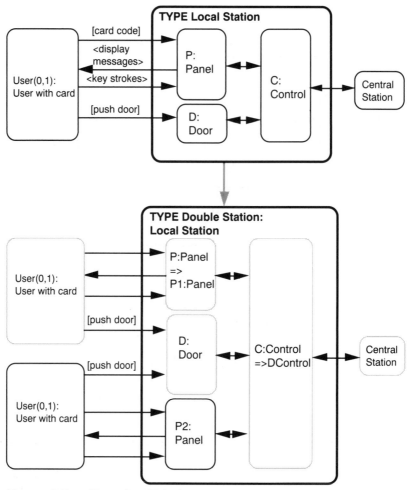

Figure 2.7   *Illustration of inheritance*

Observe that the notion of a type we have introduced here is not a set. It captures the general properties of an individual set member and is therefore different from a set. This approach has some advantages:

- The general properties of individuals may be described explicitly and equally important, the constraints pertaining to relationships between individuals can be described.
- A type may be used in many different sets of instances. The type represents the common pattern repeated for all instances.

2.4 Approaches to behaviour description

2.4.1 The problem

The quality of a real time system is determined to a very large extent by its behaviour. But, due to its dynamic and transient nature, behaviour is by far the most difficult system aspect to describe. Consequently, descriptions that help to understand, communicate and reason about behaviour are the cornerstones of quality control.

A symbolic description is a static and finite thing. As such it can represent static and finite structures quite explicitly. The challenge is to represent behaviour. How can we represent a dynamic and possibly infinite behaviour in a static and finite way?

A reader trying to understand a behaviour description must establish a mental picture of the infinite and dynamic behaviour that will occur in reality by reading a static description. Since the essential complexity of the behaviour itself is sufficient to bring most minds to their limits, the mental burden of this task must be kept to a minimum. Therefore, it is important that the description resembles the actual behaviour as much as possible.

We might start by considering an instance of behaviour. Figure 2.8(a) renders a piece of sequential behaviour where states, represented by circles, are linked by actions represented by arrows.

In systems development it is not sufficient to represent individual sequences. In order to develop a system we need to understand and analyse all the possible behaviours the system may perform some time in the future. We must somehow represent the general patterns of behaviour, the rules, that individual behaviours obey. In other words we must describe behaviour types. The critical issue is how behaviour types should be described in order to help the reader understand and analyse all possible courses of individual behaviour?

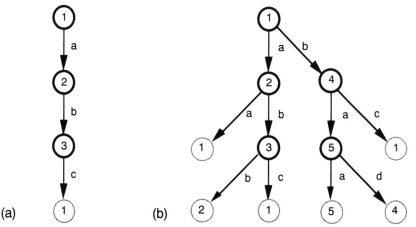

Figure 2.8 *Illustration showing the tree of all possible behaviour sequences (a) An instance of behaviour. (b) The tree of possible behaviours.*

Starting from the individual sequence in Figure 2.8(a), we may add all the possible alternative behaviours and get a behaviour tree such as the one illustrated in Figure 2.8(b). In this tree we note that instances of a given action type occur on several branches. We also note that instances of states that have occurred previously occur at the leaf nodes of the tree.

First we note that the tree represents all possible behaviours. Whenever a leaf node is reached, it is substituted by the subtree previously defined for that state. In this manner an infinite behaviour tree may be generated. A particular instance of behaviour will consist of a trace through this infinite tree where only one of the possible successor branches is selected from each node. Figure 2.8(a) illustrates part of one such trace.

The tree in Figure 2.8(b) has the advantage of being a very explicit representation of all possible behaviours. It is a state-oriented representation where each type of state occurring in the behaviour is explicitly represented and defined in terms of a behaviour subtree. Note that each trace through the tree is structurally similar to an instance of individual behaviour.

A description like Figure 2.8(b) is a *state-oriented description* where we focus first on states (values) and action instances. In this description, each state is explicitly represented by a node and each action instance by a branch.

This may be contrasted with an *action-oriented description,* where the action types and variables are in first focus and the states need not be described at all. The states may be found by analysing the actions, but they are not represented explicitly as nodes in the description.

Imperative programming languages have a natural emphasis on action types (programs define action types). Thus, they encourage an approach that focuses primarily on action types and variables. States tend to be hidden in variables that are only tested occasionally.

The consequence of hiding states is often that several states are represented by the same position in the behaviour description. This means that several state nodes in Figure 2.8 would be merged into one node in the action-oriented description. In consequence, the behaviour description would no longer be structurally similar to the actual behaviour.

In order to understand all the possible courses of behaviour, the reader would have to perform a mental simulation that generates all the states. The further away from a state-oriented description one gets, the harder it is to perform this simulation.

It is not sufficient that individual courses of behaviour may be simulated to see what will happen under all circumstances. The number of possible behaviours is so high it is normally unfeasible to simulate all the possibilities and to validate the behaviour description in that way. This is the essential problem of behaviour descriptions: how to represent behaviour such that it is easy to understand and feasible to validate?

Here, we must emphasise the difference between the needs of a human reader and those of a machine implementing the behaviour. The essential thing for the machine is that the program represents well-defined actions that it can perform. The essential thing for the human is that the program produces the desired effect. The focus of interest is therefore different. Roughly speaking the machine "thinks" in terms of actions, whereas the human user thinks in terms of results. But there is another important difference: the machine works step by step and needs not consider more than the instructions to follow at each step. The human needs to understand and analyse with a much wider scope.

In his famous paper on structured programming, Dijkstra said (Dijkstra, 1972):

"... we should restrict ourselves in all humility to the most systematic sequencing mechanisms, ensuring that "progress through the computation" is mapped on "progress through the text" in the most straightforward manner."

In other words, we should try to achieve structural similarity between description and behaviour.

We will contend that a state-oriented description is needed to achieve this goal. But this may not be as easy as it might sound. To be fully state-oriented we need to enumerate all the states of the system. For realistically sized systems this will be a formidable task. The number of states tends to explode for two main reasons:

1. The system behaviour is composed from many (independent) concurrent sub-behaviours that may interleave very freely with each other. The number of system states will therefore be close to the product of subbehaviour states. In effect the global behaviour tree grows too large to be practical.

2. The system behaviour encompasses variables with a very large number of values that are handled very similarly in the sequential behaviour. This will typically be information about objects and relationships in the environment and in other parts of the system. It may therefore be considered as spatial information or *context knowledge*, about something else existing in space, in contrast to temporal information *or control information*, about the progress of its own behaviour occurring in time. Typically the spatial information will be persistent, i.e. it has to be remembered over several states in temporal behaviour. It should therefore be stored in variables and not represented as state nodes in the behaviour description.

A case in point is the *AC-System*:

1. Individual users behave independently and are served independently by the *Local Stations*. In order to achieve structural similarity, the behaviour description should be split into parts corresponding to the concurrent threads of sequential behaviour in the system. Each part may then be described in state-oriented fashion.

2. The system needs to hold information about users, cards and access zones. This is spatial information since it represents different objects in space. It will be totally impractical to represent this information as state nodes. Instead, the spatial information must be stored in variables. This means that one state in the description will represent a set of possible values of spatial information. Readability and analysability can be increased by selecting the description states

such that narrow assertions can be made about the spatial information in each state.

These issues will be treated in more detail in Chapter 8 dealing with SDL method.

2.4.2   Some notes on the evolution of programming languages

The history of information system modelling began with the invention of the computer and the notion of a program. In fact, the first descriptions were programs at a very low level of abstraction. Thus, in the beginning there were *action sequences*. This put the algorithmic aspect into focus. Improvements in the early days sought primarily to achieve clarity and power in algorithmic expressions. Flow charts, assembly level languages and the first high level languages emerged. In these the data aspect remained very primitive.

Focus on the algorithmic aspect tended to make the data values hard to follow. Hence, it was difficult to assess the outcome of computations. Moreover, interactions taking place were hard to see and hard to understand.

It became clear that improvements were needed. Structured programming (Dijkstra, 1972) emerged as a discipline for structuring action sequences. One aspect of this was the syntactical rules for control flow, i.e. goto less programming. Another equally important aspect (but often overlooked) was the semantic rule relating actual behaviour to program text. In effect this means that the structure of the algorithm should reflect the structure of actual computations. This rule helps to follow the value sequences as they develop and to place meaningful assertions on the variables. Hence, it implies a stronger state orientation.

Structured programming did help and the rules are still valid today, but was still not sufficient. It was soon realised that the data aspect needed more consideration. More emphasis was needed on the data structures and the data types. Strongly typed languages were invented and support for user-defined data types became commonplace. But the algorithmic action sequence still remained the main structuring element in most languages. In these languages, data are arranged around the programs and access to data is limited by the scope rules of action sequences.

Some people began to wonder if data should be the main structuring element instead of action sequences. Rather than arranging data around the programs, the programs should be arranged around the data. SIMULA 67 (Dahl et al., 1968; Birtwistle et al., 1975) was the first programming language to fully employ this principle.

In his seminal paper "On the Criteria to be Used in Decomposing Systems into Modules" (Parnas, 1972) Parnas proposed the concept of *encapsulation,* i.e. that pure data should be avoided. Instead, data should be encapsulated in modules only accessible through a set of well-defined operations.

To achieve modularity it is necessary to distinguish between the module interface and the module body. For pure data there are no such distinctions. Pure data constitute the interface and the body at the same time. Therefore, pure data do not provide any encapsulation and are not well-suited as modules.

From encapsulation followed the notion of abstract data types. Data are put into focus and hidden at the same time with abstract data types. Data are seen as key structuring elements, but the structure of the pure data is hidden. Instead, an operation interface is provided whereby the data may be accessed. The main improvement here is the separation between an interface and a body provided by the operations. It is now possible to change the body without changing the interface. It is also possible to change the application without changing the interface. Consequently, the interface provides the means for independent modifications. The increased independence thus achieved gives a pay off in better prospects for reuse.

Communication, the third system aspect, is coming more into focus too. The need to communicate has been there since the beginning of computing, but its representation has been somewhat clogged by the early focus on actions. Nevertheless, systems need to communicate both internally and externally. In action-oriented descriptions communication is hidden in the way action sequences interact through data. This can be remedied to a certain extent by representing more explicitly the data flows taking place between actions and data. Data flow diagrams serve this purpose.

A characteristic feature of the world surrounding and using computer systems is that it consists of objects operating in parallel and interacting through communication and not by direct manipulation. We see a clear trend now towards modelling the behaviour of computer systems in the same way. This does not mean that action sequences are no longer relevant, only that other things come first.

2.4.3   Object orientation

Object orientation is getting popular in most areas of computer science. Starting with the creation of the simulation and system modelling language SIMULA 67, created at the Norwegian Computing Center in the 1960s, the paradigm of object orientation has spread to major breakthroughs in computer programming such as Smalltalk to AI (Artificial Intelligence), through dialects of LISP such as Loops and Flavours, to human interface designs such as the "look and feel" of Macintosh (trademark of Apple) and to standards of computer graphics through PHIGS. Now we see the Unix world turn to object orientation via C++, an extension to C (Stroustrup, 1992).

The benefits of object orientation range from the underlying philosophy of modelling the phenomena in the form of objects, to the compactness of descriptions achieved by the use of the inheritance and specialisation mechanisms. Hence, there are two separate ideas that go under the name of object orientation and both are part of the object orientation presented in this book:

1.   The notion of *object*. It conceives each object as being characterised by data items carrying state information, by local patterns of action sequences (procedures, methods) that the object may apply to these data items and by an individual sequence of actions that the object may execute on its own. The objects are thus *active* objects and not just passive data structures with associated operations. In order to directly model the different kinds of action sequencing found in a large class of application areas, the approach includes the

execution of objects as *part of* other objects (as is the case for procedures and methods), as *alternating* (one at a time) with other objects and as *concurrent* with other objects. An essential property is that objects have a well-defined interface that hides the internal structure of data items and action sequences from the environment.

2.   The notion of *hierarchical types* The approach makes a sharp distinction between *classes* and *objects*. (Other words commonly used are *types* and *instances*.) Objects are carriers of state information and behaviour, while classes are patterns defining common structure and properties of objects. A class is not regarded as a set of objects, but as a definition of a category of objects. Classes do not contribute to the total state of a system, but help in organizing objects in type hierarchies. Objects model the phenomena of the application area, while classes model the types. The importance of this aspect is that it provides effective support to reuse.

Reuse of components requires language mechanisms to support composition and adaptation of reusable components. Object-oriented concepts give answers to both of these: composition by clean interfaces between classes of objects and adaptation by inheritance and specialisation. The notion of objects and type hierarchies also promotes the definition of general classes that may be reused in many different applications.

There is no single and widely accepted definition of object orientation. The success of applying object orientation will depend upon the underlying approach.

In this book we use a very general approach to object orientation. Thus, there is not just one kind of object and the inheritance and specialisation mechanisms are applied to objects in general.

2.5   Some description approaches

2.5.1   Abstract descriptions

There are many different approaches to abstract system description. The approaches differ both in formality, abstraction and perspective. The usefulness of a particular approach depends on how well its underlying concepts fit the purpose of the description and the problem domain. There is little use in finite state machines, for instance, if the problem is complex data structures. On the other hand, there is little use for data structures if the problem is simple control sequences.

Informal descriptions are useful only for the human audience. Their advantage is the freedom to draw on the vast amounts of background information available to the human. The problem is that different human beings having different experiences may associate differently. Problems of ambiguity may easily arise. Problems of incompleteness and inconsistency are also common.

In order to resolve these problems, the dependency on human association must be reduced and replaced by more rigorous conventions. Various degrees of rigour ranging from simple structuring rules for natural languages to strict mathematical formalisms are in use.

Apparently there is a conflict between the need to formalise and the need to understand. A formal description may well be unambiguous, complete and consistent, but at the same time quite unintelligible to most human readers. The same description may however be well-suited to interpretation and analysis by a tool. Fully formal methods are required by all tools because tools operate by strictly following rules step by step. A human being, on the other hand, tries to build a global understanding beyond the scope of single rules. Formality will not help the human reader much if it is counter-intuitive.

It goes without saying that mathematical formalisms are extremely useful. We can hardly think of engineering work without their support. But in the field of behaviour description we must still trade formality against human conception when there is a conflict.

The abstract description methods that have had the strongest penetration so far have been those that emphasise the needs of the human audience. In the following sections a few popular approaches will be outlined.

2.5.2 Entity relationship descriptions

Almost every system needs to store some information about the environment. The role of a typical information system is primarily to store and process information about some enterprise in the real world surrounding it. In a typical real time system the role is primarily to control something in its environment, but even in this role most systems need to remember some information about the environment. Thus, knowledge about the environment is part of most systems. How can this aspect be described without going into the internal construction of the system?

The entity relationship (ER) description was motivated by the need to describe data in a way close to the users view in applications involving large collections of interrelated data. For this reason it has been mostly used to model typical database applications, but the current trend towards larger and more complex data in real time systems make ER descriptions increasingly useful in real time applications as well.

ER descriptions are based on the notions of entities, relationships and attributes. They are often expressed in a graphical notation called ER diagrams, of which there are many syntactical variants. A typical example is shown in Figure 2.9.

The diagram in Figure 2.9 describes data in the *Access Control* system. It represents the entities *User*, *Card*, *Door*, *Local Station* and *Access Zone* and the relations between them. It also represents the attributes of the entities. An entity in the diagram represents a collection of individuals in the real world having similar properties. An entity can therefore not be seen as a type of individual, but must be seen as a set of individuals having similar attributes and participating in the same relations.

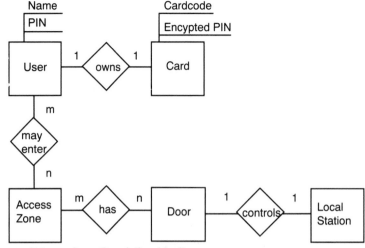

Figure 2.9   *An entity relationship diagram*

The representation of a relation in Figure 2.9 is a diamond linked to the related entities. Relations are defined in the usual mathematical way as a set of associations between individuals. The set of individuals represented by an entity will be partitioned into subsets by the relations applying to that entity. The *Users*, for instance are partitioned by the *may enter* relation to *Access Zones*. Thus, the way to arrange individuals in different sets is to define corresponding relations.

Individuals may participate in the relations in different ways. In some cases each individual is related to exactly one other individual, in other cases each individual is related to several others. It is common to classify relations as either one-to-one, one-to-many or-many-to-many and to indicate the class in the ER diagram. For instance, in Figure 2.9, the relation between *Users* and *Cards* is one-to-one, meaning that each *User* has exactly one *Card*. The relation between *Users* and *Access Zones* is many-to-many, meaning that each *User* has access to many *Zones* and that each *Zone* may be accessed by many *Users*.

ER descriptions focus on the meaning of data by representing the entities and the relationships that data refer to. They view data in the system as a description of something in the real world and try to express this part of the world in a logical way rather than as a physical storage structure. We may say that data represent context knowledge in the "mind" of the system. For this reason they are also called *conceptual schema,* in contrast to *internal schema* representing the storage structure and *external schema* representing the user interface in database applications.

ER descriptions focus entirely on the structure of data and have no way to represent behaviour. But data must be accessed, processed and communicated as part of the system behaviour in order to be useful. Consequently, one should not model everything in the world, only those aspects of the world needed by the system behaviour.

One popular solution is to combine ER diagrams with data flow diagrams (DFD) (see Section 2.5.4). In that way the ER diagram can represent the data stored in a DFD and the DFD can represent the actions performed on the data.

It is claimed(for example, Ghezzi et al., 1991), that the expressive power of ER diagrams is rather limited. One cannot express constraints on the number of individuals belonging to an entity. In the *Access Control* system, for instance, there is a maximum number of users but this limit cannot be expressed.

The same limitation applies to relations. From Figure 2.9 we can see that each *Access Zone* may be related to several *Doors*, but we cannot see how many. Nor can we express constraints on the attributes of related individuals, for instance, that the PIN code in the *Card* shall be an encrypted representation of the PIN code of the *User* owning the card.

In spite of the limitations, ER diagrams help to build understanding and overview.

2.5.3 A notation putting individuals into focus

Is it necessary to use different notations for different categories of structure? Could we not use ER diagrams to express substance structures instead of the SOON notation we introduced in Section 2.1? In many cases we need the precision lacking in ER diagrams when describing substance structures. We would like to be precise about the number of instances and their connectivities.

Figure 2.10 shows how the SOON notation can be used to express the same information as in Figure 2.9 and more. We have now added relations, represented by ovals, to the notation.

In both diagrams a box represents a set, but in Figure 2.10 it is a set of instances of a specific type. Note that the type *Door* in Figure 2.10 is different from the entity *Door* in Figure 2.9. The entity *Door* represents a set, while the type *Door* represents the properties of a single, generic door.

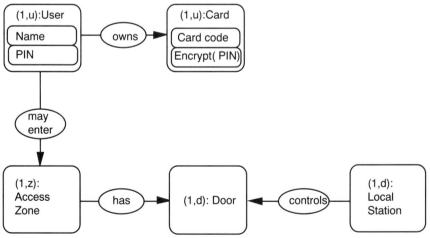

Figure 2.10   *Data description in the general structure notation SOON*

Since the notation has a clear separation between types and instances it allows us to represent individuals and types explicitly and not implicitly as in ER diagrams. Bringing the individuals forward allows us to say more about the types as well. It also provides a better basis for reuse, since individuals are used in more places than sets of individuals.

In Figure 2.10 we have expressed constraints on set cardinalities by giving a low and a high limit on the number of instances represented by each box.

Normally a relation will be one-to-one when the cardinalities of related entity sets are the same and many-to-many when they are different. One-to-many is a special case when there is just one instance in one of the sets.

We could have added the relation classification in the same way as in Figure 2.9, but we would still not be able to tell the full story. We would not know how many *Access Zones* a *Door* might be related to, only that it might be related to any number of them. To be precise we must look at the type definitions.

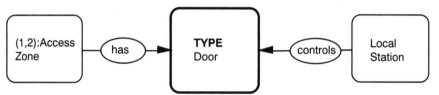

Figure 2.11   *Definition of the type Door. It implies that instances of Door shall be related to one or two Access Zones and one Local Station*

A type definition may include a prescription of what we consider a valid instance environment. The type definition for a *Door*, in Figure 2.11, prescribes that an instance of a *Door* shall be related to a minimum of one and a maximum of two, *Access Zones* and to exactly one *Local Station*. A corresponding type definition for *Access Zone*, which will be given in Figure 3.5, prescribes that an *Access Zone* may have any number of *Doors*, where some are *Way out* and some *Way in* to the *Access Zone*. From this information it follows that the relation is many-to-many with the constraint that each *Door* is related to a maximum of two *Access Zones*.

The entities and relations in the environment of a type represent *roles* that shall be played by *actors* in the environment of an instance of the type. In this case the entity roles refer to the types *Access Zone* and *Local Station*. This means that the actors have to be (subtypes of) *Access Zone* and *Local Station*. If this is not true, the instance is not in a valid environment.

The specification of roles in the type environment serves three purposes:

1.   Understanding the environment helps to understand the type.
2.   The roles help to validate the application of instances.
3.   The cardinalities of relations that an instance may participate in can be precisely specified.

2.5.4 Data flow diagrams

The first data flow diagram (DFD) notation was introduced in the SADT methodology (Ross, 1977). This is a comprehensive methodology where the data flow diagrams are one of several components. Alternative notations have been described by DeMarco (1979) , Gane and Sarson (1978) and others. Among these, the bubble diagram is a typical and popular representative (see Figure 2.12).

Data flow diagrams focus mainly on the types of actions and the types of data being stored and communicated. Actions take data as input and transform them into data delivered as output. Output from one action may then be passed on as input to other actions through a so-called data flow. In that way a system may be viewed as a collection of actions connected by flows of data, hence, the name data flow diagrams. The description focuses on the transformation of data as it flows from input to output.

In a traditional flow chart or program, the control flow is emphasised at the expense of data flow. In traditional data flow diagrams, the opposite is the case. Data flow is explicitly modelled while control flow is suppressed. The method surrounding DFD will often tell the designer not to think in terms of control initially, because control should be subordinate to data flow. Most DFD methodologies have additional notation to express control flow.

In data flow diagrams the bubbles represent actions or transformations in the DFD terminology, while arrows represent data flows. Storage is represented by two parallel lines. Information sources and receivers in the environment are represented by square boxes.

The diagram in Figure 2.12 describes the *AC-System*. The description is easy to overview and we have few problems in understanding what it is all about, but the diagram neither says anything about *when* things will happen nor *who* (what object) is supposed to do the job. Actually it does not say anything about the sequence in which things will happen nor about the substance on which it will happen. The diagram emphasises *which data* are the prerequisites for each action and which data are the outputs of each action. This is important information, but it is not sufficient if explicit interaction sequencing is considered to be of importance.

Partitioning is well-supported in DFDs. One starts modelling by showing the system as one bubble and describing the data flows to and from the environment. One continues by decomposing the system into actions and data flows. Each of these are further decomposed until the desired level of detail is reached.

The advantages of DFDs are well-known and may be summarised in the following way:

- *They are simple and general.* DFDs are simple to learn and can be used to describe a very wide range of problem domains.
- *There is good tool support.* Many commercial CASE tools are available that support DFDs in one form or another.
- *There are good textbooks and excellent courses.* Their popularity has earned them a very central position in the software engineering literature.

They are supported by methodology. DFDs are often part of wider methodologies supporting much of the software engineering process. In these methodologies one finds notations that complement the DFDs.

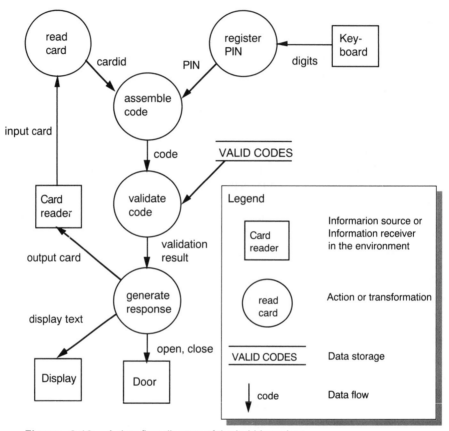

Figure 2.12   *A data flow diagram of the bubble variety*

The drawbacks are also well-known:

1. *The semantics are informal.* The meaning of actions and data flows depends on the association between names and concepts that the readers have in their minds. It is therefore a rigorous, but not fully formal approach, where misinterpretations may occur. As a consequence, the analysis performed by tools is restricted to the syntactic level. Automatic generation of action code is not possible.

2. *Implementation design is difficult.* The guidelines for going from DFDs to software design rely on heuristics that many designers find hard to apply. Most

textbooks describe implementation by a sequential program hierarchy and not by concurrent processes.

3. *No support for encapsulation, instantiation and reuse.* The notation shows action types only. It does not bother with the existence of many instances of the same action types that are around in a system or the reuse of an action type in several systems.

In this book we shall look especially at a different notation, SDL, in which a system is described as a structure of finite state machines connected by signal channels. It is possible to represent a system in a similar way using DFDs (Flo et al., 1992), but that is entirely up to the user. The DFD notation is so general that it might be used instead of other more specialised notations on the syntactic level, but it lacks the guidance towards a particular way of modelling implied by the semantics of more formal languages such as SDL.

Data flow diagrams belong to the family of action-oriented descriptions. Bubbles represent the action types and not the action instances. It is a static picture of how actions are connected through data flows and storage, not a dynamic picture of temporal behaviour. There is no concept of time or temporal ordering in the diagrams. In this sense they are declarative or constraint-oriented descriptions. As such they are valuable, but they need to be complemented by other descriptions in order to describe all aspects of a system.

Coad and Yourdon (1990) criticised the approach found in much of the software engineering literature of starting with DFDs. They contend that data modelling is more essential and should be the first issue, but they do not discard the DFDs completely. They provide a mixed notation where data modelling is blended with DFDs in an object-oriented manner. This helps to remedy the third drawback mentioned above.

2.5.5   Finite state machine (FSM)

Data flow diagrams and entity relationship diagrams are notations that focus on the time-independent structure of data and actions. In order to describe the temporal ordering in which actions will be invoked and states generated, we need other formalisms.

One of the simplest and best known is the finite state machine (FSM), which means that the machine has a finite and well-defined set of "states". The FSM focuses on the external interaction sequences and completely describes the relationship between sequences of inputs and sequences of outputs.

An FSM is defined formally by:

1. a finite set of inputs, I;
2. a finite set of outputs, O;
3. a finite set of states, S;
4. a next state function, F_S: S x I -> S;
5. an output function, F_O: S x I -> O*;
6. a designated initial state, Initial.

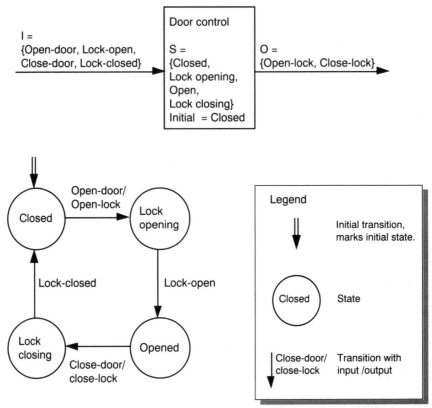

Figure 2.13   *Finite state machine describing a possible Door controller in the Access Control system*

The FSM will only accept input when it is in a state. For each input accepted it will make a transition to the next state given by the next state function and generate the outputs given by the output function. A transition is normally considered to take zero time, so all the time is spent in states.

A common way to describe an FSM is a state transition diagram (ST diagram) like the one shown in Figure 2.13.

Here the circles represent states and the arrows represent transitions. Associated with each transition is an input which triggers the transition followed by a set of outputs that will be generated during the transition.

FSMs are well-suited to describe the stimuli–response behaviour of processes. An ST diagram shows clearly and completely how sequences of inputs relate to sequences of outputs and it is done without any reference to a physical implementation. It is therefore a formalism well-suited to abstract description of externally observable behaviour.

The FSM has substance in an abstract sense due to its ability to remember a state. The state is used to represent the history of inputs and is the only memory of a pure FSM. In the object-oriented sense it is a perfect object having its own behaviour, encapsulating its data and providing a well-defined interface in terms of input and output signals.

A state transition diagram describes behaviour in a state-oriented way. The states of the diagram completely enumerate the possible states that may be reached during actual behaviour. The arrows completely enumerate all the transitions that may be performed and the actions follow from the need to generate outputs. In this manner the FSM provides the means to describe behaviour in a way that clearly shows how all the possible behaviours may evolve. It is therefore a formalism with many advantages :

1.   *External view* (observable behaviour). It is a description that focuses on external stimuli–response behaviour and not internal action sequences.
2.   *State orientation.* The explicit and complete description of all possible behaviours.
3.   *Finiteness.* It can be analysed and tested completely in finite time. The testing effort is proportional to the number of transitions.
4.   *Implementation independence.* It is not bound to a particular implementation, but may be implemented in many ways.
5.   *Implementability.* Efficient implementations can be found.
6.   *Well-developed theory.* Many theoretical results exists that can be used to analyse FSMs.

These are very strong advantages that are well worth the effort achieving. The problem is that the pure FSM falls short in practical respects:

1.   *No data.* The state is the only memory of the pure FSM. This may be sufficient for control, but is not a good way to represent knowledge about the environment. It would be highly impractical to represent the name of a user or the identity of a card, by means of the states. Therefore, the FSM is well-suited to describe control, but not to describe data.
2.   *No free ordering (concurrency).* The FSM behaves strictly sequentially. This is fine as long as inputs and outputs follow each other in a certain order. If they follow just any ordering, the FSM becomes a problem. The only way to represent free ordering with an FSM is to explicitly list all possible orderings. This is a highly inefficient way of representing the simple fact that the ordering does not matter.
3.   *No time.* Although the FSM is strong on temporal ordering, it has no concept of time. Transitions are normally assumed to take no time and there is no other reference to time. In practical systems and particularly in real time systems, time must be considered.

In order to overcome these limitations, the FSM must be extended and/or supplemented with other notations. Methodologies based on data flow diagrams, for instance, use FSMs to control the actions in a data flow diagram. (See, for instance, Yourdon, 1989.) Thus, the FSM is used for the control part while the DFD is used for the data part.

A different approach is to extend the pure FSM with concepts for data, concurrency and time. This is done in the SDL language we shall use later in this book. When the pure FSM is extended to handle data we call it an EFSM – extended finite state machine. The price we must pay for this power is non-decidability. It is not necessarily a finite task to analyse and test its properties any more. Thus, it is extremely important that the extensions are introduced and used in such a way that the advantages of the pure FSM are maintained as much as possible.

2.6   The methodology presented here

The combination of a language (notation of some sort) with rules and guidelines will be called a method in this book. In accordance with its normal definition, a methodology then is a collection of methods. Thus, the foundation for methodology is a collection of languages, rules and guidelines.

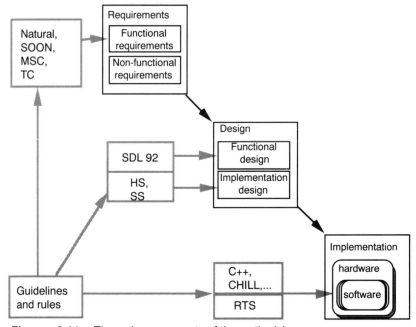

Figure 2.14   *The main components of the methodology*

The methodology presented in this book puts the emphasis on descriptions that are both comprehensible to people and implementable. To achieve this, mathematical rigour has been de-emphasised, but the descriptions are still sufficiently formal to support automatic analysis and implementation.

The methodology gives a fairly broad coverage of systems engineering, as it was described in Chapter 1. It starts with the initial needs of the future users and owners and ends with system implementation, maintenance and reuse. On the way a number of descriptions are developed using different notations supported by rules and guidelines, as illustrated in Figure 2.14.

For requirements specification we use natural language together with SOON diagrams, message sequence charts (MSC) and transition charts (TC). The guidelines are summarised in a number of analysis rules, *A-rules*.

For functional design we use SDL 92. This is the central language of the methodology and it is supported by a number of structuring rules, *S-rules* and notational rules, *N-rules*. These rules help to make well-structured descriptions that are easy to read and analyse. The resulting SDL description is used both as the basis for implementation design and to document the functionality of the system as it has been implemented. It is therefore not a description that is thrown away, but an integral part of the system documentation. It is used extensively during system testing and later reuse and maintenance.

For implementation design we use variants of the SOON notation to express hardware structures (HS) and software structures (SS). The resulting diagrams are used to express information not covered by SDL, but needed in addition to SDL to derive and document the implementation. They complement the SDL diagrams and are used together with the SDL diagrams as system documentation.

The derivation of implementations is extensively covered and a number of step-wise guidelines are provided together with some S-rules. Systems may be implemented in any programming language or in hardware. In software it is common to use an SDL run-time support system (RTS) that provides test and debug facilities in addition to support for SDL concepts.

Verification and validation is covered to some extent by the methodology. A constructive rule that helps to build consistent SDL processes is given.

The methodology employs object orientation in SDL and applies object-oriented principles to all descriptions ranging from requirements through design to implementation.

The methodology is open to almost any method for project planning and control. The same goes for document handling and quality control. The key point is that the methodology provides the tangible results that are needed to perform effective quality control and project management.

Table 2.1 summarises the languages (notations) that we use in this book and the descriptions they are used for. We have also added a column briefly showing what understanding one can expect to be achieve through the descriptions.

Table 2.1 *Summary of notations*

Language	Description	Understanding achieved
Natural	Purpose statement	Purpose, idea
Natural	Dictionary	Fragmented knowledge, concepts
SOON	Domain description,	Combined knowledge, concepts
SOON	Context description	Interfaces and environment
MSC	Interaction sequences	Temporal behaviour cases
Transition Chart	Interface behaviour, role	Behaviour projection
SDL	Functional design	Functional system behaviour
SS, HS	Implementation design	Physical system structure
Programming Language	Programs	Implementation

2.7   The SOON notation

The SISU object-oriented notation (SOON) enables us to represent different structures in a consistent and coherent way using object-oriented principles similar to those of SDL (see Chapters 4 – 7). We use this notation to describe structures where SDL is not appropriate. It is less formal and does not enforce the SDL semantics. It can therefore be used at an early stage to structure and analyse the concepts of a problem domain before the functional design is made. In that way it can be used as a help on the way from informal needs to a formal functional design expressed in SDL. In addition, it can be used to supplement SDL in the area of conceptual data models.

We shall also use variants of SOON to describe the implementation design of a system at the architectural level (see Chapters 9 and 10).

In a way SOON can be seen as a traditional box and arrow notation where general relations and types have been added. In the following we first describe the notation informally and then its graphical syntax.

Every diagram is either an entity description or a relation description. It contains a frame symbol which is an enlarged entity symbol or relation symbol representing the described entity or relation. Inside the frame symbol, in its upper left corner, the name of the described entity or relation is given. If it is a type definition the name is preceded by the keyword TYPE. If it inherits from a supertype, the name is followed by a colon and the supertype name.

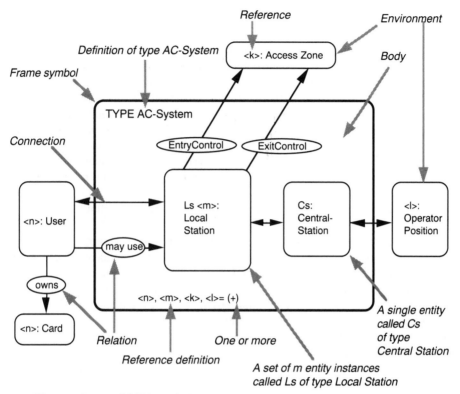

Figure 2.15 *SOON symbols*

Outside the frame one may describe the environment and inside one describes the body of the entity/relation.

A description consists of boxes, representing entities, linked by relation symbols and connection symbols. When inheritance is used, a description need only contain parts that are added or modified in relation to the supertype. Entities and relations that are inherited from a supertype are dashed. Boxes represent entities, arrows represent connections that enable entities to communicate with each other and ovals represent relations linking entities together. It is possible to define entities as well as relations separately as types. In both cases it is possible to inherit from a supertype.

A box may represent a single entity or it may represent a set of entities. The number of instances in a set is specified by a low and a high limit placed inside parentheses. For example, (1,100) which means at least one and a maximum of 100 or (3,3) which means exactly 3. The special symbols * and + represent zero or more and one or more, respectively.

(min, max)	at least *min,* at most *max*
(min,)	at least *min,* no upper bound
(+)	at least one, no upper bound

(*)   any number

The text inside an entity symbol or relation symbol consists of two parts separated by a colon. The first part, which is optional contains a local instance name followed by the number of instances. The second part contains the type name.

For entities and relations that are inherited from a supertype, the type name may be followed by a double arrow (formed by an equal sign and a right angular bracket) and a redefinition. In the redefinition it is possible to restrict the number of instances, to give instances new names and to assign a new type to the instance. This must be a subtype of the original type. (See also "redefinition" in SDL as described in Chapter 7.)

In order to save space, part of a definition may be replaced by a reference symbol, which consists of angular brackets containing a number. The definition may then be given elsewhere in the diagram by entering the same reference symbol followed by an equal sign and then the definition.

The number of connection and relation instances will often, but not always, follow from the number of connected instances. When the cardinalities are identical, one-to-one connections will be the normal case, giving just as many connections as there are instances on each side. When the cardinalities differ, each instance may potentially connect to all instances on the other side, giving many-to-many connections. More precision can be achieved in the definition of types.

In the following syntax, italics have been used to represent meta symbols and normal text and symbols to represent terminal symbols. Brackets mean an option, a slash separates alternatives and an asterisk attached to a symbol means repetition any number of times.

Entity description::=

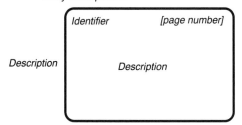

Description

An entity description is a frame symbol with entity identifier, page number, environment description and body description.

Identifier ::=
    instance name [:type name] /
    TYPE type name [:type name]

An entity identifier is either an instance identifier or the keyword TYPE followed by a type name and optionally by a colon and a new type name. The last type name refers to the supertype which is specialized.

page number ::=
    this page (number of pages)

A page number consists of the number of the current page and the total number of pages enclosed in paretheses.

Relation Description::=

Description

Identifier

Description

A relation description is a relation frame symbol, an identifier and description of the body and the environment

Description::=
    Entity*
    Relation*
    Connection*
    Inherited entity*
    Inherited relation*
    reference*
    reference definition*
    entity extension*

A description consists of any number of entities, relations and connections. It may also contain representations of entities and relations inherited from a supertype. Finally, information may be referenced in order to save space at one point.

Entity ::=

[instance name [range] :]
type name

An entity consists of an entity symbol containing a type name. It may optionally contain an instance name and a range specification for the number of instances.

Relation ::=

[instance name :]
type name

A relation consists of a relation symbol which will connect with the related entities. It contains a type name and may optionally contain an instance name.

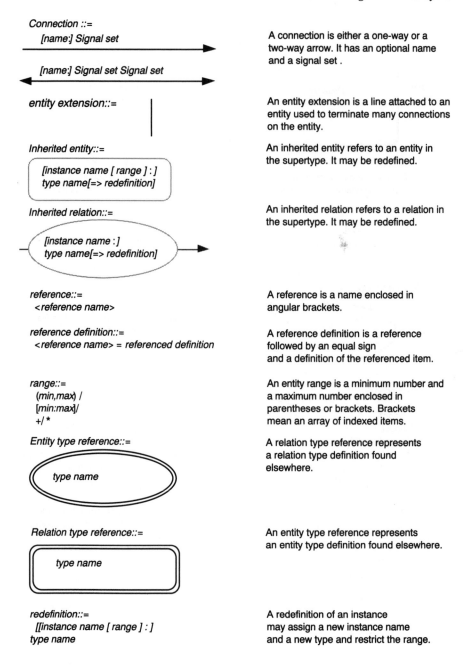

Connection ::=
   [name:] Signal set

   [name:] Signal set Signal set

A connection is either a one-way or a two-way arrow. It has an optional name and a signal set .

entity extension::=

An entity extension is a line attached to an entity used to terminate many connections on the entity.

Inherited entity::=

   [instance name [range] :]
   type name[=> redefinition]

An inherited entity refers to an entity in the supertype. It may be redefined.

Inherited relation::=

   [instance name :]
   type name[=> redefinition]

An inherited relation refers to a relation in the supertype. It may be redefined.

reference::=
   <reference name>

A reference is a name enclosed in angular brackets.

reference definition::=
   <reference name> = referenced definition

A reference definition is a reference followed by an equal sign and a definition of the referenced item.

range::=
   (min,max) /
   [min:max]/
   *+/ ***

An entity range is a minimum number and a maximum number enclosed in parentheses or brackets. Brackets mean an array of indexed items.

Entity type reference::=

   type name

A relation type reference represents a relation type definition found elsewhere.

Relation type reference::=

   type name

An entity type reference represents an entity type definition found elsewhere.

redefinition::=
   [[instance name [range] :]
   type name

A redefinition of an instance may assign a new instance name and a new type and restrict the range.

Part II

Specification

Chapter 3 treats the requirements specification or how to specify the essential external requirements to the system without going into unnecessary detail about internal operations or physical realisations. Notations for conceptual modelling and interface behaviours are introduced. Chapters 4–8 treat functional design, i.e. how to define the complete functional behaviour that can be observed at the system interfaces. First, the SDL language is described in Chapters 4–7, then methodology guidelines for using SDL to express functional designs in a clear and concise way are given in Chapter 8.

CHAPTER 3

Requirements Specifications

The objective of this chapter is to give a clear understanding of what requirements are, what to emphasise and what to avoid. It starts out by considering the main sources of requirements: the user and the owner. Since they look at the system from different angles, their requirements are not the same. The user is mainly interested in functionality, while the owners concerns are cost–benefit issues. The emphasis of this chapter is not the process of deriving requirements, but how to represent functional and non-functional requirements.

3.1   The problem

3.1.1   From needs to requirements

As we have stated already, the first and most critical step in a systems development is to get to grips with the user's and the owner's exact needs and expectations concerning the new system. This may not be easy, not even for the users and owners themselves, because "needs" and "expectations" are rather vague and nebulous matters. Nevertheless, it is essential that they are known and well-understood, not only by the users and owners, but also by the developers. To achieve this, we need descriptions that support clear thinking and precise communication about those difficult matters.

In ANSI/IEEE (1984) *requirements* are defined as follows:

1. *A condition or capability needed by a user to solve a problem or achieve an objective;*

2. *A condition or capability that must be met or possessed by a system or system component to satisfy a contract, standard, specification or other formally imposed document. The set of all requirements forms the basis for subsequent development of the system or system component.*

Requirements specifications is the collective name of descriptions used to express all kinds of requirements to the new system. They will often be collected in a document called the "requirements specification".

The scope of requirements is not to define the system properties in every detail, but to define the essential properties or attributes, required by the system environment. Some of these properties are normally specific for the system, while other properties are quite general. Some requirements are such that they cannot be altered, while other requirements may be subject to negotiation if alternatives are proposed. Most requirements state desired properties, but sometimes one needs to state non-desirable properties as well. In any case the focus is on needs and expectations emanating from sources outside the system. Among the questions that should be answered is *why* the system is needed, i.e. its purpose and role as seen by the user and the owner.

We shall make an informal distinction between *functional requirements* and *non-functional requirements*. The intuition behind this distinction is that functional requirements are concerned with the system services, i.e. the behaviour as the users will see it. They are the primary inputs to functional design. The non-functional requirements, on the other hand, are constraints on the implementation of the system. They are inputs to the implementation design.

Process requirements are concerned with the development process. They state requirements to issues such as the development methodology, the use of standards, the tools to be used, the project organisation and how quality assurance is to be carried out.

To capture and analyse needs and expectations so that they can be distilled into rigid requirements is often a difficult task that involves special skills and techniques. The approach needed for this task varies enormously from case to case and between application areas. In this book it will not be elaborated upon. We will simply assume that needs have been clarified and concentrate on how to express requirements. Of course, these tasks go hand in hand. Expressing the requirements helps in understanding the needs better, better understanding leads to a reformulation of requirements and so forth.

In ANSI/IEEE (1984) a requirements specification is defined as:

> *"A specification that sets forth the requirements for a system or system component; for example a software configuration item. Typically included are: functional requirements, performance requirements, interface requirements, design requirements and development standards."*

Requirements must have the following characteristics:

1. *Unambiguous.* There must be only one semantic interpretation. As a minimum each term used must have a unique and well-defined meaning.
2. *Complete.* No need or requirement of the user and the owner must be missing. All terms must be defined and if a particular standard is followed, the requirement specification must conform to that standard.
3. *Verifiable.* For each requirement it should be possible to check that the requirement is fulfilled in the system. Therefore, the requirements should be expressed in terms that are measurable.
4. *Consistent.* There should be no conflict between statements.
5. *Modifiable.* Requirements should be structured such that necessary changes can be made without violating the other attributes.
6. *Traceable.* The origin of each requirement should be clear and it should be possible to identify how each requirement is taken care of in the system.

In the following sections we shall have a closer look at the various kinds of requirements from the points of view of the user and the owner.

3.1.2 Domain analysis

The aim of domain analysis is to understand the problem domain independently of the particular system we intend to develop. Therefore, we do not try to draw the borderline between the system and the environment at this stage. Instead we focus on the concepts and the terminology of the application domain with a wider scope than the future system.

One way to approach domain analysis is to describe the current reality into which the system is going to be placed. The purpose of a *reality model* is to understand the current reality as a basis for designing a new reality. One may therefore start by describing the existing systems and procedures just as they are. One should at least define the concepts and the terminology of the application domain.

The next step is to identify the problems and limitations of the current reality and to clearly describe the objectives and goals one wants to achieve in the new reality. In doing that, it is important to abstract from the physical details of the current reality and to identify the problems that need to be solved in more general terms. If one fails to do so, it will be very difficult to come up with an innovative solution.

The key question to answer is *why* a new reality is needed. The answer should give the owner, the user and the developer a clear picture of what *purpose* the new system should serve. A common understanding of the purpose is the essence of quality control. It is necessary to both give the development process its proper direction and to validate the final result.

Typical activities and results of domain analysis are as follows:

1. a clear statement of purpose, i.e. objectives and goals for the new system;
2. a dictionary defining the common terminology and concepts of the problem domain;

3. description of the problem domain from a conceptual modelling viewpoint, which may include data models of the old and the desired new reality;

4. an inheritance diagram showing the relationships between concepts (types).

We shall give some examples as we go along.

3.1.3   Requirements of the environment

When the problem domain is well-understood, the next issue is to identify the new system and its environment.

So far we have been talking about "the user" in a rather unqualified manner. The term brings to mind the idea of a human user interacting with the system through a terminal. But it should not be understood in this restricted sense. What we have in mind are all kinds of objects in the surroundings that use the services that the system provides. This includes human users as well as other technical systems, such as pure software systems. Both categories give rise to requirements and both are equally important. In addition to the users, the system may need external support systems to carry out its services, e.g. operating systems, database management systems and communication media (see Figure 3.1).

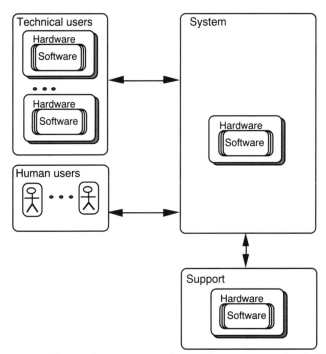

Figure 3.1   *The environment consists of human users, technical users and support. The system context consists of the system and the environment.*

There will also be physical conditions in the environment to consider, such as temperature, humidity and vibrations.

Human needs are different from the needs of machines. Human beings appreciate such things as "look and feel" where as machines simply do not care. The main difference from an engineering point of view is that human beings are not well-understood, whereas technical systems are. By studying a technical system we can derive what requirements it puts on other systems. We cannot study human users in the same way, but we may attempt to describe the existence of different user groups, their needs and the ways in which they may interact with the system.

Thus, the next thing to do is to describe the environment of the system. This is not a description of everything in the environment, only those aspects that are of importance to the system or otherwise related to it. A diagram identifying the boundary of the new system, the main users in the environment and the interaction channels will be a great help.

Note that needs and requirements go both ways. It is not only the environment that puts requirements on the system. The system will put some restrictions on its environment too and these should be expressed in the requirements specification as well (see Section 3.1.4 on roles).

Looking at the system from the outside, we see interfaces where the environment can interact with the system to obtain its services. Such interfaces will often be organised in layers with the physical interface at the bottom and the idealised services at the top. Only physical interfaces such as terminals, panels, plugs and cables are visible to the eye, but the higher layers are often more important to the user.

We can illustrate this by a simple everyday example. You want to make a telephone call to a friend, say Joe. Ideally you would prefer to ask the phone system to "get Joe" and the system would know where to find Joe and set up the connection.(This is what you could actually do in small communities back in the days of manual operators.) But modern telephone systems do not know about Joe (not yet), so you will have to look up the directory number and ask the system to "get 2753" instead. To do this you must lift your hand-set, wait for the dialling tone and dial "2753". This information is transformed into a sequence of bits and passed onto the telephone exchange over a pair of twisted wires. Thus, we have several *layers*:

1. The ideal service: "get Joe".
2. The more concrete service: "get 2753".
3. The user dialogue: lift hand-set, wait for dialling tone, ...
4. The transfer dialogue: tones, bits.
5. The physical medium: the subscriber set, twisted pair.

The two highest layers can be seen as ideal dialogues without a physical implementation. The next two are still idealised, but they have implementations. The bottom layer is the concrete physical system; the only one we can see, touch and feel.

In this picture, the user's main needs are represented by the top layer, whereas the other layers can more or less be seen as "evils" necessary to fulfil the needs. Still the user will have to cope with them, so they are subject to user requirements. In particular the user dialogue (layer 3) and the physical appearance (layer 5) will be critical for user satisfaction. This shows that requirements may have to address several layers.

Although the ideal service "get Joe" is what the user really needs, he will not get it because it is too costly to implement. Nevertheless, it is of some value to think over the ideal needs. All too often innovation is hampered because we are bound by existing solutions. Contemplating the ideal needs may help to come up with new solutions such as a terminal (holding a directory) that will call Joe when you "double click" his icon.

Note that there is some independence between the layers. The higher layers use the services of lower layers, but they do not depend on their particular form. We may change the lower layers with no effect on the higher layers as long as the same services are provided. Therefore, layering is an important structuring principle that helps to manage complexity by identifying and separating independent aspects.

What are the real and basic needs of the environment? In most cases, the ideal service is the prime thing and the interaction protocols are just a way of obtaining it. But this does not mean that the interaction protocols and the physical interfaces do not matter. It means that we should try to factor out the important abstractions and layers and express the requirements to each of them separately. This means that, to specify requirements, one will make descriptions that belong to different abstractions. Since "look and feel" are important, it may even be necessary to build a prototype in order to get the right feeling for the user interface.

In some cases, the lower layers, including the physical interface, are completely determined by systems in the environment and should therefore be completely specified in the requirements. In most cases however, they are not and should be left open for the designer to select at a later stage.

In addition to interfaces and dialogues, the system often needs conceptual knowledge about items and relationships in the environment. An accounting system, for instance, needs knowledge about customers, products, sales and the like. These play the role of subjects in relation to our system (see Section 1.1.3). A conceptual description (data-model) of the subjects and their relationships will help to clarify this aspect.

To sum up, the requirements of the user environment may be classified as follows:

1. Statement of purpose from the user point of view.
2. Functional requirements:
    (a) requirements to ideal (functional) services and dialogues, possibly on several layers of abstractions;
    (b) requirements to ideal (conceptual) knowledge about the environment;
    (c) requirements to size: number of users, terminals, etc.
3. Non-functional requirements:
    (a) requirements to (concrete) physical interfaces;
    (b) requirements to physical conditions like temperature, humidity, power consumption, etc.;
    (c) requirements to processing capacity: response times, traffic load, etc.;
    (d) requirements to exception handling.

The subclassification above may be discussed. It is not always obvious where to put the various requirements. The essential thing is not the classification, but to express all requirements as clearly and unambiguously as possible.

3.1.4 Roles

Relationships existing between the system and the environment give meaning and purpose to the system in relation to the environment. In Figure 3.1, for instance, the communication between each user and the system should serve a purpose for that user. A user who feels that the system serves its purpose well, will be satisfied and consider the system as having good quality. Another user, having other needs, might find the system poor.

The notion of quality therefore depends on the needs of a given user. (Remember that we use the term *user* in a broad sense here.) We will associate the notion of a *role* with the needs of a user. Thus, a user will expect the system to play a certain role. The role is what the user expects from the system, the *play* is what the system provides. If the play fits the role then the user will be happy. Our goal as developers is to make systems that play their roles well.

This *role-play* principle is symmetric. The system puts constraints on the user too. Unless the user follows the rules, i.e. the role required by the system, the cooperation will not work. Of course, the system should be designed to accept the dialogue form required by its users, but once designed the users cannot change the rules and expect the system to follow.

The validation of a system in relation to a user environment is to check that the system indeed plays the roles required by the users. The validation of an interface is to check that both sides play the roles they mutually require from each other. It follows from these considerations that the notions of roles and plays are closely connected to the notion of validation and thus to system quality. If we could formalise these notions, we might find better ways of achieving quality control. This is one of the ideas we will pursue in this book.

At this point we may only outline the general principle.

The role-play principle
Each type defines roles for related or connected entities. For each instance of the type, every role shall be assigned to an actor, i.e. an entity instance in the environment playing the role. We say that the play is valid when it is a proper specialisation of the role. For a system to be consistent, the play of all roles must be valid.

In other words, a system is assigned roles that it shall play in relation to its environment and vice versa. These roles are defined by the types and assigned by the connections and relations between the system and its environment. The application of an instance is valid only when the plays of all the roles given to it are valid and the plays of all the roles it gives to entities in the environment are valid.

The notion of specialisation used in the definition above has to do with inheritance in the object-oriented sense.

3.1.5   Requirements of the owners

We use the term "owner" to denote the organisation or person that asks for a system development and/or will own the system in the future. This includes companies that will own and operate an individual system installation and manufacturing companies that will own the system as a product and sell installations. Although customers and suppliers play different roles, they share a common interest in getting maximum value in return for the money they invest. Functionality and user satisfaction are more means than measures to them. Of course, they want the user to be happy with the system, but not at any cost.

The interests of the owners go beyond the initial development. It is the profits that can be made during later production, operation and maintenance that really matter. Hence, the owner is concerned with the total lifetime productivity measured as

productivity = application value/cost of resources used

Many companies have too low productivities because too many resources are spent producing, maintaining and operating system installations. Hence, if the system is to be produced and maintained, the owner will need a system where postdevelopment costs are as low as possible. However, if the system is a one-shot, the development costs are dominant. Such critical issues should be taken into account during the initial development and should be covered in the requirements.

Application value will depend strongly on the system quality in relation to the users. But in addition to the qualities needed for acceptance in the market, the time of introduction is often critical. In many cases it is more critical to minimise the development time than the development cost. A shorter development time means a longer time in the market-place. This can mean both higher prices (initially) and more sales, hence, an increase in application value that outweighs an increased development cost.

Is there a conflict between quality and productivity? Boehm has stated (Boehm, 1987):

1.   A project can reduce software development cost at the expense of quality, but only in ways that increase operational and life cycle costs.
2.   A project can simultaneously reduce software cost and improve software quality by intelligent and cost-effective use of modern software techniques.

Consequently, there need not be a conflict between quality and productivity, but the condition is that a methodology is used that helps to achieve quality without jeopardizing the cost or development time. To ensure this, the owner may state requirements to the methodology to be used, to the project organisation, to project management, quality assurance, procedures for change control, etc. It is a goal for the methodology of this book to combine quality with productivity.

Non-functional requirements will normally be expressed in natural language along with figures and measures specific to the disciplines involved, e.g. reliability engineering, performance, electromagnetic requirements, vibration and acoustics.

Since design constraints may be partially conflicting with each other, a relative priority should be assigned, so that the appropriate trade-offs can be made between, for example:

- development cost vs production cost;
- speed vs space;
- performance vs maintainability.

This may be expressed in a chart as illustrated in Figure 3.2.

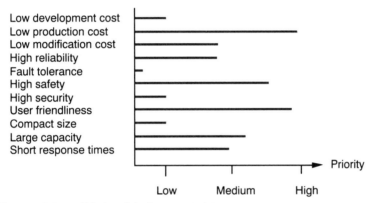

Figure 3.2 *Priority of design constraints*

We believe the most important way to increase productivity is to reuse previously developed modules (and competence). Reuse helps to improve productivity in three ways:

1. Each reuse increases the application value of a module and, thus, increases its productivity figure.
2. Each reuse saves the cost and time needed for a new development and, thus, increases the productivity figure of the application where a component is reused.
3. Each reuse of a proven component is likely to save maintenance cost.

But reuse also has a cost. It may be more expensive to build modules that are general enough to be reusable than to build special purpose modules. There will also be a cost associated with retrieval and adaptation of reusable modules. Thus, to make reuse profitable, modules must be less expensive to reuse than to build. A problem for the owner is that the cost of making reusable modules always comes before the profits may be harvested. Therefore, when pressed for time and budget, managers tend to sacrifice the long term profits for short term cost reduction.

It is an objective of the methodology presented in this book, to support reuse at minimum additional cost. To achieve this goal it is essential to take reuse into consideration at an early stage. The key to reusability seems to be a good understanding of the application domain supported by object-oriented description techniques that facilitate reuse through composition and inheritance.

Clearly, quality for the owner is more than quality for the user. The owner will put additional requirements aimed at minimizing lifetime cost and/or maximizing application value. These will be expressed in technical and economical terms such as ease of modification, production cost, portability and (re)use of existing components.

To sum up, the owner requirements include the following:

1. Statement of purpose from the owner point of view.
2. Functional requirements to the system. These should be the same as the requirements of the user environment.
3. Non-functional requirements to the system. In addition to those of the user environment, there will be requirements related to cost–benefit and to future use of the system such as:
    (a) modifiability;
    (b) producibility in different configurations;
    (c) (re) use of existing components, e.g.:
         i   operating system;
         ii   database management system;
         iii   computer system;
         iv   other hardware and software;
    (d) reusability.
4. Requirements of the project, for example:
    (a) project organisation;
    (b) management structure;
    (c) schedules;
    (d) quality assurance;
    (e) design rules and standards;
    (f) overall methodology;
    (g) cost to develop and cost to produce.

This is not an exhaustive list, but it contains common points that need consideration in most cases.

3.1.6   Requirements document

Functional requirements stem mainly from the user environment and will be the main topic of the rest of this chapter. Non-functional requirements come from both the user environment and the owner. Since they restrict the way that functional requirements may be realised, they are often called *design constraints*. To be complete, all the various requirements should be covered in a complete requirements document. Guidelines for such documents are defined in ANSI/IEEE (1984).

In the rest of this chapter we shall discuss aspects of requirements specification in the light of the access control system introduced in Chapter 2.

3.2 The *AccessControl* system

3.2.1 Project related questions

Imagine being a developer asked by an owner to develop an access control system. The owner plans to install the first system on his own premises, but wants to develop it into a product that can be sold on the open market as well. How will you proceed? Here are some questions to ask.

About the target system:
- Why develop a new system instead of buying one? It will normally be cheaper to buy than to develop. The answer to this question should clarify the main objectives of the development project and what features make the new system different from those already in the market.
- What is the environment of the new system? You need to know the different types of users in order to understand the purpose of the system and the constraints imposed on it by the environment.
- What are the overall services provided to the environment and will they depend on interactions with other systems?
- What will the physical interfaces be and what are the protocols to be used?
- What are the design constraints, e.g. requirements to fault tolerance, security, modifiability?
- Does the owner know what is wanted? If it is difficult to obtain answers to the questions above it will be necessary to sort them out. This can take a lot of effort, be careful!
- Will there be legal or social implications to consider?

About the project:
- What are the schedules? Tight schedules make the job more difficult and sometimes more expensive.
- What are the cost constraints?
- How will the owner interact with the development project?
- Will there be users available to discuss with?
- What are the commercial terms?

We assume that all questions have been answered to your satisfaction and proceed with the next step. This should be a thorough analysis of the problem domain. What are the characteristics of access control systems? What legal and operational aspects are there? What is the terminology?

In the following we will summarise the guidelines for system analysis in rules which we call *A-rules*.

3.2.2   Analysing the problem domain

Dictionary

Our first step is to identify and understand the most important concepts of the problem domain. At first we are less interested in the interrelationships than the pure concepts of the subject.

A-rule: problem statement
Make a statement that explains the problem domain. Focus on the purpose, the essential concepts, the procedures and the rules.

It will normally be sufficient to express the problem statement informally using natural language and drawings, but one should try to be as clear and precise as possible

- The main purpose of the *access control* system is to control the access of *users* to *access zones*. Only a user with known *identity* and correct *access right* shall be allowed to enter into an access zone. Other users shall be denied access.
- The authentication of a user shall be established by means of a magnetic strip *card* holding a *card code* and a secret personal identification number, *PIN*, entered by the user. The *authorisation* is performed by the system on the basis of the user identity and access rights associated with the user.
- When a user is authenticated and authorised the access zone may be entered through a *door*. The environment not controlled by the system is considered as a special zone which every user may enter. Therefore, a door is seen as a connection between two access zones. Some doors may only be passed in one direction while other doors may be passed in both directions.
- Each direction of passage through a door is considered as an *access point*. Thus, an access point controls the access from a given access zone, where the user is at present, into a neighbouring zone.
- etc.

The problem statement can often be based on existing prose descriptions. There may be descriptions of earlier systems, there may be textbooks on the subject and there may be informal statements about the system.

The problem statement leads to the very first understanding of what this application domain is all about. It helps define the purpose of the system and is suited to support an initial discussion between project participants with different backgrounds. Later in the project, prose descriptions may be needed to supplement the more formal descriptions.

But an informal problem statement is not sufficient. We will need a more precise definition of the most important concepts and the corresponding terminology. We therefore improve our understanding by listing the concepts in a *dictionary*. For some domains, dictionaries are readily available, but for other areas, an important task is to define one.

Producing a dictionary adds to the understanding of the subject being analysed. Furthermore, it will help people to communicate more precisely. A dictionary helps to bridge the gap between people with specific knowledge of the application area and people new to the area. Later in the development the concepts in the dictionary will often find their way into the system description as types (of objects). We suggest that the dictionary should be maintained along with the other permanent documents.

A-rule: dictionary
Make or obtain a dictionary for the problem domain. The dictionary should be kept updated throughout the development.

By studying the nouns in the problem statement we can make the following initial dictionary.

Access point	A point of access in one direction through a door.
Access zone	A physical zone where users are present, accessible through doors.
Authentication	To establish the identity of a user.
Authorisation	To establish the right of a user to enter an access zone.
Card	A personal identification means.
Card code	A unique identification of a card stored in machine-readable form on the card.
Door	A controlled passage from one access zone to another.
Operator	A person with known identity and authorisation to change the status of the system.
PIN	A unique personal identification number belonging to only one user. A kind of password.
User	A person with known identity with authorisation to enter specific access zones.
User name	A user name.

During the following analysis steps, the dictionary should be updated and supplemented.

Concept model/data model
A dictionary aids in starting the formalisation of the concepts, but still the understanding is "fragmented". Our next step is to study the relationships between the concepts in order to form a more "combined knowledge".

The classical notion of a concept is characterised by the following:

- *extension*, the collection of phenomena that the concept covers;
- *intention*, a collection of properties that in some way characterise the phenomena in the extension of the concept;
- *designation*, the collection of names by which the concept is known.

Representing concepts by types and instances follows this pattern: the instances belong to the extension, the type definition gives the intention and the type name represents the designation.

A-rule: concept model
Make a static conceptual description of the problem domain using the SOON notation, ER diagrams or similar.

Figure 3.3 is an instance-oriented description of the access control domain, expressed in the SOON notation. We recognise the main concepts in the dictionary as boxes in the diagram. Each box represents an instance or a set of instances, of a given type and the boxes are linked by (instances of) relationships of given types.

Clearly the relationships help to understand the problem domain. From the diagram we can also see there is an upper limit on the number of *Users* and that each *User* probably owns exactly one *Card* since the number of *Cards* is the same as the number of *Users*. From the cardinalities of *Access Zones* and *Users* we can see that a *User* may enter several *Access Zones* and that each *Access Zone* may accept several *Users*.

Note that we have not identified the *Access Control* system in this figure. It says a lot about the problem domain but nothing directly about the system. Indirectly, however, it tells us what kind of entities and relationships the system should handle. It also raises a few questions. For instance:

- Should the system keep track of where the *Users* are, i.e. know in which *Access Zone* each *User* is at any time? We decide to answer no!
- Should the system count the *Users* that pass each *Access Point*? If yes, should we ensure that the *User* really passes through? The answer is no!
- Will there be different kinds of doors and *Access Points*? It is reasonable to believe that bidirectional doors are different from unidirectional doors and that the authentication and authorisation requirements will depend on the direction. The answer is yes. There will be differences, but we will save the details to later chapters.
- How should the access rights be represented? By giving each *Access Zone* an access level and each *User* an access capability? Or by explicitly listing which *Access Zones* are open to each *User*? We decided to use the latter approach!

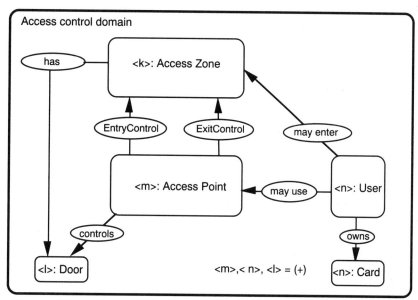

Figure 3.3 *The access control domain*

In order to understand each concept type better and describe precisely the constraints on related entities, we make explicit type definitions in the way shown in Figures 3.4 – 3.6.

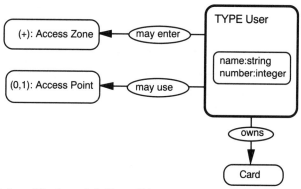

Figure 3.4 *The type definition of User*

The attributes of the *User* are defined in Figure 3.4 to be a *name* and a *number*. In our problem domain each *User* shall own a *Card* and have the right to enter at least one *Access Zone*. Such constraints on the environment can be expressed as shown in Figure 3.4. From the type environment it is clear that an instance of *User*:

1.   shall own exactly one *Card*,

2.   may enter one or more *Access Zones,*
3.   may use zero or one *Access Point* (at one time).

The following should be noted:

1.   A type definition may contain a definition of the attributes of the type (the intention).
2.   The environment of a type is important for the understanding of its purpose and constraints. Therefore, the environment of importance has been depicted outside the type. Entities in the environment represent *roles* .
3.   When the type is instantiated there will be entities in the actual instance environment that will *play* the roles. Therefore, all instances in Figure 3.3 must comply with the roles given to them by the other instances.
4.   The cardinalities and other constraints on relationships may be more explicitly represented in the type definitions (Figures 3.4–3.6) than in the instance diagram (Figure 3.3).

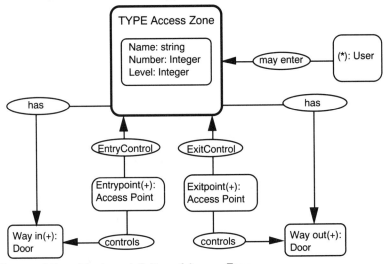

Figure 3.5   *The type definition of Access Zone*

We may give each role a local name and, in addition, specify the type of entities that are allowed to play the role. For the type *Access Zone*, defined in Figure 3.5, we have the following constraints on the environment:

1.   Zero or more *Users* have the right to enter the *Access Zone*.
2.   *Entrypoint* is a role to be played by one or more *Access Points* that controls *Doors* that play the *Way in* role.

3.   *Exitpoint* is a role to be played by one or more *Access Points* that controls the
     Way out doors.

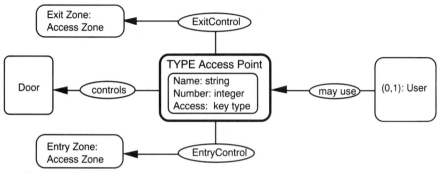

Figure 3.6   *Type definition of Access Point*

Will all the *Access Points* be similar? No, the requirements for authentication and
authorisation will vary depending on the relative access restrictions on the *Entry Zone*
compared to the *Exit Zone* (see Figure 3.6). In some cases, no authentication and
authorisation is needed at all. It is sufficient that the *User* operates a simple push key to
open the door. In other cases the *User* must enter the card and, in addition, enter a PIN.
Finally, there will be access points where the PIN is not required, only the card.

Two *Access Points* may control a single *Door* in the case when the *Door* is
bidirectional. Will the difference between *Doors* have any consequences for the *Access
Points*? We do not know that yet, but it is reasonable to believe that some extra
coordination will be needed when two *Access Points* control the same *Door*.

From this we gather that there will be different types of *Doors* and *Access Points*.
Thus, to complete our conceptual models we should define all the subtypes.

A-rule: specialisation hierarchies

*For each concept in the dictionary, ask whether all the objects that fall within the
extension of the concept have the same properties. If they have not, find specialisations,
which may or may not extend the dictionary. During the specialisation, extend the
description in the dictionary with properties which add to the understanding of the
concept.*

To do this we need the object-oriented concepts of inheritance and specialisation.
Clearly, to understand the classification of types will be important for our understanding
of the problem domain. As an illustration, Figure 3.7 expresses the type hierarchy for
Doors and *Access Points*.

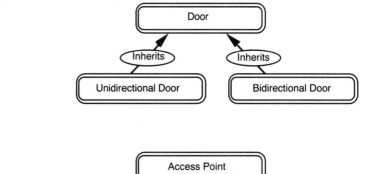

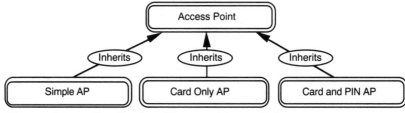

Figure 3.7   *Classification of Doors and Access Points*

3.2.3   The user environment

The next step is to identify the system and to decide what should be inside and what should be outside.

A-rule: context
Make a context diagram where the system is identified and the system environment is detailed. Describe communication interfaces and other relations the system will handle.

The system context is depicted in Figure 3.8. Here we see the system itself and the system environment. Not everything in the environment is shown, only the parts that are related to the system.

Analyzing the communication needs will normally imply that the designer finds more components to fit into the system (or its environment). We have now found the *Operators*. *Operators* were not parts of the concept models, but as soon as we started to consider the system behaviour, we realised that *Operators* would be needed to update the system with new *Users*, *Cards*, etc.

We have decided to consider the *Access Points* and the *Doors* as part of the system and the *Users* and the *Operators* as being outside. Clearly the *Users* and the *Operators* interact with the system.

The *Access Zones* are in the environment and the system performs *Entry Control* and *Exit Control* for the *Access Zones*. (Each *Access Point* will be served by a *Local Station* in the system.)

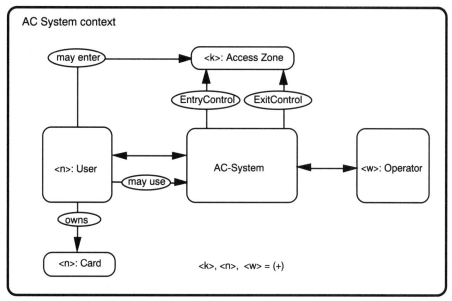

Figure 3.8   *The system context*

The *Users* physically move around in the environment, so there is a dynamic association between *Users* and *Access Points*. From Figure 3.4 we can see that a *User* may be present at not more than one *Access Point* at one time.

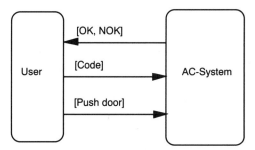

Figure 3.9   *Idealised User service interface*

Ideally, *Users* should be recognised by the system and granted or denied access depending on some unique physical attribute, such as a fingerprint. But the technology required to do that is not quite developed yet, so the system has been based on personal cards instead. But it is still a good idea to consider the idealised service interface first (Figure 3.9). As we shall see in Chapter 4 this idealised service interface will be reflected by a process in the system, the *LsControl* process. Ideally the *User* will just enter a *Code*, in one way or another and receive *OK* or *NOK* in return. If *OK* is received, the door may be pushed open.

In reality, the *User* must use a lower layer service control interface, as illustrated in Figure 3.10.

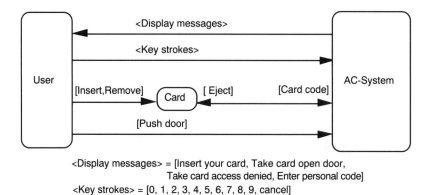

<Display messages> = [Insert your card, Take card open door,
                                          Take card access denied, Enter personal code]
<Key strokes> = [0, 1, 2, 3, 4, 5, 6, 7, 8, 9, cancel]

Figure 3.10   *User–service control interface*

Figure 3.10 depicts the static interface between a *User* and the system at an *Access Point*. Although related to physical objects, it is still a very idealised picture where the arrows represent such heterogeneous information flows as:

- physical movement – Insert card, push door;
- visual display messages;
- key strokes the user makes on a key-pad;
- electromagnetic signals from the card.

The *Card* is a plastic card with a magnetic strip holding a card identifier and, possibly, an encrypted PIN-code. To fully specify the card we have to define the logical format of the information and the encoding scheme along with its physical properties. This can most likely be done by reference to a known type of cards.

From Figures 3.9 and 3.10 we can see the static information flows, but not the dialogue between a user and the system. Our next step is therefore to define the dynamic interactions between the system and the users.

3.2.4   Message sequence charts

In order to define interface behaviour we need to describe the sequential ordering of interactions and time. A simple way to do this is by means of a message sequence chart (MSC).

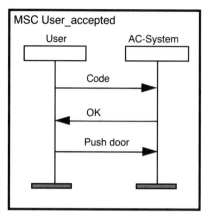

Figure 3.11 *A message sequence chart for a User being accepted at an Access Point, idealised service interface*

A-rule: message sequence charts
Make message sequence charts that describe the typical interaction sequences (protocols) at each layer of the interfaces.

We first consider the idealised layer statically described in Figure 3.9. Figure 3.11 shows an MSC for a *User* accepted at an *Access Point*. Figure 3.12 shows the sequence for a *User* not being accepted.

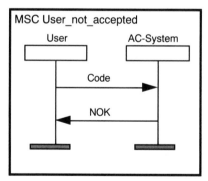

Figure 3.12 *An MSC for a User not being accepted at an Access Point*

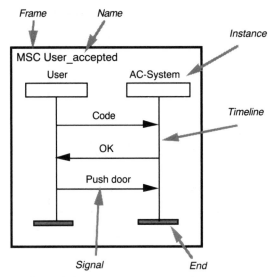

Figure 3.13   *Symbols in message sequence charts*

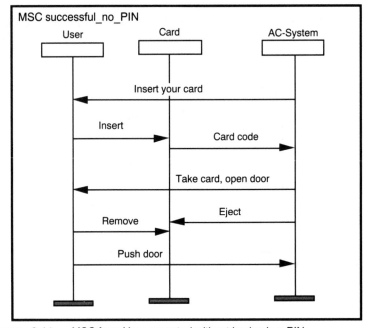

Figure 3.14   *MSC for a User accepted without keying in a PIN*

These diagrams are so intuitively understood that they hardly need any explanation. They have been widely used in various forms since the early days of electrical and communication engineering. Now they are standardised in connection with the 1992 recommendations (CCITT Z.120, 1993).

Each MSC is contained within a frame symbol. At the top of the chart the keyword MSC appears followed by the name. Then there are symbols representing the objects (instances) that participate in the behaviour. A time line runs vertically downwards from each object . This time line indicates the partial ordering of events and not a total ordering or an exact time measurement.

The arrows going between time lines represent messages exchanged between the objects. Thus, the MSC depicts a sequence of messages exchanged between objects. It represents only one trace through the tree of all possible behaviours.

Such sequence diagrams give a good overview and feeling for dialogues and protocols. But they are only capable of showing one sequence at a time and fail to show the complete behaviour of the system. Each alternative sequence must be represented separately as illustrated in Figures 3.11 and 3.12. Hence, sequence diagrams can be said to "specify by example".

What about the user–service interface described in Figure 3.10? Clearly the dialogue is more complex at this layer. Figures 3.14–3.16 depict MSCs for the concrete user dialogue. For simplicity we have represented the key strokes by a single signal: PIN.

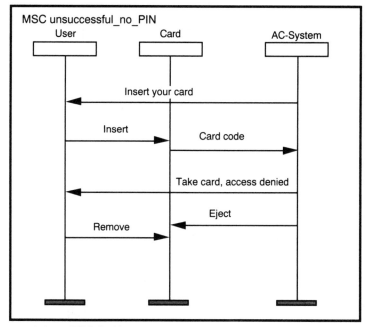

Figure 3.15 *MSC for User not accepted*

Figure 3.16 shows the sequence for accepting both a card and a personal identification number (PIN). We should continue making such MSCs until we feel confident that all the important normal and abnormal sequences have been covered.

The MSCs should be maintained for the rest of the system development for several reasons:

1. They give an overview and provide an easy path into the more complex details of the behaviour.
2. They are easy to understand, even for the user and the owner, hence they are well-suited for communicating and analysing the behaviour at the requirements stage.
3. They can be used to synthesise more detailed behaviour descriptions during functional design (see Section 3.2.5).
4. They can be used as test plans during system testing. The test should generate the same MSCs as specified in the requirements.

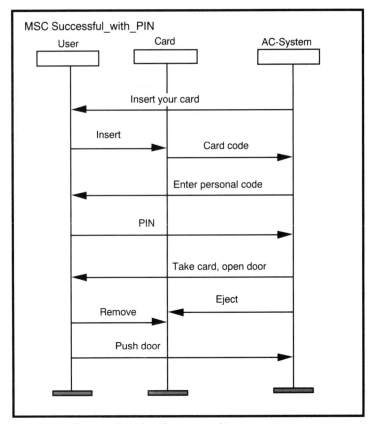

Figure 3.16 *Accepted card and secret code sequence*

However, the MSCs are only partial specifications. Could we define the interface behaviour of the system more completely using another technique?

3.2.5 Behaviour projection

In this section we shall present a way to define interface behaviours more completely. To derive a more complete definition of interface behaviour from a set of sequence charts one must focus on one object at a time and the interactions it is involved in.

If we look at the *User* in Figure 3.14 and follow its time-line downwards, we may conceive each vertical section as a state, and each arrow – starting or ending on it – as triggering an action. Hence, the time-line can be transformed into a sequential behaviour described as a *transition chart*.

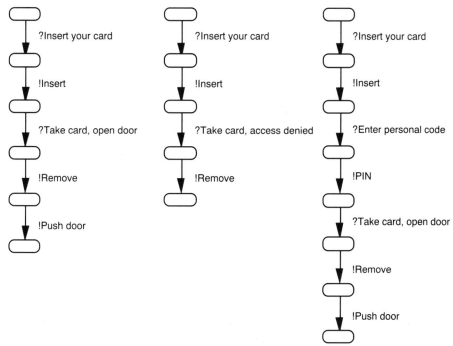

Figure 3.17 *The transition charts for the User behaviours corresponding to each of the MSCs shown in Figures 3.14 and 3.16*

The term transition chart is used in order to make a distinction with state transition diagrams used to represent the behaviour of finite state machines (see Chapter 2). In transition charts a node may be followed by output actions or input actions, while the nodes in state transition diagrams (states) may only be followed by input actions. In a transition chart there is only one action per transition. Transition charts are better suited to behaviour projections and behaviour analysis than state transition diagrams. More detail is given in Chapter 12.

Figure 3.17 shows the transition charts corresponding to each of the message sequence charts in Figures 3.14–3.16. Each transition is labelled by an interaction using the convention that output interactions are prefixed by an exclamation mark (!) and inputs with a question mark (?).

The next step is to combine the individual behaviours into a behaviour definition showing all three alternatives. Figure 3.18 illustrates how this can be done. The difficulty in this step is knowing how the individual sequences are related to each other, i.e. knowing which states are the same. In our example it is fairly obvious, but in the general case this may be more difficult.

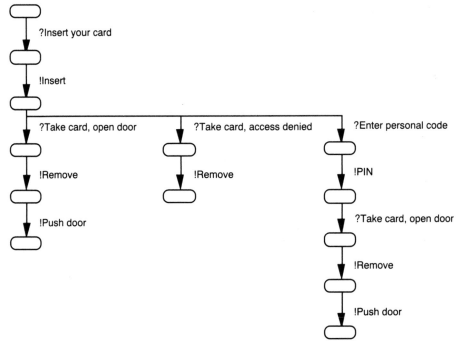

Figure 3.18 *Combining the alternative User behaviours. (This is a partial behaviour definition for the User role.)*

When different sequences are combined in this way, the result is a partial behaviour definition like the one shown in Figure 3.18. It is partial in several respects:

1. It is a projection. It is not an attempt to describe the complete behaviour of a user, only the observable user behaviour as seen from the system. It is therefore only a projection of the user behaviour. It helps to generalise the concept of a user and to concentrate only on the behaviour relevant to the system.

2.   It is incomplete. Several possible interaction sequences are not covered and must be added to make the diagram complete. For this purpose we have to analyse the diagram node by node and for each node add transitions to cover all the possible courses of behaviour that may follow that node.

3.   It is open ended. How the sequences may follow each other is not shown. In order to generate the tree of all possible behaviours the states must be labelled so that the behaviour trees may be concatenated.

Figure 3.19 describes a more complete (projection of the) user behaviour. It is our first attempt to define the *role behaviour* of the user in relation to the system. We have made the diagram more complete by adding the case where the user is denied access after entering the PIN and we have added a state name to define how the behaviour tree should be concatenated to generate an infinite behaviour tree.

There may still be more details to define before the role behaviour is complete. What if a user decides not to push the door open after all? What if the user starts to enter the PIN before the card is inserted? Such questions are important to ask and to answer. We will leave them unanswered for now, but will return to them in due time.

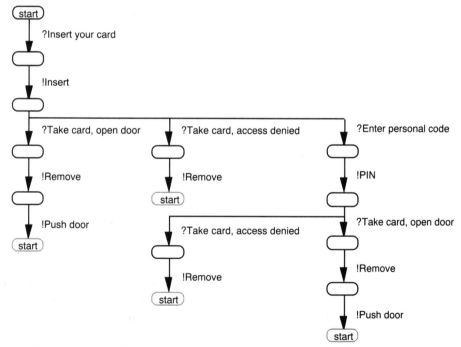

Figure 3.19   *First attempt at a User role behaviour definition*

Message sequence charts and role diagrams help:

1.   to clarify needs and problems;
2.   to express requirements.

They will be developed in an iterative process where drafts are made, questions asked and revisions made, until one is confident that all essential requirements are covered.

How is the user role behaviour related to the system behaviour? Clearly the system behaviour must match the user role behaviour in one way or another. Can we derive a role behaviour for the system from the role behaviour of the user? Yes, sometimes all we have to do is to invert the direction of the interactions (see Figure 3.20).

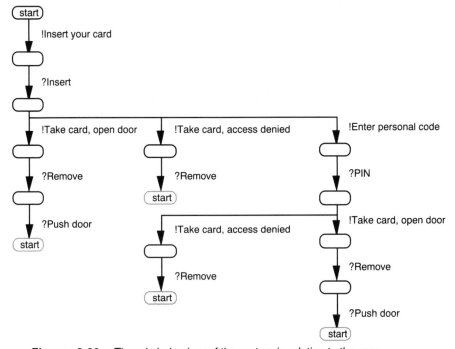

Figure 3.20   *The role behaviour of the system in relation to the user*

If the system role behaviour in relation to the user is the inverse of the user role behaviour, the user and system behaviours will fit together under given conditions. They will not necessarily fit together under all conditions (as we shall explain in Chapter 12), but the chances are good. On the other hand if the role behaviours are not inverses or equivalent to inverses, we are sure that they will not fit together.

Therefore, role behaviours can be utilised in two ways:

1.   To synthesise the system behaviour from the role behaviours in the environment.
2.   To validate the system behaviour against the role behaviour of the environment.

The second aspect will be elaborated on in Chapter 12. We summarise with the following rule:

A-rule: role behaviour
Define the interface behaviour of each role in the system and in the environment. Use the roles as a basis for behaviour synthesis and validation.

3.2.6   The owner requirements

The owner has the following non-functional requirements to the access control system:

1. *Modifiability*. The system shall be modifiable to accommodate other services than to open doors. One possible service will be an automatic teller (minibank).
2. *Size*. The system shall be flexible with respect to the number of access zones and access points. It shall be able to serve from one to 100 zones each having from one to 100 access points. The total number of access points in a system is limited to 1000 and the total number of users to 10 000.
3. *Processing capacity*. The system shall be able to serve six users a minute at each *Access Point* up to a total continuous peak load of 600 users a minute. Higher input rates shall not lead to loss or corruption of data, only to longer delays.
4) *Error handling*. A single error shall not affect the (normal) operation of more than 10 access points.
5. *Security*. The authentication and authorisation information shall be secured against unintended access.

3.2.7   The system structure

By looking at the environment we have implicitly said a lot about the system. But only in the form of external constraints, not by specifying internal details.

A-rule: sketch system structure
Sketch the system structure using SOON or similar notations. Identify the parts that are subject to requirements. Avoid describing more than required.

We know the system will provide its services at a number of *Access Points* physically distributed to where the services are needed. It will keep information about the *Users*, their access rights, their *Cards* and their PINs. It will also be possible for *Operators* to enter and remove *Users* and to change access rights and PINs. Therefore, the units serving *Access Points* must be able to communicate with the units serving *Operators* in one way or another. Thus, the requirements stated so far have implications for the system structure.

In Figure 3.21 the required overall structure is defined. Note that the concept of an *Access Point* is embodied in a *Local Station* in the system. The physical representation of an *Access Point* will be a *Panel*. A *Local Station* controls one or two *Panels* and one *Door*.

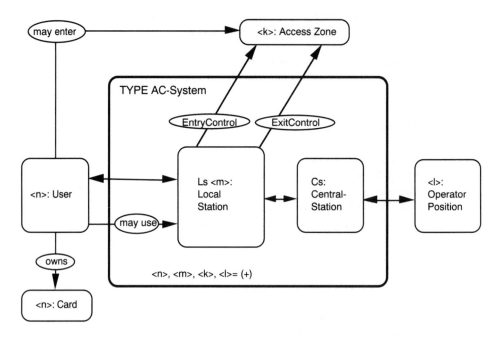

Figure 3.21   *The system structure*

In a requirements document one should not over-specify the system structure. However, the units presented in Figure 3.21 are all logical reflections of the requirements. Figure 3.22 shows a *Local Station* for unidirectional access. It can be seen that the *Local Station* has a *Panel*, that interfaces to the *User*. The physical appearance of the *Panel* to the *User* was shown in Figure 2.1. (In the case of bidirectional access we need two panels, one for each direction.)

The *Door* itself may not be so important, only the locking mechanism and the direction of passage. The exact type of lock and its electrical interface is not yet specified, but it will keep the door locked in case of power failure. (A mechanical unlocking mechanism is provided for safety reasons.)

At this point one must decide how much more to put into the requirements. The user will not care much about the *Central Unit*, but the owner may have some requirements, e.g. concerning the internal communication protocols to use, the type of processor to use and the database. This will not be elaborated upon further here.

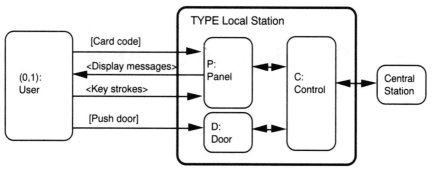

Figure 3.22 *The Local Station for unidirectional access*

Once the requirements specification is completed and has been approved by the future user and owner, the next step is to define the functional design, which is the topic of the following chapters.

CHAPTER 4

SDL – Structure and Behaviour

This chapter introduces the formal specification language SDL. Central to SDL and to our approach is the distinction between structure and behaviour. By "structure" we mean the static aspects which stay invariant during the time of study. By "behaviour", we mean the dynamic aspects, i.e. the development through states and state transitions.

4.1 SDL – CCITT Specification and Description Language

4.1.1 SDL: purpose and scope

CCITT developed The Specification and Description Language known as SDL in order to give telecommunication administrations and manufacturers a common language for precise and unambiguous communication about the behaviour of telecommunications systems. Since telecommunication systems are very complex and involve so many different aspects, a viable language has to be very general. Consequently, SDL is not restricted to telecommunications, but is generally useful for real time systems and other systems with discrete stimuli–response types of behaviour. The specifications and descriptions expressed in SDL are intended to be formal in the sense that they may be analysed and interpreted unambiguously.

As the name suggests, the SDL was developed for two purposes:

- to specify precisely the functional properties of a system to be constructed;
- to describe precisely the functional properties of a system as it has been constructed.

This distinction alludes to the purpose and use of SDL models in different phases of the system life cycle. SDL may be applied over a range of abstraction levels, starting from the very user-oriented, moving towards the very concrete and design dependent. But it is not intended as an implementation language and should not be used to bind the realisation.

SDL was first recommended in 1976 and later revised and extended in 1980, 1984 and 1988. The next recommendation is the result of the 1989–1992 study period and will be published in 1993. This textbook includes the significant new parts of SDL 92. SDL was the first specification language to be standardised by an international standardisation organisation and is gradually coming into widespread use throughout the telecommunications industry.

CCITT has defined SDL as a language and not a methodology. How SDL should be used in the various phases and how different abstractions should be related, is considered as part of "methodology" and left to the users to define. To make a methodology the user must supply rules and guidelines for how to use SDL. The SDL language is defined in the Z.100 recommendation (CCITT Z.100, 1993) a rather formal and hard-to-read document, mainly useful to the tool builder. The SDL 92 recommendation is accompanied by an appendix called *Methodology Guidelines* which is a collection of papers giving examples and advice to how SDL 92 should be applied. The CCITT SDL *Methodology Guidelines* is a good supplement to this book as well.

SDL started out in the early 1970s as a purely graphical notation to define the behaviour of a single process in the fashion of a *state transition diagram*. Later it was realised that complex systems have to be modelled as a structure of process instances and a notation for structure was added. Each aspect has two concrete syntaxes: a graphical syntax called SDL/GR and a linear (textual) form called SDL/PR. As both are concrete representations of the same SDL semantics, they are equivalent in expressing power and they share a common abstract syntax.

The definition of abstract data types follows an algebraic approach with mostly linear syntax. Operators may be described in SDL 92 by operator diagrams.

The advantage of a graphic language is that relations in two or more dimensions can be clearly visualised. For human interpretation this is extremely useful. Therefore, only the graphical notation will be presented here. The linear form is more suited to mechanical use.

4.1.2   Basic ideas of SDL

The way to manage the complexity of modern systems is to factor our independent aspects so they can be modelled and studied separately. Therefore, in the domain of complex behaviours, a way to identify and model independent behaviours is essential.

SDL models independent behaviours as (the behaviour of) concurrent processes.

The essential information one wants to convey in SDL models, is not the independence, however, but the dependency between systems. It is mutual dependencies that give systems purpose and meaning. Hence, a precise and unambiguous definition of mutual dependency is the prime concern. For this reason, all dependencies are modelled explicitly as signals interchange between the processes and their environments. There is basically no way a process and its environment may influence each other apart from sending signals through the signalroutes/channels that link the process and its environment together.

The theoretical foundation is the theory of finite state machines, which are well-suited to model behaviour based on signal communication.

An SDL *system* and its environment are conceived of as a structure of blocks connected by channels. Blocks and channels may be decomposed into blocks and channels recursively over several levels until the basic components, processes, are reached. Signalroutes are the connectors between the processes.

Processes in the system and the environment communicate with each other by sending signals through the signalroutes and channels. There are no shared data to be found outside the processes, so signals are the only means for processes to communicate. There is no way for one process to directly manipulate another process.

There is no priority among signals; signals arriving at a process will be merged into one single queue in the order in which they arrive. There is one and only one signal input queue associated with each process. This queue is called the *input port*. If two signals arrive at the same time, the conflict is resolved by selecting an arbitrary sequential order. Signals from independent sources may arrive in any order.

Each process consists of the input port and an extended finite state machine (EFSM) with a sequential behaviour defined by a process graph, which is a sort of state transition diagram. The finite state machine fetches signals from the input port in strict FIFO order except when the order is modified by the save operator (see below). For each signal it performs one transition which will take a short but undefined time.

Signals are messages that the finite state machine consumes. Each signal has a signal type identification which the FSM uses to select the next transition action. In addition, the signal carries the sender identity and possibly some additional data. (See Figure 4.1 for an illustration of an SDL process.)

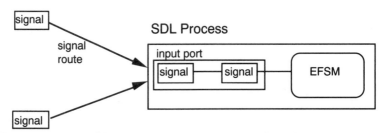

Figure 4.1   *An SDL process with signal instances in the input port*

4.2   Nested Blocks

The preceding chapter on methodology principles gave a sketch of the *Access Control* system. It also defined the terms "system" and "structure" and elaborated the difficulties in describing a system. This chapter will use SDL and we will start from the system level (the top) and gradually proceed towards greater detail.

In short SDL conceives a system as a structure of blocks connected by channels and such blocks may again be partitioned into blocks on lower levels.

SDL systems contain concurrent processes. Concurrency is an ideal model of independent behaviour. It allows independent behaviours to be described, analysed and understood separately. Interactions between concurrent behaviours causes special problems. Synchronisation is needed. If two concurrent processes may write and read the same data area, it is generally impossible to recreate an erroneous run since the sequence of events is unknown and the number of different possible event sequences is prohibitively large. It is absolutely necessary to limit the ways in which processes may interleave. Nevertheless, interactions among concurrent units are essentially what make up the interfaces between a system and its environment. Consequently, a clear and unambiguous way to define concurrency and interaction is essential for the management of complexity and quality.

4.2.1   The system level

Let us see how the *AccessControl* system may be described using SDL. The first issue is to decide on where to draw the system boundary.

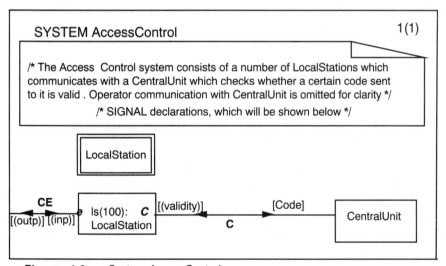

Figure 4.2   *System AccessControl*

We choose to restrict our access control system such that the access terminals (called *LocalStations*) are within the system, while the users actually getting access are outside the system. The *CentralUnit* containing the access rights is within the system, while for our current purpose, how the access rights information got into the *CentralUnit* is not described (cf. Figures 2.1 and 2.2).

In SDL systems the system components are *Blocks*, which are connected by *Channels* (Figure 4.2). In SDL blocks are represented by rectangular boxes (Figure 4.3) and channels by lines with arrow heads indicating the direction of signal transfer (Figure 4.5). Arrow heads of channels are not always at the end of the connecting line, but somewhere in between.

Figure 4.3   *Block reference to a Block definition with the name CentralUnit*

Blocks are different from processes. As they have no behaviour of their own, they are not actors, but they will eventually contain processes and as such act as if they were actors themselves. Technically, that blocks are not seen as actors follows from the fact that blocks are not described as a finite state machine. Blocks are in turn defined in block diagrams. Block diagrams may be contained directly within another (block) diagram, but normally space does not permit such nested descriptions. Instead the block is described by a *"block reference"* which is simply a rectangle with a name. The name refers to a separate block diagram which contains the actual definition of the block.

The system itself is represented by a frame symbol which represents the boundary of the system (Figure 4.4).

Figure 4.4   *Frame symbol with heading*

Channels convey signals and there may be delay on the transfer of a signal. This means that if one *LocalStation* in *ls* sends a *Code* signal before another, the signal originating from the second may very well be received first by *CentralUnit*. Channels connected to the frame symbol represent the connections to the environment. Channels may also be specified to have no delay and the symbol is then equivalent to the signal route symbol, i.e. the arrow heads are at the end (Figure 4.14).

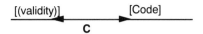

Figure 4.5 *Channel with the name C and the signal lists on the directions*

In our *AccessControl* system we have a number of access terminals which are in principle equal. These access terminals are defined to be of the same block type which we will call *LocalStation*. There is a specific symbol which indicates that there is a block type definition (Figure 4.6).

Figure 4.6 *Block type reference referring to a block type diagram with the name LocalStation*

Note that both the block reference and block type reference are merely graphical shorthands for diagrams. Block references may be substituted by block diagrams, but the surrounding diagrams would be very crowded and illegible if diagrams could not be remotely referenced by block references. The reference defines the scope of the name. In our case this means that *LocalStation* and *CentralUnit* are within *AccessControl* and the names are visible within that scope. Names within *LocalStation* are not visible within *CentralUnit* and the other way around.

Our set of *LocalStations* is called *ls* and the number (100) designates the cardinality of the set. All the block instances within a block set typically have the same relationship with its surroundings (given by the channels).

Figure 4.7 *Block set with name 'ls' with cardinality 100*

The block set is not a reference (as *CentralUnit*). It designates a set of block instances (Figure 4.7). A channel connected to a block set (via the *gates e* or *C*) will actually represent a set of channel instances. Such a channel may also be viewed as a communication bus, but this does not mean that it is practical or desirable to implement such a channel by a bus. In our example each and every one of the *LocalStations* are separately connected to the *CentralUnit* and signals may be communicated across all of these channel instances concurrently[1].

4.2.2 Signal declaration

In SDL it is necessary to declare all signals such that they are visible to the processes which handle them (Figure 4.8).

In order to explain the source and destinations of the signals, we have given these in notes in the declaration. A *note* is an explanatory text embraced by /* ... */. The surrounding frame containing the textual declaration is called a *text symbol* and there is no limit to the number of text symbols that may occur in a diagram. Text symbols are not connected to other symbols by flow lines.

```
SIGNAL
EjectCard,                        /* LocalStation      TO ENVIRONMENT */
InputCard,                        /* ENVIRONMENT  TO LocalStation */
display,                          /* Display           TO ENV */
keys;                             /* ENVIRONMENT  TO Keyboard */
SIGNAL Code(integer,integer);     /* LocalStation      TO Central */
SIGNAL OK,NOK,ERR ;               /* Central           TO LocalStation */

SIGNALLIST validity = OK, NOK, ERR ;
SIGNALLIST outp = EjectCard, display;
SIGNALLIST inp = InputCard, keys ;
```

Figure 4.8   *Signal declarations*

Often the list of signals associated with a channel is quite comprehensive and the diagram becomes crowded. Thus, it is not always obvious which list of signals is associated with what channel. We introduce *signallists*. A signallist is a list of signals which has been given a name. The list may also include timer signals or other signallist names. If a signallist contains other signallists, the signallist names will appear in parentheses. The signals of a channel are denoted by a list of signals (and signallists) in brackets (Figure 4.2).

4.2.3   Block nesting

Above we introduced "blocks". We had singular blocks like *CentralUnit* and block sets such as *ls(100):LocalStation*. A singular block may be seen as a block instance where the block instance specification and the block type definition is combined. Singular block instances may of course be specified with reference to a block type omitting the cardinality of the block set specification. Block types may contain a connectivity graph of block instances connected by channels. This makes up a structure of nested blocks. At the leaves of this structure there are blocks which contain processes. In SDL, block types may not contain both blocks and processes at the same time.

In addition to containing structures of blocks or structures of processes block types may contain other type definitions. This makes up the scoping hierarchy of SDL. Names in enclosing type definitions are the only names visible.

Block types may contain data type definitions, but no variable declarations. This follows from the fact that processes in SDL do not share data other than signal queues. They share a signal queue in the way that one process appends (output) signals to the queue (the input port), while the other process consumes (input) signals from the same queue. Appending and consuming signals are atomic, non-interuptable operations. The input port is the basic synchronisation mechanism of SDL.

Block types may contain process types, service types and procedures as well as block types and data types. We shall return to these concepts later.

W﹖ have specified an *AccessControl* system with 100 *LocalStations*. The *LocalStations* are blocks.

Let us look into one of the *LocalStation*s (Figure 4.9):

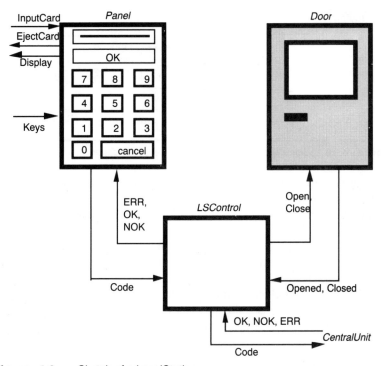

Figure 4.9   *Sketch of a LocalStation*

The user may insert a card into the slot of the *Panel*, he/she then types his/her *Personal Identity Number (PIN)* which is transmitted to the *LSControl* (Local Station Control), which furthers this information to the *CentralUnit*. From the central unit, *LSControl* receives either *OK* (access granted and the *PIN* corresponded with the card) or *NOK* (access denied or the *PIN* did not correspond with the card). Following the received results, the *LSControl* will issue a message to be put on the display of the *Panel* and the door may get a signal that it shall open. Following the acknowledgement of the *Door* being open and some seconds of waiting the *LSControl* will issue a closing signal.

If we formalise the sketch to SDL, we obtain Figure 4.10.

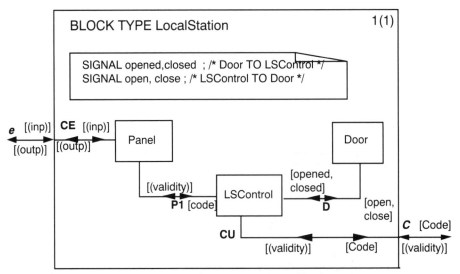

Figure 4.10   *Block Type LocalStation. Formal specification*

A block type is defined in the same way as the system itself except that the keywords BLOCK TYPE are used.

Note how the formal description of *LocalStation* corresponds with the informal description in Figure 3.22.

Note the identifiers *e* and *C* which occur both in the block type diagram *LocalStation* outside the frame and in the system diagram inside the block set *ls*. These identifiers designate *gates*. Gates are used to indicate which channels of the block type are supposed to connect to which channel connecting an instance of the type. Gates can be compared with "plugs" of household appliances. They are used to "plug" up instances correctly. The gate names are defined by the type and visible wherever the type name is visible. Note also that the gate symbols have arrows at the ends and that signal lists are associated with the arrows. The signallists will ensure that the instances of the block type are connected properly to their surroundings. We shall return to gates and gate constraints in Chapter 7.

4.3   What is a process?

The acting unit of SDL is the *process*. Most of the readers will have some notion of what "process" means. There is no canonical definition of the concept. In the literature we find several definitions and several ways to describe processes. We shall choose the definition and the description method which we find most suitable for real time software construction.

A process is a unit for sequential behaviour – "a series of actions, changes or functions that bring about a particular result" (American Heritage, 1979). It is also described as a function from substance and time to value (Haugen, 1980) – which means that the process is seen as the changing over time of variable values, i.e. the sequence of process states. In Unix systems, a process is the execution of a program, an entry in the process table (Christian, 1983). (See also definition of "behaviour" in Section 2.2.2.)

Definition : process
In SDL a process is an actor object executing his own actions and having his own local (data) attributes. Processes have discrete behaviour. Processes interact by means of signals. Signals are discrete stimuli which are actively screened and processed by the receiver.

All actions are performed by something and all data are represented by something. This something is what we, very generally, call *substance* (see Section 2.2.3).

Closely related to "process" is the notion of "behaviour". While the system and block definitions concentrated on the static relationships, the process descriptions will concentrate on what is changing. That something is changing is called its "behaviour". But that something is changing, does not mean that everything is changing. Our descriptions of behaviour will capture the change and describe the aspects of the change that do not change.

The structure of a process is what is stable when the process behaves. We choose to describe the process structure by descriptions of the possible states and the transitions between them. Our definition helps us to discriminate between processes and phenomena which are not processes and it specifies how we will describe (the structure of) processes.

SDL processes are described as FSMs, i.e. finite state machines. The process will change state, but the set of states will remain constant. The process will go through a number of transitions in a complicated sequence, but the set of transitions remains constant.

4.4   Innermost block with processes

As mentioned earlier, the leaves of the block structure will contain processes. We have chosen *Panel* to exemplify the principle. We shall start with an informal view of the *Panel* and the SIGNALs which are passed between the different processes.

From Figure 4.11 we see that the signals may carry data. In this chapter, however, we shall not go into data in detail since we are interested in the aggregation structure of a *Panel*. Data will be covered in Chapter 5.

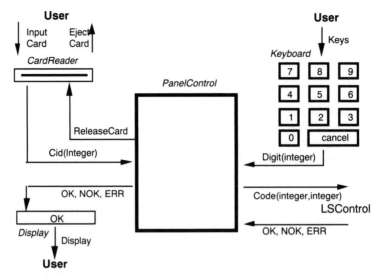

Figure 4.11   *Sketch of Panel*

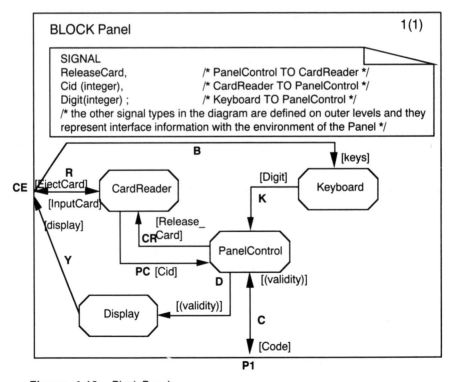

Figure 4.12   *Block Panel*

Note that the signals to and from **CE** together form the signallists *(out)* and *(inp)* which are specified on the block type *LocalStation* diagram (Figure 4.10).

Contrary to the block type diagram, the identifiers at the frame are not gates, but actual channels since *Panel* is a singular block (Figure 4.12) and not a block type (in this first version of the *AccessControl* system).

We see the *process symbols* connected together by *signalroutes*. As mentioned above, there are no blocks in this diagram since it is a leaf of the block structure tree (see also Section 4.6). The process symbols are references (Figure 4.13) as they refer to a definition of the process given in a process diagram.

Figure 4.13 *Process reference with process name*

Signalroutes convey signals, but there is no delay between the two end-points of a signalroute. Unlike the (SDL 88) channel, signalroutes have their arrow heads at the end-points (Figure 4.14).

Figure 4.14 *Signalroute **K** with signallist*

In a nutshell the kind of decomposition that we have performed here, is the "lid and magnifying glass" approach. What we see first is the box with a label on the lid. We then open the lid and look into the box as if we were using a magnifying glass. We are looking inside components as if we were using a magnifying glass on the block and process references.

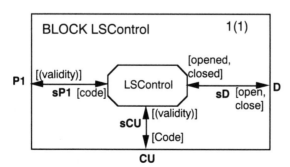

Figure 4.15 *Block LSControl, a trivial block*

The formal restriction saying that blocks and processes may not coexist in a block diagram, will in some cases mean that there are some trivial block diagrams. Our *LSControl,* for instance, is a single process shown in Figure 4.15.

Note that when blocks and processes have the same names, this causes no confusion (for SDL) as block and process are two different *entity classes* which implies different identifier name spaces.

Note that the structural decomposition of a system into blocks and processes must be seen primarily as a logical decomposition made in order to precisely define the abstract functionality of the system. It need not correspond to a physical decomposition of the real system. There are many ways to map an SDL system into a concrete implementation and some of these will be structured quite differently from the SDL system.

4.5   Process behaviour

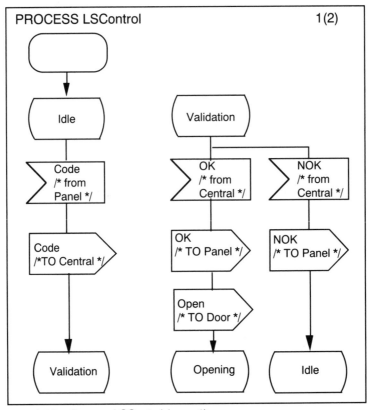

Figure 4.16   *Process LSControl (page 1)*

In this section we shall present the SDL way of describing a finite state machine (FSM). The emphasis is on dynamics in contrast with the previous sections which concentrated on the static aspects of a system.

4.5.1 *LSControl* process

In Figures 4.16 and 4.17 you find the SDL diagram for the process *LSControl*. At first glance it does not resemble the process we sketched when explaining the finite state machine (Figure 2.13), but have a closer look! In Section 4.5.2 we shall go through the individual language constructs of process diagrams and, in particular, explain the *LSControl* diagrams.

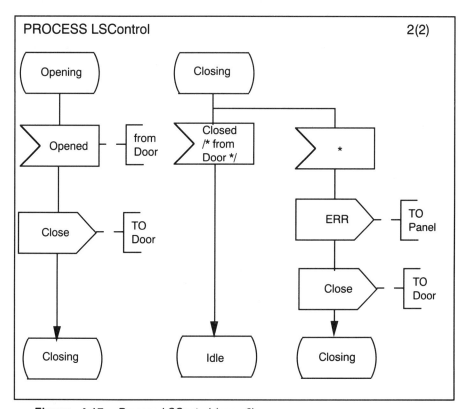

Figure 4.17   *Process LSControl (page 2)*

4.5.2   The symbols of SDL process diagrams

The idea of this section is to go through the *LSControl* diagram in detail explaining each new symbol as we go along and explaining why this diagram specifies a *LocalStation* control process.

First of all there is a *frame* surrounding the process diagram page. This frame separates the process from its environment (Figures 4.17 and 4.4).

PROCESS LSControl   1(2)

Figure 4.18 *Process Heading*

In the upper left-hand corner of the first page of the diagram, we find a *heading*. It consists of a text which starts with the keyword PROCESS followed by the name of the process (here *LSControl*). The heading identifies which diagram we have (Figure 4.18). The heading may also contain formal parameters, but this will not be covered until we have looked into data of processes in more detail.

In the upper right-hand corner there are two numbers. These are *page numbers*. The first number is the number of this page, i.e. 1 for first page and the second number is the number of pages of this diagram (i.e. 2 pages in the *LSControl* diagram).

The normal direction for reading a diagram is top to bottom. If there are deviations from this canonical direction, they will be shown by an arrow head of the *flowlines* between the symbols.

Figure 4.19 *Start symbol*

The first symbol of the process diagram (in Figure 4.16 it is just below the heading) is the *start* symbol. There is only one start symbol for a process. The transition from the start takes place when the process is generated. A process may be generated either at system start-up or as a result of a create request from another process (see also Section 5.5). Our *LSControl* will be generated at system start-up.

Figure 4.20 *State symbol*

In our process, there are no initial actions and the process will enter the *state Idle*. The state symbol resembles the start symbol, but they are not identical. The state is identified by a state name.

There are two important and useful special state names. They are *asterisk* * and *dash* - . The asterisk means "all states" and may be followed by an exception list of state names in parentheses. The dash state name means "the most recent state". Examples of their use will follow later.

A transition is the behaviour of a process which takes the process from one state to another. A transition will take place when the process consumes a signal.

Figure 4.21   *Input symbol*

Each process has one and only one *input port* which contains all signals received by the process, but not yet consumed. The signals are ordered according to their arrival times.

Our *LSControl* process will remain in the *Idle* state until it receives an input signal. It expects to receive a *Code* signal containing information about the card id and personal identity number from the Panel. It may, however, be prepared to receive other signals as well. We conclude that following a state there has to be a set of symbols referring to input. Such symbols include firstly the *input symbol* (Figure 4.21), but later we shall look into save symbols and continuous signals. In our example the *Idle* state is followed by one input symbol which describes the consumption of the signal *Code*. If the process is in the *Idle* state and signals other than *Code* are received, they will be discarded[2].

Note here that the *Code* signal according to the signal definition has two integers of data attached to it. Since data is covered in Chapter 5 and since the data carried by *Code* is not significant for *LSControl*, we have decided to omit them in the *LSControl* diagram. This cannot be done in SDL, but in order not to get involved with items not covered yet we take the liberty of doing so.

In an in-line *note* we remember which process is the sender of the signal. The note is only meant for the human reader and adds no formal meaning to the SDL description. From a testing point of view the added information of which process should be the sender is of considerable value. That the *Panel* is the sender of the *Code* signal can also be seen from the sketch of the *LocalStation*, but it helps to have that information here in the process diagram as well.

Figure 4.22   *Output symbol*

Let us follow the *Code transition* from the state *Idle*. Note that a transition is fully identified by a state and an input signal. The only thing we will do when having received a *Code* from the *Panel* is to further this *Code* to the *CentralUnit* in order to have the *Code* validated. We then output a *Code* signal to the *CentralUnit* process. We use an *output symbol* containing a signal name (Figure 4.22). The output symbol may in addition to the signal name (and actual parameters) contain a *TO-clause* and/or a *VIA-clause*. In our output symbol we have merely indicated the destination by a note. This is because the process identifier *Central* is not visible at this place in the specification.

When the TO- and VIA-clauses are omitted, there should be a unique destination for the signal based on the signal identifier. If there is a set of possible destinations, one of the destinations will be chosen non-deterministically. In our case the path and destination follow implicitly from the signalroutes and channels in the block diagrams.

When the TO-clause is explicit, it specifies a process uniquely either by its (visible) name or by a "pointer" value. This "pointer" value in SDL is known as "PId" (Process Identifier) and will be covered in Chapter 5 as it is of a predefined data type. When a process is identified by its name in the TO-clause, this means that it has to be within the same block since process names outside the block cannot be visible.

In order to specify the path the signal should follow, it is possible to append to the output statement a VIA-clause which lists the path of signalroutes and channels which the signal will be sent through. The VIA-clause may also specify a gate. Furthermore, the VIA-clause may be extended to "VIA ALL" and then if there is more than one channel instance in the path a signal instance will be generated for each channel instance. This happens for example when we have block sets. This is how we can describe a multicast message.

We summarise by means of Figure 4.23.

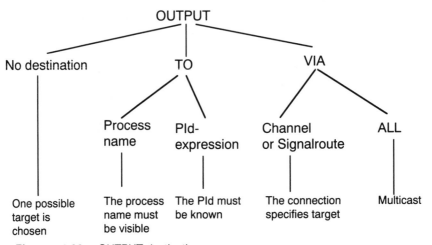

Figure 4.23   *OUTPUT destinations*

After having sent the *Code*, the *LSControl* process enters the state *Validation*. What we are expecting now, is an *OK* or Not OK (*NOK*) from the *CentralUnit*. Is the door to be opened or not? We can now easily follow the *OK* and *NOK* transitions. In the *OK* transition, we send an *OK* signal to the *Panel* to display and a request to the *Door* to *Open*. We enter *Opening* state.

If the return from *CentralUnit* is *NOK*, we pass this information on to the *Panel*, which we expect will display this before it ejects the card or requests a retyping of *PIN*. Our *LSControl* process will return to *Idle*, as its job has been done. Note that we have encountered two state symbols with the same name *Idle*. They both represent the very same state. There is no limit to how many places a state may occur in a diagram.

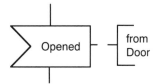

Figure 4.24   *Comment symbol associated with input*

At the top of page 2 of the diagram (Figures 4.17 and 4.24), we see a semi-formal use of comments. A *comment symbol*, may be connected to any symbol in order to give auxiliary and informal explanation. We may, for instance, let the comment symbol describe the sender of the signal.

LSControl requests the closing of the door by sending a *Close* signal to the *Door*.

Figure 4.25   *Asterisk input*

We mentioned earlier in this section that discarding unexpected signals (which is the default in SDL) may not be the most reasonable thing to do. Following the *Closing* state we have described a transition for unexpected signals which sends an error message to the *Panel*, retransmits *Close* to the *Door* and returns to the *Closing* state. The input symbol of the unexpected transition has the state name "***" (asterisk). The *asterisk input* means "any other input than listed". Our error handling here is absolutely minimal.

We have now covered all the symbols in the *LSControl* diagram and you are now able to read and understand processes described by SDL.

4.6   Substructure

In the above we have concentrated on the decomposition of a system into blocks into blocks into processes. There is a nested tree of blocks. We also said that blocks may either contain blocks or processes.

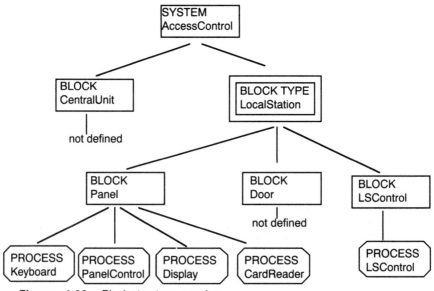

Figure 4.26   *Block structure overview*

SDL in fact has a slightly more complicated picture. Blocks may have a "block substructure" and channels may have a "channel substructure". We shall look briefly into these concepts.

4.6.1   Block substructure

We said earlier that blocks (or block types) could have blocks inside. Actually SDL says that a block has either a process graph or a substructure inside. In fact they may both be defined within the block frame.

The interpretation is that the process graph and the block substructure are *alternative* representations of the block. At configuration time the specifier will choose between the process graph and the substructure in order to define a "consistent partitioning subset" which is the total tree of blocks and processes of the actual system (similar to Figure 4.26). There is no strong semantic relationship between the process graph definition and the substructure definition (other than their external signalling interface) and we do not recommend using this mechanism. It may prove helpful on special occasions, but it may also make it more difficult to understand. Serious problems arise if the specification of some other block relies on one or the other of the two alternatives in order for it to function properly[3].

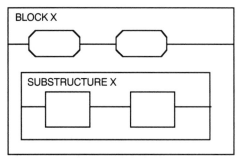

Figure 4.27 *Sketch of block substructure*

4.6.2 Channel substructure

As we can look into a block by a "magnifying glass" mechanism, the channel substructure is actually looking into a channel in the same way. The substructure is then a block definition and it may contain processes (or other blocks or substructures).

When we start to analyse our *AccessControl* system, we realise that the channel between the *LocalStations* and the *CentralUnit* is vulnerable. Therefore, we decide to encrypt the data to and from the *CentralUnit*. By using a channel substructure we see this encryption as being a property of the channel itself (Figure 4.28).

A channel substructure is equivalent to a block inserted in the channel. In the case above, however, there are encryption substructures for each channel instance of **C**.

Channel substructure may be used to model layers of SDL descriptions. We will cover this too in a later chapter.

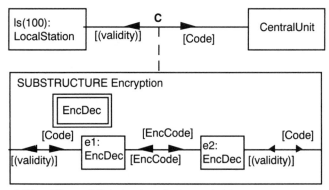

Figure 4.28 *Channel Substructure (not complete)*

At first glance this mechanism seems very attractive, but consider a return signal from *CentralUnit* that addresses the appropriate *LocalStation* controlling process by means of a PId pointer value. This signal is now routed through the substructure *Encryption* and the return signal must be consumed there in order for it to be properly encrypted. This is, however, not according to the semantics of a TO-clause, which says that the process specified in the TO-clause shall be reached as long as there is a path that leads to it. Such intercepting processes constitute a problem with SDL addressing.

4.7   Services

We shall now look at yet another SDL decomposition mechanism. Some processes have very independent parts which are candidates to be described as independent FSMs. Sometimes that is exactly what you would do; the process is made a block and the independent parts are made processes. This again has effects on upper block levels, but it can always be handled by introducing blocks with only one process. Very often, however, the independent parts are not entirely independent in fact as they may not run simultaneously. We could use a concept that covers quasi-parallelism, a concept normally called "coroutines".[4]

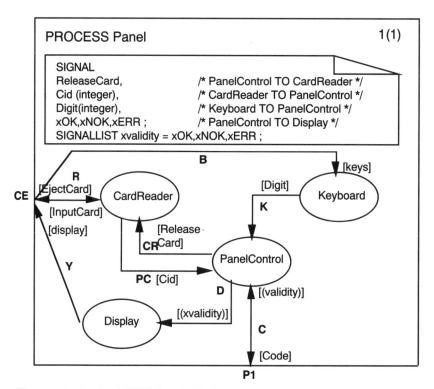

Figure 4.29   *PROCESS Panel with Services*

In SDL coroutines are called *services* which is somewhat misleading as the word is used for other purposes in other contexts. The idea behind services is that a process may be split into a set of services each of which is described as an FSM. Services operate in quasi-parallel and may share data defined on the process level.

In order to give an example we have picked the block *Panel* and said that it may well be seen as a process since the simultaneous execution of *Display*, *CardReader* and *Keyboard* is of little significance. Actually on upper block levels we would have *LSControl* and *Door* as processes directly within *LocalStation* which would make the process names more readily available for addressing (see Chapter 5).

Compared with Figure 4.12 we see that the process reference symbols are substituted by service reference symbols. The signalroutes are the same.

The process *Panel* has only one input port; the services do not have their own input ports. In order for this to function, it is required that the input signal sets of the services should be disjoint. This means that when a signal is to be consumed, the signal type identification is sufficient to determine which service should handle it. This is a serious restriction. In our example we note that we have had to define the signals *xOK, xNOK* and *xERR* in the signallist *(xvalidity)* because the *(validity)* signals cannot be used from *PanelControl* to *Display* since *(validity)* is also a part of the input signal set of *PanelControl*.

The special symbol for *priority input* in the process graphs is shown in the symbol summary below. The priority version may coexist freely with normal input and may also occur in plane process diagrams. All priority input signals are handled before other signals of the input port.

4.8   SDL symbol summary

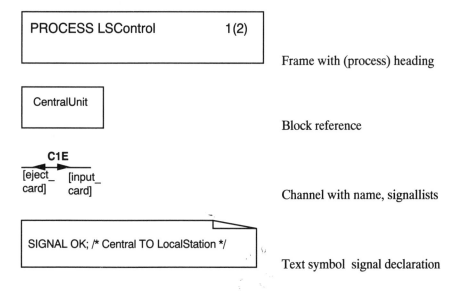

PROCESS LSControl 1(2)	Frame with (process) heading
CentralUnit	Block reference
C1E [eject_ card] [input_ card]	Channel with name, signallists
SIGNAL OK; /* Central TO LocalStation */	Text symbol signal declaration

LSControl

Process reference

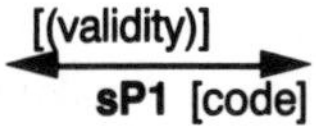

[(validity)]

sP1 [code]

Signalroute + name, signallists

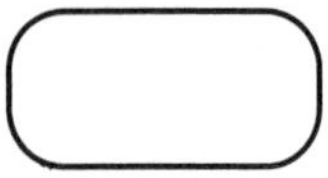

Start symbol

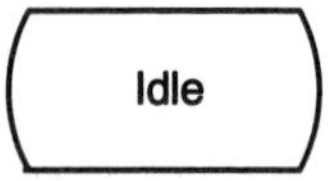

Idle

State symbol

Code
/* from
Panel */

Input symbol

Code
TO Central

Output symbol

from
Door

Comment symbol

PanelControl

Service reference symbol

Priority input symbol

Notes

[1]In SDL 88 there are no block types and block sets. It can be shown that block types and block sets can be expressed by blocks alone and as such they are "additional concepts". They do, however, represent conceptually new and valuable mechanisms which are naturally used extensively.

[2] This will in general not be the best treatment and we shall see later how we recommend that unexpected signals should be handled.

[3] Our way to describe blocks in blocks, is actually defining a substructure implicitly – a so-called "open substructure".

[4] In programming languages mechanisms for coroutines are found in e.g. SIMULA.

CHAPTER 5

SDL – Data

In this chapter we will try to show that data in SDL is no more difficult than normal programming languages if only traditional use is required. We will also show that SDL data is flexible and has strong expressive powers. We will also touch upon the theoretical foundations of SDL data, the theory about abstract data types.

5.1   What is data?

Everybody "knows" what data is. Data is stored in a computer system. Bits and bytes are data. Integers, reals and character strings are data. Pointers are also data. Pointers and integers are represented by bits in a computer and they often have the same number of bits as well. But pointers are not integers and integers are not reals, even though they may use the same number of bits, e.g. 32. In order to make use of data we have to attach an interpretation to the bits that represent the data.

How do we "store" things in an SDL process? Can we talk about "SDL bits"? We will shortly return to these intricate matters after we have looked briefly into *why* we need data.

The bytes of a computer normally play two somewhat different roles. Some bytes are parts of the program, while others are manipulated by the programs. This leads to the common distinction between *control* and *data*[1]. In an SDL process the control information is represented by the process graph.

118

In the *LSControl* process (described so far), we did not care about data, but implicitly there is data in the process. The *LSControl* received the *Code* signal from the *Panel* and furthered it to the *Central*. Because the *Code* signal was not handled within the *LSControl* process, we overlooked the fact that the *Code* would contain data. The *Code* signal represents what we referred to as "spatial information" in Chapter 2. It represents something existing in space outside the process. Data is normally used to store spatial information whereas control is used for temporal information about behaviour progress. It would contain the card identity read by the *Panel* and the *Personal Identity Number* (*PIN*) typed in by the user. We could have declared one signal for each value of the card identity and one signal for each value of the *PIN*, but this would have been very cumbersome and virtually impossible in practice.

Data have the desired feature that they may be used to *generalise*. We talk about *pin* and *cardid* and we know that we refer to the *PIN* and the read card identification. It is of no relevance whether the *PIN* is 3144 or 2155 or whether the card identification was 5533 or 6789.

Furthermore, *data exists over time*. By using data we keep information for the time period when it is needed.

Let us now return to the intriguing question of the existence of "SDL bits". There is no such thing as an "SDL bit"! There is no least SDL storage unit. SDL is a specification language and will not care about the way data is stored in physical machines. What is important to SDL is the behaviour of real time systems and, consequently, the behaviour of data units.

When we talk about integers versus reals, we are interested in the difference in the operation of the two types, not their representations. Very few have to know the IEEE floating point number format and we seldom care whether the integers are 1-complement or 2-complement. What we care about is that 2+2 is 4 and that 2.5 * 3.1 = 7.75. This means that we are interested in the operations of integers and reals with respect to addition and multiplication. When we define our data types with respect to their operations and not with respect to their actual representations, we say that we have *abstract data types*. This will be covered in more depth (but not to the very bottom of the theory) in a later section, but first we shall have a look at how simple data is handled in SDL.

5.2 Simple data in SDL

5.2.1 *AccessControl*: sketch of *Panel*

Let us now have a look at another very central part of the *AccessControl* system. We shall use the *Panel* to exemplify simple data in SDL processes. The reader is urged to recall the block diagram of *Panel* which was presented in Chapter 4 (Figure 4.12).

We note that the BLOCK *Panel* represents an abstraction of a panel which in a uniform fashion represents both electronic hardware, electromechanical devices and computer software. Actually it is up to the design phase to decide what actual media the processes should be realised on!

From the signal definition, we see that some of the signals carry data. We need only very simple data in this example and may use the predefined type *integer*.

The *Cid* signal will carry an integer which is the card identification code read from the card by the *CardReader*. The *Digit* signal will carry an integer which is a digit, i.e. a value between 0 and 9.

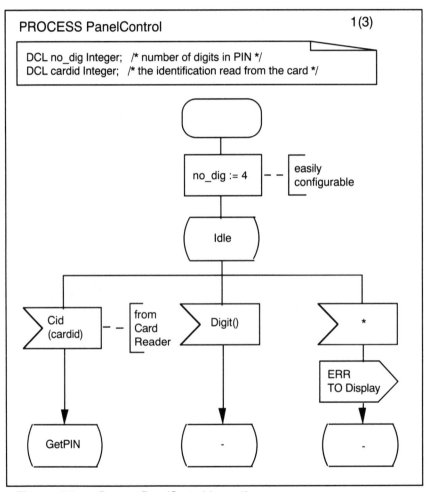

Figure 5.1   *Process PanelControl (page 1)*

Formerly, we have considered the *Code* signal, but we have intentionally overlooked its data attributes. Now we shall look more closely into how it is built up. It consists of two integers, one of which is the card *internal identification* (read by the *CardReader* originally) and the other is the personal identification number (*PIN*) which the user types in on the keyboard.

The PanelControl process uses two local variables.

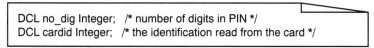

Figure 5.2   *Declaration of variables*

The text symbol includes declarations of the two integers *no_dig* and *cardid. DCL* is the keyword which precedes data declarations. A list of names follows and the line is terminated by the *sort* name. "*Sort*" is the SDL technical term for what is normally called "type". We shall use both terms to mean the same.

Variables in SDL are declared in very much the same way as in programming languages. Furthermore, we see that SDL has predefined types which are quite similar to those we are used to from programming languages. The common predefined types are: *Boolean, Character, Charstring, Integer, Natural and Real*. These types have operations such as we know from algorithmic languages such as Algol, FORTRAN, C, etc.

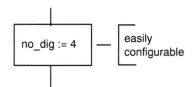

Figure 5.3   *Task symbol with simple assignment*

The rectangle following the process start symbol is called a *task symbol* and it is used to set the values of data by assignments. A task symbol may contain a list of assignments separated by commas. Alternatively a task symbol may contain informal text, where formal assignments are not considered appropriate.

At start-up time the variable *no_dig* is assigned the value '4'. Its value will remain 4 (in this example) during the life of the process since no other assignments alter its value.

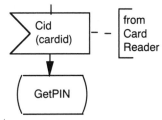

Figure 5.4   *Input signal with data*

We have declared the integer *cardid* which is used to record the card identification. When the *Cid* signal is consumed, *cardid* is assigned the value of the data attribute of the consumed signal. Note that parameter values carried by input signals must be transferred to local variables. There is no way to access the input signal again after it has been consumed, i.e. after the input symbol. When the *PanelControl* has recorded the *card identification* it is ready to handle the *personal identification number (PIN)*. This is described by the state *GetPIN*.

If the user types digits before entering the card into the *CardReader*, the *PanelControl* process will discard the digits. Note that the integer associated with the signal *Digit* in this case will be discarded since no variable is specified to hold it.

Any other input signals constitute errors and cause an error message to be issued before the process returns to *Idle*.

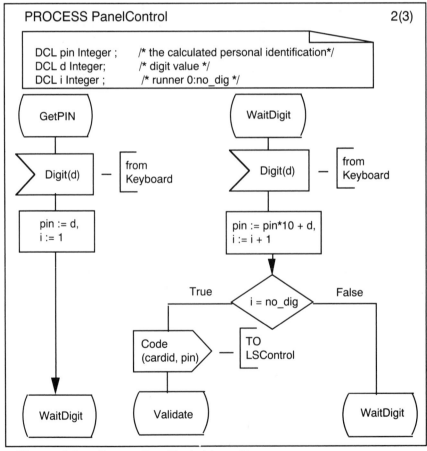

Figure 5.5   *Process PanelControl (page 2)*

We declare three data variables in order to keep track of the situation at all times. The *pin* variable is used to build up the *personal identity number* from individual digits *d* which are received from the *Keyboard* through the signal *Digit*.

When the process is in state *GetPIN*, all signals other than *Digit* are discarded. This holds also for the state *WaitDigit*. We could have described this explicitly by an asterisk input signal leading directly to a dash state.

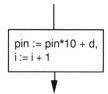

Figure 5.6   *Task symbol with list of assignments*

In the task symbol of Figure 5.6 we see examples of assignments where variables are assigned integer values obtained from expressions. This indeed looks like any other programming language. It may seem trivial, but we shall go through the first assignment in more detail because this will facilitate the understanding of more advanced data concepts. The right side of the assignment operator symbol represents the expression. *pin* means we will extract the current value of the *pin* variable. This value will be multiplied by the value of the constant *10*. Thereafter the value of *d* is extracted and added to the first arithmetic result. The expression value is then used to modify the *pin* variable. We have applied the two operators * (multiplication) and + (addition) to *pin*, *10* and *d*. This is all right since multiplication and addition are defined for integers and *pin* and *d* are integer variables and *10* is an integer literal. We could not have applied the operators *AND* or *OR*. Those operators are defined for the Boolean type, but not for integer.

We summarise in brief:

- Variable occurrences on the right of an assignment operator means extracting the value from the variable.
- Operations are associated with types.
- Variables on the left of the assignment operator are modified to become the expression value of the right-hand side.

Figure 5.7   *Decision symbol with formal values in question and answers*

We introduced a new symbol at the bottom of page 2 (Figure 5.5). The diamond symbol is the *decision symbol* which is used to choose between different alternative courses of action upon a *question*. The question is written within the decision symbol and may be either a formal expression (such as the one in our example) or informal text. On each of the flow lines from the decision symbol there is an *answer*. The course of action will follow the line where the correct answer is associated.

Decisions change the control flow according to values of internal variables, while state–input constructs change control flow according to external stimuli. Often it is a matter of design whether we use state/signals or decisions. It is quite possible to always specify a process with no more than one state and where decisions on "state variables" will branch the control flow. That would be an action-oriented and not a state-oriented description. As we shall state in more detail later, we do not consider that a good design strategy.

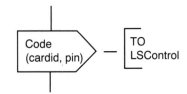

Figure 5.8   *Output signal with data*

The above output signal puts the values of *cardid* and *pin* into the signal which is sent to *LSControl* process. There could equally well have been full expressions in the signal parameters, not only variables.

Note that there is a special initialisation construct used in the declaration on page 3 (Figure 5.9) where *trial_no* is initialised to *0*. If there is no such initialisation value in the declaration, the value is undefined. Of course we can achieve the same result by initialising *trial_no* in the task just following the start symbol.

The initialization of *trial_no* has only effect when the process is created. Thus, whenever a trial sequence has terminated, successfully or not, *trial_no* must be assigned *0* again.

In Figure 5.9 we see examples of output-symbols where the destination is a process name. The *validity* signals can be addressed to the *Display* directly since the *Display* is in the same block as *PanelControl* and, thus, visible within *PanelControl*.

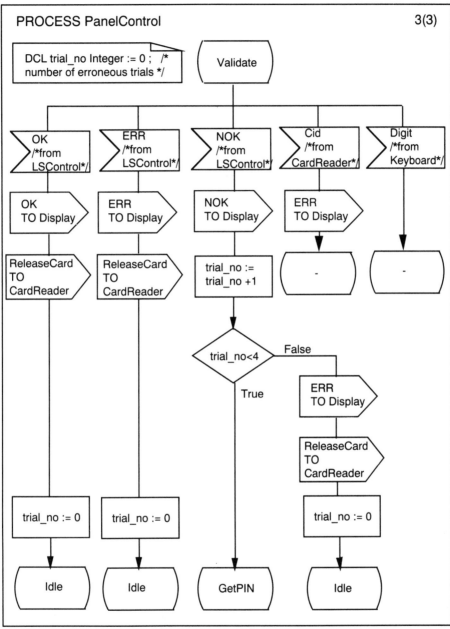

Figure 5.9 *Process PanelControl (page 3)*

5.2.2 TIME, duration and TIMERs

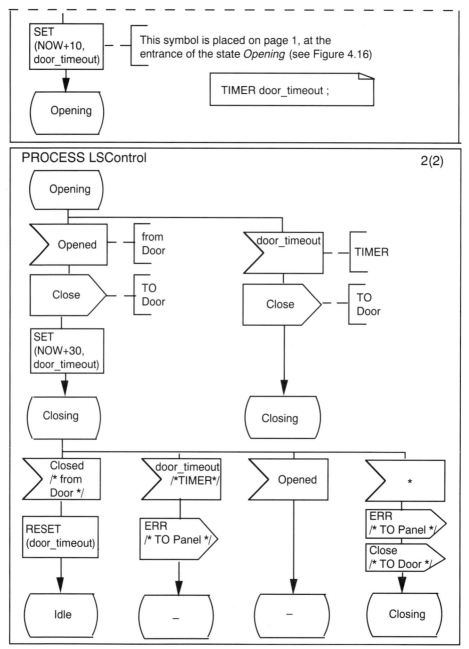

Figure 5.10 *A simple TIMER. A revisit to a part of LSControl*

SDL offers more than the common data types. SDL is used in cases where explicit specification of time-related matters is of great importance. It is therefore important to have concepts to handle time.

In the *LSControl* process we had the opening and closing of the *Door*. We shall now take a look at a version of the process *LSControl* which uses a TIMER.

Tasks in SDL are often considered to have no time duration; the only places in a process where time elapses are in the states.

Timers are just like alarm clocks. The process is passively waiting since the process needs not sample them. They will issue time-out signals when their time is reached. There may well be several different timers active at the same time. Active timers do not affect the behaviour of the process until the timer signal is consumed by the process.

A *timer* is declared similarly to a variable (Figure 5.10)[2]. When a timer has not been SET, it is *inactive*. When it is SET, it becomes *active*. A timer is set with a *TIME* value. TIME is a special data type and is mainly used in connection with timers. The expression "*NOW+10*" is a TIME value and it adds the TIME expression *NOW* and the duration *10* (here:seconds). *NOW* is an operator of the TIME data type and it returns the current real TIME. *Duration* is another special data type and it is also mainly used in connection with timers. You may add or subtract duration to TIME and get TIME. You may divide or multiply duration by a real and get duration. You may subtract a TIME value from another TIME value and get duration.

The semantics of timers is this: a time value is set in a timer and it becomes active. When the time is reached, a signal with the same name as the timer itself will be sent to the process itself. Then the timer becomes inactive.

A timer may be RESET and it then becomes inactive and no signal will be issued. (If an inactive timer is RESET, then it remains inactive.) A RESET will also remove a timer signal instance already in the input port. This happens when the timer has expired, but the time-out signal has not been consumed.

If an active Timer is SET, the TIME value associated with the timer receives a new value. The timer is still active. If a timer is SET to a TIME which is already passed, the timer will immediately issue the time-out signal.

There is an operator *ACTIVE* which has a timer as a parameter and which returns a Boolean that can be used to check whether a certain timer is active or not.

Timer signals may contain data as other signals may contain data. Different parameter values in SET means generation of several timer instances. RESET must match these parameter values to eliminate the correct timer instance.

We summarise by a sketch of a finite state machine the behaviour of a timer (Figure 5.11).

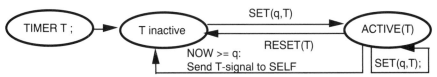

Figure 5.11   *The automata of a TIMER*

Let us now go through the example in Figure 5.10 in some detail. We have taken the liberty of placing a task symbol at the very top of the page doing a SET operation. This should be on the former page, but the point is that the SET operation must be performed before the process enters the state *Opening*. The timer (*door_timeout*) is first used to control that the person actually opens the *Door* when it is unlocked. If he does not open the *Door*, then it should not stay open for anybody to enter. If the timer expires, a *door_timeout* signal is issued from the process to itself and we have a transition (upper right of Figure 5.10) which results in sending a signal to lock the *Door* again and entering the *closing* state. The other, normal result is that the person opens the *Door* and the *Door* issues an *opened* signal. Then again the signal to lock the *Door* is sent and the timer is SET again. This time the timer is used in order to avoid somebody keeping the *Door* open physically.

In the *Closing* state, there are four transitions. The most normal one is that the user closes the *Door*, the timer is then RESET and the process returns to the *Idle* state. The second case is that the timer expires and an error message is sent to the panel. The third case may at first glance seem impossible and erroneous. But there is a chance that the person succeeds to open the *Door* after the *close* signal has been sent from *LSControl* due to the first timer expiring, but before the *closing* signal has been consumed by the *Door*. We just stay in the *Closing* state. The fourth possibility covers all other signals which occur and they represent internal errors.

5.2.3   Process identification (Pid)

Each SDL process has a unique identification. This identification is a value of the data type *Pid*. To the PId type there is associated one literal *Null* which means "no process" and one operator *unique!* which returns a new unique PId. (The operator cannot be used by users directly.) A PId value may be seen as a unique pointer value to the process instance.

PId expressions are used mainly as the destination of output. We recall that an output may have a TO-clause giving an explicit destination of the signal. One variant of the TO-clause has a PId value as the destination indicator.

PId values are obtained from the following PId expressions which are predefined in all processes:

- *SELF* – the process itself.
- *OFFSPRING* – the most recent process instance created by SELF. If no processes have been created by SELF, then OFFSPRING is NULL.
- *PARENT* – SELF is the OFFSPRING of PARENT. If SELF is not generated dynamically, then PARENT is NULL.
- *SENDER* – the process which sent the signal most recently consumed by SELF. If no signal has been consumed yet, SENDER is NULL.

In order to give a short example of the use of PId, assume that a *LocalStation* consists of not only one *Panel*, but two (or more). This is often the case where passing the door either way requires validation. Then the *LSControl* process will have to know which panel it is validating in order to issue the reply message to the correct panel. Figure 5.12 shows a part of the *LSControl* specification for this modified requirement.

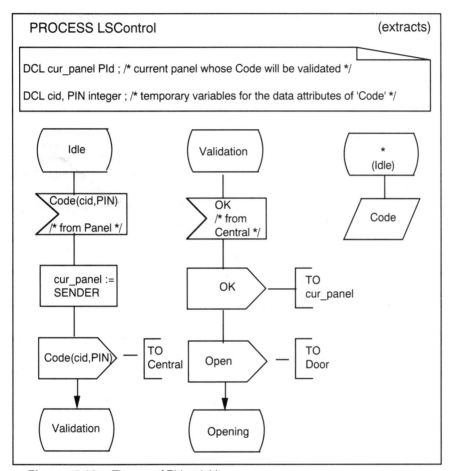

Figure 5.12   *The use of Pld variables*

While in *Idle*, the *LSControl* receives a *Code* signal from a *Panel*. Which *PanelControl* process that sent the *Code* signal is recorded by the task shown in Figure 5.13.

Figure 5.13   *Task including Pld expression SENDER*

Then the *Code*-signal is furthered to the *CentralUnit* by an output statement (Figure 5.14).

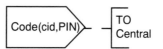

Figure 5.14   *Output symbol with commented TO-clause*

We note here that the TO-clause here is only a comment and not a part of the output statement itself since the identification *Central* is neither a PId-expression, nor a visible process name. For a human reader, however, it makes sense as we know that the *CentralUnit* is a block in which the validation is taking place. The output signal will still find its way since it has only one path to follow. The *CentralUnit* may in turn record which *LSControl* process it has received a validation request from through the same means (using the PId expression *SENDER*).

When the reply comes from the *CentralUnit* (here we show only the *OK* reply), we may direct the message to the right panel (see Figure 5.15).

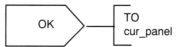

Figure 5.15   *Output symbol with Text Extension and TO-clause*

Note that even though the symbol associated to the right of the output symbol resembles a comment symbol, it is not. It is a *text extension symbol*, distinguishable from a comment symbol by the association line. The association line for a comment symbol is dashed, while for a text extension it is solid. As the name suggests, a text extension is an extension of the text within the symbol. The text in the text extension is appended to the text in the symbol itself and it is considered as part of the symbol. In our case above, the TO-clause resides in the text extension in order to graphically put it apart. It is definitely a part of the output-statement and significantly it tells to which panel control process to send the reply message.

Note also that using the expression SENDER directly in the TO-clause above will yield the wrong result as SENDER in *LSControl* now points to the process in *CentralUnit* which issued the *OK*-signal!

Alternatively, instead of a PId expression a TO-clause may specify a process name. In the *PanelControl* the *OK* signal leads to Figure 5.16.

Within the *PanelControl* process both *Display* and *CardReader* are visible names of processes.[3] Of course this is only useful when there is a static relation between processes.

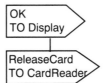

Figure 5.16   *Output symbols with TO-clauses with process names*

Let us now recapture the two main problems with the SDL addressing scheme:

1.   The name of the desired destination process is not visible at the output point.
2.   The signal may be intercepted on its way to its final destination, e.g. in a channel substructure.

A simple, but efficient way to handle these two problems is to introduce a routing process for each block with processes. The routing processes are known to the implementation given their input channels. The routing process will further signals according to a final destination through explicit knowledge of the topology of its block environment or because the final destination PId is transmitted as data in the signal. The original Sender should also be transmitted as data, since SENDER at the final destination will point to some intermediate routing process. Chapter 8 will give an example of routing processes (see Section 8.6).

Let us now return to our extended *LSControl* process and introduce a mechanism that is often encountered, but which has nothing to do with PId or addressing.

What if *LSControl* receives a *Code* signal while in *Validation*? Is this an error? The *LSControl* may receive *Code* from two *Panels* and it is not erroneous to receive a *Code* from the second *panel*, when validating a *Code* from the first *Panel*.

The *save* symbol assures that a set of signals will be bypassed until the process has entered a different state. Then the saved signals will be processed, as they have remained in the input port in their original order.

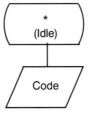

Figure 5.17   *Save symbol*

The construct above says that in all states except *Idle*, the *Code* signal will be saved. (Remember the asterisk state with exception list?) This means that the *Code* signal will only be handled when in *Idle*. This is how synchronisation between the two *Panels* is well taken care of. If the save construct was not here, the *Code* signal would have been discarded while the *LSControl* was handling the other *Panel's Code*. What would then happen to the inserted *Card*?

The save construct may have time-consuming implementation, its effects may be difficult to overview and some people find it awkward to understand. This has led us to suggest that save should be used with modesty and care. It is, however, the only SDL mechanism that helps rearrange the consumption of signals.

5.3   Advanced data in SDL

5.3.1   Abstract data types

In the introduction we argued that for a specification language such as SDL, it is practical to keep a conceptual distance to the implementation representation of data. In this section we will see how abstract data types are defined in SDL.

Let us again recall what we said in the introduction to this chapter. We said that what we are mainly interested in when we talk about integers is that 2+2=4. What we just said may be rephrased more formally as:

1.   We have a *data type* 'integer'.
2.   We have some basic values of integer (*literals*) and we know two '*2*' and '*4*'.
3.   There is an operation '+' which takes two integers and returns an integer value.
4.   We know one basic fact about addition (an axiom) and that is *2 + 2 = 4* .

We have actually defined above an abstract data type. We have called it 'integer', but it is very restricted. The reader understands immediately that 2+2=4 is not sufficient to tell all about integers. From the definition we cannot know anything about 3+1 as we have not defined '3' and '1' as literals and we have no axiom to tell us how to add 3 and 1. Furthermore, we can say nothing about 4-2, since we have not defined the '-' operator.

This illustrates one major difficulty with abstract data types. It is not easy to validate that the definition covers exactly what you have in your mind. Sometimes the definition does not cover the whole idea, e.g. the above definition does not cover the whole idea of an integer and sometimes the definition covers more than intended. We shall now give two examples of complete abstract data types, one is quite simple and hopefully easy to understand, while the other is more complicated and suited for readers with stronger interests in formalisms.

We return now to the *AccessControl* example. In the description of *Panel* we have seen that the *Display* is instructed to put up an error message. *PanelControl* issues an *ERR* signal and the *Display* shows "ERROR". There is, however, not only one error situation and the *PanelControl* knows more than it transmits when issuing *ERR*. We can transmit this extra information by adding a data attribute to the *ERR* signal and that data attribute shall be of the data type *ErrMessage*.

```
NEWTYPE ErrMessage
LITERALS
  Idle_Not_Cid_Digit, Validate_ERR_from_LSC,
  Validate_Cid_from_CR,
  Validate_tried3
OPERATORS
  Message:  ErrMessage -> CharString;
AXIOMS
  Message(Idle_Not_Cid_Digit)     ==
    'Idle:    neither Cid nor Digit';
  Message(Validate_ERR_from_LSC)  ==
    'Validate:  received ERR from LSC';
  Message(Validate_Cid_from_CR)   ==
    'Validate:  Cid, now?';
  Message(Validate_tried3)        ==
    'Validate:  Wrong PIN 3 times';
ENDNEWTYPE ErrMessage ;
```

The type definition will be contained in a text symbol in the SDL/GR (graphic syntax).

We shall go through the type definition above in some detail. The first line (starting with NEWTYPE) tells the name of the data type. The next line (starting with LITERALS) give the constant values of the data type *ErrMessage*. In this type, the literals are the only values of the type.

There is one OPERATOR which is called *Message* and which takes an *ErrMessage* as an argument and produces a character string. The syntax of operator signatures may look unfamiliar to readers who are mostly used to programming. The equivalent operator declaration in C++ would read:

```
CharString Message(ErrMessage);
```
        // given that CharString and ErrMessage were already declared as types (classes).

The AXIOMS give the correspondence between the values of the *ErrMessage* data type and character strings. This *Message* operator may then be used by the *Display* in order to show the character string corresponding to an error value.

5.3.2   Abstract data type with inductive operator definitions

This section is meant to show that abstract data types are very powerful and compact, but that the axioms may be quite difficult to understand. The reader who does not want to spend his time with the theory of abstract data types can skip to the next section. as SDL offers predefined data type generators that will do the trick in almost all cases. This section is only meant for those intending to build data types from scratch and for those who want a thorough background for understanding (SDL) data types.

In order to show a more complicated data type we introduce another modification of the requirements. Assume that the users find it too cumbersome to wait for central validation. One *LocalStation* is visited by the same people all the time and they have to pass access control quite frequently. They propose that it should be possible as a feature of the *LSControl* to let frequent users be validated by a local database of card identifications. When the database is established, it will be sufficient for frequent users to put their card into the *CardReader* and the validation will be swift. No *PIN* is necessary.

We shall model the database as one object of a data type *QuickBase*. We will not go into the details of the user interface for the establishment and use of the database.

```
NEWTYPE QuickBase
LITERALS EmptyBase
OPERATORS
   Insert: QuickBase, Integer -> QuickBase
   Delete: QuickBase, Integer -> QuickBase
   Valid:   QuickBase, Integer -> Boolean
AXIOMS
FOR ALL q IN QuickBase (
FOR ALL i,j IN Integer (
/*1*/ Insert(Insert(q,i),j) ==  Insert(Insert(q,j),i);
/*2*/ Insert(Insert(q,i),i) ==  Insert(q,i);

/*3*/ Delete(EmptyBase,i)     ==   EmptyBase;
/*4*/ Delete(Insert(q,j),i) ==
IF i=j THEN Delete(q,i) ELSE Insert(Delete(q,i),j) FI;

/*5*/ Valid(EmptyBase,i)        ==  False;
/*6*/ Valid(Insert(q,j),i)  ==  i=j OR Valid(q,i);
))
ENDNEWTYPE QuickBase;
```

This data type definition is far more intricate. Actually it is the general definition of a set. There is only one literal, namely the *EmptyBase*, the database with no elements, the empty set. There are two modifiers: *Insert* and *Delete*. There is one extractor: *Valid*.

Axiom 1 says that if we start with a *QuickBase q* and add integers i and then j , that is equivalent to adding j first and then i. Axiom 2 says that adding i twice to q is equivalent to adding it once. Axiom 3 says that deleting anything from the empty base leaves the base empty. Axiom 4 is the really tricky one to understand. It says that if you first add j to q and then delete i, that is equivalent to one of two cases: the first case is when $i=j$ then you delete what you just have inserted and this is equivalent to deleting it from q (NOTE that it is not equivalent to q itself, because the element i (or j) may have been inserted before and may already be an element of q (see axiom 2)); the second case is when i and j are different, then you may do the deleting first and the inserting afterwards. This all seems quite plausible, but the really tricky part is understanding why this defines the *delete* operation! Axioms 1 and 2 tells us that we may see a

QuickBase as a sequence of *Insert* operations. Axiom 4 defines *Delete* by itself (recursively), but the expression on the right is less complex (with respect to *Delete*) than the left side. It tells how you may derive the sequence of *Insert* operations equivalent to the *QuickBase* which has suffered a *Delete*.

Axiom 5 says that you may find no elements in the *EmptyBase*, trying to find an element that returns *False*. Axiom 6 is another example of a recursive definition where the right side is less complex than the left side. If you add *j* to *q* and then ask whether *i* is in the *QuickBase*, this is simple if *i=j* where it is obviously *True*, but it is less obvious if they are not equal, but the problem is now reduced to finding out whether *i* is within *q*.

We assume that many of our readers found the last example far from obvious and, therefore, we shall give a concrete example of a *QuickBase* which is being manipulated.

Assume that the set {1, 2, 4} is our *QuickBase*. According to our literals and axioms, we may not write the *QuickBase* in that fashion. We write:

```
    i.   Insert(Insert(Insert(EmptyBase,1),2),4)
```
Let us now delete the element 2
```
    ii.  Delete(Insert(Insert(Insert(EmptyBase,1),2),4),2)==

       Insert(Delete(Insert(Insert(EmptyBase,1),2),2),4)==
         /* from axiom 4, second branch*/
         Insert(Delete(Insert(EmptyBase,1),2),4)==
         /* from axiom 4, first branch */
         Insert(Insert(Delete(EmptyBase,2),1),4)==
         /* from axiom 4, second branch*/
         Insert(Insert(EmptyBase,1),4)
         /* from axiom 3 */
```

which we may write {1, 4} which is what we expected.
Let us now check whether 1 is in the *QuickBase*
```
    iii.   Valid(Insert(Insert(EmptyBase,1),4),1)==
           Valid(Insert(EmptyBase,1),1)==
           /* from axiom 6, second branch */
           True
           /* from axiom 6, first branch */
```

Yes, 1 was in the *QuickBase*.
The following shows how the *QuickBase* data type could be used in the *AccessControl* system.
```
    /* Declaring the database in process LSControl*/
    DCL quickcards QuickBase;
    ...
    /* Some transition must store cardid's in the base */
    quickcards := Insert(quickcards, 1533);
    quickcards := Insert(quickcards, 1566);
```

```
...
/* Sometimes some cardid's must be removed */
quickcards := Delete(quickcards, 1566);
...
/* Checking for valid cardid in the database */
validity := Valid(quickcards);
/* where validity is a Boolean */
```

5.3.3   Generators

Let us now summarise some of the positive and negative features of the abstract data type approach.

Positive	**Negative**
• Independent of implementations	• Axioms are hard to understand
• Well-defined interface through operators	• Automatic generation of constructive code difficult

We shall see that the negative effects may be remedied to a large extent by SDL having a predefined set of sorts and generators which are quite similar to mechanisms found in most modern programming languages. That it is well-understood actually means that the axioms have been internalised in the designer. He/she finds the interpretation trivial. This helps to overcome the first negative effect. The second negative effect is minimised because these predefined concepts already have corresponding implementations in the target languages such as C, C++ and CHILL.

In common programming languages we have ways of combining simple data attributes into more aggregated constructs such as arrays and sets. In SDL such aggregation concepts are described as *GENERATORs* which may be seen as parameterised types.[4] SDL has predefined three kinds of such generators: String, Array and Powerset.

The String is used to define a list (sequence) of items of a specified sort. Array is used to define an array sort with no upper index bound. Powerset is used to define set types with elements of any sort. (The readers familiar with set theory will see that "POWERSET" is not the correct term since the SDL generator with that name describes a set rather than a set of sets.) Having these three mechanisms and the STRUCT construct (see Section 5.3.4) a wide range of dynamic data structures can be expressed.

```
GENERATOR String
/* a sequence of items of specified sort */
(TYPE Itemsort,
/* the sort of the items in the sequence */
LITERAL Emptystring)  /* the only literal */
/* here we define the generator by the same means as a
normal type, with literals, operators and axioms*/
LITERALS Emptystring
```

```
OPERATORS
  MkString: Itemsort  -> String;
    /* make a string from an item */
  Length:   String    -> Integer;
    /* number of elements in string */
  First:    String    -> Itemsort;
    /* first item in string */
  Last:     String    -> Itemsort;
    /* last item in string */
  "//"      String,String -> String;
    /* concatenation */
  Extract!: String,Integer  -> Itemsort;
    /* get indexed item from string */
  Modify!:  String,Integer,Itemsort->String;
    /* modify one item in string */
  Substring:  String, Integer,Integer->String;
    /* make substring */
AXIOMS
  /* left to the reader as night exercises */
ENDGENERATOR String ;
```

Note that the operator "//" is surrounded by double quotes. It is an *infix operator* which means that concatenation of strings look like: "*string1 := string2 // string3 ;*".

Strings are sequences of any kinds of items. The most prominent use of String is of course Charstring – the character string which is defined by using the generator:

```
NEWTYPE Charstring
String ( Character, '')
  /* formal Itemsort is Character, Emptystring is '' */
/* LITERALS are strings of any length separated by
single quotes */
/* here additions to the general String is specified */
ENDNEWTYPE Charstring ;


GENERATOR Array
/* an array of items of the sort Itemsort, indexed by
type Index */
(TYPE Index,  /* the type of the indexing expression */
TYPE Itemsort)  /*the type of the items of the array */
OPERATORS
  Make!:    Itemsort  -> Array;
    /* make an (unbounded) array of items */
  Modify!: Array, Index, Itemsort -> Array;
    /* update one item of the array */
```

```
    Extract!: Array, Index  -> Itemsort;
      /* read one value of an item */
  AXIOMS
    /* left to the reader as night exercises */
  ENDGENERATOR Array ;
```

To use this generator, we shall first make types and then declare instances of that type. Let us assume we want an array of Integers indexed by Character.

```
  NEWTYPE IntXChar
  Array(Character, Integer)
  ENDNEWTYPE IntXChar ;

  DCL chrval IntXChar ;
  /* declaring array variable for the conversion of
  characters to integers */
```

Within a TASK:
```
  chrval('X') := chrval('Y')-1 ;
  /* which uses the short form of the operators Extract!
  and Modify! */
```

The long form would look like:
```
  chrval:=Modify!(chrval,'X', Extract!(chrval,'Y') - 1 );
```

The long form shall be used in axioms, while in TASKs the short form must be used. Strings use the same short form as arrays. Arrays of more than one dimension must be described as arrays of arrays.

```
  GENERATOR Powerset   /* represents mathematical sets, of
  any type */
  (TYPE Itemsort)
  LITERALS Empty;
  OPERATORS
    "IN": Itemsort, Powerset  -> Boolean;
      /* is the item in the set? */
    Incl: Itemsort, Powerset  -> Powerset;
      /* include an item in the set */
    Del:   Itemsort, Powerset  -> Powerset;
      /* delete an item in the set */
    "<":   Powerset, Powerset  -> Boolean;
      /* is proper subset? */
    ">":   Powerset, Powerset  -> Boolean;
      /* is proper superset? */
```

```
   "<=": Powerset, Powerset  -> Boolean;
     /* is subset? */
   ">=": Powerset, Powerset  -> Boolean;
     /* is superset? */
   "AND":  Powerset, Powerset  -> Powerset;
     /* intersection of sets */
   "OR": Powerset, Powerset  -> Powerset;
     /* union of sets */
 AXIOMS
   /* left to the reader as night exercises */
 ENDGENERATOR Powerset ;
```

We understand now that we can define our *QuickBase* as an instance of this generator:

```
 NEWTYPE QuickBase
 Powerset(Integer)
 /* The operators have different names: Insert is called
 Incl, Delete is called Del and Valid is called IN */
 ENDNEWTYPE QuickBase ;
```

5.3.4   STRUCT

In order to make use of SDL data more practical, SDL has introduced a shorthand for defining types which have aggregates of fields of different types. It is quite common to want a type which has multiple fields of varying types with operators defined for extracting and modifying single fields.

In our *AccessControl* example, we have the *Code* signal that contains a *card identification* and a *personal identification number*. Suppose that we find it desirable to collect those two pieces of data in one structured type.

```
 NEWTYPE AccessCode
 STRUCT
 cardid, pin Integer ;
 ENDNEWTYPE AccessCode;
```

will be equivalent to the following (long) definition

```
 NEWTYPE AccessCode
 OPERATORS
   Make!:  Integer, Integer -> AccessCode;
   cardidModify!: AccessCode, Integer-> AccessCode;
   pinModify! : AccessCode, Integer -> AccessCode;
   cardidExtract! : AccessCode -> Integer ;
   pinExtract! : AccessCode -> Integer ;
```

```
AXIOMS
/* we have omitted them here */
ENDNEWTYPE AccessCode ;
```

Having introduced the STRUCT shorthand, we should use the shorthand notation for Modify! and Extract! with respect to STRUCTs.

If *AC* is a variable of sort *AccessCode* then we may have the following assignments:

```
AC!cardid := 1234 ;
   /* long form: AC := cardidModify!(AC, 1234);   */
temp_pin := AC!pin ;
   /* long form: temp_pin := pinExtract!(AC);     */
```

Furthermore, we can use the STRUCT construct and then add new operators and corresponding axioms. Let us now extend our *AccessCode* type to include an operator which will check whether the card identification is in a *QuickBase*.

```
NEWTYPE AccessCode
STRUCT
cardid, pin Integer ;
ADDING
OPERATORS
   QuickValid: AccessCode, QuickBase -> Boolean;
   /* is card identification in base? */
AXIOMS
   QuickValid(AC, QB) == Valid(QB, cardidExtract!(AC) );
ENDNEWTYPE AccessCode;
```

This is an example of a data type which is not trivial and which may serve some practical purpose, but which is neither difficult to understand nor to implement (automatically). We have used the STRUCT predefined shorthand and we have added a "constructive" axiom to define the added operator. The axiom looks nearly exactly like the way one would implement the operation in a programming language.

5.3.5   Constructive operators in SDL 92

Recognising the fact that abstract data types relying solely on axioms for the definition of user defined operators is considered impossible by the large majority of SDL users, SDL 92 introduces constructive operators.

We shall use our *QuickBase* as an example and define that we want to "implement" the set by means of an array.

```
NEWTYPE intarr
/*"local" sort: an integer array indexed by integers */
   Array(integer, integer)
ENDNEWTYPE intarr;
```

```
NEWTYPE QuickBase
STRUCT
  A intarr;
  /* a local array of integers, indexed by integers */
  cardinal integer; /* the number of integers */
/* data invariant: the set of integers will be in the
first elements of the array. There will be no
duplicates and no ordering */
ADDING
LITERALS EmptyBase
OPERATORS
  Insert: QuickBase, Integer -> QuickBase ;
  Delete: QuickBase, Integer -> QuickBase ;
  Valid:   QuickBase, Integer -> Boolean ;

  Index!: QuickBase, Integer -> Integer ;
    /* help function */

OPERATOR Index!
  FPAR qb QuickBase, elem Integer
  RETURNS inx Integer
  REFERENCED ;
  /* help function returning index of found elem */
OPERATOR Insert
  FPAR qb QuickBase, elem Integer
  RETURNS qbr QuickBase
  REFERENCED ;
OPERATOR Delete
  FPAR qb QuickBase, elem Integer
  RETURNS qbr QuickBase
  REFERENCED ;
OPERATOR Valid
  FPAR qb QuickBase, elem Integer
  RETURNS res Boolean
  REFERENCED ;

ENDNEWTYPE QuickBase ;
```

We define in Figure 5.18 the operator *Index!* which we will also use in the other operators.

The operator diagram resembles a procedure diagram (which we will go through in greater detail in Chapter 6), but it may not include states and signal handling which means that it will mainly consist of decisions, tasks and operator calls in addition to operator start and operator return. Specifying a constructive operator will be very much like programming by flow charts.[5]

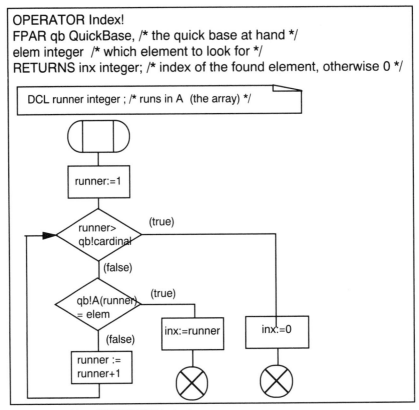

Figure 5.18 *OPERATOR Index!*

5.4 Shared variables and enabling conditions

We have emphasised that in SDL data is not shared among the processes other than the buffers (input ports). This is definitely true for basic SDL. There is, however, sometimes a need for simulating shared memory and this must be done by signalling the values between the processes. Only one process can own one piece of data. Since this has been felt as a general need, SDL has offered a shorthand for the sharing of data in order to minimise the specification errors made in specifying the somewhat cumbersome signalling needed and to minimise the number of (insignificant) signals and signalroutes.

In our example below we will combine the need for shared variables with the need to be able to check whether a certain input is "welcome" or not. We call the latter "enabling condition" which indicates that it specifies a condition (a Boolean expression) which must be fulfilled in order to enable the transition. We will also introduce "continuous signals" which is an enabling condition with no initial input, i.e. whenever there are no inputs in the input port, the continuous signal condition is evaluated and the corresponding transition performed if it is evaluated to true.

Our starting point is our *LocalStation* with the *LSControl* process and the corresponding *Door*. Assume that we have an *LSControl* which can have more than one *Panel* as we suggested earlier in this chapter. We have not specified *Door*, but implicitly we have assumed that the *Door* will issue a signal *Opened* when it has been opened and *Closed* when it has been closed. This may or may not be how a *Door* functions. Let us now for our new purpose assume that the *Door* does not issue signals all by itself. It can only issue replies to requests from the *LSControl* process and the only reply it can issue is the value of a Boolean variable called *closed_door*. In an implementation this means that *LSControl* may poll this variable of the *Door*.

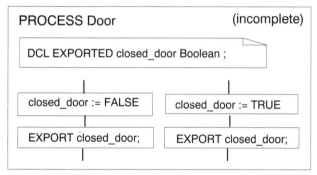

Figure 5.19   *PROCESS Door (incomplete)*

The exporter must declare his/her variable exported which means that an extra variable will be made holding the value to be exported. This extra variable will be updated every time an EXPORT statement is performed. All intermediate assignments to the variable will have no effect on the exported value!

Our (incomplete) *LSControl* in Figure 5.20 shows how the new logic works. After having unlocked the *Door* by issuing *Open*, *LSControl* enters state *Opening* and waits for the door to open. Any *Code* signals will be saved, while all other signals (*validity* signals) will be discarded (they are actually erroneous). Whenever there are no signals in the input port, the imported value is polled.

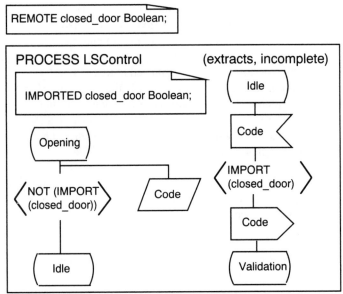

Figure 5.20   *Process LSControl with continuous signal, enabling condition and imported variable*

The IMPORTED definition in Figure 5.21 declares a pseudo-variable to hold the imported value. The variable is updated for each IMPORT expression.

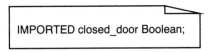

Figure 5.21   *IMPORTED definition*

In order to comply fully with the general SDL scope rules the imported/exported variable should be specified on a higher (block) level. In our case this means that in block type *LocalStation* there will be a remote variable specification:

```
REMOTE closed_door Boolean;
```

The exported declaration and the imported specification must both be equal to the remote variable specification.

Whenever the *closed_door* variable becomes FALSE, the transition is initiated leaving the process in the *Idle* state (see Figures 5.20 and 5.22).

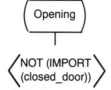

Figure 5.22   *Continuous signal with IMPORT expression*

Normally in the *Idle* state the process would expect a *Code* signal, but now we specify that *Code* is not welcome before the door is closed.

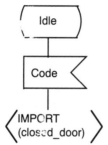

Figure 5.23   *Enabling condition with IMPORT expression*

The mechanisms covered in this section are SDL additional concepts and it is possible to show that one can transform a system description such that the semantics is equivalent, but the continuous signals, enabling conditions, IMPORT and EXPORT are eliminated. The transformation is not trivial and the resulting description is not good for people to read! Still we feel that more explicit signalling makes subsequent implementation easier, but there are certainly situations where the above mechanisms will defend their use.

5.5   Dynamic generation of process instances

Up to now we have only considered systems where all the constituent parts are known at system generation time. For many reasons static systems are still the most common ones, but modern object-oriented technology makes dynamics more common. Historically, dynamic procedure instances were introduced by Algol60 and SIMULA had dynamic data objects. In the seventies and eighties, Unix with its very dynamical process concept became more popular.

SDL has dynamics since processes may *create* other processes and procedures are called dynamically. Note that blocks cannot be generated dynamically. They are not "actors" and have "life" only as a consequence of the lives of their contained processes. Neither is data as such dynamically allocated in SDL as SDL data merely specify declared variables (within processes and procedures) and their (possibly complex) values. An *implementation* of variables of SDL data types such as, e.g. String will, however, often result in dynamic memory allocation.

In our *AccessControl* example we have the BLOCK *CentralUnit* which is to perform validation of the *Code* signals in order to return validity-signals. If we assume that the validation involves heavy work, it may be wise to have more than one validation process. In general we may talk about a set of validation processes. In SDL 88 a set of processes can be expressed simply by one process reference symbol. In SDL 92 creation can be expressed on a process set which has a reference to a pure process type.[6]

We see that on Block diagrams (see Figure 5.24), the creation is shown by a dashed line from the PARENT to the OFFSPRING. The parenthesis of *Validation(0,)* means that the *Validation* process set has zero members at system start-up and there is no limit to the maximum number of processes it may have. We further note the signal declarations which show that the *CUControl* is an intermediate communicating process between the original requester of validation (some *LSControl* process) and the actual *Validation* process. The intermediate signals transmit the PId of the requester together with the rest of the information between the requester and the *Validation* process. In this case the requester PId will be known by the validation process, but the inverse relation is not needed as the requester is only interested in the result and not in which process produced it.

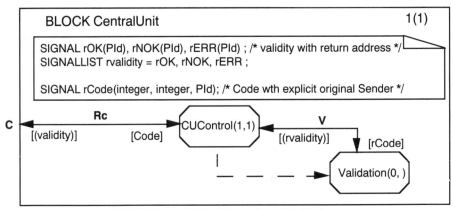

Figure 5.24   *BLOCK CentralUnit with creation of Validation processes*

The *CUControl* process (Figure 5.25) will keep track of the resource pool of *Validation* processes and direct the *Code* signal to a free process. When the *validity* returns, *CUControl* knows that the *Validation* process sending it is ready for another *Code* signal.

We note the *Create symbol* and the use of the available expressions SENDER and OFFSPRING. The reader will recall that SENDER is the PId of the process which sent the input which was most recently consumed by this process. *OFFSPRING* is the PId of the process most recently created by this process.

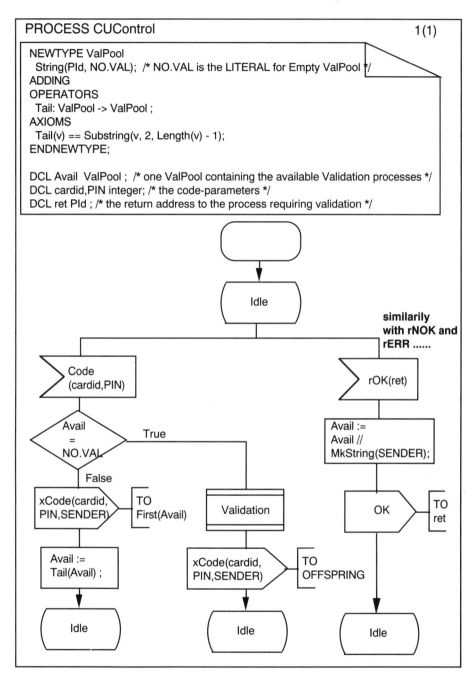

Figure 5.25 *PROCESS CUControl*

The reader may also note the definition and use of the data type *ValPool*. The type is made from a predefined generator *String* and we have added one operator which gives the tail of the string when the first element is excluded. The axiom is constructive. Note also that the LITERAL for an empty *ValPool* is *NO.VAL*.

When we are talking about the creation of processes, it becomes natural to look at the other end of the life span as well. How are processes terminated. While processes are created by their parent (or implicitly at start-up time), processes may not kill each other. Processes terminate when they reach a *Stop* symbol.

Figure 5.26   *Stop symbol*

When a process has terminated all referencing of that process will result in an error. The PId of the terminated process will not be used again within the same system instance.

In our case above, a simpler description could be reached if the *Validation* process would terminate after having performed the validation. Then there would be no reason to have the *Avail* variable since a new *Validation* process would be generated each time a validation takes place. The reason for not implementing it this way is the overhead required for creating and terminating processes.

5.6   SDL symbol summary

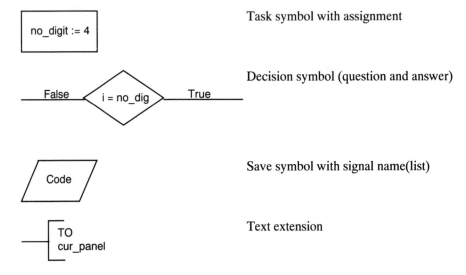

Task symbol with assignment

Decision symbol (question and answer)

Save symbol with signal name(list)

Text extension

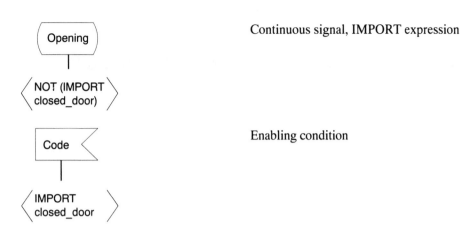

Continuous signal, IMPORT expression

Enabling condition

Notes

[1]Actually the difference is not as fundamental as it may seem as programs may be seen as data to an interpreting program execution.

[2]A timer is not a variable and TIMER is not a data type. Timer is an SDL primitive different from both variables and data types and processes.

[3]In SDL 88 the TO-clause may not include process names and, therefore, addressing becomes even more cumbersome. The alternative is to use VIA-clause instead of TO-clause, but addressing channels/signalroutes are not what the specifier normally wants

[4] SDL 92 has "parameterized" types and the GENERATORs can be expressed as such. This gives a technically more uniform approach to user defined types as derivatives of predefined concepts.

[5]Actually when we decide to implement *Index!* as an operator diagram, we must also define all operators using *Index!* as operator diagrams because there is a restriction in SDL 92 that operators defined by operator diagrams cannot be used in axioms. The making of the diagrams for the other operators should be trivial and are left to the reader.

[6]The process set which is generated from a process type will typically look like: 'setname(startno, maxno):typename'.

CHAPTER 6

SDL – Macros and Procedures

This chapter will cover the mechanisms in pure SDL which handle patterns in the description which recur at several places in the system. We shall look at the similarities and the differences between the very flexible, but dangerous macro construction and the more restricted, but safer procedure concept.

6.1   Similarities

There are two very different ways to describe similarities:

- macro;
- type.

We introduced block types in Chapter 4 and in Chapter 5 we covered abstract data types. A type is a pattern that may be used to generate instances and the instances will refer to their type for their semantics. In this chapter we shall cover "procedures" which are behavioural patterns to be used at several places within a process.

A *macro* is a pattern which is replicated (expanded) where the macro calls are. When the macro is expanded the macro call does not exist any more and the semantics is in the expanded macro. A macro is a shorthand notation, not a semantic concept within the language. Macros with parameters are extremely powerful. SDL has macros (as an additional concept) and they may be applied at any level.

6.2   Macro

In SDL 88 macros were the only mechanisms to describe similarities on a block level and our block set of *LocalStations* had to be expressed with a number of macro calls of a macrodefinition containing a block definition corresponding closely to our block type *LocalStation*. Figure 6.1 is how it could look in SDL 88.

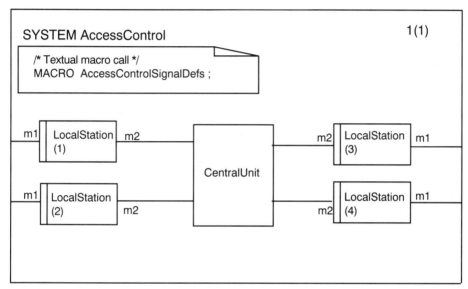

Figure 6.1   *Macro calls on structure level*

Let us first give the textual macrodefinition:

```
MACRODEFINITION   AccessControlSignalDefs;
SIGNAL         /* sender TO receiver */
EjectCard,   /* LocalStation TO ENV */
InputCard;  /* ENV TO LocalStation */
SIGNAL Code(integer,integer); /*LocalStationTOCentral*/
SIGNAL OK,NOK,ERR;   /* Central TO LocalStation */
SIGNALLIST validity  = OK, NOK, ERR ;
ENDMACRO AccessControlSignalDefs ;
```

Then we give the graphical macrodefinition in Figure 6.20.

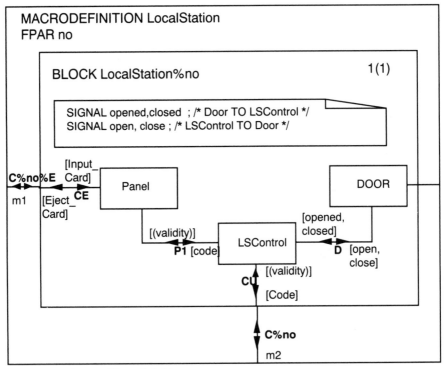

Figure 6.2   *Macrodefinition*

Let us go through the diagram (Figure 6.2) in some detail. The macrodefinition is a diagram that may be referenced from anywhere in the whole system. The macrodefinition has one parameter *no* which designates the individual *LocalStation*, just to ensure different identifiers . When the macro is expanded the formal parameter will be substituted by the actual text parameter. The '%' is a concatenation operator that concatenates the actual macro parameters with other strings. Thus, *C%no%E* expands to *C2E* when *LocalStation(2)* is expanded. *m1* and *m2* are macro *inlet/outlet* indicators and they are used to match the macro call surroundings.

It is a matter of taste, but we find that extensive use of macros to define similarities on a block level may prevent understanding more than it helps conception.

A common use of textual macros is to split up the text in text symbols into manageable macros. In this way the text is separate and the text symbols become smaller. Since SDL does not have data type diagrams, to use macros for the purpose of having one "entity" for each data type is quite sensible. The alternative is to use several text symbols and several pages.

NOTE that a macro is **not** a scope unit. No reasoning about the diagram may in principle take place before the macro is expanded.

6.3 Procedure

Unlike the macro mechanism, procedures are type concepts, which means that their semantics can be determined without expansion. Procedures are scope units and they may have their own variable declarations and the local names are confined to this procedure.[1]

In Figure 6.3 we rewrite the *PanelControl* and use procedures.

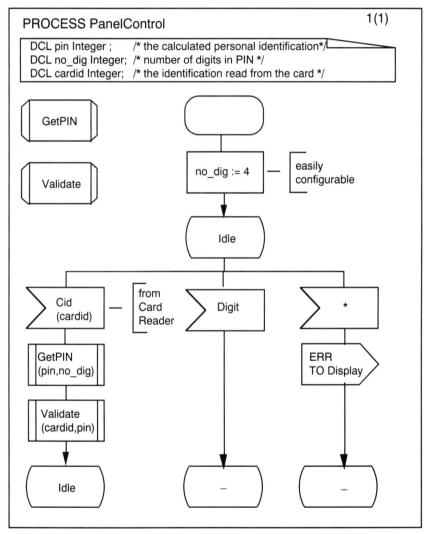

Figure 6.3 *Process PanelControl with procedures*

Procedures contain the same mechanisms for describing behaviour that are found in processes and as such they may be considered subprocesses. But procedures are not actors of their own, the interpretation is performed by the process in which they are declared.

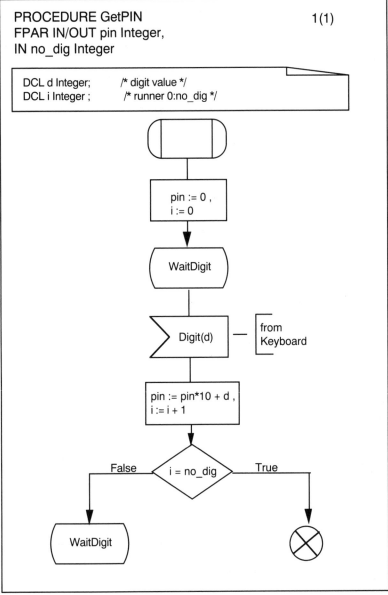

Figure 6.4   *Procedure GetPIN*

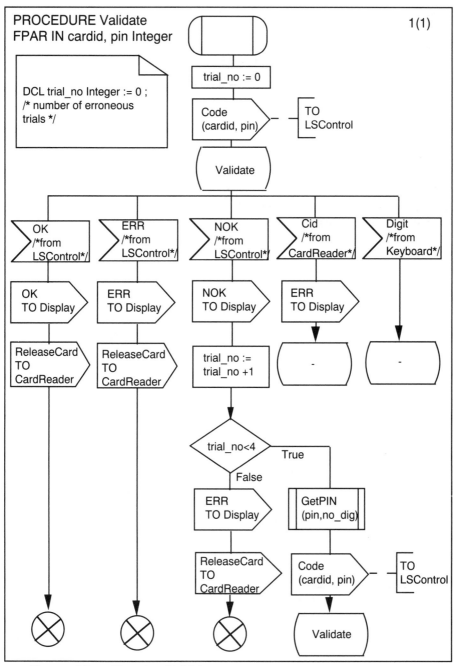

Figure 6.5 *Procedure Validate*

Let us go through the process procedure diagrams in some detail.

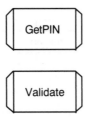

Figure 6.6   *Procedure symbols for localisation of procedures in the SDL scope*

Firstly, we observe that there are two *procedure (declaration) symbols* in the upper
left-hand corner of the process diagram (Figure 6.3) with the names of the procedures.
Note that there is no counterpart for macros. This is because macros are not scope units,
whereas procedures are. The scope unit containing the procedure symbols (in this case
process *PanelControl*) defines the scope of the procedure use. (Remember that the scope
of the macrodefinition is the whole system always[2].)

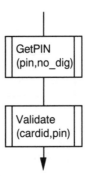

Figure 6.7   *Procedure calls*

Secondly, observe the procedure call symbols in the process diagram (Figures 6.3
and 6.7) and in the *Validate* procedure (Figure 6.5). The *procedure call symbols*
resemble the procedure (declaration) symbols, but their corners are different. Note that a
procedure call symbol has one and only one entrance and one and only one exit[3].

Figure 6.8   *Procedure heading with formal parameter specification*

Thirdly, observe the *procedure diagram* of *GetPIN*. There are two parameters: *pin* and *no_dig* which are both Integers. The *pin* parameter is *IN/OUT* which means that the actual parameter corresponding to formal *pin* will be updated whenever the formal *pin* is updated within *GetPIN*. This is just like **var** parameters in Pascal or **reference** parameters in C++. The *no_dig* parameter is an *IN* parameter which means that the procedure will have a local variable with the name of the parameter. This variable will assume the value of its corresponding actual argument at entry. Changes in the value of IN parameters will not be transmitted to the actual argument. This is just like traditional **value** parameters.

Fourthly, observe in the procedure *Validate* (Figure 6.5) that the procedure name coincides with a name of an internal state of *Validate*. This is not an error, since procedure names and state names fall into different entity classes and therefore have different name spaces.

State names are not visible outside the procedure. The process states are not visible within the procedure.

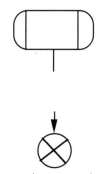

Figure 6.9 *Procedure start and return symbols*

Fifthly, observe the two special symbols which represent the start of the procedure and the return from the procedure (Figure 6.9). The *procedure start symbol* designates the starting point of a procedure. Then the transition from the procedure start symbol is interpreted. The control will return back to the caller when the *return symbol* is encountered.

6.4   Differences between macro and procedure

	Macro	**Procedure**
Main characteristic	Syntactic substitution	Type: semantic substitution
Symbols	Macro call	Procedure, procedure call
	▯	◗ , ▯
Diagram	MACRODEFINITION	PROCEDURE

Parameters	Textual substitution	IN or IN/OUT
Scope unit?	No	Yes
Scope of definition	The total system	Process of the procedure symbol
Scope of use	In all diagrams	Only in process and procedures
Entries	Possibly multiple	1
Exits	Possibly multiple	1
Reasoning	Macro must be expanded	Procedure is unit of reasoning

Macros are merely syntactic substitutions and as such a way to partition the description, while procedures are types and as such they partition the process (i.e. the semantics of the process). The difference may not be simple to grasp, but think about the fact that macros must be expanded before any analysis can be done! In fact few tools support macros in full (textual macros may be supported) and no tools support a graphical expansion such that the user can see the expanded result. In fact it is often impossible to know exactly how the expansion will turn out. Despite the innate hazards of using macros, they are still used. They are analysed separately and the resulting systems are consequently error prone.

Procedures in contrast are supported by all tools. Procedures are types which may be understood by analysing their definitions independently of their use. They can be used in several different places and as such constitute reuse of a definition in an orderly and constructive manner. In our *PanelControl* example above we see that *GetPIN* is called both from the process body itself and from the procedure *Validate*.

Those readers still not certain about the difference between macros and procedures should consider whether macros could have been used in the *PanelControl* example above. The diagrams can be modified by substituting procedure call symbols with macro call symbols and substituting the procedure diagrams with macro diagrams (with only the heading slightly different and the entry and exit symbols substituted by the corresponding macro inlet and outlet symbols).

How would the expanded diagram look? It would not be totally correct as there would be multiple declarations of variables. This is due to the fact that when macros are expanded the result is "flat", while a corresponding procedure use will yield a layered world where each procedure layer will have its own visible identifiers.

Thus, the "flatness" of macros caused multiple declaration problems. We have a complementary problem with the hierarchy of procedure calls. Each procedure sees only its own set of states. Any odd, unexpected signal must be handled where it is consumed whether it is in a procedure or in the process body itself. This means that exception handling must be propagated into every procedure. Since the procedure is the behavioural context this seems reasonable, but in practice exceptions should imply a change of the action sequence which is incompatible with the "one entry – one exit" style of procedures. If the exceptions are not time-critical, simple save will normally do the trick making sure that the exceptions will be handled after the procedure has exited. Still the exceptions must be explicitly covered by the save symbols in each procedure state. When a decision on data uncovers an exception, the situation is even more difficult. The procedure cannot direct the next state of the calling process and, thus, the exception information must be exported from the procedure and rechecked within the scope which can handle it.

6.5 Value returning procedures

SDL 92 offers value returning procedures, i.e. procedures which can be called as integral parts of expressions. We saw in Chapter 5 that SDL 92 offers operator diagrams which in fact are procedure diagrams containing only one (start) transition. Value returning procedures can be used very much like an operator, but they may contain states just like an ordinary procedure.

In our example we could make *GetPIN* a value returning procedure. The diagram would be slightly modified in its heading (Figure 6.10) and optionally in the return area where the returning expression may be associated with the return symbol (Figure 6.11).

Figure 6.10   *Heading of ValueReturning GetPIN*

Figure 6.11   *Returning from a value returning procedure*

The call will look somewhat different (Figure 6.12).

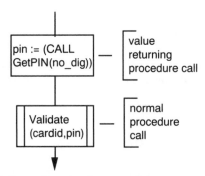

Figure 6.12 *Calling value returning procedure*

Note in Figure 6.12 that the value returning procedure call is within an expression. The procedure name is preceded by the keyword *CALL*. A value returning procedure call must be enclosed in parentheses when it does not constitute the whole expression. In our example, the value returning procedure call could have been without enclosing parentheses. Alternatively we could have called the *GetPIN* procedure directly within the parameter list of *Validate*.

6.6   Remote procedures

Procedures are behaviour patterns defined within a process (type). As such they may be seen as possible behaviour patterns which the process can perform. The next step in our chain of reasoning would be to suggest that the process could perform procedures upon requests from other processes. It would function as a "server" of behaviour. It would be simple to make up a signalling scheme to support this scenario: each procedure would have its input request signal and its output result signal. Where to send the result would be given by the SENDER of the input request.

The "server scenario" is so attractive that SDL decided to provide a shorthand for such signal sending. The mechanism is called "remote procedure" and functions the same way as import and export of values. In the same fashion some signals and signalroutes will be generated implicitly. This will in some cases make the descriptions easier to overview.

In our example the *CentralUnit* could contain a process which had a procedure *Validation* which took a couple of integers as input parameters (the same parameters as the *Code*-signal) and gave the *validity* result back as an integer (for instance). Then the *LSControl* would not do explicit signal sending, but would call a remote procedure instead. In our case there would be little difference between the two approaches, but in the signal sending case *LSControl* could continue doing other business while waiting for the explicit *validity* signal return. The remote procedure case would require that *LSControl* waits inactively for the return of the remote procedure call. Consequently, remote procedures are mechanisms for synchronous communication between processes.

The remote procedure mechanism consists of four interdependent language constructs:

1. *The exporting of a procedure.* A procedure which is made visible by other processes is marked with the keyword 'EXPORTED' preceding the procedure heading, e.g. "EXPORTED PROCEDURE Validate ...". The exporting process can control in which states it will accept the remote request. It may also specify to save the request to other states. The controlling of the acceptance is done by using input and save symbols with the remote procedure name preceded by the keyword *PROCEDURE*.

2. *The importing of a procedure.* When a process, service or procedure wants to import a remote procedure, it must specify the signature of this procedure in an "imported procedure specification" in a text area. The specification in our case would read: "IMPORTED PROCEDURE Validate; RETURNS integer;" where the integer returned would give the result of the validation (unlike the version suggested earlier in the book, where explicit signals represent the result).

3. *The specification of remote procedure.* In SDL all names must be defined in a specific scope. Thus, the names remote procedures must be defined in the context in which the actual definition of the procedure and the calls will be contained. In our case the definition of the procedure *Validate* is within the *CentralUnit* and the call is in *LSControl* of the *LocalStations*. The scope unit enclosing all these is the system itself. There we will find a text area with the following text: "*REMOTE PROCEDURE Validate; RETURNS integer;*".

4. *The calling of a remote procedure.* The calling of the remote procedure is indistinguishable from local procedure calls unless the caller explicitly states which process it will request the procedure executed by. This can be done by a TO-clause with a PId following the procedure name of the call.

Remote procedures may be value returning (as in our example above) and they may be virtual.

6.7   SDL symbol summary

| LocalStation (1) |

Macro call symbol

| GetPIN (pin,no_dig) |

Procedure call symbol

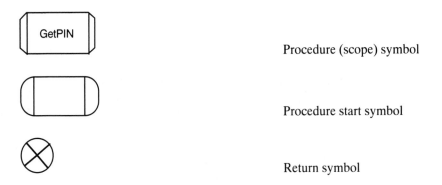

Procedure (scope) symbol

Procedure start symbol

Return symbol

Notes

[1] In SDL 88 procedures may, however, not be applied on the block level.

[2] The scope of a name in SDL is within its defining context. The defining context is where the identifier is declared. Thus, when a procedure has its procedure symbol within a process *PanelControl*, the procedure will be visible within the whole *PanelControl* and within all procedures of *PanelControl*. If the procedure symbol had been within a procedure, the scope would have been limited to that procedure. The same principle holds for most names in SDL. Exceptions include state names which are only visible within the exact scope where they are defined and not in inner scope units.

[3] This is quite different from macros, where any number of inlets and outlets may occur. The effect is that it is impossible to specify a separate error exit from a procedure, while this is possible from a macro. Conversely entry and exit assertions of procedures are more easily established.

CHAPTER 7

Object-oriented SDL

In this chapter we shall focus on the object-oriented concepts which were introduced in SDL 92. They include more versatile mechanisms for the specification of types, inheritance between types, mechanisms for redefinition of (virtual) types and parameterised types. The chapter will also give an introduction to *packages*, the SDL 92 library concept.

7.1   Introduction

Real time systems are characterised by being very large and very complex and specifications of such systems are correspondingly large and complex. However, many elements of these systems share common characteristics. Object-oriented constructs are especially devised to express this.

Reuse requires language mechanisms to support composition and adaptation of reusable components of specification. Object-oriented concepts provide both of these: composition by clean interfaces between types of objects and adaptation by specialisation. The emphasis on making types used for specialisation also tends to motivate the definition of general types that may be reused in many different applications. This will be even more encouraged by generic parameters to types, making them independent of specific applications.

Object-oriented extensions of SDL were first introduced in the Mjølner project (Knudsen et al., 1992) The Mjølner project was a 3 year Nordic research project with funding from the Nordic Industry Fund. Participants were companies and research institutions from Norway, Sweden and Denmark. In the SDL context, major contributors were EB Technology of Oslo, Norway[1] with its subcontractor the Norwegian Computing Center and from Sweden: TeleLOGIC[2]. The development of object-oriented SDL was also sponsored by the Norwegian Telecom.

The work on object-oriented extensions of SDL was continued both in the SPECS project[3] and in the SISU project. The current book conforms to SDL 92.

The object-oriented perspective used in SDL 92 is based upon the ideas behind SIMULA (Dahl et al., 1968) generalised in Nygaard (1986) and BETA (Kristensen et al., 1987). Introducing object orientation, generic parameters and library packages in SDL calls for new elements of an SDL method. It will no longer be the rule that only full system descriptions are the targets, but also reusable components of specifications.

7.2   Types and instances revisited

We are now going to use our *AccessControl* system to illustrate the different object-oriented mechanisms of SDL 92. The central diagrams of the *AccessControl* system are the system diagram, the diagram describing *LocalStations* and the process diagram of the "brain" of the *LocalStation*, the *LSControl*.

7.2.1   The difference between types, sets and singular instances

We recall the system diagram of the *AccessControl* system in Figure 7.1.

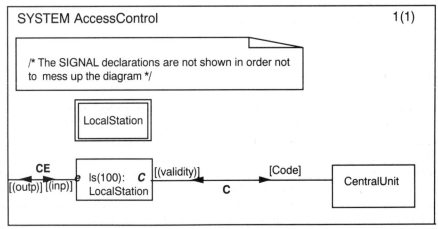

Figure 7.1   *System AccessControl (as known)*

We recall that this diagram describes a system with 100 *LocalStations* each one connected to a *CentralUnit*. The local stations are similar as they are derived from the same type *LocalStation*.

CentralUnit is a (singular) *block reference* (in SDL, often only called "block").There is only one *CentralUnit* in the system. The block reference refers to a block diagram (which will not be shown in this chapter as it has been shown earlier).

Figure 7.2   *Block CentralUnit – a singular block reference*

LocalStation is a *block type reference* and it refers to a block type diagram. As far as the type is concerned, there may be zero or more local stations in the system.

Figure 7.3   *Block type reference to block type LocalStation*

ls is a block set comprising 100 *LocalStations*. They do not share the same channel instances, but they share the same general understanding of its surroundings.

e   ls(100):   *C*
    LocalStation

Figure 7.4   *Block set of 100 LocalStations (called 'ls') with gates **e** and **C***

The reader should make sure that he/she recognises the difference between a block reference, a block type reference and a block set.

A block type is a general description of the properties of block instances. Block sets or block instances may be instantiated from this type description (Figure 7.4). The block type itself is not affected by where the type description is used. It may sound trivial, but it is of major importance that the description of the type is conceptually separated from the instances of the type. Block types are described by block type diagrams.

Just like we have the distinction between block reference, block type and block set, we have the distinction between process reference, process type and process set. This distinction follows exactly the same conceptual lines, but it is blurred by the old SDL 88 definition which made an awkward equivalence between process reference and process set. In SDL 88 it was possible to describe a process set of several process instances by a process reference. In order to keep the SDL 88 compatibility SDL 92 allows this, too, but our recommendation is that process sets should be described with reference to a process type.

Figure 7.5   *Process reference which is a process set (SDL 88)*

Figure 7.6   *Process type Validation and a process set (SDL 92)*

7.2.2   Gates and gate constraints

Now we continue by looking at the type definition (Figure 7.7).

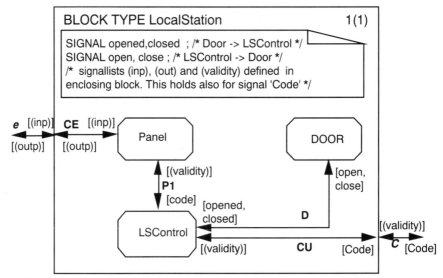

Figure 7.7   *Block type definition with gates and gate constraints*

We have shown another version of this block type diagram in Figure 4.10, but we have now used processes directly inside (Figure 4.10 had *Panel*, *LSControl* and *Door* as blocks). This is according to the strategy that *Panel* will be divided into services. The important thing here is that we get one block level less, which simplifies the example.

Furthermore, we have elaborated the description of the interface. A block type has no connectors (channels) connected to it, but instances of the type will have. In order to connect the instances correctly to its surrounding, we need a way to describe the connections. These connections are called *gates* and the output symbols of the processes within the type can refer to the gates in VIA-constructs.

The gates need not be more than a name associated with where a channel/signalroute connects to the frame. This has been shown in Chapter 4. Gates may, however, also describe invariants which should hold in the actual connections where the instances are. We say that we have *gate constraints*. Gate symbols are signalroute symbols and they may have signallists associated with the directions. The constraint is that the actual connections must have the signals mentioned in the constraints.

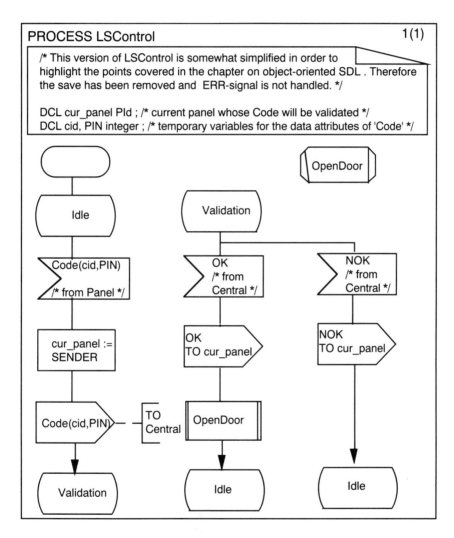

Figure 7.8 *Process diagram of LSControl (simplified)*

In order to have the reader updated about our starting situation, we show the *LSControl* process diagram in Figure 7.8, which is somewhat simplified from the versions we have shown earlier. We have done this to highlight the points that we are going to make later in this chapter.

7.3   Inheritance and modification

Having now presented our starting point including types, instances and sets, we shall go on to elaborate our example incrementally in order to show how object-oriented mechanisms in SDL can be effectively applied to describe and modify a description.

Let us assume that we find that there is a need for some of the stations to be disabled upon request from the *CentralUnit*. These doors will then remain locked until they are enabled from the *CentralUnit*.

It is quite obvious that we now need to distinguish between stations with this ability and stations without this ability. Since we may have several such *BlockingStations* as well as plain local stations in our system, we will describe *BlockingStation* as a type and make a set of *BlockingStations* in addition to what we have from before.

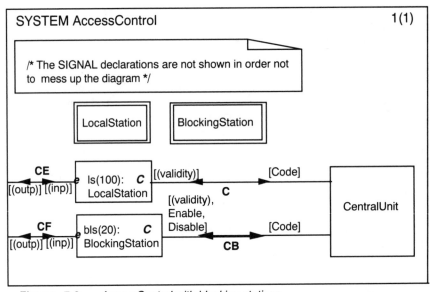

Figure 7.9   *AccessControl with blocking stations*

7.3.1   Types that are almost similar

BlockingStations are quite similar to the plain *LocalStations*. Our specification (in prose) above indicates that the only difference is that the *BlockingStations* shall be able to react to signals from the *CentralUnit* that plain *LocalStations* will not recognise. *BlockingStation* will have a *Door* (which should not have a new definition), a *Panel* (which could have a new definition, but need not have a new definition) and a control process *LSControl* which should be able to do extended controlling.

We conclude that a *BlockingStation* is a specialised *LocalStation* where *LSControl* should be extended or modified. In SDL 92 this is exactly what is expressed by Figure 7.10.

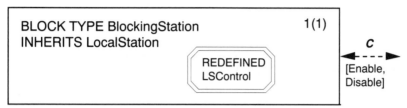

Figure 7.10 *BlockingStation diagram*

In prose Figure 7.10 says that *BlockingStation* inherits everything from *LocalStation*, but it adds a redefinition of *LSControl* and it adds two signal types onto gate *C* namely *Enable* and *Disable*. This looks simple, straightforward and compact and that is exactly what object orientation is all about.

There is, however, a snag. The observant reader may have spotted that *LSControl* in the definition of *LocalStation* above was not a type, but a process reference. The redefinition is a type.

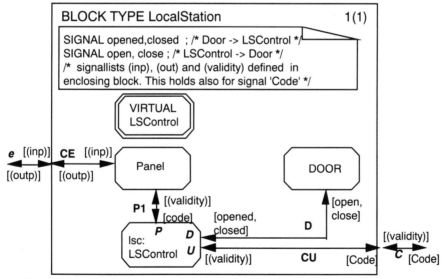

Figure 7.11 *Slightly altered LocalStation definition*

Furthermore, one may ask whether any component can be redefined in a specialisation just by prefixing the reference by the keyword *REDEFINED*. The truth is that only types specifically marked can be redefined. Therefore, our original definition of *LocalStation* must be altered slightly (see Figure 7.11).

Firstly, we have to make an *LSControl* process type and a (singular) instance *lsc* of that type at the very same place as the process reference was at in the original definition. Secondly we have marked the process type with the keyword *VIRTUAL* to show that specialisations of *LocalStation* may replace that definition with their own definition.

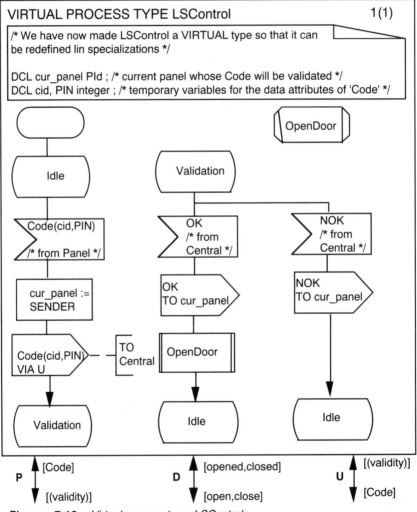

Figure 7.12   *Virtual process type LSControl*

Plain *LocalStations* have their own (default) definitions of *LSControl* (see Figure 7.12). We see that the definition of the process type *LSControl* is almost identical to the process diagram *LSControl* given in Figure 7.8, but we notice that we have defined three process gates *P*, *D* and *U* with associated process gate constraints. We note that the enclosing *LocalStation* definition uses these gates in connection with the instance *lsc* of *LSControl*.

Within the process type diagrams, the gates appear as identifiers in the VIA-clause of the output symbols.

When we want to analyse the type enclosing the virtual type (here, block type *LocalStation*) we wish to know something about the instances of the virtual types even though we know they may be redefined in subtypes. At least we must know the static interface, i.e. the gates. Very often we would like to know more about the type and, therefore, the header of a virtual type may include a *virtuality constraint*. The virtuality constraint is of the form "**atleast** type-identifier". All "matches" (redefinitions and finalisations) of the virtual must be specialisations of the type referred to by the type-identifier of the constraint.

When there is no constraint, the default is that the type itself is the constraint. This applies here and, therefore, all redefinitions must be specialisations of the *LSControl* type of *LocalStation*. In the following we will show that this holds.

7.3.2   Extensions by specialisation (inheritance)

We have still not solved our *BlockingStation* problem completely. We have made it clear that the process type *LSControl* can be redefined and we have indicated in the *BlockingStation* diagram that it has a redefinition.

Just as it was reasonable to describe *BlockingStation* as derived from *LocalStation* by using inheritance (the INHERIT-clause of the heading), it seems reasonable that the redefinition of *LSControl* in *BlockingStation* should be derived from *LSControl* of *LocalStation*.

It is also evident from the informal requirement specification that *LSControl* of *BlockingStation* should be a pure extension of what *LSControl* of *LocalStation* can do.

Furthermore, the (default) virtuality constraint requires that the redefinition should be a specialisation of the original virtual type (see end of Section 7.3.1).

What is special about the *BlockingStation* variant is that it can handle two new signals which are never sent to *LocalStations*.

Let us go through the specialised *LSControl* in some detail (Figure 7.13). Firstly, we see that the heading looks much more complicated than we are used to. The problem is that the redefined definition must have the same name as the original or one could not tell what it is a redefinition of. On the other hand, this definition must be distinguishable from the one in *LocalStation* and that is why we must qualify the names. When a tool is used, the tool will keep track of the enclosing relation and it will also produce the appropriate headings[4].

Secondly, we notice how the gate **U** is extended by adding the two signals *Disable* and *Enable*. The process gate symbol is dashed in order to show that this gate has already been defined in a diagram from which this diagram is specialised.

Thirdly, we notice how this extension of the basic *LSControl* "connects to" the part from which it inherits. The asterisk state refers to all the states in both the parent type and the specialised part. Here we have added a number of transitions to the ones of the basic *LSControl*. None of the existing transitions are altered.

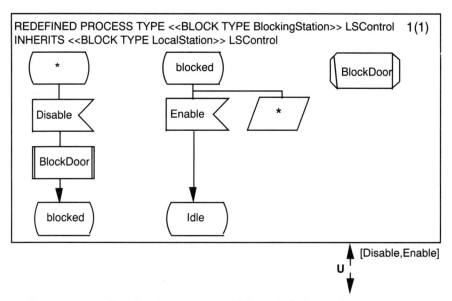

Figure 7.13 *Redefined process type LSControl of BlockingStation*

Figure 7.14 shows how the transitions of basic *LSControl* are a subset of the transitions of the specialised *LSControl*[5].

The reader will appreciate how the FSM technique makes it possible to extend behavioural descriptions. In normal programming languages this is not at all simple. Often the more basic description must know about potential extensions to come. It is a strong point that FSMs need not know about which new transitions will be added in an extension. The clue lies in the fact that FSMs have a finite set of states which can be used as "hooks" for new transitions. The asterisk state serves as a means to let the new transitions refer to all the old states. The old states can also simply be repeated in the specialisation. Conversely an asterisk state in a supertype will refer to all states – also those states which are defined in a subtype!

LSControl of LocalStation:

	code	OK	NOK	opened	closed
Idle					
Validation					

LSControl of BlockingStation:

	code	OK	NOK	opened	closed	Disable	Enable
Idle							
Validation	LSControl of LocalStation						
Blocked							

Figure 7.14 *State transition matrices of LSControl*

7.3.3 The need for modifications

We have now seen that SDL has powerful mechanisms to extend the process definitions, but sometimes this is not quite enough.

Assume now that the *AccessControl* system should log the transactions on some of the *LocalStations*. The owner wants to attach a logging device to the *LSControl* and he wants to trace all the transactions performed by the *LSControl* (see Figure 7.15).

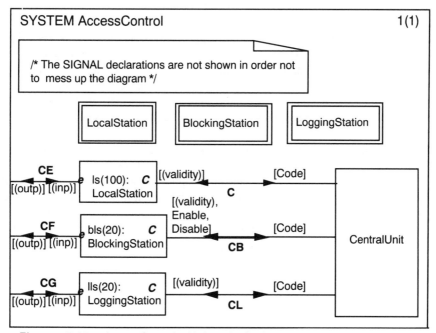

Figure 7.15 *AccessControl with LoggingStations*

We recognise that on a certain abstraction level, the job to make *LoggingStation* seems similar to what we did with *BlockingStation*. As for *BlockingStation* the *LoggingStation* will be a specialisation of *LocalStation* (see Figure 7.16).

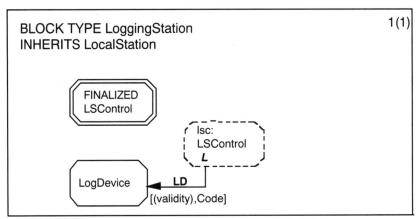

Figure 7.16   *LoggingStation*

With *LoggingStation* it is not sufficient to only modify the *LSControl*, since there is an addition to the block, namely the *LogDevice*. The *LogDevice* must be connected to the *LSControl* along a signalroute that we did not have before. *lsc* has been defined in the *LocalStation* definition and is dashed here.

We notice the keyword *FINALIZED* in the process type reference. This has a slightly different meaning than *REDEFINED*. A redefined type can be redefined again in yet another specialisation. A finalised type cannot be redefined. There is a subtle point to making this distinction. Virtual and redefined types are very flexible, but analysis becomes more uncertain since some components may not be entirely known. Finalised types are not flexible any more, they are completely known and, therefore, analysis can be certain.

The new signalroute **LD** indicates that it is not be possible to derive the finalised *LSControl* by only adding a number of new transitions to the basic *LSControl*. In order to get new transitions, we need either new input signals or new states. The *LSControl* of *LoggingStation* has neither new signals, which can be seen from the channels to the *lls* set of logging stations, nor new states. In fact the *LogDevice* should be invoked for most transitions since the requirement was to trace the transactions. Then our need is to modify (redefine) some of the existing transitions.

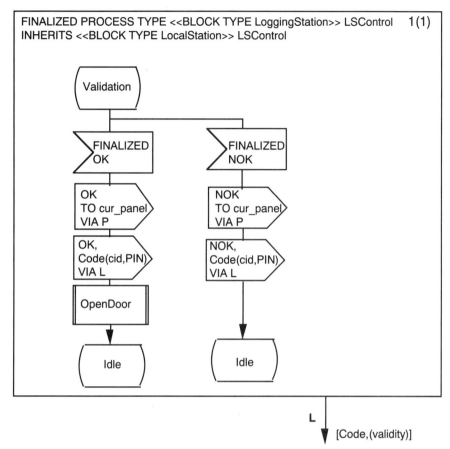

Figure 7.17 *LSControl of LoggingStation with virtual transitions*

We now begin to see the parallel with the specialisations on block level. We have used the virtuality concept to redefine processes of the block type. We now use the virtuality concept to redefine transitions of the process type (Figure 7.17). We conclude that we need only redefine the transitions returning *validity* to the *panels* and we will send both the *Code* and the *validity* signal to the *LogDevice*.

We have specified the redefined transitions as finalised to make sure that they will not be redefined again.

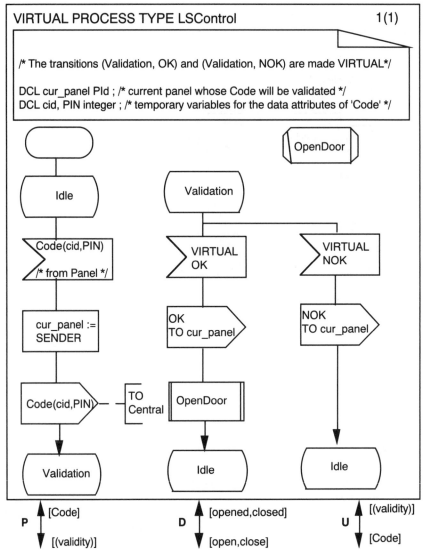

Figure 7.18 *LSControl altered with virtual transitions*

Just like in the case of the virtuality on the block level, we must indicate which transitions can be modified, which means that we must alter the original *LSControl* slightly.

7.3.4   Summary of inheritance, virtuality and their interrelationship

We will now summarise some of the major points of object orientation in SDL 92:

- **Inheritance** means specialisation of type. Pure additions require no modifications of the supertype.
- Modifications of the supertype will have an automatic effect on the inherited type.
- SDL 92 provides an efficient form of inheritance of behaviour (inheritance of process and service types and procedures) which is rarely found in other object-oriented languages. The states serve as place holders for the modifications and wild card notations (asterisk and dash state) serve as powerful entries into the super- or subtype.
- Inheritance can be applied to system, block, process, service types and to procedures and signals (in addition to data types).
- Virtual types may have virtuality constraints given by an **atleast**-clause which specifies a minimum type which the analysis of the enclosing type may take for granted. When no atleast-clause is given, the default is that the original virtual type itself is the constraint type.
- A **redefined** type is a type which is specified as **virtual** in a supertype of the type enclosing the redefined type. A redefined type must be a specialisation of the virtuality constraint. A redefined type may be further redefined in specialisations of its encloser.
- A **finalized** type is a type which is specified as **virtual** in a supertype of the encloser. A finalised type must be a specialisation of the virtuality constraint. A finalised type may not be defined again in specialisations of its encloser.
- Specifying a type as virtual, decreases the degree of analysis which can be performed on its encloser (since the instances of the virtual type may be of a type which is actually not known at the analysis of the encloser). However, it increases the flexibility of specialisations.
- Finalising a type increases the degree of analysis which can be performed on the encloser.
- Virtual, redefined and finalised can also be used for individual transitions in processes. The virtuality specification can occur in input symbols, start symbols and save symbols.

7.4   Packages

Up to now in this chapter we have worked within the framework of one system – the *AccessControl* system. We have altered the original definition and put new concepts into it, but still – we have only one system.

This may or may not be a problem. If you are actually only making one system, all is well. There is, however, a fair chance that you will hope to sell more than one system. Of course you can replicate your system completely and again there seems to be no problem, but in fact what you have done is to define a system type and more than one instance of that type.

System types are almost identical to block types. A system instance is made with a frame symbol containing solely the following text: "SYSTEM systemname: systemtype". System types may contain virtual block types which can be used for modification.

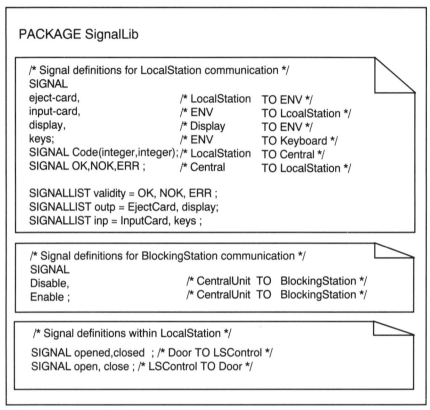

```
PACKAGE SignalLib

  /* Signal definitions for LocalStation communication */
  SIGNAL
  eject-card,                    /* LocalStation  TO ENV */
  input-card,                    /* ENV           TO LcoalStation */
  display,                       /* Display       TO ENV */
  keys;                          /* ENV           TO Keyboard */
  SIGNAL Code(integer,integer);  /* LocalStation  TO Central */
  SIGNAL OK,NOK,ERR ;            /* Central       TO LocalStation */

  SIGNALLIST validity = OK, NOK, ERR ;
  SIGNALLIST outp = EjectCard, display;
  SIGNALLIST inp = InputCard, keys ;


  /* Signal definitions for BlockingStation communication */
  SIGNAL
  Disable,                       /* CentralUnit  TO  BlockingStation */
  Enable ;                       /* CentralUnit  TO  BlockingStation */


  /* Signal definitions within LocalStation */
  SIGNAL opened,closed  ; /* Door TO LSControl */
  SIGNAL open, close ; /* LSControl TO Door */
```

Figure 7.19   *Signal library package*

Still you may think that the system structure is too monolithic. You would like to have a freer collection of types which you could use in different contexts. This would make it simpler to merge the *AccessControl* mechanisms with other desires.

In SDL, type definitions and type diagrams may be collected into packages. These packages may then be used in other packages or in systems. The types found in packages will exist on a level conceptually outside the system level. We may say that you may collect "global" types in packages.

We have altered the *AccessControl* system slightly to fit this new approach and have decided to follow a strategy that is quite common in some companies, namely to collect all the signal definitions in one place – in one package.

Using a package *SignalLib* as in Figure 7.19 makes all the signal type definitions become global. It is of course possible to let additional signals be defined locally in order to restrict the contexts in which they will occur.

A package definition which uses this *SignalLib* is the package collecting the *Stations* (Figure 7.20).

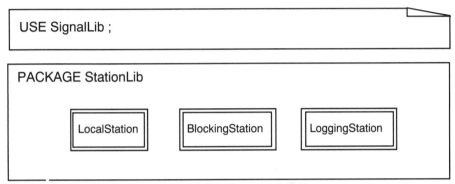

Figure 7.20 *Package containing station type definitions*

We notice how the USE-clause is placed in a text symbol outside the package frame. This means that it is the package that uses other packages. The system diagram then may use both these libraries and the diagram becomes quite compact.

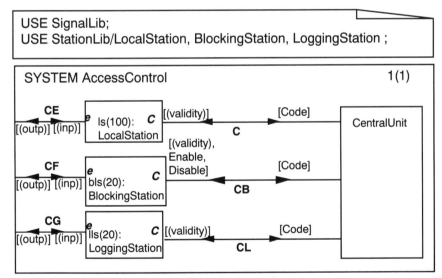

Figure 7.21 *System AccessControl using packages*

One obvious result of organising descriptions in packages is that the description tend to become "flat" since all packages have to be "global". Hierarchical structure may be better for navigation and overview.

7.5   Context parameters

The *AccessControl* system has become more disintegrated as bits and pieces have been put into packages. Some relations which were formerly aggregate relations of the monolithic system, have now become USE-relations between packages. It is a matter of taste whether we have really achieved more freedom and flexibility by substituting an intrinsic language relation (nesting) with an extrinsic relation on the topmost level (USE).

Take the *LocalStation* type for example. It is now dependent upon the *SignalLib* package, but it should be possible to describe those signals necessary for the *LocalStation* within the type itself, too. Figure 7.22 shows how SDL offers parameterised types with context parameters.

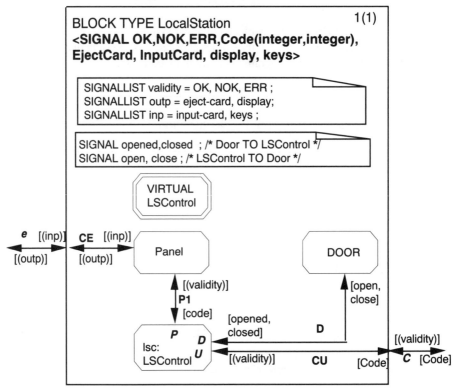

Figure 7.22 *LocalStation with context parameters*

Parameterised types may occur anywhere in the system. As the context parameters are normally types themselves, the parameterised type is a higher order type. Only first order types can give instances and parameterised types must have their context parameters bound before they become a first order type.

The formal context parameters in Figure 7.22. are given the same names as the original signal definitions. This is by no means necessary since these parameters are just formal and have no connection yet to the actual signal definitions.

The formal context parameter *Code* includes a specification of the parameters and this is the *signal constraint* indicating that the actual match of *Code* must have two integers. This kind of constraint is called a *signal signature*.

We also note that all the individual signal types must be mentioned in the parameter list, it is not legal to have signallists in the formal context parameter list. That is why we must declare the signallists again within the parameterised type. Do remember that signallists are only shorthand for a sequence of signal names.

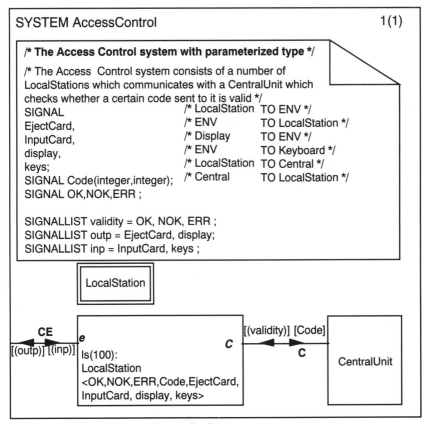

Figure 7.23 *Using a parameterised type*

The application of a parameterised type is straightforward, shown in Figure 7.23.

The actual context parameters are visible signal types.

Let us now try to emphasise the difference between first order types and parameterised types. When first order types are specialised the result remains a first order type. First order types can be directly used in order to instantiate instances. When parameterised types are specialised by adding new properties, the result remains a parameterised type. When formal context parameters are bound, the resulting type is first order if all formal context parameters are bound, otherwise the type is still parameterised. First order types coming from binding all context parameters may be anonymous. For example, *LocalStation<...>* of Figure 7.23 is in fact a first order type with no explicit name.

If the resulting first order type should be named, one may define such a name by a block diagram using an INHERIT-clause where the anonymous type is the base type.

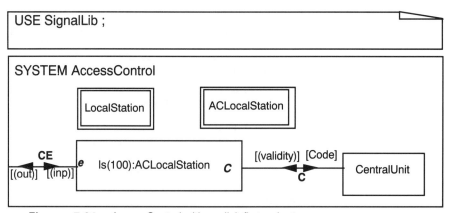

Figure 7.24   *AccessControl with explicit first order type*

Notice that parameterised types and packages are orthogonal concepts. Parameterised types may reside in packages. Together using both parameterised types and packages one may achieve both flexibility and clarity. First order types can be contained in the nesting while the parameterised types are in the packages.

```
BLOCK TYPE ACLocalStation
INHERITS LocalStation
<OK,NOK,ERR,Code, EjectCard, InputCard, display, keys>
```

Figure 7.25   *ACLocalStation: naming the first order type*

There is no supertype/subtype relation between *LocalStation* and *ACLocalStation*. *LocalStation* is a parameterised type, while *ACLocalStation* is a first order type. The distinction may seem peculiar, but for consistency of the language it is quite important.

To summarise: binding context parameters is not the same as specialising! The relations between the type concepts of SDL 92 are given in Figure 7.26.

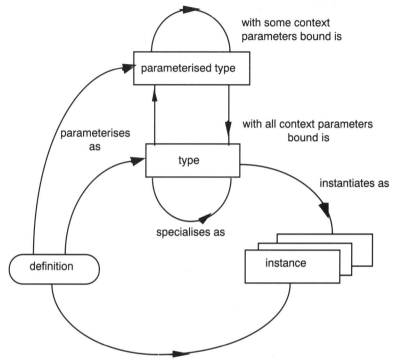

Figure 7.26   *The type concepts of SDL 92*[6]

Notes

[1]EB Technology is now ABB Corporate Research Norway.

[2]The vendor of SDT, SDL Tool. Parts of TeleLOGIC of 1988 are now in Telia Research.

[3]SPECS is a European project in the RACE project.

[4]In Figure 7.13 we could have omitted the inheritance clause as the default is that the virtuality constraint is the supertype. Furthermore, introducing a second process type diagram with the name *LSControl* makes it necessary to also qualify the original (Figure 7.12), but that is not shown here.

[5]The observant reader will notice that most of the new transitions are empty.

[6]This figure is copied from the Z.100 Recommendation (CCITT Z.100, 1993).

CHAPTER 8

SDL Method

This chapter provides guidelines that help to use SDL effectively during functional design. It tries to answer the questions that most people ask once they start to use the SDL language. How should a system be partitioned into blocks and processes? How should a process graph be structured in states and transitions? When and how should SDL data be used?

8.1   Objectives

SDL may be used in many ways to describe a system. Some of them will be easy to read and comprehend. Others will be hard. The difference lies in how one chooses to structure a system. Some structures give clear and concise descriptions of reasonable size, others give unintelligible descriptions that are either very compact or enormously big. The trick is to strike the right balance between size and clarity. This chapter describes rules that will help you to do exactly that; structure your SDL descriptions so that they will fulfil their purpose in the systems engineering context.

Our goal is to make a product that fulfils its explicit and implicit purposes. A methodology must contain a set of mechanisms that will aid us on the way from an idea to the finished (software) product. The SDL method provides guidelines for the functional design step.

To achieve our purpose we must *understand*. We must understand what the owner and the user want and we must understand how the part of the world affected by our system works. In order to understand, we *describe*. We describe the objectives (the requirement specification). We describe the surrounding world and we describe the system.

Understanding and describing are two sides of the same coin. In the beginning our understanding is as vague as our description, but ultimately we have a clear and accurate description and a correspondingly good understanding. Our aim is to achieve the collective understanding among the owners, the users and the developers needed to build a quality system.

SDL is used primarily to make functional designs. As stated in Chapters 1 and 2 the purpose of a functional design is to describe the system behaviour at an abstraction level where it can be understood and analysed independently of a particular implementation. Thus, the functional design is the main vehicle for communication and understanding of the functionality. At a later stage, described in the following chapters, the functional design will be used to design an optimum implementation satisfying both the functional and non-functional requirements of the user and the owner. We therefore seek to achieve functional designs that are the following:

1. *Readable* in the deep semantic sense that it supports collective understanding in a project team. It should support unambiguous communication among project members and in-depth understanding by the individual.
2. *Analysable* in the sense that properties can be derived and compared with requirements.
3. *Implementable* in the sense that the described functionality can be implemented in a way that satisfies non-functional requirements.

Due to its dynamic and transient nature, behaviour is difficult to describe and understand. The kind of complex behaviours performed by modern real time systems are extremely hard to understand to their full extent. But we cannot hope to develop a system that behaves reliably to the users satisfaction unless we fully understand its behaviour. The prime concern of the SDL method is therefore to make behaviour descriptions that are easy to understand, analyse and implement.

To this end we shall give a number of rules that fall into three major categories: *analysis rules* (A-rules), *structuring rules* (S-rules) and *notation rules"* (N-rules). Analysis rules tell you how to understand your system, structuring rules tell you how to structure a system, while notation rules direct your use of the SDL notation.

The semantics differ between languages, meaning that some languages are more suited for one purpose while others are more suited for other purposes. Musical notes are well-suited for describing classical music, while they are not very appropriate for describing a telecommunication system. SDL is well-suited for the latter purpose, but writing a symphony in SDL is probably futile. We have found that even within our limited realm of real time systems, it is favourable to use more than one language to describe the system. We have in the preceding chapters shown how SDL can be used to specify the functionality of the system, while in earlier chapters we have introduced more informal notations such as SOON and MSC to aid the early stages. The implementation will use a programming language such as C++. In this book we have limited ourselves (on purpose) to languages adhering basically to the object-oriented paradigm.

A *paradigm* is a way of thinking. This gives rise to a number of techniques that will hold for all the languages adhering to the paradigm. The techniques or approaches we present in this book characterise object orientation. Our languages have mechanisms that correspond to the techniques. In this chapter we will concentrate on SDL, but the reader should understand that most of the guidelines, i.e. the A-rules and S-rules, are independent of a particular language. Thus, even if you do not use SDL, but a language based on similar concepts, the rules will still apply.

But remember; even though you have a good hammer, you should not use nails if nuts and bolts are what you really need! A good system and an effective development are achieved only when the human understanding is well-supported. When making descriptions, there is always "*conceptualizing*" going on in parallel, which means to improve the understanding of the subject matter.

Understanding is not like painting a house where you may know exactly how much you have covered and how much there is left. Understanding is more like trying to explore a maze – first you try a little in one direction and then a little in another. You evaluate how you are doing and gradually you build a map of the maze, but you do not know how much is left until you have covered it all.

8.2   System versus product

Most system development is not concerned with a singular system, but rather with a product that will be used to generate a family of systems. Are there differences between the guidelines we should follow in the two cases?

Clearly the need to understand the system behaviour is the same. Therefore, the guidelines aiming at understanding behaviour should be the same. But for a product, there are additional considerations regarding its adaptation and (re)use in different applications. The big difference is that a product has to be more general and adaptable than a singular system. Since a product must consider a range of applications, where a singular system only needs to consider one, the scope of product related guidelines is wider.

Additional considerations will be needed both to *design for reuse* and to *design with reuse*. These considerations will be discussed in Chapter 13. In this chapter we will concentrate on the guidelines for singular systems. But, as we shall see, there is no fundamental conflict here. Correct application of the rules for singular systems will be a precondition for a successful product. The reason for this fortunate situation is that in both cases the underlying criteria for system partitioning are *independence* and *generality*.

Even for a singular system, adaptation to changing requirements will be required. It is quite normal that the environment of a real time system undergoes changes during the lifetime of the system and that enhancements and modifications are required. Therefore, adaptation and change are still criteria for a singular system. For some systems it may even be required that adaptation and change be performed on-line without interruption of its normal services.

8.3 Behaviour

8.3.1 State orientation

What principles can we give to guide the designer in finding adequate processes and states in the system description?

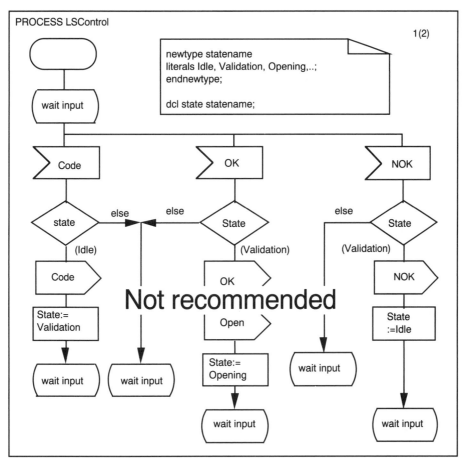

Figure 8.1 *Action-oriented description of LsControl (first page only)*

In Chapter 2 we contended that a structural similarity between the description and the system is essential and, therefore, we should prefer to use a state-oriented description rather than an action-oriented description of behaviour. This is the common underlying principle we shall use to guide our system partitioning. In this section we shall explain what structural similarity means in SDL terms and then see how it leads to specific guidelines.

All the SDL process graphs presented so far have been state-oriented descriptions. They have represented the control states of the processes explicitly, thereby helping us to get a clear picture of all the possible courses of behaviour. But SDL may also be used to make action-oriented descriptions. Figure 8.1 illustrates an action-oriented description of the *LsControl* process (only the first page is shown). Note that this process graph contains only one state, whereas the original description of *LsControl* in Figures 4.16 and 4.17 contained four states.

At first glance, Figure 8.1 may look quite attractive. But when it comes to the meaning in terms of actual behaviour it is not so good. To understand all possible behaviours we have to do a (mental) simulation to generate the same pictures as represented in Figures 4.16 and 4.17. This is because we have hidden the control states in a variable, called *state*, in Figure 8.1.

S-rule: state orientation
Represent what the environment may distinguish as control states of the process, as states in the process graph.

If the interactions with the environment are to follow a sequential protocol, this protocol should be clearly described in the process graph. This means that control states must be chosen to reflect the sequential interface behaviour of the process.

Some will claim that to describe control states is to reveal internal details belonging to the process implementation, therefore, control states should be avoided in a specification. We strongly believe this to be wrong. Using the rule above, the control states are necessary means to represent the required interface behaviour. What should be avoided in a specification is describing internal states necessary only for the purpose of internal action sequences not directly related to external interactions.

How does the environment see the process, in what situations does the environment perceive the process of being stable?

When approaching a panel in an *AccessControl* system, we perceive that the panel is waiting idly for our card. When we have inserted our card, we believe that the panel is waiting for the PIN to be typed in. Then we deduce that it is waiting for central validation and after we have received our card and the door has been opened, we assume that the panel is back on idle vacation again. This informal description of the panel, leads naturally to the state space that we had in the first description of *PanelControl*, namely *{Idle, GetPIN, WaitDigit, Validate}*.

A symptom of the state hiding is the high number of decision symbols in Figure 8.1. A decision is used to map information from the data domain into the control domain.

Therefore, when control states are hidden in data as in Figure 8.1, many decisions will be needed to achieve the same control.

S-rule: decisions
Critically review all decisions to ensure that they are not symptoms of undesirable state hiding.

What to put into the data will be treated in Section 8.3.2. Having given a rule for the states of the process, it seems natural to continue with the other kernel concept of SDL, the signals. Signals may carry additional information as parameter values. Often the designer is free to decide whether information should be represented by the value of a signal parameter or by distinct signal types. The underlying principle should be the same here as above; represent what the environment may distinguish as explicitly as possible.

S-rule: signal set
Represent what the environment may distinguish as different control signals by different signal types.

This means avoiding putting control information into the signal parameters.

In pure FSMs, a state and an input signal are sufficient to determine which state the process will enter next. In SDL however, a process may include decisions which branch on data values. With respect to the control structure, we recommend that the designer keeps his/her EFSM as close as possible to a pure FSM. Thus, we may summarise the considerations above in one rule.

S-rule: control flow
Branch on input signals in states rather than on decisions.

SDL generalises more easily on data than on signal types and states. Therefore, the rules above may sometimes be in conflict with the needs of adapting a process to changing requirements.

Clearly, for any realistically sized system, data (and signal parameters) will be needed. The question is what kind of information to represent in data and what kind to represent in states. This is the topic of the next section.

8.3.2   Process data (variables)
In SDL, the pure FSM model has been extended in two directions.

1.   Data and timers have been added to make the FSM into a very general and powerful sequential machine, the extended finite state machine, EFSM.
2.   Parallel composition of EFSMs has been added in order to model complex concurrent behaviours.

By extending the FSM with data, the power and generality increases, but so does the opportunity to describe action-oriented behaviour. In the previous section we emphasised that data should not be used to hide control information. What should data be used for then?

> *S-rule: data*
> *Use data*
> *   *when the process graph structure is not dependent on the data values (non-decisive data);*
> *   *to keep information about the situation and structure of the environment (context knowledge);*
> *   *to control loops that are not terminated by specific signals (loop control data).*

Examples of non-decisive data are *cardid* and *pin* of the *PanelControl* process. These data are never involved in decisions. They represent information about the current user and can therefore be seen as knowledge about an entity external to the process. Hence, they are also representatives of context data. Another example of context data, is the *LsControl* process modified to handle two panels (controlling a bidirectional door) where *cur_panel* keeps track of which panel process is currently active.

Context data may be seen as information about entities existing in space (and time) outside the process, whereas loop control is about the temporal progression of the process behaviour itself. Thus, loop control data belong to the control domain together with control states and signal types, whereas context data belong to the data domain.

In the PanelControl process we have used the data *trial_no* to control the loop of repetitive attempts to type the *PIN*. This has made the diagram more compact, but more importantly, it has made the diagram structure independent of the number of iterations. Hence, loop control helps to make the diagram more general.

In order to send a signal to another process, the identity of the receiver must either be specified using a TO-clause or it must be uniquely identifiable from the signal type and, possibly, the channels and signal routes specified by a VIA-clause. In many cases the actual receiver is variable and must be specified using a PId expression in a TO-clause. Therefore, a process needs PId variables to represent the processes it may send signals to. Often the process needs a PId variable for each process it may interact with. Each of these variables represents a role that a process in its environment will play. The actual PId value represents the actor of the role.

As a general rule we recommend specifying the receiver using a TO-clause. We also recommend giving the PId variable the same name as the external process role it refers to. This may be a process name in a context where all actors have the same name, e.g. *LsControl* or it may be a more general role name such as *B-subscriber*, when the role may be played by processes with different names.

S-rule: PId variables
Use a PId variable to represent each process role in the environment of a process type. Give the variable the same name as the role.

Using this rule each process will have a mirror image of its process environment represented as PId variables.

8.3.3 Concurrent behaviour

The next question is when and how to use concurrency. Concurrency is the other main extension of the basic FSM made in SDL.

Different processes behave concurrently and signals on separate channels are transferred concurrently. In this context "concurrent" is synonymous with "independent". Concurrent behaviours proceed independently of each other without any mutual ties apart from those imposed by explicit interactions, i.e. signal interchange in SDL. Thus, concurrent processes are excellently suited to model independent behaviours.

S-rule: concurrency
Model independent and parallel behaviours as separate processes.

Even though there are potential analytical difficulties associated with concurrency, there are major advantages as well.

1. Parallelism is a real world fact (see Chapter 2). Objects in the real world behave truly in parallel. Therefore, concurrent processes are natural representations of their behaviour. By using concurrent processes in the description we achieve structural similarity between the system and the description.
2. Parallel processes are disjoint and, thus, do not interfere with each other at all. In our *AccessControl* system we have used one *LsControl* process to control each *LocalStation*. Each of these behaves independently of the other *LsControl* processes in the system. Having one process per local station enables us to focus on the behaviour of each station without considering the other stations. Thus, by decomposing into independent behaviours we are able to focus on the essential sequential behaviour of each process.
3. Concurrent processes help to achieve encapsulation and modularity. The interactions with other processes are explicitly described by input and output signals. Thus, each process has a clear interface across which only explicit interactions take place. Thereby, the mutual dependencies and interactions become clearly visible in our description. At the same time the signal interface hides the details of the process behaviour from the environment. As long as the interface is the same, the process behaviour may be replaced by another without any change needed to the environment.
4. Concurrency implies a logical separation of substance. Thus, concurrency is the natural way to model physically separate behaviours. In our *AccessControl*

system, we know that *Panels* are physically distributed, therefore it is natural to represent these as separate processes in the system.

Let us consider two independent behaviours A and B, each represented as a sequence of state transitions as indicated in Figure 8.2. In a description we may either choose to describe the resulting behaviour as two concurrent processes or as one process. If we choose to describe the behaviour as one process, its process graph will be the *behaviour product* A*B of the independent behaviours (see Figure 8.2). This product is generated by exploring all the possible ways that transitions in A and B may combine. (It is common to consider only the possible interleavings of transitions in behaviour products assuming that transitions are mutually exclusive and atomic. We have, therefore, not considered simultaneous transitions in Figure 8.2 although this may happen in a truly parallel system.)

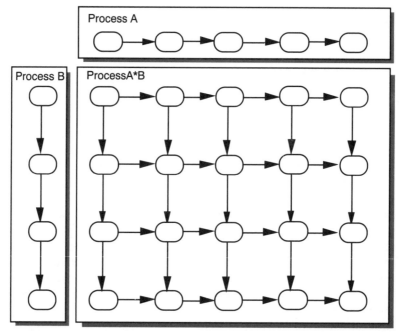

Figure 8.2 *Two independent behaviours A and B may be described either as separate concurrent processes or as a single sequential process with the process graph A*B*

We make the following observations:

- *Size*. The behaviour product A*B is larger than the sum of the independent behaviours. The number of states in A*B is the product of the number of states in A and B. This effect is often referred to as the "*state explosion*". When independent behaviours are combined, the state space tends to explode. Just consider combining two behaviours each having 100 states or combining many processes even if each of them has few states. In the *AccessControl* system, for instance, there are 5 *LsControl* processes, each having 4 states. This combines to 4x4x4x4x4 = 1024 states.

- *Clarity.* Compared to the component behaviours A and B, the behaviour product is harder to overview. It is a complex way to express the simple fact that the component behaviours are independent.

- *Analysability.* The behaviour product describes all the possible courses of behaviour very explicitly. Therefore, the generation of a behaviour product is a basic technique used to analyse the properties of a system (see Chapter 12). However, the generation of behaviour products has little value when the component behaviours are fully independent as in this example.

- *Modularity.* The behaviour product depends on the number of processes. Adding a new process to the product is far more complex than adding a concurrent process described separately.

From these observations we conclude that we may reduce the size and increase the clarity as well as the modularity of behaviour descriptions by partitioning a system such that independent behaviours are described by separate processes. It is illustrated in Figure 8.3 that increasing the number of processes according to this rule helps to make a better description. There is, however, an optimum beyond which it does not help to add processes any more. This happens when a sequential behaviour is split between two processes so that additional coordination among the processes is necessary.

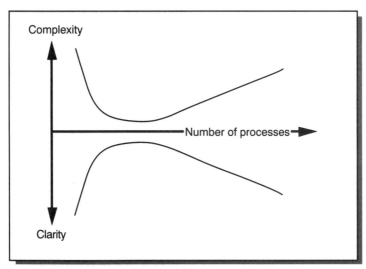

Figure 8.3   *There is an optimum decomposition that gives maximal clarity and minimal complexity in behaviour descriptions*

S-rule: golden rule of partitioning
The golden rule is to partition along the lines of independence and not across dependencies.

This is in accordance with the principle saying that a system should be decomposed into modules with low external coupling and strong internal cohesion (see, for example, Yourdon and Constantine, 1975).

By way of illustration we may consider dependency as a kind of cohesive force working to keep the substance of a system together and our attempt to partition the system as an opposite force trying to tear it apart. The more independent the parts of the substance are, the more easily they fall apart. The stronger the dependency is, the harder they are to separate. In a good partitioning we exercise just enough partitioning force to separate the substance into parts that are independent or moderately dependent, keeping strongly dependent parts together.

As we start to apply the partitioning force, we experience that totally independent parts separate without resistance. The first resistance we feel comes from relationships in data, but it is not strong enough to keep the substance together. As we apply force, the substance will partition, but we will see fine lines of conceptual relationships (or references) linking the parts together. They represent what the parts need to know about each other. Parts that are only linked by conceptual relations may behave concurrently and independently of each other. To further partition the substance, we must overcome the resistance of behavioural dependency. When the substance breaks apart this time, we will see communication channels between the parts. The cohesive force now rapidly increases with the amount of behavioural dependency. The strongest cohesive force exists between the states and transitions of a "naturally" sequential behaviour. We should not try to break that apart.

The goal is to partition into parts that can be understood, modified and (re)used as independently as possible.

A consequence of these considerations is that we partition into processes such that each individual sequence can be clearly described in a state-oriented way. Even though the *LsControl* processes are similar, we partition the system such that each individual process is identified. Each process encapsulates control information and data that forms a unit of independent sequential behaviour. Our rules, therefore, enforce a data- or object-oriented approach and not an action-oriented approach.

Let us briefly consider the action-oriented description of *LsControl* given in Figure 8.1 again. In this type of description it is easy to handle many process instances simply by adding an array of states instead of using a single state as in Figure 8.1. Thus, it is possible to describe many independent behaviours using only one process without the penalty of a state explosion. Does this mean that an action-oriented style is better in this case?

We claim it is not:

- • because the existence of concurrent processes is hidden in the data;
- • because the states of these concurrent processes are hidden in data;
- • because a signal interface is not enforced among the concurrent processes described as a single SDL process;
- • because the structural similarity between description and system is lost;
- • because the SDL process depends on the number of concurrent processes it describes. Therefore, the SDL process becomes a less basic unit of reuse and configuration than each of the concurrent processes it describes. As a matter of fact, the SDL process effectively blocks the concurrent processes it describes from being reused and configured as separate units.

In the action-oriented solution the readability as well as the modularity is reduced because logical units of behaviour and reuse are hidden. It tends to mix two jobs that should be separated: describing sequential behaviour and multiplexing between sequential behaviours.

S-rule: similar process instances
Do not hide similar behaviours in data. Decompose such that similar independent behaviours are described explicitly as separate instances of a process type.

Thus, we strive to achieve explicit representation of each independent process, its interfaces and all its state transitions.

But how should a designer go about identifying the independent behaviours in a system? The answer is to look at the environment. The system is there to play a number of roles that the environment requires; nothing more, nothing less.

We should therefore start by studying the actors in the environment and the roles they demand the system to play. Independent actors operating in parallel normally demand to be served independently and concurrently, hence they give the system independent and concurrent roles to play. For each of those roles there should normally be (at least) one process in the system. Therefore, as a first step towards a process structure we assign a process to play each independent (concurrent) behaviour role demanded by the environment.

S-rule: interaction processes
Use one process to play each independent behaviour role required by the environment.

Using this rule we start with the environment; we identify each independent behaviour role and we assign a process or a block of processes, to play each role.

Going back to the requirement specification and the description of the *AC-System context* in Figure 3.8 we identify behaviour roles associated with the *Users* and the *Operators*.

The *AC-System* has a large number of *Users*, but only the *Users* present at *AccessPoints* interact with the system concurrently. Therefore, we primarily need concurrent processes to serve each *AccessPoint*. These are the processes in the *LocalStations*. We also need concurrent processes to serve each *Operator position* in the *CentralUnit*, since the *Operator positions* operate concurrently.

We then consider the interconnections needed to carry interactions between the actors in the environment and the actors in the system. We use a similar criterion here and use one channel/signal route for each independent interaction dialogue.

S-rule: interconnections
Use one channel and/or signal route to carry each independent and concurrent interaction dialogue.

Using these rules on the *AccessControl* system leads to the structure outlined in Figure 8.4. Note that this is an incomplete sketch. Also note that it is not possible to describe the environment of a system formally in SDL. We have included the environment here for illustration purposes only.

So far we have not concerned ourselves with the internal dependencies in the system, therefore there are no internal connections as yet. Note that this structure corresponds to the idealised user–service interface described in Figures 3.9, 3.11 and 3.12.

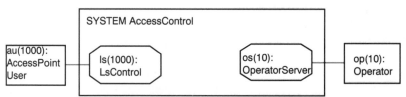

Figure 8.4   *First step in system structuring: assign a process in the system to play each independent behaviour role and a channel/signal route to carry each independent dialogue*

8.3.4   Layering

The next thing to consider is layering. From Chapter 3 we are familiar with layering as another principle for division. We recommended making a clear separation between the high level services the system provides, the service control protocols and the signal transfer protocols. For the *AC-System*, two layers were identified in Chapter 3; the abstract services and the concrete user dialogue (see Figures 3.9 and 3.10). In order to take care of the concrete user dialogue, we have introduced a separate process, the *PanelControl* process on the *User* side and a *TerminalServer* on the *Operator* side.

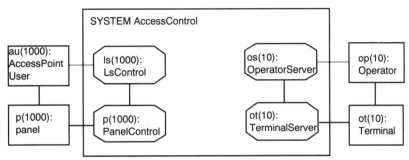

Figure 8.5   *The next step is to consider interaction layering. Here PanelControl and TerminalServer processes are introduced to serve the concrete (physical) layer*

The concrete user dialogue is served by the *PanelControl* processes in the *LocalStations* and the abstract service is served by the *LsControl* process. Thus, we have used the conceptual layering of the interface to structure the system. This has two advantages:

1.   The conceptual service needs of the user are handled in one place explicitly described in the system. Modifications to the services can (probably) be confined to that process.
2.   The protocol is described separately and may therefore be modified separately from the service control process. Thus, if the magnetic card scheme is replaced by something like an identification tag that responds to radio signals, the modification may (hopefully) be confined to the *Panel* block.

In addition to the advantages above, the separation of concerns often leads to a simpler behaviour description. This was not clearly demonstrated for *LsControl* and *PanelControl*, but there are cases where this effect is much more pronounced. (When we consider the signal transfer protocol needed between *LocalStations* and the *CentralUnit* this point becomes more clear. It would not be a very good idea to embed this protocol in the *LocalStation* behaviour, not only for the reasons mentioned above, but also because the process graph for the *LsControl* would become more complex.) Thus, layering helps to reduce the complexity, improve the clarity and increase the modularity of descriptions and systems.

Layering is useful wherever it is possible to identify interfaces that allow applications to be separated from service primitives needed to carry out the application. This separation between services and applications is a fundamental principle in systems engineering. The independence between services and applications means that the services may be reused in many applications. Provided that the services have the necessary generality, they are excellent units of reuse. Therefore, layering is an important technique in increasing the amount of reuse. It also helps to improve maintainability, as it allows the layers to be modified independently as long as the interface is kept stable.

S-rule: protocol layering
Protocols should be decomposed by layering, such that each layer hides the details of the protocols used on that layer from higher layers. Lower layers should provide application independent transfer services for the upper layers.

In SDL we may use channel substructuring to describe the layered approach (see Section 4.6.2 where we described *encryption* as a lower level).

How to model protocol layering in SDL? There are two mechanisms available:

1. *Separate processes*. This has been illustrated in Figure 8.5.
2. *Procedures*. Instead of separate processes, layering can be accomplished by procedures. The transfer protocol is described in procedures that provide services to the application described in the calling process graph. Procedures may only be used where the behaviour on different layers alternates sequentially. If the behaviours are concurrent, processes should be used.

Each layer that provides a general service is a candidate for reuse and should be defined separately as a type.

8.3.5   Context knowledge

We have now identified actors in the system that will interact with the *Users* at *AccessPoints* and the *Operators*.

The next thing to consider is the knowledge about the environment needed by the system in order to provide its services. For the *AccessControl* system this knowledge was described on a conceptual level in Chapter 3. Figure 3.8 tells us that the system needs to know all the *Users*, what *Cards* they have and what *Access Zones* they may enter. Therefore, we need internal representations for this knowledge. The next question is how and where to represent this information?

Clearly this information needs to be accessed by all the *LocalStations* and the *Operators*. In SDL there is an underlying principle saying that all data should be owned by one and only one process. By keeping each data item under the control of one sequential behaviour it is simpler to keep it consistent and to analyse its behaviour. By avoiding shared data one is forced to describe all interactions between processes clearly by means of signals. Therefore, the principle helps to describe more clearly everything that may happen during actual behaviour. In a way the principle helps to achieve structural similarity between the description and the actual system behaviour. It is a well-known experience that undisciplined use of shared data often leads to problems that are difficult to reveal.

Since there is no way to share data between processes in SDL, there are only two options when several processes need to access the same data:

1.   *Duplication.* Duplicating the same data in all processes needing the data. We might duplicate the validation data in all *LocalStations*, for instance, but this would require more resources for data storage and make it more difficult to update and safeguard the data.

2.   *Shared processes.* Encapsulating the data in special processes and accessing the data by normal signals or remote procedures. (Reveal/view expressions or export/import expressions may be used too.)

In the *AccessControl* system we have decided to use shared processes. We have encapsulated the shared information in central validation processes. The next issue is how to allocate the information to processes. As one extreme we may use one SDL process to model each independent piece of information. We could map each *User*, each *Card* and each *AccessZone* into a process in the system as indicated in Figure 8.6. Another extreme would be to represent all the information by context data within one process as indicated in Figure 8.7.

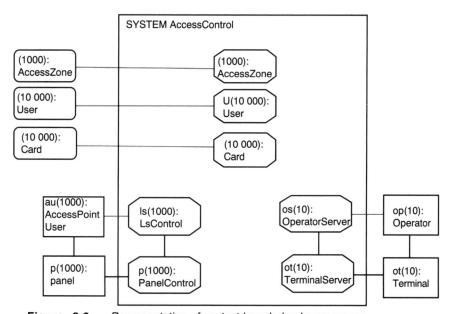

Figure 8.6   *Representation of context knowledge by processes*

Since the users are actors in the environment that will demand service from time to time, representing users by processes may seem natural. The responsibility of a *User* process would be to know the access rights and the *PIN* of that user and to perform the actual check on authenticity and authority.

When to use processes and when to use data? This depends on the behaviour associated with context knowledge. If it includes independent signal sending, signal reception and/or timing, a process is needed. If the behaviour only needs operations of the kind supported by SDL data types, then data is appropriate. This is the case in the *AccessControl* system and, therefore, we initially decided to put the knowledge inside one process.

S-rule: shared data
Introduce special processes to encapsulate shared data. Encapsulate data needing independent access in separate processes.

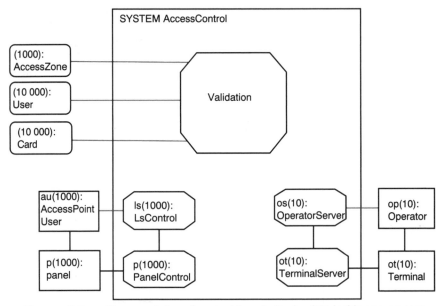

Figure 8.7   *Representation of context knowledge by data inside one process*

8.3.6   Interprocess dependencies

We have now found processes and data that follow directly from the external dependencies between the system and the environment. The next issue is how to take care of dependencies between the processes by means of signal communication. This means to connect the processes by signal routes and define signals for interprocess communication. For the *AccessControl* system, signal routes might be as illustrated in Figure 8.8. Note that this diagram is not correct SDL as yet. There has to be at least one level of blocks between the system and the processes. We also need to include signal definitions in the diagram.

Before we make the diagram more complete, however, we should check if this solution gives us the maximal clarity and minimal complexity in behaviour descriptions that we are looking for (see Figure 8.3).

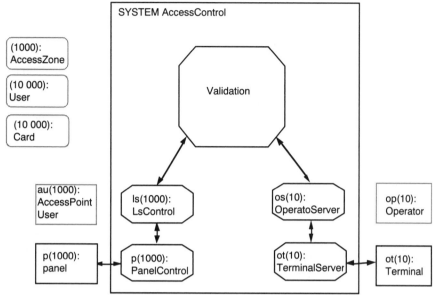

Figure 8.8   *The signal routes in the AccessControl system*

8.3.7   Resource allocation

A special class of shared information has to do with the access to shared resources. In many systems logical resources are dynamically assigned to processes on demand. The two *Validation* processes in the *CentralUnit* is one example motivated by the need to speed up computations.

In other cases resources are shared for functional or economic reasons. The subscribers to a telephone system, for instance, may be seen as shared resources. There may be several calls directed to the same subscriber at the same time, but only one of them will succeed. Therefore, a kind of contention control is needed for the access to a subscriber. This could be embedded in the behaviour of a subscriber process, but it is often better treated in a separate resource allocation process. The reason is that requests for the subscriber may arrive at any time while the subscriber is busy with another call. By directing the requests to a resource allocator, the subscriber process is shielded from them while it is busy. This helps to separate concerns and to make the description simpler and more modular.

Another typical example is trunk lines in a telephone system. In order to make a connection between two telephone exchanges, a trunk line must be allocated from a pool of trunk lines going in that direction. For an outgoing call it does not matter which line it gets, as long as it gets one of the lines. Thus, it is necessary to allocate and release trunk lines dynamically. In order to ensure a safe and fair discipline one needs shared information about the busy/free status of trunk lines. This is best achieved by encapsulating the shared information in a resource allocator process controlling the access to the pool of trunk lines.

A similar example could be part of the *AccessControl* system. If we decide to use a connection-oriented communication service between the *LocalStations* and the *CentralUnit*, we need to allocate a connection each time we need to do a validation.

Quite often we have a general picture like the one indicated in Figure 8.9 where there are a number of requesting processes contending for the access to different pools of resource processes. We recommend using a separate resource allocator for each pool of resources as indicated in Figure 8.9.

S-rule: resource allocation
Introduce a special resource allocator process to control the access to each pool of functionally equivalent resources.

The rules and guidelines given so far enable us to define the structures of processes and context data that will perform the actual system behaviour. We have focused initially on the processes and data in order to fulfil our first two goals; readability and analysability of behaviour descriptions.

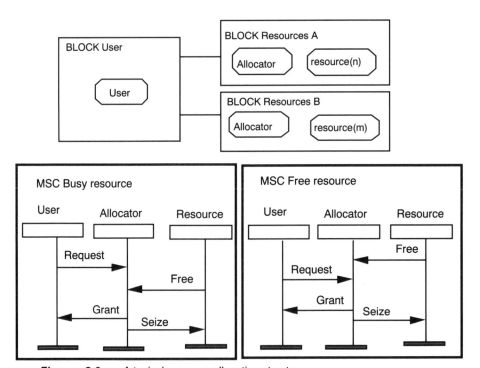

Figure 8.9   *A typical resource allocation structure*

The reader may now wonder why we have said nothing about blocks? The reason is that blocks are not essential for those goals. But blocks are important for other reasons; they serve to structure the description into units suitable for gradual approach to detail, independent reuse and implementation. This is the topic of Section 8.5. Before that we will consider the internal structuring of process behaviours and the use of abstract data types.

8.3.8   Procedures, macros and services

Procedures and macros serve the same purposes in SDL as in programming languages: to provide clarity through a level structure and to provide compactness by describing repetitive behaviours once only. In contrast to macros, procedures are conceptual units and they represent a level of reasoning. When procedures represent good functional units, then the overview on the calling level is improved, not only geometrically, but also conceptually. Procedures may therefore be used to chop up the description in order to obtain a better overview.

In the *AccessControl* system we have the *GetPIN* procedure which is called both from the process *PanelControl* and from the *Validation* procedure. The *GetPIN* procedure appears as an operation that is intuitively understood as a unit at the calling level. By describing subbehaviours that can be seen as natural operations at the calling level as procedures we achieve a form of layering in the process graph.

The procedures will represent a lower layer of operations that can be used to describe the higher layers in a clear and concise way. To fully take advantage of this the procedure layer should be as independent of the calling layer as possible, allowing a procedure to be called from many places. When this is achieved we also achieve the usual advantage of layering, i.e. that lower layers (the procedure definition) may be modified independently from the higher layer (the calling diagram) as long as the interface is the same.

S-rule: procedures
Model independent subbehaviours within a process as procedures. Look for sub-behaviours that can be perceived as one operation at the calling level.

Procedures may also be used to generalise. Formal parameters are used to adapt the procedure to slightly different call surroundings, so that the procedure specification may be reused in more places. This ensures a more compact description of the process behaviour without loss of readability.

S-rule: similarities within processes
Use procedures within processes to single out patterns that recur in the process.

Having advocated strongly in favour of procedures, the reader may wonder whether macros could have deserved the same enthusiasm. We have signalled scepticism against macros for several reasons, but we should not deny that macros can play a good structuring role, especially if their use is accompanied by strong invariants.

S-rule: macros
Never use macros where procedures are applicable. When macros must be used,
formulate and keep strong invariants about their use. Try to use macros very similarly to
the use of procedures. Be careful with "fancy" use of parameters.

Since a macro is not a formal scope unit, one cannot reason about the macro before it
is expanded in the calling context. In practice, however, the specifier does reason about
a macro without expanding it and this is the major deficiency with the macro concept.
Restricting your own use, is one way to ensure that macro use is within control. The
following N-rule may help:

N-rule: names in macros
Let each macro call have a unique number (throughout the system) as parameter and
let all the varying names that are visible at the macro border include that number.

Unlike macros, services are scope units, but there are strong semantic limitations on
the use of services. We try to summarise the desired use of services in an S-rule which
gives two requirements for the application of services:

S-rule: services
When the following two requirements are met, services may be applied:
1. The process is naturally divided into quasi-parallel subbehaviours having
separate state spaces (services).
2. The decision of which service to apply is given uniquely by the input signal
type.

We remember that services only run one at a time (within one process). Which
service is to run on a given input signal must be determined uniquely by the type of the
input signal. The major gain by using services is that more than one state space can be
described within one process.

8.3.9   Process graph aesthetics

We rely exclusively on the graphic notation of SDL. The graphical notation is more
voluminous than the textual, but it gives a better overview. The overview may,
however, get lost if the pages are crammed with symbols and the connectors are messy.
Much can be gained by splitting the diagrams into a set of pages where each page is easy
to overview.

N-rule: state subdiagrams
Consider one state and the transitions from it as a subdiagram which is described in
one place.

This rule is more geometrical than conceptual. Division into pages is one way to chop up one process into manageable pieces, introducing procedures is another.

There is an even stricter version of this N-rule:

N-rule: State and Nextstate
Each page of an FSM should have only one State and it should be at the top of the page. All the inputs should be aligned horizontally just below the State. All Nextstates shall be aligned horizontally at the bottom of the page. All transition actions should be encapsulated in procedures described separately.

This stricter N-rule gives diagrams which may have a larger number of pages, but which are easy to maintain manually.

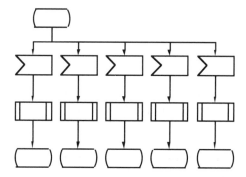

Figure 8.10 *Organisation of process graph*

We pose a notation rule to facilitate the documentation of signals.

N-rule: source and destination
Specify the sender of an input signal by means of a comment symbol and the receiver of an output signal by means of a text extension symbol (or a comment symbol, if the TO-clause is not formally specified).

Often this N-rule comes into conflict with the desire to see the total set of transitions from a state in one page. When the overview is the most important, the sender/receiver should be put in a note in the symbol itself.

8.4   Data types

Many SDL users are afraid of abstract data types. In many cases the fear is so big that they refuse to use the SDL data concepts at all and substitute SDL data with data concepts taken from the ultimate implementation languages such as C, C++, Pascal or

CHILL. As we have already pointed out in the Chapter 5, this approach should not be necessary and we believe it may not be wise for the following reasons:

1. By mixing languages the overall semantics is based not only on the SDL semantics, but also on some other language's semantics. Tools will normally have weak support for mixed languages and there may be problems porting such an SDL description to other implementations.
2. By introducing target language constructs in the specification, programming activities are mixed up with the specification.
3. The fear of SDL data comes from the difficulty of writing and understanding axioms. As we have seen, SDL offers powerful predefined data types which can be used without knowing the axioms. Predefined aggregate concepts such as *Powerset* and *STRUCT*, very often have counterparts in implementation languages or in available libraries.

Abstract data types follow the principles of object orientation by focusing especially on encapsulation.

S-rule: data types
1. *Use predefined data types whenever applicable;*
2. *Use predefined generators to make arrays, sequences (String) and sets (Powerset);*
3. *Use STRUCT to make more advanced data types;*
4. *For user-defined operators, always specify the signature formally and the semantics informally;*
5. *Use constructive operators (SDL 92) for user-defined operator semantics;*
6. *Use axiomatic description of very advanced data types. Use experts.*

The general syntax of abstract data types is prefix, which means that the operation precedes the operators. This is not common in normal arithmetic and SDL has allowed infix notation for normal arithmetic just as we know it from programming languages.

8.5   Block structure

In the previous sections of this chapter we have focused on behaviour. We have shown how to partition the behaviour description into concurrent processes and how to describe the processes using data, procedures and macros. We shall now consider how the processes should be aggregated into blocks.

A system contains blocks and a block may contain inner blocks. On the leaves of this block tree, the blocks will contain processes. Thus, the blocks serve to provide intermediate levels between the system level and the process level. In this section we shall go into the principles by which we recommend that you partition your system into nested blocks and block types.

Starting on the system level we first have the question of where to draw the system boundary. In system theory there is usually a distinction between open and closed systems. Open systems interact with their environments, while closed systems have no significant contact with the outside. SDL is a framework for open systems. It is therefore of utmost importance to have a notion of what the environment is like. The purpose of the system is to fulfil requirements from its environment. The very same principle is applied to the components: their purpose is relative to their (immediate) surroundings.

For our *AccessControl* system, the purpose is defined by the environment of eligible and ineligible persons and the desire of the management to discriminate between them. Persons are represented by their *Cards* and their typed *PIN*. On a lower level, the purpose of the *Panel* is to receive the *Card* and the *PIN* and assemble them for the *LocalStation* control unit. Furthermore, it communicates back to the person through the *Display*. The *Panel* is unaware of the purpose of the total system to discriminate between persons. The *Panel* responds only to its purpose in its local context.

The specifier may decide to place elements at the system periphery inside the system rather than in the environment because it increases the possibilities of describing these elements. The behaviour of elements in the environment is normally described indirectly through the signal interface, while elements within the system are specified in detail in SDL. There is no absolute requirement that what is eventually implemented must be the total system!

S-rule: system and environment
For the elements at the periphery of your concern, place them inside the system if you wish to describe their behaviour in detail. If you are merely interested in their signal interface, place them in the environment which means they will not be identified explicitly in SDL.

In SDL block types and process types have gates where constraints on the connected blocks may be specified using an ATLEAST-clause. Thus, for block and process types, SDL 92 provides us with the means to say more about the environment than the signal interface.

In our *AccessControl* system we have placed the *Doors* inside our system (the *Door* is described within the *LocalStation* block type), while the actual persons using the *Doors* are placed in the environment. It is debatable whether we are very interested in the detailed behaviour of the *Door*, but we found that describing the *Door* inside the system improved the description of the block type *LocalStation*.

The key question now is how we determine what should be a block. Following our discussion of the nature of a system (see Chapter 2), the decomposition of a block is also a matter of choice. There is not one single partitioning which is "the right one", but some are better than others. The criteria for what is a good partitioning depend on what purposes one wants to achieve:

1. *Gradual approach to detail.* A block is an aggregate concept representing a substructure of blocks and processes as one unit. By partitioning a system into blocks the description is organised in a level structure that may help the reader to gain an overview and a gradual approach to the full details of the system. This purpose is mainly descriptive.

2. *Unit of reuse (and repetition).* Being an aggregate concept, the block is a potential unit of reuse and repetition on a higher level than the process. In the *AccessControl* system, the concept of a *LocalStation* is used repeatedly. Block types are conceptual components that may be used to build new block types, system types and systems by *composition*. They may also be used to define new types by *inheritance.*

3. *Unit of adaptation and change.* A block is a unit of encapsulation that may hide its internal structure from the environment. Therefore, a block may be modified or replaced with no impact on the environment, as long as the interface remains the same. In the *AccessControl* system we use different subtypes of *LocalStation*, i.e. *BlockingStation* and *LoggingStation*, which all look the same from the central validation point of view.

4. *Scope of process creation.* It is only possible for a process to create processes within the same block. Therefore, a block restricts the scope of process creation.

5. *Scope of communication.* SDL signals can be passed between two blocks only if there is a path of channels connecting the blocks. Hence, the structure of blocks and channels limits the scope of communication within a system. (In addition, processes within the same block are allowed to communicate shared values using REVEAL/VIEW expressions, while processes in different blocks must use EXPORT/IMPORT for the same purpose.)

6. *Unit of implementation and physical separation.* The SDL block is an abstract concept belonging to the functional system. There is no implementation bias in the block concept as such. However, all but the first purpose above are also relevant for implementation units. Therefore, it is natural in a description (see Chapter 9), to have blocks that correspond with implementation units serving similar purposes. It is also natural to describe parts of a system that are known to be physically apart in separate blocks, if the physical separation is significant. The reason is that an SDL channel can model a physical channel more realistically than a signal route.

In the block partitioning we must consider all these purposes and select a block structure that fulfils the various purposes in the best possible way. This may involve compromises where there are conflicts. In the *AccessControl* system we chose to partition the system into a number of *LocalStations* and a *CentralUnit* and to further partition the *LocalStations* into *LsControl*, *Panel* and *Door*.

This partitioning fulfils several of the purposes above. The *LocalStation* is clearly a natural unit of description providing a gradual approach to detail. In fact, the *LocalStation* mirrors the concept of one or two *AccessPoints* controlling a *Door* described in the conceptual model in Chapter 3. It is also a unit of repetition and reuse as well as a unit of modification within the system. Finally it is likely that *LocalStations* will be physically separated. Inside the *LocalStation* the *LsControl* and the *Panel* were represented as blocks although they contain only one process each. In that way we may introduce more processes at a later stage if need be. The *Panel*, for instance, encapsulates the lower layers in the user interface. In addition to the layer discussed so far, handlers for the physical devices (the *Keyboard*, the *CardReader* and the *Display*) may be added later on.

To a large extent the block partitioning follows the guidelines given for behaviour decomposition, on a higher level only. We study the environment first and identify blocks in the environment interacting independently with the system. Such blocks impose block roles on the system and we introduce corresponding blocks into the system to play the roles.

Next we consider the context knowledge and introduce additional blocks to handle shared data if necessary. We then make the necessary internal and external channel connections between the blocks. The result is a block structure, where each block may be considered as a system of its own. We may now repeat the approach above for each block recursively until the blocks contain only processes. In doing this we take layering into account. On higher levels we try to encapsulate lower layers inside blocks. The layers will then appear gradually.

In the following we shall give some S-rules which may help to put the designer on the proper track.

S-rule: block purposes
Use blocks to achieve one or more of the following purposes:
1.   *Gradual approach to detail;*
2.   *Units of reuse and repetition;*
3.   *Encapsulation of layering;*
4.   *Encapsulation of independent adaptation and change;*
5.   *Limited scope of process creation and communication;*
6.   *Correspondence with the physical system.*

Blocks have substance. Therefore, the blocks partition the substance of the system:

S-rule: substance division
Decompose blocks into lower level blocks by subdividing the substance of the block.
Consider the following substances:
1.   *Substance of the environment and the interfaces. Partition into blocks in a manner that mirrors the substance of the environment and the interfaces.*
2.   *Substance of system implementation. Partition to reflect the physical substance of the implementation. NB this consideration should not be taken too early. It is an issue for implementation design (see Chapter 9).*
3.   *Abstract substance in terms of processes and channels.*

The following rules summarise the steps one may take to derive a block partitioning.

S-rule: step 1, partition the environment behaviour
Partition the significant environment behaviour into nested blocks in a way that fulfils
the desired block purposes.

S-rule: Step 2, identify behaviour roles
Identify nested behaviour roles that blocks in the environment give to the system.

S-rule: step 3, mirror the behaviour roles by actors in the system
Partition the system into actors corresponding to the behaviour roles.

S-rule: step 4 , context knowledge
Make a conceptual description of context knowledge needed by the system. Allocate
the knowledge to blocks and processes in the system.

S-rule: step 5, shared resources.
Identify shared resources and introduce corresponding resource allocation processes.

For each block the same rules apply as if it was a system. The decomposition process continues recursively until processes are reached. The structuring of blocks results in a tree of blocks. The leaves of this tree will contain the real actors of our system, the processes.

S-rule: control processes
Let leaf blocks have
- *one process for each independent communication with its context;*
- *one process for each pool of shared resources to be dynamically allocated;*
- *one process for each block of shared data accessed and controlled*
  independently.

Note that our rules do not focus on the number of blocks to use on each level, nor the number of levels in the decomposition. We believe that such rules are of a "cosmetic" nature and less important than the rules given above.

8.6   Signal routing

Localisation independence is a central idea in distributed systems. It means that types should be described in a way that allows instances to be freely distributed on physical units. The consequence is that SDL process and block types should be defined independently of the physical localisation of their instances. A process should be able to send a signal to another process and to receive a response without knowing its physical localisation.

The concept of Process Identifiers (PId) in SDL is intended to hide the physical localisation. It is a logical identifier telling *who* the receiver of a signal is, not *where* it is. The problem is that the PId expression stated in a TO-clause identifies the first process to receive the signal. When the signal needs to be transferred through several layers of protocol processes, it is the first process in the chain that must be identified in the TO-clause and not the destination process at the other end. Whenever a signal has to be routed through intermediate processes, the final destination must be transferred as an ordinary parameter in the signal.

Consequently, we need a two-level identification scheme:

1.   The first receiver, which is expressed in the TO-clause;
2.   The final destination, which is a parameter of the signal.

The idea is that the first receiver knows the next receiver down the chain and may substitute the first receiver accordingly. On the last leg of a signal transfer, the first receiver and the final destination will be identical.

In order to achieve localisation independence we recommend adopting this two-level scheme as a default. It implies that the first receiver is statically known and may serve as a signal router that passes the signal either directly to a local receiver or through a chain of protocol processes.

S-rule: routing processes
For each block where there is a choice between local and remote communication, use a two-level addressing scheme and hide the routing knowledge in a routing process.

The role of the routing process is to know where to send a signal so it may eventually reach its final destination. To this end the routing process needs to know something about localisation. At least it must know what final destinations are local and can be reached directly and where to send the signal if the final destination is remote. Using this approach there will be a routing process located centrally in all blocks where such routing decisions need to be made.

In Chapter 9 we shall discuss the physical distribution of the *AccessControl* system and we shall decide to use an underlying physical structure which is reflected in the block structure sketched in Figure 8.11. Here the routing blocks serve to hide the localisation of the *Validation* processes from the *LsControl* processes.

Note that the introduction of separate routing processes also helps to structure the description. Where there are complex many-to-many connections between blocks, this means considerable simplification and improved clarity in the graphical appearance.

To some extent the routing problem may be solved in the implementation of the PId data type. But if one wants to analyse or simulate an SDL system formally, the routing problem must be solved on the SDL level.

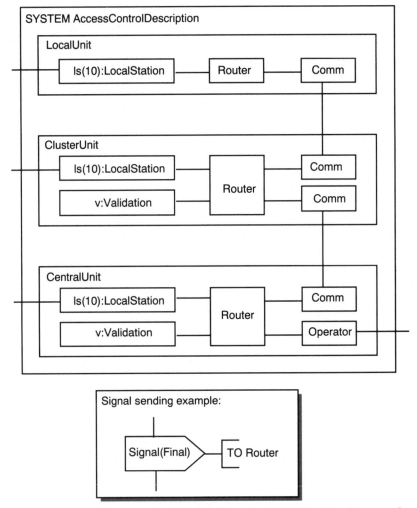

Figure 8.11   *A sketch of the AccessControl system showing the use of routing
blocks containing routing processes*

8.7   Types

We use types for the following purposes:

1.   To describe separately a concept we want to understand, identify and (re)use as
     a whole independently of its applications;
2.   To describe a concept we (re)use many places once only;
3.   To enable reasoning about the concept independently of its applications;

4. To facilitate the consistency checking of applications composed from instances of types;

5. To encapsulate units of variation and change.

Keywords in our search for types are similarity, independence and encapsulation. We look for concepts that capture the similarities between phenomena in the real world. We look for concepts that are as independent as possible from particular applications, i.e. concepts that have a certain generality and we look for concepts that encapsulate properties behind an interface.

By using the partitioning rules presented so far it is very likely that good candidates for types have been identified. Our *AccessControl* system consists of a number of similar *LocalStations* and a *CentralUnit*. The very fact that we have distinguished independent parts and similarities within the system, reassures us that we may have chosen a fruitful angle.

S-rule: similarity
Look for similarities, which will make type concepts. Re-examine components that are partially similar, but partially dissimilar.

The rule applies to the system environment as well as to the system itself. It even applies to more abstract concept models of the problem domain and to more concrete implementation descriptions. In Chapter 3 we identified many similar concepts in the problem domain, e.g. *Access Points*, that were later reflected in the system, i.e. *Panels*. Similar concepts in the problem domain are often represented by similar concepts in the system.

On the block level, the block types will represent such "repetitive" concepts. In our *AccessControl* system we have found the block type *LocalStation* which in turn consists of three singular block definitions (*Panel*, *LsControl* and *Door*). Describing the same world, we could have made a *Panel* type, an *LsControl* type and a *Door* type.

We should choose to describe blocks and processes separately as types whenever they are likely to be used in more than one place. We should also reconsider blocks and processes that seem to be unique. Trying to describe them as types independently of the actual application may in fact give a different view leading to improved insight and generality.

In this chapter we have focused mainly on the use of types in composition. In Chapter 13 we shall look more closely at inheritance.

8.8   Step-wise guidelines

The guidelines and rules presented in the previous sections are summarised in a step-wise procedure as follows:

1. *Describe the environment.* Decompose the environment into blocks and processes. Identify the behaviour roles these blocks impose on the system and the knowledge they require in the system.

2. *Mirror the environment behaviour.* Mirror the behaviour roles imposed by the environment, by actor blocks and actor processes within the system. Be sure to allocate independent and concurrent roles to separate processes. Avoid splitting a naturally sequential behaviour between two processes.

3. *Mirror the environment knowledge.* Assign the knowledge about the environment to processes in the system. If the knowledge needs to be shared, define one process for each block of shared data that shall be accessed and controlled independently. Use one process to allocate each independent group of shared resources.

4. *Analyse the behaviour.* Can the behaviour be clearly and concisely described in state-oriented form? If not, analyse the reasons and modify the structure to solve the problem either by splitting processes, adding processes or combining processes.

5. *Analyse the block structure.* Check that the blocks fulfil the block purposes. Check that the block structure encapsulates units of independent adaptation, change and reuse.

6. *Look for similarities.* Identify types and type hierarchies. Organise the types into libraries. Check if existing types or type libraries may be used either as they are or adapted to this application.

7. *Analyse the variability.* What variability is needed in the product? Check that it can be accommodated by the types developed.

8. *Iterate until satisfaction.*

Note that the steps above, in principle, apply to each block in the same way as to the system. To derive a good system and product structure is an iteration process. We therefore recommend going through the steps several times, gradually adding detail to the description. In the first pass, only sketches of the block and process structure may be needed. Instead of describing the process behaviour in detail it is a good idea to develop MSCs that show the internal and external interactions first. When the MSCs look fine, proceed to make detailed process graphs.

For the data part we recommend describing data informally to begin with and to gradually formalise the data during later passes as the description becomes more stable and complete, but to always encapsulate data using the concept of abstract data types.

A precondition for the guidelines presented here is that a conceptual understanding of the application domain and the system environment is established before the SDL descriptions are developed.

Part III

Design and Implementation

Chapter 9 introduces the implementation design problem. It discusses the common difficulties and the main design steps in going from an abstract functional design to an implementation satisfying requirements to non-functional properties such as performance, exception handling and modularity. A graphic notation used to describe hardware and software designs on the architectural level is also introduced. Chapter 10, treats software design in more detail and Chapter 11 provides implementation examples in C++. Finally, in Chapter 12 the verification and validation issues are treated.

CHAPTER 9

Implementation Design

The topic of this chapter is how an abstract functional design can be mapped into a concrete implementation in hardware and software. The problem is to bridge the gap between the abstract system, modelled in the functional design and the concrete components available in the real world. Since the properties of real world components often differ from the properties of abstract components, it may be necessary to restructure and refine the functional design to a form that is more suitable for implementation. Documentation, in addition to pure SDL, is needed to define the concrete system and its relationships to the abstract SDL system. For this purpose notations for hardware and software design definitions are introduced. This chapter outlines the major steps in deriving implementations and how the implementations may be documented on the architectural level. Step-wise guidelines are summarised at the end of the chapter.

9.1   What is implementation design?

9.1.1   The problem

The development model presented in Chapter 1 puts the user needs into focus. The idea is to define functional requirements first and then develop a functional design which can be validated against the user needs (see Figure 9.1).

In the previous part (Chapters 3–8) methods for functional requirements and functional design have been presented. We now turn to the next step in the development process: to design a physical system that will implement the specified functionality. This can be seen as mapping the abstract system defined in the functional design to a concrete system made up of hardware and software components. The goal of *implementation design* is to define this mapping and the concrete technical system.

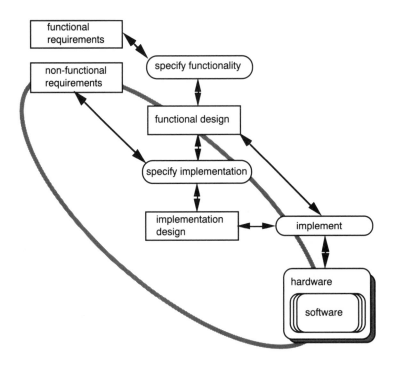

Figure 9.1   *The scope of implementation design*

It is in the nature of a functional design to model the system on an abstract level from where many alternative implementations are possible. In fact, one purpose of a functional design is to provide a basis for selecting the best possible implementation among many alternatives. As a consequence there will be several possible implementations corresponding to each functional design.

Take the *LocalStation* illustrated in Figure 9.2 as an example. The diagram does not tell us anything about the implementation, although it is clear from the requirements that the *Door* and part of the *Panel* will be mechanical devices. The *LSControl*, for instance, might be either a dedicated hardware unit or it might be software running on a general purpose computer. (One may even implement both alternatives.) If software is chosen, a host of more detailed decisions need to be made. Where to put the hardware–software interface? What kind of software platform should be used? Which programming style to use? How shall errors be handled? What about performance, fault tolerance and safety?

Of course, one cannot design the various parts of a system independently. Each decision concerning one component may have an impact on the interface with other components. For instance, if *LSControl* is implemented in software and the *Panel* is hardware, then there will be a hardware–software interface somewhere between them.

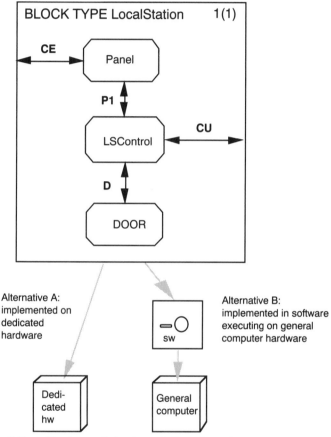

Figure 9.2 *The two main implementation alternatives*

It is the task of implementation design to make all the necessary decisions and to document the concrete system in sufficient detail to make the implementation well-defined. The result of implementation design is an *implementation design description*, where the concrete system is defined on the architectural level and related to the abstract system. Thus, the implementation design description explains HOW the abstract functions are realised.

9.1.2   Different views on implementation design

In the software engineering literature one finds at least two different views on implementation design:

1. The functional design is made rather informal and, therefore, normally incomplete and ambiguous. Many decisions concerning functionality therefore need to be made as one proceeds with implementation design and implementation. Design and implementation are often seen as processes of gradual refinement and restructuring towards the final implementation. In this case, there is no clear separation between WHAT the functionality is and HOW it is implemented.

2. The functional design is complete and unambiguous. Implementation design and implementation is mainly concerned with the concrete system. Even if some refinement and restructuring of the functional design takes place, there is a clear separation between WHAT and HOW. The implementation design description only tells how the functions are realised and not what they are. The final functional design tells what the functionality is, not how it is implemented. In other words, the two definitions are orthogonal.

The second approach is the one recommended in this book, because:

*   the functionality can be understood independently of the implementation;
*   the functionality can be reused in different implementations;
*   the transformation from a functional design to an implementation may be automated.

As long as the functional design is informal we cannot hope to achieve automatic implementation. Thus, the second paradigm is essential to automatic implementation and therefore necessary to design-oriented work. But automatic implementation will need to be controlled by implementation design information. We therefore believe that a formalisation of implementation descriptions will become increasingly important as the effort is gradually shifted from traditional programming towards functional design.

9.1.3   The role of functional design

The functional design serves at least three purposes:

1. at an early stage to specify and to validate the functionality (behaviour) required by the user environment;
2. then to provide a firm basis for implementation design, i.e. designing the optimum implementation;
3. after implementation design, to describe (document) the complete functional properties of the system as implemented.

SDL is based on concepts well-suited for the first purpose above; to define the observable behaviour of systems in a clear and unambiguous way. For this purpose, the external behaviour should be emphasised and irrelevant internal design details should be avoided.

SDL is also well-suited for the second purpose; to be a basis for implementation design. SDL has the nice property of combining implementation independence with implementability (except for infinite data types). For this purpose no premature design decisions should be embedded in the SDL specifications, but so called non-functional requirements, i.e. properties the implementation shall have in addition to those expressed in the SDL specifications, may be given as additional guidance.

If the real system is functionally equivalent to the SDL system, the third purpose above is also achieved. This is well worth aiming for, not only because it saves documentation effort, but also because the SDL descriptions will be useful during system testing, operation and maintenance. When designers and programmers find the SDL descriptions useful in their daily work, they will be motivated to keep them up to date and avoid changes on the implementation level that degenerate the documentation value.

9.1.4   The forward and the feedback aspects

There are two major aspects involved in designing the implementation of an SDL system:

1. *The forward aspect* of selecting among implementation alternatives being functionally equivalent to the SDL system. Normally there will be several such alternatives from which the designer should select an optimum implementation with respect to non-functional requirements.

2. *The feedback aspect* of adapting the SDL description in the case when the selected implementation is not functionally equivalent. There are important differences between the abstract world of SDL and the real world that sometimes will show up in the observable behaviour of the system. In such cases the complete SDL description of the system should be adapted to maintain functional equivalence.

The forward aspect

Figure 9.3 illustrates the forward aspect. The SDL specification and the non-functional requirements are used together to select and specify an implementation. The implementation description resulting from this activity defines the mapping from the SDL specification to the real system implementation. It is orthogonal to the SDL specification and is therefore shown as a separate box in Figure 9.3. The separation is not the key point here, but the orthogonal nature of the information. In practice the implementation description might be embedded as annotations to the SDL description.

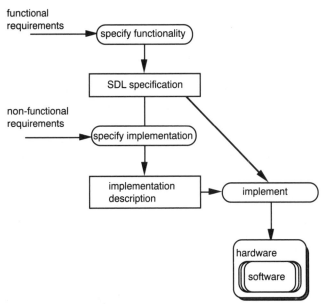

Figure 9.3 *The forward aspect; non-functional requirements are used to select a functionally equivalent implementation*

A few observations can be made in relation to Figure 9.3:

- The SDL specification fulfils all the three roles of SDL definitions described in Section 9.1.3.
- Alternative implementations may be derived from the same SDL specification by providing alternative implementation descriptions.
- If the implementation activity is automated, the implementation will be kept consistent with the specification at all times (provided the translation is correct).

The feedback aspect

In many practical instances the somewhat idealised picture of Figure 9.3 will be modified by the feedback aspect. Ideally, the decisions made during implementation design should be completely orthogonal to the original functional design, but alas, this is not always possible. Feedback from the implementation design will occur, leading to restructuring and refinement of the functional design.

If the *AccessControl* system is to be realised by a distributed computer network, for instance, some of the SDL channels will be implemented using network protocols. These protocols are needed in a distributed implementation, but not in a centralised solution. Since parts of a distributed system can go down while other parts remain operational, error handling is different in a distributed system compared to a centralised system. Therefore, in order to define the complete functionality actually implemented, the SDL description of a distributed system may differ from that of a centralised system.

Figure 9.4 illustrates the interplay between the forward and the feedback aspect. As in Figure 9.3, the non-functional properties are used to derive an implementation description. Knowledge about the implementation is then used to refine and restructure the SDL specification to a complete *SDL description*. But even this latter SDL description will leave room for alternative, functionally equivalent, implementations. Therefore, the implementation description is still needed to direct the implementation step just as in Figure 9.3.

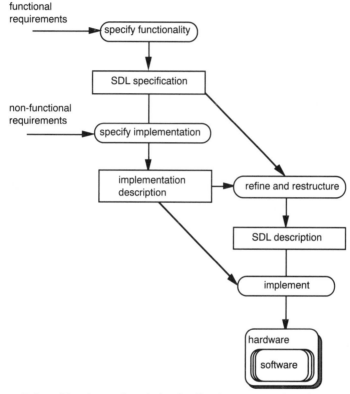

Figure 9.4 *The forward and the feedback aspects of implementation design combined*

The following observations apply to Figure 9.4:

- Two SDL definitions, the *specification* and the *description,* are needed to fulfil all three roles of SDL (see Section 9.1.3).
- For a given SDL specification, several SDL descriptions may be derived depending on the implementation description.
- For a given SDL description several implementations are possible.
- The implementation step may be automated.

The first, most user-oriented, functional design – the SDL specification – will often conceal aspects that are irrelevant to the user. In the extreme this may lead to functional designs that are not implementable with existing hardware and software technology. They may well contain infinite data types, for instance. In fact, all SDL systems are potentially unimplementable, because each SDL process has an unbounded signal queue in its input port. Depending on input rates and processing speeds this queue may grow *ad infinitum*. In most practical cases, however, it is possible to design load control and overflow mechanisms that handle these problems in a satisfactory way.

One may have to modify the functional design to properly take care of such problems. The task of implementation design involves finding a technical solution and providing the necessary feedback to the functional design. After that select the best implementation based on the implementable functional design and the non-functional design constraints expressed in the requirement specification.

This step may lead to additional functionality needed to support the implementation. Typical examples are the protocols needed in a distributed implementation, the operating system on a computer, the input–output mechanisms needed at the hardware–software interface, exception handling, diagnostics and maintenance functions. In order to document the complete functionality and to also implement automatically, the final functional design may have to be updated to cover such additional functions.

Finally, insight gained during implementation design may lead to adjustment of the functional design. Altogether one may end up with a refined and restructured functional design, the SDL description, that is considerably more complete and design-oriented than the original user-oriented version. This will be elaborated on in later sections of this chapter.

When a new system is developed from scratch, it is desirable that the SDL specification is implementation-independent. This can mean considerable feedback when the implementation is chosen. (But it does not mean that everything in the specification is changed. Often the refinement and restructuring needed can be confined to limited parts of the system.) When an existing system is extended or enhanced, however, more is known about the implementation, so one may aim more directly at the SDL description and avoid feedback.

The role of the implementation description is to define the mapping from the refined and restructured functional design to the concrete implementation. It contains information that is orthogonal to and needed in addition to the functional design. It is a goal that implementation can be done automatically on the basis of the final functional design and the implementation design.

9.1.5   The role of design constraints

Although the realisation alternatives for a given functional design are functionally equivalent, the choice of the designer is normally restricted by the non-functional requirements or design constraints, put down in the requirements specification (see Chapter 3).

If no constraints exist or all solutions are equivalent, the designer is free to choose among the solutions.

Each implementation alternative may be characterised by non-functional properties such as execution speed and memory requirements. Such properties may be quite important for the user and the system owner. Design constraints should therefore be put down in the requirement specification, to ascertain that the right kind of implementation is chosen from the (functionally equivalent) alternatives. The design constraints may be seen as a first step towards an implementation design.

An important class of constraints originates from the concrete user environment. When the system being developed is to be part of an existing system, the implementation design and implementation is heavily constrained by the existing product environment. This will often imply detailed engineering and programming practices, as well as concrete interfaces.

Although the design constraints reduce the number of implementation alternatives, there will still be many alternatives to choose from.

Four questions may now be asked:

1. What are the essential differences between SDL systems and real systems that need consideration?
2. How should the implementation descriptions be expressed; as annotations to the SDL descriptions or separately from the SDL descriptions?
3. What are the main implementation alternatives to choose from?
4. What are the main considerations and rules to apply during implementation design on the architectural level.

These questions will be discussed in the remainder of this chapter. The next chapter treats software design in more detail.

9.2   Differences between real systems and SDL systems

The physical structure depicted in Figure 9.5 is quite typical for modern real time systems. Clearly the components in the real system are different from the components of the SDL system. The real system is composed from physical computers, buses, process interfaces and communication networks, while the SDL system is composed from abstract channels and extended finite state machines. Still, the physical system will implement the SDL system in one way or another.

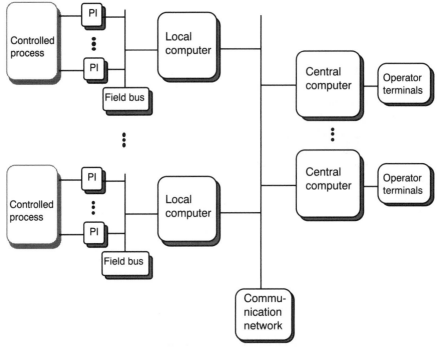

Figure 9.5   *A typical physical realisation of a modern real time system*

A good designer is well aware of the differences between the real and the abstract world. There are two main categories of such differences:

1. *Fundamental differences* in the nature of components. Physical components are rather imperfect compared to the more ideal properties of SDL components. They develop errors over time, they are subject to noise and they need time to perform their processing tasks.
2. *Conceptual differences* in the functioning of components. In both worlds there are concepts for concurrency, communication, sequential behaviour and data, but they are not necessarily the same.

9.2.1   Fundamental differences

Processing time

An SDL system is not limited by processing resources. Consequently, the balance between the traffic load offered to the system and its processing capacity need not be considered. One simply assumes that the system is fast enough to process the load it is offered.

The real world is vastly different on this point. Each signal transfer and each transition of a process, will take some time and require some processing resources. Due to these differences, the focal point of implementation design is quite different from that of the functional specification. The challenge is to find implementations for the SDL concepts that are sufficiently fast to meet the traffic load and response time requirements without destroying the validity of the SDL descriptions.

One major issue is to balance the processing capacity of the implementation against the offered traffic load.

In the *AccessControl* system, for instance, the average peak load is 600 validations a minute. This means that a central computer must process each validation in less than one-tenth of a second. How much less will depend on the other tasks the computer has to do and the margin one wants against overloading the system.

A related issue is to balance the processing capacity against the requirements to response times. Again the SDL system has no problems, but the implementation may be highly pressed to meet response time requirements. One must be able to perform time-critical processing, e.g. fetching input samples, process the sampled information and respond in a feedback loop, all within a maximum time frame. Such requirements may increase the demands on processing speed beyond the speed required to handle the traffic load.

In the *AccessControl* system, it is required that each *LocalStation* is able to serve 6 clients per minute. Therefore, the total response time per client must be less than 10 seconds. This is a fairly relaxed requirement, but there may be stricter subrequirements associated with interactions. The input rate from the key-pad, for instance, may be as high as 5 key strokes per second. Internal communication channels in the system may possibly use time-dependent synchronisation (see Section 9.2.2), needing even faster responses.

When one knows the speed required, the next task is to find hardware–software solutions that will be fast enough. This can mean a simple general purpose microcomputer in some cases and a network of high performance computers in other cases. Consequently, non-functional requirements to traffic handling capacity and response times have a strong impact on the implementation design.

The hardware–software interfaces need special consideration. It is not unusual that the larger part of a computer's capacity is spent doing input–output. Much can therefore be achieved by carefully designing the input–output interface.

A special class of time constraints originates from channels assuming time-dependent synchronisation (see Section 9.2.2). This means that the receiver has to be fast enough to catch all relevant signal information at the speed it is passed over the channel.

Since SDL descriptions clearly specify the external and internal interactions needed to perform given functions, they provide an excellent basis for estimating the processing capacity needed to meet load and timing requirements. This is elaborated on in Section 9.4.2.

Errors and noise

SDL systems may suffer from specification errors, but the abstract world of SDL does not suffer from physical errors. It is simply assumed that processes and channels always operate according to their specifications. It is not assumed that processes will stop from time to time or that channels will distort the content of signals. But in the real world such things happen. From time to time errors will manifest themselves as faults in the operation of channels and processes.

Of course, logical errors and inconsistencies may be part of an SDL system too. It may, for instance, contain internal deadlocks. But these are not the kind of errors we have in mind here. What we mean is the kind of errors that are introduced when the abstract system is implemented. A purpose of the design method being introduced in this book is to minimise the number of design and implementation errors. But even with a good method it would be rather naive to believe that the number can be reduced to zero.

In addition to the logical errors, we will have to cope with physical errors. Hardware errors, physical damage and noise are caused by physical phenomena entirely outside the realm of SDL. Consequently, the implementation will contain errors that are not part of the SDL system.

The effect of errors and noise will often need to be handled explicitly in the SDL description, however. One must consider what may happen, how it can be detected and how the damages may be limited. If one process goes down, for instance, how should the environment react? One must consider what a process should do if it never gets a response to a request or if it gets an erroneous response. What should the reaction to a channel going down be? What if a process starts to produce crazy signals? What if a signal is sent to a non-existing receiver?

To some extent the answers depend on the physical distribution of SDL processes in the real system and the physical distances that SDL channels must cover.

Physical distribution

Physically separate processes and channels may fail independently of each other. Channels covering long physical distances are subject to more noise and errors than channels implemented in software within one computer.

An SDL description does not tell anything about the physical distance covered by a channel. In reality, however, there may (or may not) be large physical distances. This means that transmission equipment and protocols are needed to implement the channel reliably. Thus, physical distance may introduce new functions needed to support the implementation of channels.

In the *AccessControl* system we can expect *LocalStations* to be distributed physically and to be far away from the *CentralUnit*. Thus, there will be a need for communication protocols on the channels between the *LocalStations* and the *CentralUnit*.

A positive effect of physical separation is that errors are isolated. Errors in one unit need not affect the other units in the system, provided that erroneous information is not propagated into them. Thus, physical separation may improve the error handling. But there is no free lunch. Errors need to be detected and isolated to allow the operational parts to continue operating with the error present. Proper handling of this aspect can be quite complex and will normally require additional functionality in the SDL description.

Finite resources

All resources in a real system are finite. There may be a maximum number of processes the operating system can handle or a maximum number of buffers for sending messages. The word length is restricted and the memory space too. Even primitive data like integers are finite.

SDL, on the other hand, has an unbounded queue in the input port of each process and allows infinite data to be specified. Hence, the designer must find ways to implement potentially infinite SDL systems using finite resources. One way is to restrict the use of SDL such that all values are certain to be bounded. Another is to deal with resource limitations in the implementation, preferably in a manner transparent to the SDL level. In cases where transparency cannot be achieved, one must either accept deviation from the SDL semantics or explicitly handle the limitations in the SDL description.

9.2.2   Conceptual differences

Concurrency

The model of concurrency used in SDL assumes that processes behave independently and asynchronously. There is no relative ordering of operations in different processes except the ordering implied by the sending and reception of signals.

This permits SDL processes to be implemented either truly in parallel on separate hardware units or in quasi-parallel on shared hardware.

Physical objects in the real world truly behave in parallel. This means that operations within different objects proceed in parallel to each other at the speed of the performing hardware. We may distinguish between two cases:

1.   *Synchronous operation,* where the operations of parallel objects are performed at the same time. This is mostly used on the electronic circuit level where operations may be controlled by common clock signals. In relation to the SDL semantics this may be seen as a special case.
2.   *Asynchronous operation,* where the operations of parallel objects are performed independently and possibly at different times. Unless we have detailed knowledge of the processing speeds we cannot know the exact ordering of operations. This corresponds well to the SDL semantics.

A "natural" implementation is therefore to map each SDL process to a separate physical object. This is not always cost-effective. An alternative approach is to implement many processes in software sharing the same computer hardware. The implications of this are two-fold:

1.   The processes and channels will not truly operate in parallel, but in quasi-parallel, meaning that they will operate one at a time, according to some scheduling strategy.
2.   Additional support will be needed to perform scheduling and multiplexing on top of the sequential machine.

Quasi-parallelism means that only one process will be active at a time and that the active process will block the operation of other processes as long as it is allowed to remain active. This will affect the response times of the blocked processes. This is an acceptable approximation to the SDL semantics only as long as the delays this introduces are acceptable to the environment.

Normally, the scheduling and multiplexing are handled by an operating system. The operating system can be seen as a layer that implements a quasi-parallel virtual machine on top of the physical machine. Chapter 10 contains a brief introduction to a simple real time operating system.

Communication

Very basically there are two different categories of information we need to communicate:

1.   events;
2.   states.

In the first case, the sequential ordering is often important while in the second case, the sequence will often not matter, only the current value at each instant in time. There are also two ways to communicate:

1.   by *signal units* or messages transferred as discrete information packages;
2.   by *continuous signals* or values transferred continuously.

Continuous signals may be read over and over again, whereas signal units are normally read only once. There are also two kinds of communication media:

1.   *unit-oriented media*, such as message queues in software;
2.   *continuous media*, such as a physical line in hardware or a shared variable in software.

The various forms of communication needs, communication signals and media may be combined in different ways in a system.

A user approaching the *AccessControl* system needs to know that the system is in a state where a new user will be accepted. This state information should be communicated as a continuous signal (in the form of a text) on the display unit. The system, on the other hand, needs to know the sequence of events generated by the user in order to respond properly. For this purpose a signal unit should be transferred for each event, e.g. when the card is inserted and a key is pushed. Thus, in the *AccessControl* system we need to communicate events as well as states and to use signal units as well as continuous signals.

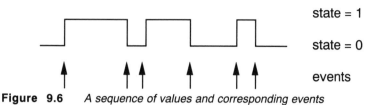

Figure 9.6 *A sequence of values and corresponding events*

Figure 9.6 illustrates that a continuous signal embodies a sequence of events. Therefore, a continuous signal implicitly carries both events and states.

A designer may well choose to transmit event sequences by means of continuous signals, but this implies overheads needed to derive the events from the continuous signal at the receiving end. Conversely state values may well be transmitted by means of signal units, but again some overhead is needed to integrate the received signal units to a state value at the receiving end. (This principle is applied in the SDL EXPORT/IMPORT mechanism.) Consequently, the signal form should preferably correspond to the communication need.

Consider input from a key-pad as an example. The output signal from each button is basically a continuous "1" when pushed and a continuous "0" when not pushed. But the system needs to know the sequence of key strokes and not the instant values. Thus, the value changes (events) need to be detected and converted to signal units representing complete key strokes. This kind of *event detection* is often needed at the interfaces of a real time system. It may either be performed in software or in hardware.

Visual signals on a display screen are another example. The user wants information presented as continuous values and not as messages flickering across the screen. Hence, the SDL signal has to be converted to a continuous value on the screen.

SDL signals are signal units. Therefore, they are implemented most directly by using a unit-oriented medium such as a message queue. But this will not always be the most cost-effective form in the real system. Sometimes the SDL signals have to be implemented by means of continuous signals.

The VIEW/REVEAL construct in SDL belongs to the continuous signal category. The natural implementation is a continuous medium. The EXPORT/IMPORT construct looks similar, but is a shorthand representation of an underlying protocol of signals enabling the receiver to keep track of a continuous value. When EXPORT/IMPORT is used in SDL, it may be better to use "real" continuous signals in the implementation (e.g. values in variables) rather than the signal protocol assumed in SDL. (This changes the SDL semantics slightly, so one should be careful. But normally it will be acceptable to the user and far more efficient.)

Channels crossing the hardware–software boundary need special attention. A channel, represented by a line in SDL, may turn out to be a mixture of physical lines, electronic equipment and software in the real system. The communication and synchronisation primitives used in hardware will often differ from those used in software.

The sampling needed to convert analogous signals to digital form resembles event detection. Sampling will normally have to be done at regular and often frequent, intervals. Thus, the requirements for sampling and/or event detection may have a strong impact on the processing capacity needed and, thus, the implementation design.

To sum up: we cannot expect to find SDL-type signals at all interfaces and must therefore be prepared to adapt and convert. Conversion from one form to another will be necessary. This is often a time-critical task needing careful optimisation.

Synchronisation

The act of aligning the operations of different concurrent processes in relation to each other is generally called *synchronisation*. Synchronisation is necessary not only to achieve correctness in communication, but also to control the access to shared resources in the physical system.

In SDL, synchronisation is achieved by means of the signal queues of processes and channels.

Consider two SDL processes that communicate. The sending process may send a signal at any time because it will be buffered in the input port of the receiving process. The receiving process may then consume the signal at a later time.

This is a buffered communication scheme in which the sender may produce infinitely many signals without waiting for the receiver to consume them. It is often referred to as *asynchronous communication*.

Asynchronous communication may be contrasted with so-called *synchronous communication*, in which the sending operation and the consuming operation occur at the same time. This is necessary when there is no buffer between the processes.

Synchronisation of interactions can be classified in the following categories:

1. *Time-dependent synchronisation*, in which the interaction operations are not explicitly synchronised. Therefore, the correctness of an interaction depends on the relative timing of operations. The operations have to be performed at the same time, more or less. There are two subcategories depending on the medium that connects the interacting objects:

    (a) *Synchronous medium.* In this case the transmission medium itself is synchronous as, for instance, the channels in a PCM (pulse code modulation) system. The sender and the receiver have to keep in step with the common timing of the transmission medium. This puts real time constraints on the sender as well as on the receiver.

    (b) *Asynchronous medium.* The transmission medium itself is asynchronous, with no explicit synchronisation mechanism on the medium. This scheme depends on the relative speed of the receiver compared to the sender. The sender must produce output at a rate the receiver is able to follow. A typical example is the decadic pulse dialling on old telephone subscriber lines. This scheme is much used in physical communication links (and is a notorious cause of real time problems).

2. *Time-independent synchronisation*, which depends on an explicit synchronisation of operations:

    (a) *Synchronous medium.* In this case the processes are locked together during interaction. Processes may have to wait for the interaction to be enabled. Once it is enabled, the interaction takes place by operations that are simultaneously performed by both processes. This is the synchronisation mechanism of LOTOS (ISO 8807) and process formalisms such as CCS (Milner, 1980) and CSP (Hoare, 1978).

    (b) *Asynchronous medium.* In this case there is a buffer, normally a FIFO queue, between the interacting processes. The sender puts (a sequence of) values (signals) into the buffer and the receiver removes the (sequence of) values at some later time. The buffer capacity determines how many values the sender may produce ahead of the receiver. SDL signal communication is in this category. It is much used in software systems, but is less common in hardware. A synchronous medium is a special case where the buffer capacity is zero.

SDL synchronisation is time-independent, using an asynchronous medium with infinite buffer capacity. This means that the sender may be infinitely many signals ahead of the receiver. In practice, however, the queue will be finite, so in the case of a full queue the sender will either have to wait or signals will be lost.

Full queues can be avoided in several ways. Sometimes the application is such that the number of signals the producer is able to generate ahead of the consumer will always be limited. In other cases the consumer is fast enough to prevent the queues from growing too long. Careful engineering is needed to ensure a smooth load control without severe performance degradation in overflow situations.

To be general, one must deal with the buffer overflow problem by delaying the producer when the buffer reaches its maximum capacity. In consequence, output from an SDL process may have to be delayed until the receiving buffer is ready. This deviation from the SDL semantics can hardly be avoided in a finite implementation. Care is needed to reduce to a minimum the practical problems this may cause.

The synchronisation of SDL rests on a basic synchronisation mechanism, called *mutual exclusion.* Only one process at a time can gain access to the input queue. Only one service at a time can get access to shared data within the process and only one process at a time gets access to revealed data. Mutual exclusion is generally needed in the access to shared resources.

One will often find mechanisms that differ from the SDL mechanisms at the physical interfaces to the system. It is fairly typical to find time-dependent synchronisation on physical channels. This implies that time-critical event monitoring and event generation will be necessary.

The synchronisation of SDL has to be implemented in the concrete system. How this should be done depends on the kind of concurrency employed and the basic mechanisms available in the concrete system.

A designer will be faced on one hand by the synchronisation primitives available in the real system and on the other hand by the synchronisation implied by the SDL specification. Additional functionality will often be needed to glue the various forms together.

Data

SDL data is based on the notion of abstract data types where operations may be defined by means of axioms. An implementation will normally need concrete data types where the operations are defined operationally. Therefore, the designer may need to transform the abstract data types of SDL into more concrete data types suitable for implementation.

9.2.3 Summary

The table below summarises the differences between SDL systems and real systems.

Table 9.1   *The difference between SDL systems and real systems*

	SDL system	Real system
Concurrency		
Synchronous		x
Asynchronous	x	x
Communication		
Unit oriented	x	x
Continuous	x	x
Synchronisation		
Synchronous time-dependent		x
Synchronous time-independent		x
Asynchronous time-dependent		x
Asynchronous time-independent	x	x
Mutual exclusion	x	x
Processing time		x
Errors and noise		x
Physical distribution		x
Finite resources		x

9.3 Implementation descriptions

It follows from the implementation independence that the same SDL specification may be reused in several different implementations and that the physical structures of these implementations may vary considerably. In one case each SDL process may be implemented on a separate physical chip, in another they may all be software running on the same computer. The way this is done is something that needs to be documented.

9.3.1   Rationale

In order to bind the implementation it is necessary to add information relating the blocks and channels of SDL to hardware and software units. This kind of information is outside the scope of SDL.

We will argue that it should remain outside SDL too. Firstly, because this kind of information is orthogonal to SDL and secondly, because there are important aspects of an implementation that cannot be defined by SDL without changing the semantics of SDL. The construction of an electronic circuit board is one example. The construction of a software system in terms of procedures and data is another.

Implementation languages such as hardware description languages and programming languages are needed to fully define the concrete system. In addition, we need to define the mapping from the abstract SDL system to the concrete system.

How should this be done? By gradually adding information to the functional design or by switching to a different kind of model?

One possibility is to add implementation descriptions as annotations to SDL descriptions. The advantage of that solution is that all the information describing the system can found in one place. The disadvantage is that the SDL descriptions are tied to particular implementation designs. By describing the implementation separately it will be easier to reuse SDL descriptions in systems having different implementations. It will also be easier to put the particular aspects of implementation design into focus during the implementation design activity.

If one abstracts from the details and looks at the overall architecture of hardware and software, one will find many similarities between implementations written in different languages. At this level one can model important design alternatives independently of specific implementation languages. Therefore, it is useful to look at the architecture before entering into the detailed implementations.

The following aspects need consideration:

1.   *The architecture* of the real system in terms of hardware and software structures.
2.   *The non-functional properties* of the real components and the resulting system. In particular, its performance in terms of traffic handling capacity, response times and error handling.
3.   *The mapping* from the abstract SDL system into components of the real system.

It may be an advantage to describe and analyse these aspects somewhat decoupled from the functional structure of SDL systems. The main structuring criteria for real systems are related to performance, cost and physical properties, whereas the criteria for SDL descriptions are clarity and completeness of behaviour. These criteria are so different by nature that they will not always yield similar structures. Moreover, there are aspects of real systems that are complex enough by themselves to justify a separate description.

In order to discuss aspects of implementation design independently of SDL descriptions without going into the details of particular implementations a notation for implementation descriptions will be informally introduced in the next section.

9.3.2   Notation

The boxes and arrows of SDL block interaction diagrams represent abstract blocks and channels with well-defined semantics. They may be understood and analysed in their own terms, independently of the realisation.

The purpose of the implementation description is to define the mapping from SDL descriptions to the realisation. For this purpose it does not need a semantics in the sense that SDL has a semantics. Its meaning comes from what it represents in the real world. For the real world itself we have other formalisms, such as programming languages and hardware description languages with well-defined semantics. Therefore, the scope of the implementation description can be limited to a syntactic mapping (see Figure 9.7).

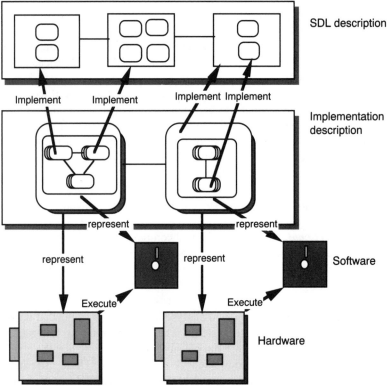

Figure 9.7   *Implementation descriptions represent the real system implementing SDL descriptions*

By representing the structure of the realisation using a graphical notation, we gain an overview and insight into the structure of the physical system.

The notation we shall use is based on SOON (Chapter 2) adapted to represent hardware and software structures and mappings.

A hardware structure example is depicted in Figure 9.8.

Boxes represent instances of concrete hardware units such as computers or circuit boards. Arrows represent physical connections, such as cables. With this notation, the hardware definition may be decomposed to provide a gradual approach to details. The idea is to use this notation to define the overall structure and then refer to special hardware notations such as circuit diagrams for the details. In that manner, a well-structured hardware definition can be made.

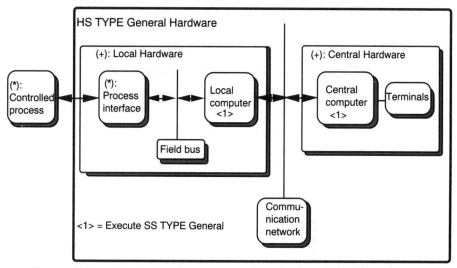

Figure 9.8 *A typical hardware structure for a distributed control system*

Arrow heads indicate the direction of signals flowing through a connection. Two-way connections are possible.

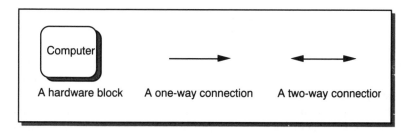

A hardware block   A one-way connection   A two-way connection

Blocks and connections may be decomposed recursively over many levels. A decomposition may either be described separately or directly inside a box.

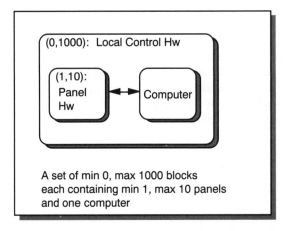

One purpose is to relate the concrete blocks and connections represented in the hardware structure to the abstract SDL blocks and channels they implement. It may also be useful to relate the hardware blocks to software units and to more detailed hardware descriptions expressed in other notations, such as circuit diagrams and mechanical layout diagrams. This is achieved by representing the relations in the diagram below.

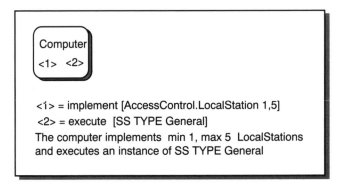

(See the table of hardware diagram symbols at the end of the section.)

The notation for software structures is based on the same principles as the hardware structure notation, but the boxes come in different shapes. This is used to distinguish characteristically different types of software units (see Figure 9.9).

The software structure depicted in Figure 9.9 is quite general. It contains a number of software processes, some of which do application functions while some perform input or output and some handle intercomputer communication. These processes are scheduled by an operating system and communicate by passing messages to each other through a message routing procedure.

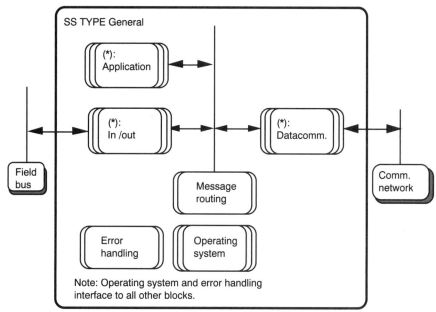

Figure 9.9 *A software structure example*

The triple sided box represents a software unit containing at least one non-terminating program. Such programs will be executed as quasi-parallel processes under an operating system. The triple sided boxes therefore represent concurrent units. Units that contains only terminating programs such as procedures are represented by the double-sided box and pure data are represented by a single-sided box.

The arrows used to represent data flows, references and activations between software units are differently shaped.

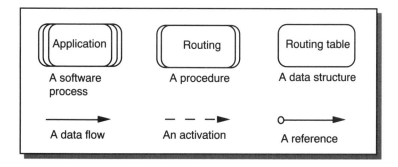

The software structure notation is used to give an overview and to provide a gradual approach to software system details. The idea is to define the overall structure of programs and data in this way and to use other notations such as program text for procedural details.

This notation combines data structures and program structures in a unified notation. It allows network-structured relations to be represented and can express concurrency.

Because the relations are hard to see in a linear program text, they are useful to represent graphically. Since activation (or control flow) is quite clear from the program text, it is considered the least important relation to represent in the software structure. Emphasis should be on data flows and references.

In the upper left-hand corner inside the frame symbol, one shall put the type of diagram and the name of the defined entity:

HS TYPE *name*   definition of a hardware structure type
SS TYPE *name*   definition of a software structure type
HS *name*   definition of a hardware structure instance
SS *name*   definition of a software structure instance

In order to define the mapping from the SDL system to the real system, it is necessary to add mapping information to the hardware and software structure diagrams.

There are several mappings to take into account:

1.   Source code *is translated* from source specification.
2.   Object code *is compiled* from source code.
3.   Executeable code *is loaded* from object code.
4.   Physical hardware *executes* executable code.
5.   Physical hardware + executable code *implement* source specification.

To fully control and document the design and implementation, all levels must be considered. For most practical documentation purposes, however, some levels may be omitted.

In order to save space in boxes and on arrows, mapping expressions may be split into two parts, a (mapping) reference and a mapping definition:

<1>   reference
<1> = implement [SYSTEM AccessControl.LocalStation]   mapping definition

The following mapping types are used (*node identifier* identifies the related entity):

Implement [*node identifier*]
Implemented-by [*node identifier*]
Execute [*node identifier*]   (implies that the software is loaded)
Executed-by [*node identifier*]

9.3.3   Symbol summary

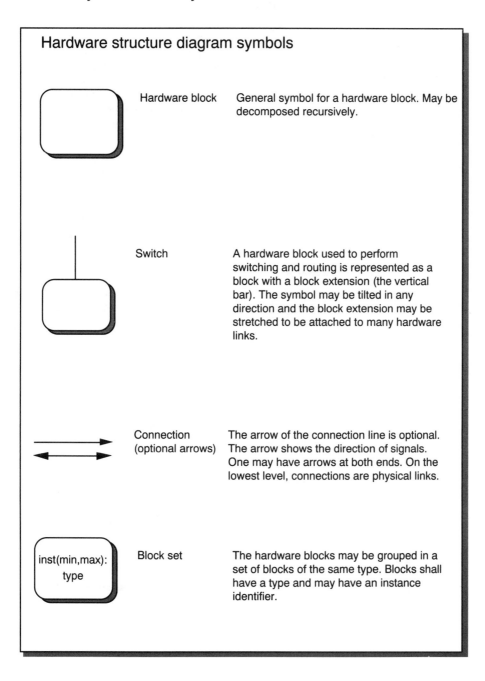

Hardware structure diagram symbols

Hardware block — General symbol for a hardware block. May be decomposed recursively.

Switch — A hardware block used to perform switching and routing is represented as a block with a block extension (the vertical bar). The symbol may be tilted in any direction and the block extension may be stretched to be attached to many hardware links.

Connection (optional arrows) — The arrow of the connection line is optional. The arrow shows the direction of signals. One may have arrows at both ends. On the lowest level, connections are physical links.

Block set — The hardware blocks may be grouped in a set of blocks of the same type. Blocks shall have a type and may have an instance identifier.

inst(min,max): type

Software structure diagram symbols

Symbol	Name	Description
(software process block)	Software process block	A software unit containing at least one non-terminating program. May contain procedures and data.
(procedure block)	Procedure block	A software unit containing at least one terminating program, but no non-terminating program. May contain data.
(data block)	Data block	A pure data element or a group of data elements. May not contain programs.
→————→	Data flow	Arrow denotes direction of flow.
– – – →	Activation	Activation or call. Cannot connect to data blocks.
○——→	Reference	Reference or pointer.
(data flow by reference symbol)	Data flow by reference to message buffer	The line denotes data flow and the referenced square denotes the message buffer.
C(n,m): B	Set of data elements of type B	A set of min n, max m elements of type B
C[n:m] : B	Indexed array of data elements	An array of n elements called $C(n)$–$C(m)$ of type B
A B:BT C:CT D:DT	Structure of data elements; record	A composite data structure (A) consisting of elements of different types. Each data element has a type and an instance identifier.

9.4 Design considerations

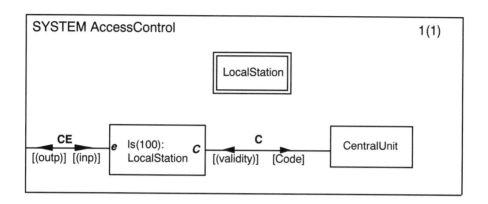

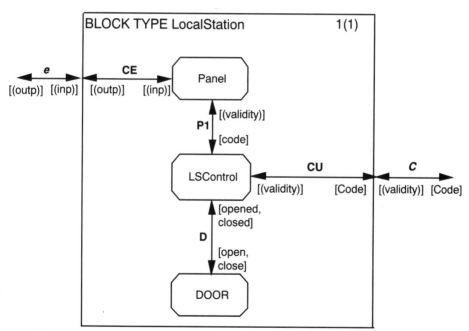

Figure 9.10 *Outline of the functional design*

There are four objectives of this section:

1. The reader should get to understand the purpose of implementation design and the interplay between implementation design, functional design and implementation.

2.   The reader should get a feeling for the major design issues and the major steps in implementation design, as well as some generic solutions that can be used as the basis for actual designs.

3.   The reader should learn notations that enable him/her to describe and discuss implementation alternatives on an abstract implementation level.

4.   The reader should appreciate that there is a lot of freedom in the mapping from SDL to implementation. An example will be given, but this is by no means the only possible solution.

We shall now embark on a standard approach to implementation design that will be presented by means of the *AccessControl* system example.

9.4.1   The starting point

The starting point for implementation design is made up of the design constraints (Chapter 3) and the functional design (Chapters 4–8). Figure 9.10 shows, slightly simplified, the top levels of the functional design. It shows a system consisting of a *CentralUnit* and a number of *LocalStations*.

The functional design also contains process graphs, data and signal definitions we have seen in the preceding chapters.

9.4.2   Step 1: trade-off between hardware and software

There is a close interplay and many trade-offs to be made between hardware and software. Indeed a main objective of the methodology is to enable the designer to make well-founded trade-offs during implementation design.

This will normally require a cut and try procedure, where the designer first selects a hardware architecture and then evaluates its ability to fulfil the non-functional requirements. Thereafter the architecture is restructured and refined until it is satisfactory. With experience one learns to home in on a good solution quite rapidly.

Once a suitable hardware structure has been selected, the consequences it has on the software design must be considered. Peripheral hardware, for instance, has consequences for the input–output software. If the functions are distributed on many computers, we will need additional software for intercomputer communication and distributed error handling. Therefore, before all the software can be designed, it is necessary to know the overall hardware structure.

Hardware should not be designed without considering the software structure either. Coordination and trade-off between hardware and software design is necessary. The first step in implementation design is to perform this trade-off and to design the overall architecture of the hardware and software taking the non-functional requirements into account.

The major considerations in this step are as follows:

1.   Physical distribution and physical interfaces;
2.   Time constraints versus processing capacity;
3.   Error handling requirements, i.e detection, isolation and recovery from errors;

4. Security against unauthorised access to information;
5. Operation and maintenance;
6. Cost to develop, cost to produce, cost to modify and maintain;
7. (Re)use of existing components.

Physical distribution and physical interfaces

The SDL specification should not prematurely assume an internal physical partitioning of the system. But sometimes the physical location of interfaces implies a physical distribution of the system. The subscribers to a telematics system, for instance, will be physically distributed. Consequently, the user interfaces at least, will be physically distributed.

The physical user interfaces of the *AccessControl* system are the *Panels* and *Doors*. The *Panels* have to be physically located at the *Doors* where the users need them. Does this mean that the *LocalStations* should be physically distributed as well? Or should they be physically centralised in the vicinity of the *CentralUnit*?

To answer these questions one should look at the channels represented in the functional design to find which ones are best suited to cover physical distances. SDL signals are defined independently of physical distances. One is therefore free to localise processes physically apart. But there will always be a certain delay and cost associated with signal transfer over distances. One should therefore look for channels carrying a low signal traffic without strict timing constraints. Such channels may sometimes be found at the external system interfaces, but more often they will be found internally in the system.

This generalises to a rule saying that we should distribute along the channels with few interactions and relaxed timing constraints. We should keep strongly coupled processes together. This will often mean that a fair bit of processing should be performed physically close to the external interfaces.

S-rule: physical distribution
Distribute processes in a way that minimises the bandwidth needed over physical channels.

In our system the channels between the *LocalStations* and the *CentralUnit* satisfy these criteria best. We therefore decided to let these channels be the ones that cover distances.

Does this mean that each *LocalStation* should be a physically separate unit? Not necessarily. We may implement several *LocalStations* in one computer when their *Panels* and *Doors* are located close to each other.

Perhaps some *LocalStations* can be colocated with the *CentralUnit* too? This could be a solution for small installations. A scheme that can be physically distributed or centralised depending on the physical distances and the size of each installation seems attractive. We therefore select the structure shown in Figure 9.11 as our first attempt at a hardware architecture.

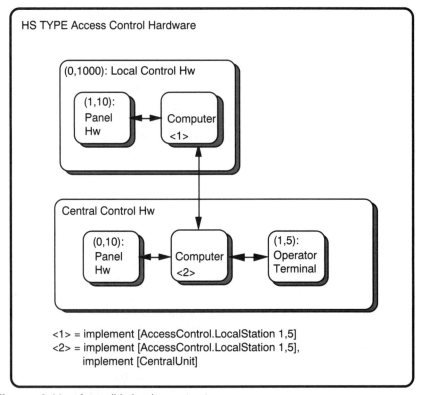

Figure 9.11   *A possible hardware structure*

There will be at least one block of *Central Control Hardware* and from zero up to 1000 blocks of *Local Control Hardware*. In this architecture we intend to implement the *LSControl* processes and the *CentralUnit* processes in software running on the various computers. We are not sure as yet how to implement the *PanelControl* processes, but software seems to be most likely option if the computer capacity permits.

At this stage of design there are still many open questions. What kind of computer to use, what kind of communication links to use and so on.

Before we carry on, we make two general observations:

1.   The hardware architecture is different in structure from the functional design.
2.   Some communication protocols will be needed to support the communication between the local and central hardware.

Time constraints versus processing capacity

Intuitively, a standard computer should have no problem in handling one *LocalStation* since the maximum load at a *LocalStation* is just 6 validations a minute. The heavy workload seems to be on the *Central Computer*. But is this intuition correct? How can this problem be approached systematically?

For this purpose we need to estimate processing times and then calculate the processing load represented by the SDL application and its response times. Simple mean value calculations may be performed as follows:

1. For each SDL process, P, estimate a mean transition time t_P. This figure depends on the size of the software and the execution speed of the hardware. One may for instance calculate the mean number of operations, o_P, per transition (sending signals, timer operations, data operations) and then estimate a mean number of instructions, i_P, per operation. If the execution speed of the hardware is S seconds per instruction, then $t_P = i_P * o_P * S$.

2. Calculate the mean number of transitions, n_P, that each SDL process will perform per second at peak load. This figure can be found by counting the number of transitions needed to carry out a given function, e.g. handle a telephone call, multiplied by the number of such functions the process will perform per second.

3. Calculate the normalised, mean peak load for each process:
   $$l_P = n_P * t_P$$
   This is a measure for how much processing time this process will need per second, i.e. the fraction of the processing capacity needed by this process (Erlang measure).

4. Calculate a corresponding load figure for each channel, C and signal route, R:
   $$l_C = n_C * t_C$$
   $$l_R = n_R * t_R$$
   Here n_C and n_R are the number of signals per second and t_C and t_R the processing times per signal transfer.

5. Calculate the mean peak load of the system by adding together the channel, signal route and process loads. If the sum is higher than one, the mean load is higher than the processing capacity of a single computer. In that case the capacity must be increased either by optimisation of the software, speeding up the hardware or by distributing the system. As a rule of thumb the mean peak load on a single computer should not exceed 0.3 in order to give room for statistical peak loads exceeding the mean peak load.

Note that the real load will vary statistically and have peak values considerably higher than the mean values we have been looking at. The system may therefore be overloaded for periods of time even though the mean load is handled with a good margin. A strategy for load control should therefore be part of the implementation design.

If the system can be run on a single computer, this should be preferred (unless other considerations demand something else). If it cannot be run on a single computer for performance reasons, it must be distributed. This will add communication overheads that must be included in revised load figures.

S-rule: mean peak load
Calculate the mean peak load for each SDL process, channel and signal route. Allocate SDL processes to computers such that the sum peak load for each computer is less than a given load limit (typically 0.2–0.3).

In addition to the load calculations above, it is necessary to check that the system will meet real time constraints. Will there be speed-dependent synchronisation with time-critical input rates? Are there constraints on response times?

To answer the first question we must compare the processing time needed per input signal with the minimum arrival interval between input signals, t_A. To answer the second question we must compare the maximum allowed response time, t_R, with the composite processing time needed to generate the response. Both calculations will be based on the estimated time to perform transitions, t_P, multiplied by the number of transitions that must be performed sequentially in each case. The number of transitions and signal transfers per time-critical transaction must be found from the SDL diagrams and the corresponding processing times calculated. Again it is necessary to make room for statistical variations.

From the requirements specification we know that a *LocalStation* will be able to handle 6 validations a minute, i.e. 0.1 validation per second, while the *CentralUnit* will handle 600 validations per minute, i.e. 10 validations per second.

From the SDL process graphs we find the number of transitions each process must perform in order to carry out one normal validation.

1. *LSControl*:   5 transitions per accepted client
2. *PanelControl*:   6 transitions per normal validation
3. *CuControl*:   2 transitions per validation
4. *Validation*:   1 transition per validation

In order to be accurate we need to distinguish between the alternative paths through the process graphs. It is not sufficient to know the number of validations per second. We also need to know how many of those will be successful and how many will be unsuccessful. As a rough estimate, we may select the worst case, however. If we assume that the mean transition time is 0.01 seconds, we get the following load estimates:

1. $l_{LSControl}$ $= 5*0.1*0.01$ $= 0.05$
2. $l_{PanelControl}$ $= 6*0.1*0.01$ $= 0.06$
3. $l_{CuControl}$ $= 2*10*0.01$ $= 0.2$
4. $l_{Validation}$ $= 1*10*0.01$ $= 0.1$

Consequently, the *Central Computer* will have a mean load of $l_{CuControl} + l_{Validation} = 0.3$ doing validation alone. This seem to be too high considering that the *Central Computer* will have to handle the transfer protocols and the operator interactions as well.

Therefore, we must either reduce the transition time by speeding up the computation or distribute the load over several computers.

The question now is how the performance of the *CentralUnit* may be increased. For small installations there will be no problem, but for large installations validation needs to be done in parallel. We therefore decided to distribute the validation load to a number of *ClusterStations*, each serving a group of *LocalStations*.

Figure 9.12 shows the new hardware structure we propose to use for large installations. The *Central Hardware* will be without *Panels* in this case. The clusters will be connected to the central hardware through a local area network, the *LAN* in Figure 9.12.

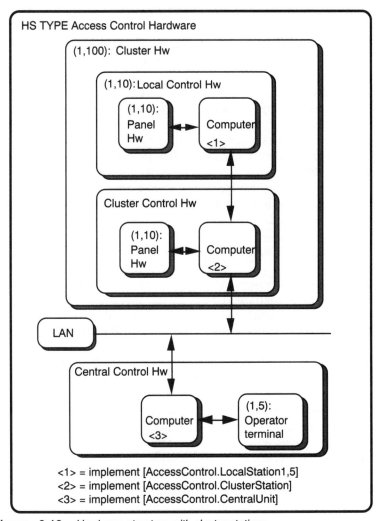

Figure 9.12 *Hardware structure with cluster stations*

In this solution the validation database will be distributed. There will be a copy of the central *Validation* process (and its database) in each cluster. This means that the *CentralUnit* must handle updates in a distributed database. This introduces a new problem to solve in the functional design, but the *LocalStations* and the *Validation* processes in each cluster may (hopefully) work just as before.

The next step is to consider real time constraints. Will the system be able to process its inputs fast enough?

As one proceeds with hardware and software design, the estimates for tp may be improved. One may also include the loads represented by the operating system, by signal transfer between processes, etc. in order to get a better load estimate for each computer. Note that the real load will vary statistically having peak values considerably higher than the mean values we have been looking at.

Error handling, that is detection, isolation and recovery from errors
Requirements to reliability may impact on the hardware structure in several ways:

1.   Fault tolerance means redundancy. At least two hardware units and facilities for error detection, diagnostics and switch-over are needed to implement fault tolerance.
2.   Fault sectioning means distributing the functions over separate hardware units in a way that limits the number of SDL processes that may be blocked by a single hardware error.
3.   Fail-safeness means that the system must always fail to a safe state where it does no harm to its environment. Some sort of supervisory hardware will normally be needed.

The requirement specification of the *AC-System* states the following:

1.   Errors should not cause access to be granted to unauthorised persons.
2.   Errors should be confined to the unit where they occur.
3.   Not more than 10 panels and 5 doors should be blocked by a single error.
4.   Doors shall be locked, not open, under error conditions.

The first and second requirement must be met by carefully designed hardware and software. A defensive style where inputs are mistrusted and checked, as far as possible, by each process is essential.

The last requirement implies that doors should lock automatically in the case of errors. It will be necessary to have hardware mechanisms that automatically lock the doors when malfunctioning is detected. One cannot rely on software alone to do this.

The third requirement is met by the introduction of clusters if each cluster is allowed to serve a maximum of 10 panels and 5 doors. This illustrates how physical distribution helps to reduce the effect of errors. But it may lead to a stronger partitioning into physical units than required for performance reasons alone.

The general problem is to identify how much and what kind of service degradation one can accept from a single error. If no degradation is acceptable, the system has to be fault tolerant, i.e. be able to continue operation in the presence of errors.

Security against unauthorised access to information

The security in this system rests on the cards being kept personal and the card identifier as well as the personal code being kept secret. An intruder may get hold of the last two items by listening in on the communication links. We assume that the local area network is the weak point in this respect. It is therefore necessary to encrypt information that is passed over the local area network. This will add encryption–decryption to the functional design. Security against unauthorised access to or modification of, information may also demand some special measures in the hardware.

Operation and maintenance of the hardware

Extensibility is to some extent already taken care of. Important questions now are whether extensions will be possible during operation or not? Should it be possible to block down hardware units, replace them by others or add new ones as the system is running?

Cost to develop, cost to produce, cost to modify and maintain

Hardware design, more than software design, must take production costs into consideration. This will depend on both the complexity of the hardware itself and the production volume. A high volume will mean lower unit cost. One therefore needs to minimise the number of different designs in order to take advantage of a high production volume. One will often be able to find a generic hardware design that can be used to implement a wide range of SDL systems.

There are several options available to the hardware designer:

1. develop a completely new design;
2. specialise or instantiate an existing design;
3. combine existing design solutions with new ones.

Normally the last two are far more cost-effective than the first.

It can be seen from Figure 9.12 that there are considerable similarities among the hardware units. Much can be achieved by reducing the number of different types that need to be developed, produced and maintained. If existing components may be used, so much the better.

S-rule: hardware similarity

Look for similarities between hardware modules. Increase cost–benefit by using similarity to minimise the number of different component types needed and maximise the reuse of each.

9.4.3   Step 2: define the hardware architecture

From the considerations above, the overall hardware architecture needed to implement the SDL system should be defined. This may be documented by means of hardware structure diagrams, as illustrated in Figure 9.12. The emphasis at this stage is the overall hardware structure in terms of computers, peripheral equipment and communication channels.

The protocols, the signal formats and the synchronisation schemes used on all physical interconnections should be defined, as this is important input to the software design.

Finally, the allocation of SDL processes to physical units should be documented. Once this is done, we know the functionality as well as the physical environment of the software in the system.

One aim of the notation introduced here is to facilitate the reuse of existing designs. It supports the definition of types and the specialisation and inheritance of properties in a manner similar to the object-oriented extensions to SDL.

9.4.4   Step 3: define the software architecture

In the example we have assumed that the majority of SDL processes are implemented in software running on the various computers. Each of these computers will contain software that implements the local functions, the cluster functions and the central functions. In addition, they will have software for intercomputer communications, local input–output and error handling. Finally, they will most likely have an operating system.

A typical software structure for one computer is presented in Figure 9.9.

The task of a software designer is to select a structure of software processes that will implement the desired functions. How to go about this task is treated in Chapter 10.

Presently, we simply assume that a software structure has been defined and consider the additional functionality introduced by the design.

9.4.5   Step 4: restructure and refine the functional design

As illustrated in the previous sections, additional functionality will normally be needed to support the concrete system. This functionalities will depend on design decisions and cannot be defined before the overall design is made. Ideally, it should all be invisible to the users, but some functionalities are likely to be visible. In any case, it may be complex enough to warrant a separate functional definition.

Some functions that are normally visible to the user are:

1.   Error handling, e.g. error reports, missing services;
2.   Operation and maintenance of the real system, e.g. blocking units, testing units;

3.　　Access to limited resources.

Some functions that should be invisible to the user are:

1.　　Multiplexing of computers and channels;
2.　　Synchronisation and mutual exclusion;
3.　　Communication services;
4.　　Load control.

After the overall hardware and software structures are defined, the additional functionality should be incorporated into the functional design. As our next step, we therefore return to functional design to make a refined and restructured definition of the complete functional properties that are visible to the user. Figure 9.13 illustrates the top level of the resulting SDL description.

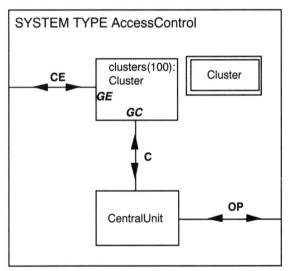

Figure 9.13 *The top level diagram of the complete, SDL description*

The initial functional design was structured to render the functional properties with minimum complexity and maximum clarity, while the implementation design was structured to render the physical construction. It is hardly surprising that these criteria lead to different structures. We contend that this is how it should be too!

Once the implementation design has been defined, the functional consequences should be reflected in the functional design. This also serves to simplify the mapping from the abstract functions to the concrete implementation. The functional blocks in Figure 9.13, for instance, map directly to the hardware blocks in Figure 9.12.

Figure 9.13 reflects the concrete system structure, but it is still an abstract system description that can be *understood independently of the concrete system.* Indeed, considerable freedom still remains for the detailed design and implementation.

After this stage, the SDL description becomes a key element in the system documentation. (Often it is the only functional design that is maintained.)

Note that the restructuring does not mean that everything has to be redefined. A majority of the processes from the first functional design may be left unchanged. If they are defined as stand alone types, it is a simple matter to put them into a new structural context together with some new processes.

Indeed, to be generally useful, a type must not be too dependent on its immediate environment. In Figure 9.14 we take *LocalStation* as an example. We will use instances of *LocalStation* in the *LocalUnits* as well as in the *ClusterUnits*. Those in the *ClusterUnits* will have direct, local access to the validation process, whereas those in the *LocalUnits* must communicate via physical links and protocols.

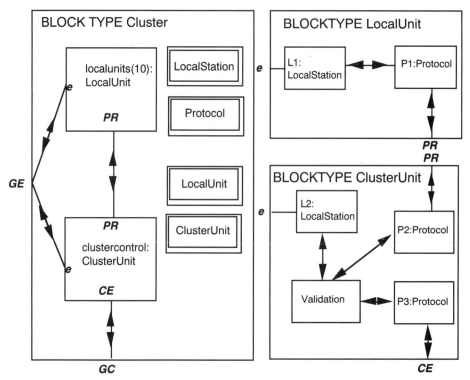

Figure 9.14   *The LSControl should see no difference between local and remote access to the validation.*

To summarise, the main steps of implementation design are:

1. Hardware–software trade-off;
2. Define hardware;
3. Define software;
4. Define design adjusted and complete functions in the SDL description.

Note that we have presented the main design steps only. In practice, more iterations may be needed.

After completion of these steps, detailed design and implementation may proceed. While the main design steps rely on high level decisions which are likely to remain manual, the detailed design and implementation are subject to gradual automation.

CHAPTER 10

Software Design

The objectives of this chapter are to describe some of the general problems a software designer must solve, to present some alternative solutions and finally to give some guidelines for software design. A short section on hardware design is included.

10.1 The problem

In the trade-off between hardware and software design (Chapter 9) we started by looking at the physical interfaces. By analysing their physical distribution, their traffic load and their real time constraints we were able to design a suitable hardware architecture. In software design we will do likewise by starting at the hardware–software interfaces and work towards an internal software structure.

From the trade-off between hardware and software we know the physical interfaces to each computer and the functionality, in terms of SDL processes, to be implemented by its software. Figure 10.1 serves to illustrate the context of software design.

The software designer is faced with three interrelated problems (see Figure 10.1):

1. *Input–output*. How to handle the communication with the environment across the hardware–software interface.
2. *Application*. How to implement (the functionality of) the SDL (sub)system within the software system of each computer.

3. *Concurrency*. How to handle the concurrency required by the input–output and the application. In short, how to handle time, priorities, scheduling and synchronisation.

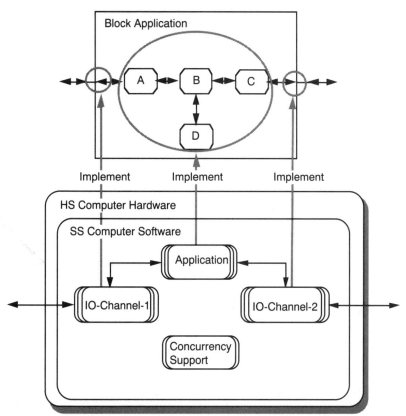

Figure 10.1 *The software design is constrained by the functional design and the hardware interfaces.*

Input–output needs special attention mainly because of the differences in concurrency, communication and synchronisation primitives used at either side of the hardware–software interface. A computer is basically a sequential machine executing a sequential program, whereas its environment consists of physical objects truly operating in parallel. Likewise, SDL processes implemented in software on the same computer will operate in quasi-parallel, but they will interact with objects in the physical environment truly operating in parallel. At the hardware–software boundary different forms of concurrency, communication and synchronisation will meet each other. The problems of overcoming these differences have a strong influence on the overall software structure.

To be precise we should bear in mind the difference between a description and a system. Software is not a system, it is a description. The computer that executes the software is a system. When we talk about implementation of SDL systems, we always have the executing software in mind. The task of the software designer, however, is to generate a description in a programming language, i.e. to map the SDL description to a description in a programming language that will execute in a way that is functionally equivalent to the SDL system.

There are considerable semantic differences between SDL and most (if not all) programming languages:

1.   *Concurrency*. Sequential programming languages like C and PASCAL give no support to the concurrency of SDL. Some languages like CHILL and ADA support concurrency, but do so differently from SDL.
2.   *Time*. Very few programming languages support time at all. SDL-like time is not directly supported by any language, not even CHILL.
3.   *Communication*. SDL-like signal communication is not supported by any language.
3.   *Sequential behaviour*. An SDL process graph specifies state-transition behaviour in the fashion of an extended finite state machine, while programming languages specify action sequences.
4.   *Data*. SDL data are abstract and possibly infinite. The implementation in a programming language has to be operational and finite.

A usual way to overcome such differences is to adapt the underlying machine and programming language to the SDL semantics by means of support software.

Three levels of support are in common use when implementing SDL system (see Figure 10.2):

1.   *No support*. SDL concepts are mapped directly to concepts supported by a sequential programming language.
2.   *Real time operating system*. Basic facilities to support concurrency, time and communication are provided by a real time operating system. This also includes the run-time support provided for concurrent languages like CHILL and ADA.
3.   *SDL run-time support system RTS*. Additional run-time support for SDL concepts like timers, signals and channels.

In the first case, the SDL specification is transformed into a sequential program that can be run on a "naked" computer. In the second and third cases, the SDL specification is transformed to application software running on top of virtual machines that facilitate the implementation of the SDL application.

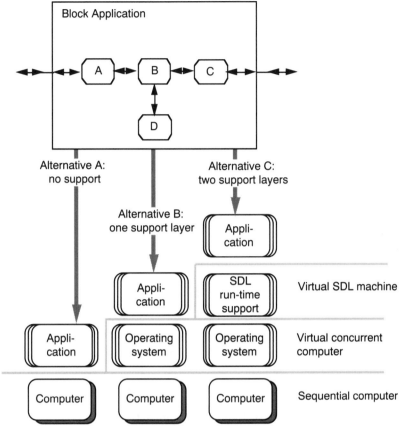

Figure 10.2 *One may either adapt the application to the machine or adapt the machine to the application using layers of support software.*

Although the use of an operating system is the most common approach today, there are cases where the overhead this introduces is unacceptable either because of speed constraints, memory size constraints or cost.

We shall therefore look at all the possibilities.

The level of support needed is not dictated by the needs of the SDL application alone. The input–output requirements are important too. In fact, the requirements to event detection and synchronisation at the hardware–software interface compared to the time needed for internal processing, determine the kind of scheduling mechanisms and priorities needed.

10.2   Concurrency and time

10.2.1   Levels of support

In principle, an SDL description containing several processes may be transformed into an equivalent description containing only one. This process may then be implemented as a sequential program in a sequential programming language.

Due to the problem of "state explosion" and the lack of modularity in this approach, it is only practical in very restricted cases. Therefore, one will normally seek an implementation that retains the original process structure of the SDL description. This means that the concurrency and the communication in SDL must be implemented.

A very simple solution is to implement SDL processes in modules that communicate by means of procedure calls. A procedure call is a way to communicate information and transfer control at the same time. Procedure calls implement the asynchronous communication of SDL by means of synchronous communication. In addition, procedure calls imply a transfer of control from the calling to the called module. Therefore, procedure calls provide a combined communication and scheduling mechanism that can implement special cases of SDL communication and concurrency. The lowest level of support is therefore to use procedure calls as the basic scheduling and communication mechanism. This approach is outlined in Section 10.3.2. It is strongly limited in its ability to support SDL communication in general, to handle time and to meet real time constraints.

In order to implement more general SDL systems, it is necessary to introduce a buffered, asynchronous, communication scheme. This can be achieved within the framework of a purely sequential program system using, for instance, a main program that schedules the activation of modules implementing SDL processes that communicate through message buffers. The limitation of that approach lies in its ability to handle time and real time constraints.

A general purpose operating system that schedules concurrent processes according to priority and supports SDL-like communication and timing, will provide the easiest and most general platform to implement the concurrency of SDL systems.

The basic facilities needed from a real time operating system are as follows:

1.   Multiplexing and scheduling of processes, i.e.:
   (a)   context switching between processes;
   (b)   scheduling with pre-emptive and non-pre-emptive priorities to meet response time requirements;
   (c)   interrupt handling to provide passive waiting on external events.
2.   Synchronisation of interactions, i.e.:
   (a)   communication;
   (b)   access to shared resources.
3.   Time measurement.

These facilities are provided in one way or another by many commercial operating systems. They are also supported by concurrent programming languages such as CHILL and ADA. A small operating system that supports these functions will be described in the following to provide an example and a frame of reference.

10.2.2 A simple operating system example

The operating system sees the software system as a collection of *software processes* that synchronise and communicate by means of general *semaphores* (see Figure 10.3). It performs multiplexing and scheduling of the processes on the basis of external and internal events. These events are either external interrupts (including time interrupts) or internal operations on the semaphores.

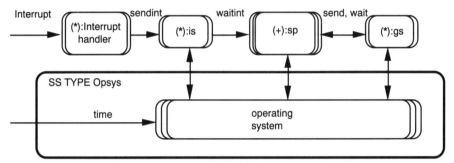

Figure 10.3 *The operating system schedules a number of software processes, sp, that interact through general semaphores, gs. Interrupts are signalled through interrupt semaphores, is.*

The semaphores administer buffers and waiting processes. Buffers are shared data records used both for message communication and to represent (other) shared resources. The general semaphore is a mechanism that can be used both to allocate free buffers, possibly representing some other resources and to provide asynchronous communication. In both cases the buffers will be managed by the semaphore in a FIFO queue order.

In order to send a message a process will first fetch a free buffer from a semaphore (keeping a free-pool of buffers), then fill in the message content and, finally, send the buffer to another semaphore. The message will be received, in due time, by another process waiting to receive the message from that semaphore.

The processes may perform two operations on the general semaphores:

- send(semaphore, buffer) and
- wait(semaphore, max_time) -> (buffer, time).

On a *send* operation a buffer is appended to the end of the FIFO queue of the semaphore. On a *wait* operation a buffer is removed from the front of the queue. If there are no buffers in the queue when a process performs a *wait* operation, the process will be suspended until a buffer is entered by a *send* operation performed by another process. When a process performs a send operation on an empty semaphore where another process is waiting, the relative priority of the two processes determines which should be activated. If the sender has the higher priority, it will continue. However, if the receiver has the higher priority, the sender will be suspended and the receiver activated. In this way the *send* and *wait* operations are linked to the scheduler of the operating system. Both operations may lead to suspension of the performing process.

The wait operation specifies a maximum waiting time. If no buffer is entered before the time expires, the operation will return with a time-out indication. By waiting on a special semaphore, SUSPEND, that never returns a buffer, a process may suspend itself for a specified time.

The general semaphore can be seen as an abstract data type with two operations, *send* and *wait*, implemented by procedure calls. It will use a data structure, a linked list, to hold the queue of buffers. It will also keep a queue of references to waiting software processes in the case when the buffer queue is empty and there are processes waiting to receive buffers.

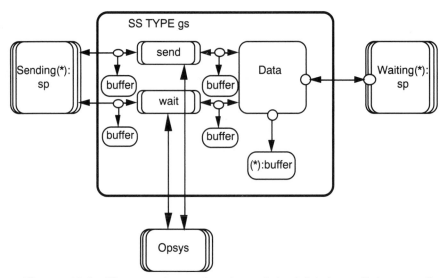

Figure 10.4   *The general semaphore is an abstract data type with two operations; send and wait.*

This kind of semaphore is a generalisation of the classic semaphores described in Dijkstra (1968) and Brinch Hansen (1973).

In order to implement SDL-like communication, the buffers may be encoded with SDL signals.

A special type of semaphore, the interrupt semaphores, are used for interrupt signals. There are two operations on interrupt semaphores:

- sendint(semaphore);
- waitint(semaphore, max_time) -> (time).

In contrast to the general semaphore, no buffer is passed through the interrupt semaphore. The reason is that we want to signal an interrupt as quickly as possible, spending as little time as possible in the interrupt handling routine.

SDL timing is different from suspension of processes, since an SDL process may be active doing transitions while a timer is running. To support this, the operating system provides an SDL-like timer facility:

- starttimer(time, timer-id, PId) -> message(PId, timer-id);
- stoptimer (timer_id, PId);
- now-> time.

When a timer is started it will run until the specified time is reached and then generate a time-out message addressed to the specified process. *Stoptimer* will reset the timer or remove the time-out message if it is already sent but not yet consumed.

The timer facility basically operates on a list of times and corresponding processes waiting to receive a time-out message when the time is reached. By using *starttimer* a process in reality orders the timer facility to make an entry in this list. The timer facility will monitor the actual time and compare the actual time with the times in the list. When a time specified in the list is reached, a time-out message is sent to the corresponding process and the entry is taken out of the list.

Stoptimer will order an entry to be taken out of the list in a similar way. What will happen if a *stoptimer* is issued in the short time interval after a time-out has occurred and before the time-out message has been received? The time-out message is still under way and will be received by the process, if nothing is done to prevent it. The best solution is to let *stoptimer* remove the time-out message, wherever it is.

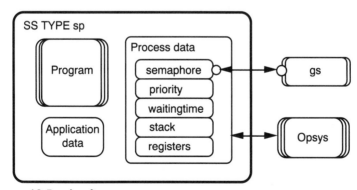

Figure 10.5 *A software process*

Each software process will have *Process data* that the operating system uses during scheduling and context switching. Some of the information in the *Process data* is shown in Figure 10.5.

The scheduler in the operating system will keep a list of processes that are ready to run and will always start the one with the highest priority. (In the case of equal priorities, it may choose to alternate, e.g. in round robin fashion.) Whenever a *send* or *wait* operation is performed, a new process may become ready to run and/or the running process may have to wait. Each semaphore operation may therefore cause a new process to be activated and the running process to be stopped. Interrupts may have the same effect through the use of *sendint* and *waitint* operations. Likewise time interrupts may cause time-outs.

In addition to the basic set of operations described so far, operations to dynamically create and delete software processes and semaphores may be needed in some applications.

10.2.3   Priority

In SDL there is no priority among processes. But this does not mean that priority cannot be used in the implementation. Priority is needed for several reasons:

1.   There are external real time constraints that can only be met by giving high priority to certain processes.
2.   There are internal error situations that should be treated with the highest priority.
3.   There are situations where priority helps to simplify and speed up computations.

Normally, real time constraints must be met by giving high priority to the time-critical processes. Therefore, one will normally have to treat time-critical input–output as high priority, while the internal processing is allowed to proceed at a lower priority. This is one reason why input–output should be separated from the application processes.

In error situations one must react quickly in order to isolate the error, reduce the damage and give alarms. This means that some processing needs to be done immediately and that the error should be reported as quickly as possible. In order to report quickly, it is not sufficient that processes have high priority. We need priority on the message transfer as well. This can be achieved in the operating system either by giving each message a priority attribute or by sending high priority messages through semaphores that are served with high priority.

Services in SDL operate in quasi-parallel and communicate by means of priority signals. This can be implemented by giving equal priority to services and allowing their internal signals to have priority over external signals.

If internal messages within a software system have priority over external messages arriving from the environment, the internal processing order will become more deterministic. This helps to reduce the number of ways that operations of processes will actually interleave. In turn, this reduces the probability that certain interaction errors will occur. More importantly, it sometimes helps to reduce the overhead and increase the speed of internal communications. Finally, load control is improved if services already accepted take priority over fresh service requests.

S-rule: external signal priority
Give time-critical external events priority over internal processing.

S-rule: internal processing priority
Give the processing of internal signals priority over the processing of external signals

S-rule: load control
When overload occurs, give priority to service requests already in progress and delay fresh requests.

Corollary:
Stop fresh traffic where it originates, i.e. at the user interfaces.

10.3 Communication

We believe that software design should start by considering the communication aspect.

S-rule: communication-oriented design
Start software design by deciding on communication mechanisms for all external and internal interfaces.

10.3.1 Input–output

Input–output communication poses special problems that will influence the software design to a large extent. Since the hardware environment of a computer operates truly concurrently with the software system, interactions across the software–hardware interface need to be synchronised.

As discussed in Chapter 9, synchronisation may either be time-dependent or time-independent. The communication medium may either be unit-oriented or continuous (Section 9.2.2). Physical channels are often continuous media with time-dependent synchronisation.

In either case, synchronisation implies that processes sometimes need to wait for certain events to occur. Such events may either be related to time, e.g. that a specific duration is reached or to events on the channels, such as a change in a continuous value.

Conversions are often needed, not only to convert data from one format to another, but also to overcome differences between communication needs, signal forms and communication media (see Section 9.2.2). One may, for instance, need to scan external variables at regular intervals in order to detect events and generate SDL-like messages for the internal communication.

Event detection can be performed either actively, semi-actively or passively:

1. *Active waiting.* The program runs in a loop where it continuously monitors the state of a variable to detect whether an event (a change) has occurred. This mode of waiting consumes all the computing capacity and prevents other processing from taking place. It is only acceptable if the computer has nothing else to do or the waiting times are very short. An example:

```
DO FOREVER
BEGIN
  newstate := input(channel);
  IF newstate NEQ laststate
    THEN process_event;
  laststate := newstate;
END;
```

2. *Semi-active waiting.* The program is periodically activated to read the current value and detect events. Between each activation, other processing may take place. An example:

```
DO FOREVER
BEGIN
  newstate := input(channel);
  IF newstate NEQ laststate
    THEN process_event;
  laststate := newstate;
  DO "something_else";
END;
```

In this case, "something_else" must not take so much time that we cannot be sure to detect all events. A normal way to ensure this is by simply suspending the process for a period of time:

```
DO FOREVER
BEGIN
  newstate := input(channel);
  IF newstate NEQ laststate
    THEN process_event;
  laststate := newstate;
  wait(suspend, time);
END;
```

3. *Passive waiting.* The program is suspended and not activated before an event has occurred. In this case the event detection is performed by an external hardware unit, which generates an interrupt to the computer. An example:

```
DO FOREVER
BEGIN
  waitint(channelevent, max_time);
  process_event;
END;
```

In all the examples above, there is a possibility that input events may be lost if the time needed to process an event is too long. If the minimum time between events is t_A and the time to process an event is t_R then, t_R should be less than t_A.

In many cases this can not be guaranteed. In order to detect all new events, it may therefore be necessary to interrupt the processing of already detected events. This means that event detection must be performed with pre-emptive priority over event processing.

This can be achieved with our operating system by performing event detection and event processing in different software processes as illustrated in Figure 10.6.

Interrupts are the basic means to provide pre-emptive priority and to enable passive waiting on external events. But the interrupts introduce a non-deterministic execution order into a software system. The operations of the interrupted and the interrupting software units can be interleaved in almost any order, which makes the conditions between these units similar to the conditions between truly parallel units. Consequently, synchronisation is necessary on internal interactions between concurrent software units. This has to be a buffered, asynchronous scheme in the cases where events (for short periods) may be produced faster than they are consumed.

The concurrency and priority needed to serve input–output interfaces therefore determines the degree of concurrency needed inside the software system. On the other hand, it is desirable to separate the problems of the physical interface from the problems of the application. One would like to implement SDL processes internally in a manner that is independent of the physical signal transfer across the input–output interface.

Because of the priorities and speed needed to meet real time and performance requirements, input–output must often be implemented by separate software processes in the way illustrated in Figure 10.6.

The input process, *IN* in Figure 10.6, is in charge of the actual input of data. It waits passively on input events by performing a *waitint* operation on the interrupt semaphore, *II*. When an input event occurs, the interrupt will activate the interrupt routine, *Inhandler*, which will signal the interrupt by performing a *sendint* operation on *II*. When this occurs, the *IN* process will be activated as soon as its priority permits. It will then input the data and put the information into a message buffer which is sent to the *Application* by performing a *send* operation on *IS*. Due to the buffer capacity of the general semaphore, the *IN* process may produce several input messages while the *Application* is busy processing.

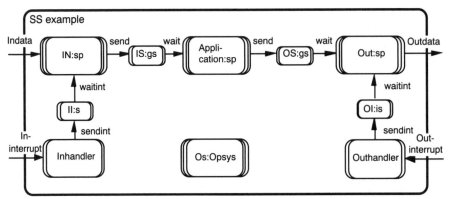

Figure 10.6   *Input–output and application in separate software processes. In this figure the handling of free message buffers has been omitted (see Figures 10.9 and 10.10.)*

Towards the output side, the *Application* can generate output messages independently of the speed of the output channel due to the buffering performed by the output semaphore *OS*. The output process, *Out*, will wait for output interrupts and for each interrupt it will output a new set of output data to the channel. It will fetch new output data by performing *wait* operations on the output semaphore, *OS*.

The scheme outlined above serves to hide the inside of the input–output interface from the application part. All time-critical operations are performed with high priority by the input–output processes. The *Application* process simply waits for inputs at the input semaphore and sends outputs to the output semaphore. It may process inputs and produce outputs at its own rate without considering the input–output timing problems.

High priority is normally needed on input–output interactions in order to:

- ensure that all external events are detected;
- make efficient use of slow input–output channels;
- reduce response times.

S-rule: input–output layering
Try to hide the physical details of input–output in separate software modules that handle the physical layer and provide an SDL-like signal transfer service to the application software.

S-rule: input–output processes
When input–output modules are time-critical or need to perform event detection or need to wait, they should be implemented in software processes that may be scheduled independently from the application software.

S-rule: max waiting time

Always specify a max waiting time when waiting on external events in order to avoid infinite waiting in error situations. This applies to the input–output modules as well as SDL processes.

10.3.2 Procedure calls

Procedure calls provide the most straightforward way of communication among software modules. They are supported by all programming languages and can be used to implement SDL signals directly. Each signal type may be represented as a procedure belonging to the receiving process. The signal *Code(cardid, pin)*, for instance, can be implemented by the procedure CODE(CARDID, PIN). This implies that the receiving SDL process is implemented with one procedure for each input signal.

As an example, consider the three SDL processes P1, P2, P3 represented in Figure 10.7.

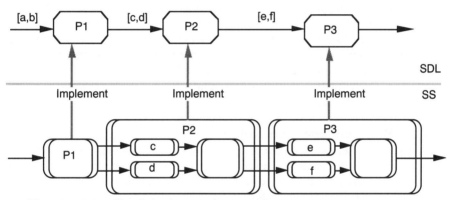

Figure 10.7 *Signals implemented as procedures*

For each process, there may be one procedure for each input signal or there may be one common procedure with the signal type encoded as a parameter. In either case, the activation of processes will follow the procedure calls. When a signal is sent, the receiver will take pre-emptive priority over the sender and finish its transitions before control is returned to the sender.

Procedure calls can be seen as a special case of synchronous communication, where the scheduling is such that the receiver takes pre-emptive priority over the sender. This puts a rather severe restriction on the use of SDL.

If this solution is to work, the following conditions must hold:

1. The SDL (sub) system must behave like a procedure call tree.
2. Only one process, the input process at the root of the tree, may wait to receive signals from the environment or perform time measurements, unless the waiting time is negligible.

3.   For each signal sent down the tree, not more than one reply signal is returned to the sender (implemented as a procedure return value).

4.   There is sufficient time between each external input signal to process all signals and outputs that follow from it and to return to the input process. Consequently, there is no need to give pre-emptive priority to the input process.

Due to these restrictions, this simple and fast solution will not work in all cases. In general, SDL communication needs a more general and flexible scheme than procedure calls provide. Therefore, procedure calls are rarely suitable for an entire SDL system. But the conditions may hold for a limited part of a system. This may help to speed up communication in time-critical parts where the conditions hold.

We may now ask if procedure calls may be used within the *AccessControl* system? We may start with the *PanelControl* and the *LsControl* processes (see Chapters 4 and 5). These parts of the SDL system will behave like a procedure call tree with the *PanelControl* as the input process, so the first condition holds. Only the input process waits to receive inputs from the environment, but the *LsControl* performs time measurement. Therefore, the second condition does not hold. The third condition seems to hold, but the fourth may be critical. Responses from *LsControl* to the *PanelControl* depend on responses from the *Validation* process. Since this will take some time, the *PanelControl* may have problems at the input side. In conclusion, we cannot use procedure calls for this system.

10.3.3   Buffered communication

In the general case, we must separate activation from communication. To obtain this, the communicated values must be passed through shared data records, called buffers and the activation through control programs that schedule the activation. Therefore, as soon as we move away from direct procedure calls, the notion of scheduling is introduced.

The simplest case of buffered communication applies a single buffer where one value may be stored. Each time the producer puts a new value into the buffer, the receiver must read the value. The producer and consumer, therefore, must alternate. But, in contrast to the direct procedure call, the consumer need not have pre-emptive priority. It is possible to delay activation of the receiver until the producer has finished its task, as long as it is activated before the next value is entered into the buffer.

When the buffer capacity increases, the sender and receiver need not alternate strictly any more. The sender may produce several signals before the receiver is activated. Buffered communication with sufficient buffer capacity is therefore a very general and flexible solution.

The drawback with buffered communication is that it is slower, in most cases, than direct procedure calls and that it is not supported by many programming languages. One therefore has to acquire the additional software needed to support buffered communication and to have computing resources for the additional processing.

A tree-structured design where all communication passes up and down through a procedure hierarchy will normally use a form of buffered communication, as indicated in Figure 10.8.

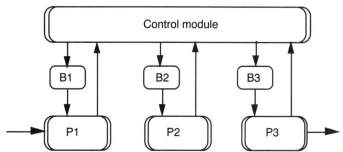

Figure 10.8 *Tree-structured software with a control module that takes care of buffered communication and scheduling. For each process, P1, P2 and P3, there is an input buffer B1, B2 and B3.*

In the simplest case, the return values from one procedure are immediately passed on to the next procedure to be called. But since the communication follows the procedure hierarchy and is passed through the control module, it is possible for this module to perform more elaborate buffering and scheduling. This structure is more general and flexible than the direct procedure call solution and is therefore recommended in the traditional design methods for sequential programs (see for instance Pressman, 1982 and Yourdon, 1989).

If this solution is to work the following condition must hold:

- The timing requirements must be such that there is no need to give pre-emptive priority to any of the processes.

The basically sequential organisation depicted in Figure 10.8 can therefore be used where there is no need for pre-emptive priority. If you try to use it where pre-emption is necessary, the control module will become more and more like an operating system that supports concurrent processes.

In those cases, one should prefer a real time operating system that schedules concurrent processes according to priority and supports buffered communication. This will provide the easiest and most general way to implement the concurrency of SDL definitions. Such an operating system was described briefly in Section 10.2.2.

SDL-like communication is easily accomplished by sending message buffers through a queue. The general semaphores of our operating system may be used for this purpose (see Figure 10.9).

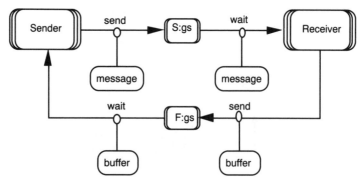

Figure 10.9 *Communication by message buffers. Free buffers are fetched from the free-pool semaphore, F, filled with information, passed through the signal semaphore, S and finally returned to F.*

The communication scheme depicted in Figure 10.9 uses the general semaphores introduced in Section 10.2.2. SDL signals are encoded in buffers and passed as messages through semaphore *S*. Free buffers are managed by another semaphore, *F*. The scheme is quite general and has been used to implement many real time systems specified with SDL. Two aspects need consideration:

1. *Load control.* The circulating buffers provide an opportunity to perform a simple form of load control. In overload situations, the message queue between the sender and the receiver will grow until all free buffers are used. This prevents the sender from generating more messages before the receiver has managed to process some of the messages already in the queue. By careful dimensioning of the free-pools, one can control the internal load in a software system.

2. *Deadlock possibilities.* When several processes compete for the same resources, deadlock may be possible. Consider an overload situation where the free-pool in Figure 10.9 is empty. If the receiver now needs an additional buffer from the free-pool, the system may deadlock with both processes waiting for an empty buffer. One should therefore prefer to use separate free-pools to avoid this problem.

Figure 10.10 illustrates how free-pools may be added to the structure shown in Figure 10.6.

S-rule: free-pool limits
Limit the size (the number of free buffers) of free-pools where it helps to control the internal load in a system, in particular at the input side.

S-rule: separate free-pools
Use a separate message buffer free-pool for each consumer of message buffers.

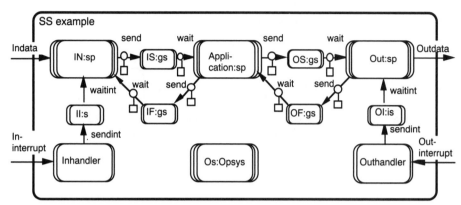

Figure 10.10 *Using separate free-pools*

As explained in Chapter 9 there are two categories of information one wants to communicate: state values and event sequences and two corresponding categories of signals: continuous signals and signal units.

A single buffer, i.e. a shared variable, is the most direct way to convey continuous signals. The producer may set the value when it should be changed and the user may read it when needed (see Figure 10.11). Reading a current value can only be done when the user is active and executes a read operation. There should be no waiting involved, because the user wants to know the value at the reading instant.

Figure 10.11 *Continuous value communication through a shared variable*

In case the producer and user are concurrent processes, the write and read operations must be mutually exclusive. This may be achieved in several ways:

1. Ensuring that the read and write operations are atomic with respect to each other:
    (a) use primitive instructions;
    (b) turn off interrupts;
    (c) schedule such that the sender and receiver never interrupt each other.
2. Controlling the access to the shared variable by means of a resource allocator. The producer and the receiver must ask the allocator to get access before they start an operation on the shared variable and return the access immediately after

the operation is finished. This can be achieved by means of the general semaphore and *wait* and *send* operations as illustrated in Figure 10.12.

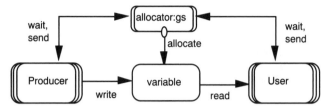

Figure **10.12** *Process communication through a shared variable controlled by a resource allocator*

Corresponding pseudo-code for the producer and user may be:

```
producer:
   . . . .
   wait(allocator, indefinite);
   write(variable, value);
   send(allocator);
   . . .
user:
   . . . .
   wait(allocator, indefinite);
   input := read(variable);
   send(allocator);
   . . .
```

10.3.4   Routing

When an SDL process sends a signal, it must somehow be routed to the receiver. SDL signals identify their sender and receiver by PId values and the signals are routed by the blocks on the basis of *who* the receiver is, not *where* it is, except when the route is specified by the VIA-clause. At the abstract level this is sufficient, but in the realisation we must know the physical location of the receiver in order to route the signal correctly from the sending to the receiving process.

The physical process location is determined by the physical computer, the software process inside the computer and possibly the local address inside the software process.

It should, however, be a goal to keep the software as independent as possible of the physical location of processes. A process should know as little as possible about the path a signal is routed through to get to a destination. Ideally it should only know *who* the receiver is, not *where* it is.

To some extent this is solved by the concept of PId variables. The data structure of a process contains PId variables representing the processes it can send signals to. These variables are bound either at process creation time or dynamically during process behaviour. Thanks to the concept of abstract data types in SDL, the actual representation of PId values can be hidden from the process code.

But the implementation of the PId data type will depend on how PId values are represented. How the PId values are generated and represented is not defined in SDL. This is left to the designer to decide. One of the major design questions is therefore how PId values shall be represented and allocated.

One common solution is to represent PId values (signal addresses) by an identifier for the process type and another for the process individual. But this will be a logical and not a physical address. We will therefore need some support to map the logical addresses into physical locations.

In Figure 9.9 there is a separate software block, called message routing, that performs the actual routing on the software process level. Its purpose is to hide the physical addresses from the application processes, allowing messages to be routed on the basis of logical destination addresses. Hence, an SDL process needs not know where other processes are located. It is sufficient to know their logical identifiers. Moreover, the implementation of the PId data type is independent of the physical address structure. The routing system will use the logical identifier and an address map to select a semaphore through which the message is sent. Thus, knowledge of physical routing is centralised to the address map.

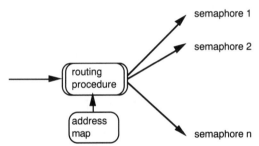

Figure 10.13 *The routing procedure uses an address map telling which logical process identifiers are reached through which semaphores.*

If there is no need to hide the physical addresses, a separate routing system is not needed.

One advantage of this approach is that it is simple to reroute messages in cases of on-line (or off-line) system extension and restructuring.

10.4   Implementing the SDL processes

10.4.1   Sequential behaviour

In this section we first consider the implementation of extended finite state machines (EFSMs) in general. Thereafter we look at the special features of SDL, i.e. services, procedures, decisions and dynamic process creation.

The FSM behaviour of SDL processes may be implemented in many ways. One is to encode the control part directly as IF-THEN-ELSE expressions or CASE expressions in a programming language. Another is to encode the control part in state transition tables. In between those there is a whole range of intermediate solutions.

Direct code implementation of finite state machines

In this approach we may distinguish between two ways to represent the state:

1.   by a position in the program text;
2.   by a value stored in a variable.

In the first case the program will be state-oriented. In the second case it will be action-oriented. In Chapters 2 and 8 we contended that for the human reader, a state-oriented form is preferable to an action-oriented form. Therefore, state orientation is essential in an abstract functional design where human understanding and analysis is the first issue. In the implementation, however, other considerations such as efficiency in time and space may be more important. Given that the functionality is well-defined in the functional design (using SDL), it may be acceptable to trade some readability in the programs against higher efficiency. Of course, readability is still important and should be emphasised, but if a simple and clear mapping from the functional design to the code can be defined, an action-oriented style may be acceptable.

State-oriented. Let us first consider the state-oriented style. The principle is to express the state transition diagram directly in the programming language. A typical implementation goes like this:

```
begin
  state_1: wait(input);
    case input of
        signal_a: call Action_1; goto state_3;
        signal_b: call Action_2; goto state_5;
        else:     call Action_3; goto state_1;
      end case;
  state_2: wait(input);
      case input of
        signal_c: ...
  ....
```

```
end
```

Be a bit careful with *case* statements if time is critical; some compilers will produce slow and/or voluminous code.

A state transition diagram is not normally structured in a manner that will map directly to a "structured program". A direct mapping will normally lead to a program containing *goto* statements as indicated above. Since the state transition diagram is a clear definition of the behaviour, this is not a problem. One should not try to make the program *goto*-less, because that would lead to a more complex program with a less obvious mapping to the specification. One should therefore use *goto* to get to the next state and be careful to ensure that the program faithfully implements the specification.

If decisions can affect the next state, the necessary *goto state_n* statements must be added to the *Action* procedures above. In the state-oriented style, SDL procedures may be supported in a straightforward manner by using procedures in the programming language.

Since the state is represented by the program position, this technique implies that each SDL process is implemented as a separate software process, e.g. a CHILL process. This may be too space-consuming if the number of processes is high.

Action-oriented. In the action-oriented style, the state is stored in a variable. This will typically lead to a program that waits for input in only one place:

```
repeat forever
begin
  wait(input);
  case state of
     state_1:
        case input of
           signal_a: call Action_1; state:= state_3;
           signal_b: call Action_2; state:= state_5;
           else:     call Action_3; state:= state_1;
        end case;
     state_2:
        case input of
           signal_c: ...
        ....
  end case;
end;
```

If decisions may change the next state, the next state assignment must be moved inside the `Action` procedures above. SDL procedures can easily be supported here too if one can accept waiting for input inside the procedures.

This approach may be extended to handle many SDL processes simply by introducing an array of states indexed by the process identifier. Since each instance is represented simply by an element in the state array, this is a space-efficient solution. It is also quite time-efficient. By putting process instances together in one software process, the internal communication between them can be quick if it is done locally, instead of invoking the support of the operating system. In this way the synchronisation and context switching between software processes is avoided.

The disadvantage of this solution is that pre-emptive priority among the process instances cannot be supported. Once a signal is received and a transition is started, the active process instance blocks all the other instances for the duration of the *Action* procedure. Thus, the *Action* procedures should not take too long to execute and they should not involve waiting on external events.

Another disadvantage is that the implementation of general SDL procedures becomes more difficult. The problem is to keep track of return addresses when the SDL procedures contain states. If the program is shared between many process instances, this has to be handled explicitly using a stack of return addresses.

The state-oriented style cannot be easily combined with communication by means of procedure calls (Section 10.3.2.). In the case of communication by procedure calls, the state has to be stored in a variable. It is necessary to use an action-oriented style with a procedure corresponding to each input signal to the process. Each procedure must first test on the state and then perform the corresponding transition.

Table-driven implementation of finite state machines

When SDL is translated into statements in a programming language, the same two options exist as when the programming language is translated to machine code. One can either compile to directly executable machine code or translate to a form that can be interpreted by a run-time support system.

Thus, one can either map SDL directly to executable code or to interpretable code for a virtual SDL machine running on top of the target computer. Since the process model of SDL is based on the extended finite state machine (EFSM) model, this virtual machine can be based on the general properties of EFSMs.

Such machines are well-suited for table-driven implementation. Their behaviour may be conveniently defined in a state transition table (see Figure 10.14) which is equivalent to the graphical form used in state transition diagrams.

signal/ state	signal 1	signal 2
state 1	state 2/ action 1	state 3/ action 3
state 2	state 3/ action 5	state 1/ action 2
state 3	state2/ action 3	state 1/ action 2

Figure   10.14 *A state transition table*

Such a table can be implemented by a two-dimensional array indexed by the current state and the input signal, where each element specifies a next state and an action to be taken for each combination of current state and input. One may easily design a general program that uses such an array to determine the next state and the action, given a current state and an input signal. This is the general idea behind table-driven implementation of FSMs.

Normally the table will contain many open cells because one does not expect all input signals to arrive in all states. A straightforward implementation as an array may therefore be too space-consuming. It is usually better to implement the table in a more space-efficient way. Some searching must then be done in order to access the proper element.

One way to design table-driven implementation of an extended finite state machine is outlined by the software structure diagram in Figure 10.15. It contains a general program called *FSM-Support* which interprets a data structure, *ST-Table*, representing the state transition table of the finite state machines it implements.

The software described in Figure 10.15 provides a concurrent implementation platform for processes described as extended finite state machines. Scheduling is performed on the basis of input messages, called *Signals*. Each *Signal* contains an *Address* that identifies the receiver process instance. The *FSM-Support* program will use the *Address* to activate the process instance by selecting first the appropriate *Process Type* and then the *Process Instance* record. The *Process Instance* record holds the current *State* and the optional *Data* objects an extended finite state machine may have in addition to the state (i.e. the extension of the pure FSM).

The input *Signal* carries a *Signalname*, which is used to select a transition. For each input *Signal*, the addressed SDL process instance is allowed to perform one transition.

In the ST-*Table* each state is represented by a *State Record* that contains a (variable) number of *Transition* records, one for each transition from the state (see Figure 10.16). Each *Transition* record specifies the input *Signalname* that may cause the transition, the corresponding *Action* and the *next:State* (see the example in Figure 10.17).

The *FSM-Support* program will wait for input *Signals* and respond to the *Signals* in the order in which they arrive. For each *Signal* it will access the *State-Record* (Figure 10.16) in the *ST-Table* referred to by the (current) *State* of the *Process Instance* and search there for a *Transition* record having the same *Signalname* as the input *Signal*.

If a *Transition* record with the same *Signalname* is found, this transition is selected. If not, the transition for unspecified reception is selected. This transition is identified with an asterisk (*) as *Signalname*. The *FSM-Support* will then call the *Action* procedure referenced in the selected transition, and, finally, assign the *next:State* value to the *State* of the *Process Instance*. This ends the transition and the *FSM-Support* will wait for a new input *Signal*.

When a new *Signal* addressed to the same process instance arrives, the next transition will be performed in the same manner, but it will be selected according to the new *State* value.

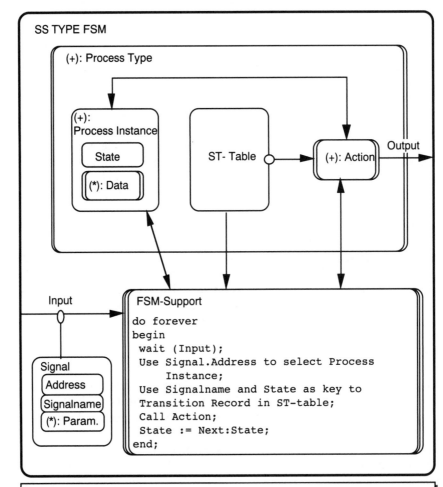

The Process Type block represents software for an SDL process type. The Process Instance block holds the variables of an SDL process instance.
The Signal is the input signal. The Address is the receiver process identification (Pld implementation).

Figure   10.15 *Table-driven implementation of finite state machines.*

Actions may, in principle, either be encoded as interpreted code or as directly executable code in the programming language. We shall use the latter approach here. Hence, interpretation is limited to the state transition table which represents the control part. The action part is then performed by calling the *Action* procedure referred to in the *Transition* record.

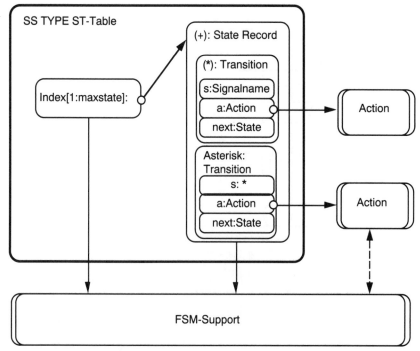

Figure 10.16 *ST-Table definition.*

Normally a number of distinct operations will be carried out during a transition. In general, the operations that an SDL process may perform are as follows:

1. sending signals to other processes or external equipment;
2. performing operations on local data;
3. setting and resetting timers.

The action procedures perform all these operations. Each operation will normally be implemented as a procedure. Hence, the action procedure mainly consists of procedure calls to more primitive operation procedures. In addition, there may be simple assignments and expressions corresponding to the data operations specified, e.g.:

```
PROCEDURE action-1
BEGIN
   send-signal(ok, panel);
   send-signal(open, door);
   starttimer(now+10, t1, self);
   pin:=pin*10+d;
END;
```

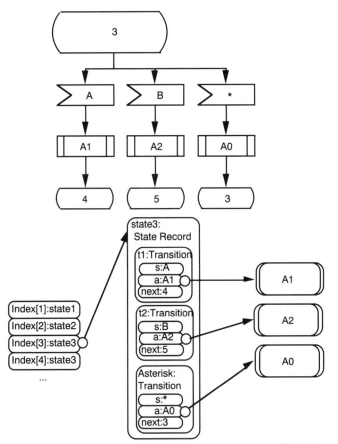

Figure **10.17** *Example showing how one state is encoded in ST- Tables.*

It can be seen that the operation procedures may be designed to constitute a language level which is very close to the SDL description (This is not particular to the table-driven approach, however. Direct code implementations may use a similar approach to the action code.) This simplifies the effort needed to generate and read action code.

What are the limitations of the approach exemplified by *FSM* (the type *FSM* is described in Figure 10.15)? Since other processes are blocked during a transition, the *Actions* should not wait on external events or perform very time-consuming operations. For the same reason, SDL processes implemented on the same instance of *FSM* should have equal priority (since they cannot interrupt each other.) If pre-emptive priority is needed, it can be achieved by using several instances of *FSM* which are scheduled with different priority by the operating system.

A disadvantage is the time overhead needed to search for transition records. To reduce this overhead one can arrange the records in the order of the most frequent signals. One may alternatively encode the state transition table as a two-dimensional array where the state and the input signal are used as indexes. This will give fast access, but may be too space-consuming.

When all aspects of an application are taken into consideration it often turns out that the overhead is negligible. When implementing several SDL processes on one software process like *FSM*, there may even be a net gain compared to other solutions due to a saved communication overhead. *Signals* passed between processes implemented on the same instance of *FSM*, may be given priority over external messages by sending such messages through a queue internal to the *FSM-Support* program. This will speed up internal communication since one avoids external synchronisation and calls to the operating system (*wait* and *send* operations). The *FSM-Support* program is a suitable candidate for speed optimisation, if need be.

The reader may try to implement *FSM* as an exercise. The *FSM-support* program is not large, but writing it will give a useful programming experience and help to understand how table-driven implementations work.

The table-driven solution exemplified by *FSM*, has several virtues:

1. *It facilitates implementation and documentation.* The coding of control structures, which is normally difficult and error prone, is done easily and reliably in the state transition table. The mapping from the SDL description to the code is easy to follow. If the code is reasonably well-structured and commented, the SDL process graph together with the source code listing may be sufficient documentation.

2. *It enhances modularity and eases maintenance.* The support module (*FSM*) itself can be instantiated in many different applications. Thus, it is a highly reusable module. When the SDL processes are implemented in a standard way they too become more easy to reuse in new applications. Modifications are easy to make without side-effects. This is largely due to the clear separation between action code and control structures. Normal practice is to modify the process graph (*ST-Table*) first and then to add the action procedures that are needed.

3. *It is reliable.* The standard support program will be thoroughly tested in many applications and is therefore likely to be very reliable. The application is also likely to be reliable because it is derived from a presumably correct, functional design in a direct way that tends to introduce few implementation errors.

4. *It is robust.* Robustness is partly due to the message communication mechanism and partly due to the table-driven approach. When signals are passed as messages, the receiver may always check the input before it is used. Thus, the support program (*FSM-Support*) may check incoming messages for consistency before they are accepted. The table-driven approach is a robust way to encode control structures because the asterisk transition ensures that all non-expected inputs will be handled in a proper way.

5. *It supports testing.* The support module (*FSM*) may be implemented in a test version that allows the tester to simulate input messages and to trace the transition actions and output messages that are generated. Thus, an SDL

process may be conveniently tested on a host computer in an environment that looks exactly like the real target environment to the process itself (see Chapter 12).

Many projects have experienced that this kind of implementation technique helps to use the SDL process graphs as the primary documentation and the source code as secondary documentation which are consulted only when errors have to be debugged. Thus, the approach stimulates people to keep the functional design updated.

Although we approached this implementation technique from functional designs expressed using SDL, it is by no means particular for SDL. It is useful whenever one needs a dispatcher that selects actions on the basis of input events. If we specify with data flow diagrams, for instance, it can be used to implement so-called transaction centres (Pressman, 1982). (If we compare with the usual data flow design, the *FSM-Support* takes the place of the main control program.)

In summary, the implementation of SDL processes can benefit from a layer of SDL support functions. We will refer to this as an SDL run-time support system, RTS, in the following. The *FSM* we have described above illustrates one way to provide an RTS. A slightly different way will be described in Chapter 11. In addition to the functionality we have described so far, an RTS will normally embody a library of procedures supporting SDL concepts like signal sending, timer operations and built-in data types. It will also provide support for testing (see Chapter 12).

10.4.2   Implementation of other SDL features

SDL has some features which are different from the ordinary, extended finite state machines. Examples are decisions, save, procedures, services and dynamic process creation. We shall see that these may all be implemented on top of the FSM implementations described so far.

Decisions

Decisions in the SDL specification can be encoded as states when the table-driven approach is used. This is not strictly necessary, but it makes the action procedures independent of particular states.

When there is a decision that affects the next state, treat it as if it was a state. Do the question operation before the decision "state" is entered and send the answer as an input signal to be received in the decision "state". In that manner, the branching on internal values and external signals is treated similarly. In order to speed up the decision making and to finish decisions before new inputs, decision signals should be given priority over external signals. When a decision signal has been issued, the corresponding transition should be performed immediately. When a transition contains a decision that does not affect the next state, it should be encoded as an internal decision in the procedure of the transition action.

Save

The save mechanism implies that each process has a logical queue of saved signals. This queue may be implemented as part of the process data. A save symbol may then be encoded as a transition to the current state (next state := current state), where the action is to put the signal in the save queue. Whenever a process makes a transition to a new state, the signals in the save queue are moved back to the front of the input queue and treated as normal input signals. Hence, save may be implemented by adding a save queue to the data of each process and by moving input from this queue to the front of the normal input queue at the end of each transition to a new state. Since this may be rather time-consuming, save should be avoided in time-critical applications.

The idea of a save queue is to postpone some signals until it is time to treat them. This can be implemented in other ways too, for instance, using separate signal queues. The reader should think over the purpose of using save before implementation takes place and look for solutions that avoid time-consuming activities.

SDL procedures

Procedures in SDL may contain states. In those cases, the procedure introduces a level structure into the process graphs. This is easily implemented in the direct code approach when SDL procedures can be directly mapped to programming language procedures.

But in the cases where several SDL process instances are mapped on one software process instance this is not possible. In order to implement this case, each process will need a stack to store states, action addresses and data local to the procedures. When a procedure is called, the current context (state, action address and data) is pushed onto the stack and the procedure is entered. Upon return, the opposite operation takes place. This is simpler to implement if procedure calls always occur at the end of a transition, because the return will be to a state and not to an arbitrary action address.

Services

Services in SDL are basically finite state machines that execute in quasi-parallel and use priority signals to communicate among each other. They are easily implemented within one software process using either the table-driven or the direct code approach. In order to identify the service to receive a given input signal, the signal name may have to be considered in addition to the PId.

Dynamic process creation

In the case when there is one software process instance per SDL process instance, dynamic process creation requires the support of the operating system. Within one software process, dynamic process creation amounts to the allocation and initialisation of a record from free memory that can store the process instance data.

Inheritance

Inheritance and specialisation can be handled in different ways. One way is to perform a translation to an SDL description without inheritance before the system is implemented. In that way the implementation may use any of the principles described above.

Another way is to use implementations that support inheritance. This can be achieved using the direct code approach in combination with an object-oriented programming language such as C++. This will be outlined in Chapter 11.

Inheritance can also be supported using the table-driven approach. In order to specialise a process it is necessary to use data structures that will support the additions and replacements needed when a process type is specialised.

10.4.3 Data

Now we come to the non-trivial problem of implementing SDL data. SDL data has three aspects (see Chapter 5):

1. the abstract data types, defined in terms of operations and axioms;
2. instantiation of the data types as SDL process variables;
3. instantiation of the operations on variables, which is specified in the transitions of SDL process graphs.

In SDL descriptions, abstract data types help to focus on functionality and to remove irrelevant details of the implementation while in the software implementation, the notion of abstract data types helps to increase modularity and reuse. In the implementation the main benefits are *encapsulation* and *information hiding* (Parnas, 1972).

The idea is to encapsulate data in modules that offer a set of well-defined operations to the environment. This means that data structures cannot be accessed directly, but only by invoking the operations. The operations are normally implemented as procedures. In this way the internal data structures are hidden from the environment.

The instantiation of operations specified in the SDL process graphs will therefore be implemented by calls to the operation procedures. This means that the transition actions are independent of the particular data structure used to implement the data types.

Even if data is informally defined at the SDL level, the notion of abstract data types is useful because it helps to achieve independence and modularity.

S-rule: abstract data types as software modules
Encapsulate data in modules that offer a set of well-defined operations (procedures) to the environment.

The first step in software design for an abstract data type is to define the operation interface. Consider as an example the SDL data type *AccessCode*:

```
NEWTYPE AccessCode
OPERATORS
  Make : Integer, Integer -> AccessCode;
  PardidModify : AccessCode, Integer -> AccessCode;
  PinModify : AccessCode, Integer -> AccessCode;
```

```
    CardidExtract : AccessCode -> Integer ;
    PinExtract : AccessCode -> Integer ;
AXIOMS
/* we have omitted them here */
ENDNEWTYPE AccessCode;
```

The corresponding operation interface in terms of procedure definition heads may be:

```
MAKE(integer, Integer) -> AccessCode
CARDIDMODIFY(AccessCode, Integer) -> AccessCode
PINMODIFY(AccessCode, Integer) -> AccessCode
CARDIDEXTRACT(AccessCode) -> Integer
PINEXTRACT(AccessCode) -> Integer
```

The next step is to choose an appropriate data structure. This choice is important since it will have a major influence on the algorithms used to implement the operations and hence influence the performance. The choice will depend on non-functional design constraints. Several implementations corresponding to different design constraints are feasible, all reachable through identical operation interfaces. This is the advantage of encapsulation.

In the formal SDL definition, the meanings of the operations are defined either by means of axioms or by operational operator definitions. There is as yet no general and straightforward way to turn an axiomatic definition into an efficient implementation. Consequently, if axioms are used, we have to be pragmatic about the design of data structures and algorithms.

First, we must consider alternative data structures and select one that meets the performance requirements. Next, we design a procedure corresponding to each operation.

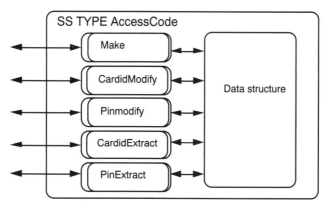

Figure 10.18 *The implementation of an abstract data type is a module that encapsulates the data structure behind a set of operation procedures.*

The design approach of this example has been to define a procedure for each operation of the abstract data type. Alternatively, one might consider using a macro or even a simple statement, if the data type is directly supported in the programming language. This will be the case for many of the built-in data types of SDL. In real time systems, many data structures and algorithms are simple and supported by the built-in types.

In the complex cases, more effort will be needed. For data types with complex data structures, it is useful to represent the logical data structure in conceptual data models as part of functional requirements or functional design. In our example, an entity relationship model of the validation database could be useful.

The next step would then be to map the conceptual model into SDL data. Since the operation interface of data objects hides the internal data structure from the environment, a database management system may be used without the environment knowing it. In fact, the notion of abstract data types can be successfully used for very elaborate data structures.

Abstract data types are supported by SDL, but the notion is not particular for SDL. In fact, the above guidelines will be useful in any software design, regardless of specification method. They help to decompose a design into modules with low coupling and high cohesion.

10.5   Overall software design

10.5.1   General approach

In this chapter and the previous one we have looked at some fragmented problems and solutions concerning the design of software implementations. In this section we shall present an overall approach to software design.

The input information to software design are:

1.   the functional design;
2.   the architectural hardware design;
3.   the design constraints.

In the functional design we define the functional interfaces and the functionality of the software system. From the hardware design we know the physical interfaces. From the design constraints we know time and performance restrictions.

The first step is to look at the internal and the external communication and design a solution for each interface. (Recall the following S-rule: *start software design by deciding on communication mechanisms for all external and internal interfaces.*)

On one hand we have the problems of the physical interfaces and the functional communication they carry, on the other hand, we have the internal communication needs. These two aspect may be studied separately to begin with:

- Look at the physical interfaces and identify software modules that can take care of the physical layer, i.e. synchronisation, waiting, event detection, timing, format conversion. For each module, indicate whether it should be a concurrent software process or can be performed in sequence with other modules. If it is a separate process, define its priority with respect to other processes and how it may communicate towards the application.
- Look at the internal interfaces and choose a suitable communication mechanism for each. Consider the time needed to process a signal in relation to the arrival interval between signals. May synchronous communication (by procedure calls) be used or is buffered communication necessary? Is pre-emptive scheduling required?

The next step is to study the application part, i.e. the implementation of SDL processes:

- Look at the SDL (sub)system and allocate SDL processes to software processes. What kind of priority is needed among the application processes? Is processing speed-critical or is memory size more important? Will dynamic process creation be needed? Identify each software module in the application part and which part of the SDL system it implements. For each module, indicate whether it should be a software process or a procedure block.
- Link the modules indicated up to this point together. Define the communication links between the input–output part and the application part, as well as the internal links within the application part. Consider the addressing scheme and the use of a routing module.

The next step is to consider the need for an operating system and other support software:

- Consider the needs for priority scheduling, timing and synchronisation. From this, decide on the functionality needed from an operating system. Take the need for testing support into the consideration (see Chapter 12).

Finally, consider the implementation technique to use for each SDL process: direct code or table-driven code.

These considerations will lead to an overall software structure, such as the one shown in Figure 10.20.

At this point we should take another look at the estimated mean execution times per transition, t_P, (see Section 9.4.2). The estimates may now be improved and we may also estimate the time needed to transfer signals across the input–output interface. From these figures we may recalculate the mean peak load of the computer. If this figure is above the load limit, we must reconsider the design, e.g.:

- allocate SDL processes differently to computers;

- use a faster computer;
- optimise the software for high execution speed.

If the load figures look fine, proceed by checking real time constraints against the maximum execution times needed to respond as required. When this too looks fine, proceed with the detailed design of each module and of the support software.

The best way to implement the extended finite state machines defined with SDL depends on the design constraints. If the speed constraints allow, one should use the table-driven implementation. This is a compact, flexible and reliable solution. If processing speed is critical, one should consider using the direct code implementation and implementing signals by procedures.

The data part should be implemented in modules corresponding to abstract data types.

One may implement each SDL process instance in a separate software process instance, but this is necessary only when pre-emptive priority is needed.

Our general guideline is to map the functional design as directly as possible into the software design.

Use the most general and flexible communication scheme, i.e. buffered communication, unless you are certain that direct procedure calls are needed and will work.

Use general support systems whenever possible, to ease the implementation of application functions and to increase reliability.

Use a general operating system that supports concurrent processes and buffered communication except when a simple sequential program structure is obviously sufficient.

S-rule: generality
Preferably use the most general and flexible implementation techniques wherever they satisfy the design constraints, i.e. implement :
- *communication by messages;*
- *SDL processes by FSM-Support;*
- *basic support by a general operating system.*

Optimisation to meet real time constraints may be necessary, but this should be confined as much as possible to modules where it is really needed. All too often time optimisation is allowed to pervade the entire design, leading to a solution that is hard to understand and impossible to modify.

S-rule: optimisation
Confine time-critical functions to modules that can be optimised separately. Do not optimise more than necessary.

S-rule: messages
Prefer to communicate events (and SDL signals) by messages in order to achieve generality and flexibility (and tracability of communication in the system behaviour).

S-rule: shared variables
Use shared variables to communicate continuous signals.

S-rule: ownership of variables
Let all variables and peripheral equipment be controlled (i.e. changed) by one and only one process.

These rules can be applied in all software design, regardless of the functional design method. They apply equally well to data flow-based design as to SDL-based design.

As a final advice, do not fear concurrency, but use it to your advantage. When the functional system is concurrent, as data flow or SDL systems are, a concurrent software structure is the simplest and most modular solution. Software processes that interact by buffered communication provide a message interface to their environment and hide the internal structure. They are therefore relatively independent modules, convenient to handle and easy to integrate and to test.

10.5.2 Example

So what will the software design for the *AccessControl* system look like? Let us design the software system for the *Computer* in a *Local Control Hw* unit (see Figure 9.12).

It has hardware interfaces to a maximum of 10 *Panels* and to an intercomputer channel towards the *Cluster Control Hw*. We need corresponding software modules to handle these interfaces:

- *Keyboards* will produce input events at the human rate of maximum 5 key strokes per second. An interrupt will be generated for each key stroke.
- *Card readers* will produce an input event for each card they read. Interrupt will be generated when a card has been inserted and read.
- *Displays* will receive new text directly without delay. No waiting needed.
- *Door locks* will accept open and close signals without delay. The status of the lock may be input as a continuous value. It takes approximately 100 ms for the lock to open and close. In order to generate the *Opened* and *Closed* signals expected by *LsControl*, we must detect the events by semi-active waiting.
- *Intercomputer channels* will transfer one signal at a time. Interrupts are generated when a new signal arrives and when a signal has been sent. Arrival time between signals is a minimum of 10 ms from the beginning of one signal to the beginning of the next.

The physical interfaces to keyboards, card readers and intercomputer channels are interrupt-driven and need priority over internal processing. We therefore decided to use separate software processes for these functions. The door lock needs event detection by semi-active waiting, so we use a separate software process for the door lock module. The display may be operated directly without any waiting, so this interface module may be a procedure.

The result of these considerations is the software structure depicted in Figure 10.19.

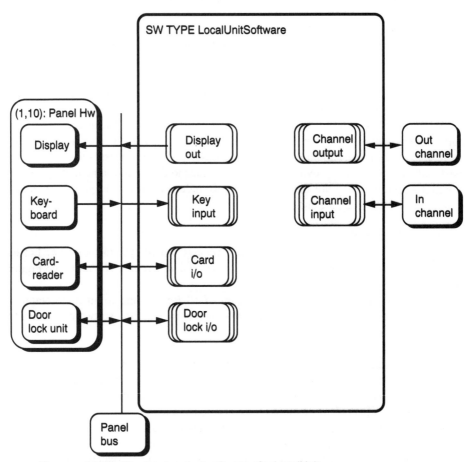

Figure   10.19 *The input–output software of a LocalUnit*

The next step is to decide on the internal communication channels. Due to the synchronisation requirements, we will use asynchronous message communication on internal interfaces, except for the interface to the display module. Since no waiting is involved, we decided to use synchronous communication by procedure calls on that interface.

We now consider the concurrency issue. The design decisions we have reached so far imply that pre-emptive priority will be needed to serve the input–output interface.

Moreover, asynchronous communication will be needed on internal interfaces. Therefore, a general operating system will be used to support concurrency.

What about the application part? There is no need to give any SDL processes pre-emptive priority over other SDL processes. We assume that there will be no load problems and decide to implement all the SDL processes in one software process using an instance of *FSM* (described in Figure 10.15). The result is the software solution outlined in Figure 10.20.

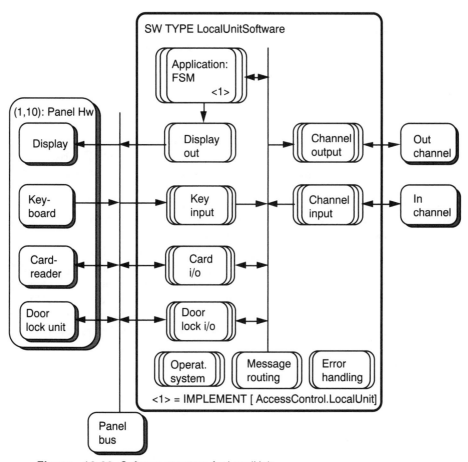

Figure 10.20 *Software structure for LocalUnit*

This software solution can be seen as a specialisation of the general software system depicted in Figure 9.9.

From this overall structure, the design work proceeds with the internal details of each software block in the diagram. Some blocks will be instances of predefined types, e.g.

the *Application* is an instance of *FSM*. For these it is sufficient to define the specialisation, i.e. the the actual configuration of the *Process Type* blocks.

For the application we use a standard mapping into the *ST-Table*, *Process Instance* data and *Actions*. It may therefore be sufficient to refer to the source code for details. One should indicate the implementation chosen for each data type.

The software modules in general should be related to the source code, either by naming convention or by explicit references.

The operating system will most likely be an instance of a predefined type. Its configuration in terms of software processes can be seen from Figure 10.20. When the software blocks are opened, we will see the semaphores and interrupt routines. In addition, priorities must be assigned to each software process.

10.6   Hardware design

In Section 9.4 we discussed the high level design of the hardware architecture. But SDL may also be used for more detailed hardware design.

Hardware, in contrast to software, is fundamentally different from SDL. Hardware is physical. As such it develops errors over time, needs time to perform tasks and is subject to noise.

But there are conceptual similarities between SDL and hardware. Concurrency, for instance, comes naturally with hardware and there is a long tradition for specifying and implementing hardware by means of finite state machines.

There exist hardware description languages, such as VHDL (IEEE 1076, 1987), that resemble programming languages. Therefore, up to a point, hardware design is similar to software design. It is a matter of mapping the SDL definition into a corresponding definition in the hardware description language. This can be achieved by automatic translation tools in the same manner as for software. But the hardware designer is faced with another set of constraints that makes the task different from software design.

10.6.1   Concurrency and time

On the circuit level, hardware components will often operate synchronously and interact synchronously using continuous values. These mechanisms must then be used to implement the asynchronous operation and asynchronous interaction assumed in the SDL system.

Therefore, either the SDL system must be restricted in a way that complies with the hardware mechanisms or the hardware must provide the mechanisms used in SDL.

In principle it is possible to implement most SDL mechanisms in hardware. We can build asynchronous components corresponding to SDL process communicating asynchronously through SDL-like channels.

For technical and economical reasons, however, it will normally not be practical to implement general SDL systems in hardware. Therefore, it is more common to restrict the use of SDL in a way suitable for hardware implementation. This may mean restricting the communication structure such that synchronous communication can be used.

In a synchronous system the clock signal gives a natural time reference. Time measurements can then be implemented by counting clock ticks.

10.6.2 Sequential behaviour

There is no fundamental problem in implementing finite state machines in hardware. In fact, finite state machines were used for hardware design before they were used to design software.

Provided that the use of data is restricted to the data types supported in the hardware description language, there is no fundamental problem in the implementation of tasks and decisions.

Procedures may cause problems. In particular if dynamic data allocation is needed to support them. Therefore, the use of procedures should be restricted.

Dynamic process creation is unfeasible if it means creating a physical unit, but it may be simulated by activating and passivating processes built into the hardware from the beginning.

10.7   Step-wise guidelines to implementation design

10.7.1   Overview

The main steps of implementation design are as follows:

1.   Perform the trade-off between hardware and software.
2.   Define the hardware architecture.
3.   Define the software architecture.
4.   Restructure and refine the SDL specification to a complete SDL description.

After these steps, detailed design and implementation of hardware and software is performed.

Note that these are the main design steps only. In practice, iterations may be needed. After completion of these steps, detailed design and implementation may proceed. While the main design steps rely on high level decisions and are likely to remain the job of a human designer, the detailed design and implementation that follows are candidates for automation.

10.7.2   Step 1: trade-off between hardware and software

Inputs are (1) the SDL specification and (2) the non-functional requirements.
Considerations and rules:

- Physical distribution requirement. Analyse requirements to physical distribution of interfaces and services. Select a physical system structure to support this. Minimise the band width needed over channels covering physical distances.
- Performance. Calculate the mean peak processing loads for each SDL channel, signalroute and process. Allocate processes to computers such that the mean peak load on a single computer does not exceed about 0.3 of its total capacity.
- Real time response. Calculate the response times for time-critical functions and check that requirements will be satisfied. Use priority to ensure fast response. Isolate time-critical parts as much as possible.
- Reliability. Consider the need for redundancy. Add redundant units and restructure the system until requirements can be met.

10.7.3   Step 2: hardware design

The task here is to define the overall (architectural) hardware design. It is based on the division into hardware and software where the main hardware units were identified.

- Describe the overall structure of computers and other hardware units.
- Describe the physical interconnections between the hardware units.
- Describe the signal synchronisation schemes and protocols to be used on the physical interconnections, to the extent they are not already covered in the requirement specification or the functional design.

10.7.4   Step 3: software design

The task of a software designer is to select a structure of software processes that will implement the SDL (sub)system.

Considerations and rules:

- Map the SDL description as directly as possible into the software implementation.
- Look at the physical interfaces and design software modules that can take care of the physical layer, i.e. synchronisation, event detection, timing and format conversion.
- Look at the internal interfaces and choose a suitable communication mechanism for each, i.e. procedure calls, message buffers and continuous values.
- Use the most general and flexible communication scheme for SDL signals, i.e. buffered communication, unless direct procedure calls can do the job.
- Use a general operating system that supports concurrent processes and buffered communication except when a simple sequential program structure is obviously sufficient.
- Select the implementation method for each SDL process. Use general support systems, RTS, whenever possible, to ease the implementation of application functions and to increase reliability.

10.7.5 Restructure and refine the functional design

All functional properties of the implementation should be reflected in the SDL description. This serves to ensure equivalence.

The SDL description should reflect the concrete system structure. This serves to simplify the mapping from the SDL description to the implementation.

CHAPTER 11

Implementation in C++

The objective of this chapter is to carry out an example of an implementation of selected pieces of our *AccessControl* system. In this chapter we concentrate on the implementation of the object-oriented concepts of SDL 92 and we will select the pieces for implementation which were described in Chapter 7.

11.1   Coding principles

Our starting point is an SDL specification which we are reasonably certain corresponds to the user's will and the budget of the requester. Furthermore, we have a description of the architectural and software designs such that the strategy is laid for the actual implementation.

At this stage it is utterly important to maintain the intimate connections between the different descriptions on different implementation levels. Let us have a schematic look at the pieces of software present in the implementation.

Figure 11.1 corresponds to Figures 9.3 and 9.4, but the implementation activity has been expanded. In the following, we shall go through this figure in order to highlight how a successful SDL specification is turned into a successful running system which produces the desired results.

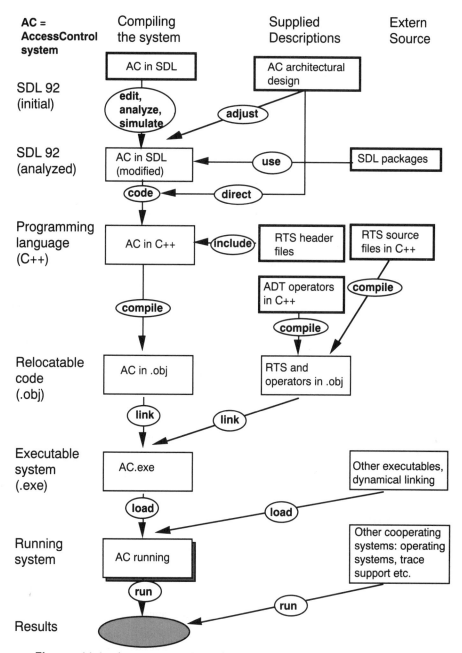

Figure 11.1 *Languages and transformations*

11.1.1 Choosing target language

The ultimate aim is the absolute code running on the target hardware. To generate the executable code, however, we must use an intermediate level programming language. In the future we may go automatically from the SDL specifications all the way down to the running system. For the time being state of the art is to code the SDL system in a programming language such as CHILL, C or C++ even if the code is automatically generated from SDL.

The target language for the implementation may be given by external requirements. We find that defence applications demand the system implemented in Ada, while telecommunication administrations may demand CHILL as the target language. In recent years C has become the favourite choice due to its popularity in general for technical applications and because compilers from C to any hardware are most likely available. Actually several C environments may be available on the same hardware.

The principal questions when choosing a target language are "what will produce the code?" and "what will use the code?".

The production of the code may be automatic or manual. If it is manual, the competence of the programmer is one factor to consider. The use of the code is normally for both men and machines. The code will be fed into a compiler and checked rigorously. Furthermore, the code will be read and validated by humans. The competence of these validators is also a factor in the decision.

Furthermore, the hardware and the basic software may pose important constraints. If the hardware is such that only assemblers are available, then assembly code must be produced as the target code. If the chosen run-time support system is made in C++, the target language should preferably also be C++.

Telecommunication administrations have wanted their switching systems to be implemented in CHILL (CCITT Z.200, 1993). CHILL is the CCITT recommended implementation language for telecommunication systems and its standardisation body is the same study group as SDL. SDL and CHILL both emerged in the seventies from the same CCITT language question, but in recent years their developments have departed as SDL has introduced object orientation while CHILL has not reached recommendation for object-oriented concepts yet, but they have had contributions on the matter. Technically CHILL has powerful process and signal concepts which are well-suited for the implementation of SDL. CHILL has not reached widespread use outside telecommunication and the CHILL support tools are often proprietary tools of the large vendors of telecommunication systems.

We have chosen C++ as the example target language because we believe it has properties which will be important in the future as an implementation language for time-critical software. Furthermore, given the basic object orientation of this book, C++ code can be understood without detailed knowledge of the language. Finally, since we have set out to implement object-oriented features of SDL 92, choosing an object-oriented target language gives us a significant advantage. The major disadvantage of using C++ is that the language has no standard concurrency mechanisms such that concurrency must be delegated to the operating system.

C++ was developed at AT&T Bell Laboratories in the early eighties and is still evolving. The main designer of the language was Bjarne Stroustrup, a Dane, who, well-acquainted with SIMULA, set out to make an object-oriented language with no performance degradation compared with C (Stroustrup, 1992). Actually C++ is a superset of C and AT&T offers a translator which translates C++ into C. This translator is used for some compilers commercially available today. There are, however, several native[1] compilers in the market as well. Compilers exist for more than 50 machines. It seems today that C++ is the object-oriented language with the most commercial support.

11.1.2 Manual, automatic or mixed code generation?

We shall now concentrate on the activity **code** in Figure 11.1.

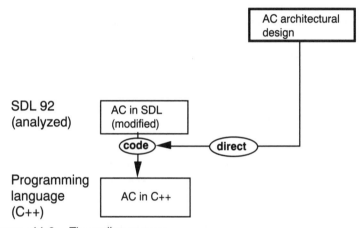

Figure 11.2 *The coding process*

The desire for automatic code generation is easy to understand, but not quite as easy to accomplish. The development has been, however, to obtain more of the target code directly from the SDL diagrams. The reasons why there are few automatic code generators available that covers the whole SDL properly are as follows:

- SDL does not specify everything needed for making target code. We must add implementation information such as the size of arrays.
- The semantics of the complete SDL language is so complex that making code generation automatic for all cases is rather complicated and time-consuming. The vendors have settled for major subsets of the language which can be implemented more easily and more efficiently than complete SDL.
- Different hardware (or software) bases may require different implementations within the same system. The tools normally provide only one canonical implementation method.
- Coding directions (given by the activity **direct** above) are not yet standardised, but the notation used in this book will be given as suggestions in the appendix

to Z.100 which is called "*Methodology Guidelines*" (CCITT Z.100, 1993). Some vendors add annotations to the SDL symbols which are seen as comments by the SDL analyser, but are used by the code generator to make specific code.

- There is sometimes a need to be able to tailor the code in great detail. The tools are just starting to give the users full control of the coding schemas, but still they lack the ability to specify different coding for different parts of the system.

In summary, provided that implementation directives can be given for each part of the SDL system, there is no reason why the code generation cannot be largely automated. In practice even the manual code generation is rather automatic meaning that the programmers follow rather strict coding rules and a well-described programming methodology.

The following pieces are normally tailored to the application:

- The implementation of signal sending to and from the system environment (this is normally known as programming "drivers", "I/O processes" and "the user interface");
- The algorithmic implementation of operators (if the operators are defined axiomatically in SDL);
- Addressing in distributed systems (see Section 11.2.6);
- The implementation of – and the interfaces with – parts of the SDL system which are implemented externally (such parts may include database systems which are integrated in the system, but specified as a process or a complex variable (see Section 11.3)).

Experience data suggest that as much as half of the code volume is spent on implementing the application tailored parts. However, these parts are often reused in later projects (see also Chapter 13).

For the subsequent sections of this chapter, it is irrelevant whether the coding is done manually or automatically.

11.2   Run-time support systems

A run-time support system (hereafter also denoted as RTS) can be described as software (and possibly hardware) which makes up an execution fundament which can be seen as an "SDL machine". The RTS will also assist during debugging and simulation by providing a set of facilities for tracing and observation. The principles behind an SDL RTS are found in Section 10.4.

The SDL machine (the SDL run-time support system) can be reused among different applications of the same company and, therefore, making a stable and versatile run-time system is cost-effective. There are also commercial run-time systems available.

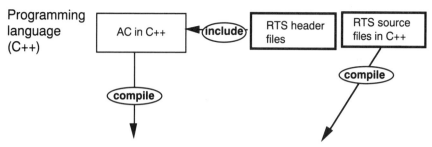

Figure 11.3 *SDL run-time system*

The RTS is brought into the system on a level below SDL since it forms a base for SDL. The example RTS is built in C++ and contains the following three distinct parts:

1. An SDL-machine, an interpreter for the SDL system (it also controls the debugging and tracing facilities (see also Figure 10.15));
2. A number of SDL concepts from which the C++ classes of the application will be derived corresponding to SDL types;
3. A number of functions which corresponds closely to the SDL primitives.

We shall go into the details of each of these parts below, but here we summarise the benefits and potential problems with using an RTS (see also Section 10.4.1).

The benefits are as follows:

1. *Ease of coding.* The coding is done according to templates such that even when the coding is done manually, it can be done swiftly and without errors. SDL primitives have directly corresponding RTS functions.
2. *Ease of reading.* The code can be easily read by anybody familiar with either SDL or C++. New project participants can be brought into the code quickly.
3. *Ease of maintenance.* Due to the simple methodology, alterations can be done easily from the alterations in the SDL specifications. The logical maintenance should not be initiated from the C++ code. By encouraging SDL level maintenance, the code is kept consistent at all times.
4. *Organisational concurrency.* When the SDL specification is known, any number of project participants can make the C++ code in parallel.
5. *Ease of testing and tracing.* The RTS supports a tracing facility which can easily be disabled at release compilation. Signal queues and transition sequences can be followed closely.
6. *Correctness.* The programming of control is done once in the RTS. The RTS code is widely reused and, therefore, continuously tested and improved.

The most common problem areas include the following:

1. *Execution speed.* The handling of signals and starting a transition take some time and this overhead may sometimes be critical. The user should, however, bear in mind that this "overhead" also carries information and that it can never be eliminated completely. There are some remedies to limit the overhead associated with signal handling. Firstly, it may be cost-effective to use more powerful hardware. Secondly, some signal sending may be optimised through use of function calls. Thirdly, the number of signals sent can possibly be decreased by using more data in each signal (which in turn may be contrary to our SDL methodology).

2. *Dynamics.* Signals in SDL are generated and consumed dynamically. In general there is no guarantee that the number of unconsumed signals in a system is less than some predefined limit. Nevertheless, the application must be finite and, thus, overflow is a potential problem. In C++, dynamics can be controlled closely by overloading the operators "new" (for generation) and "delete" (for deletion) for each class. In our example, RTS overloading is done for signals and possibly processes and procedures.

11.2.1   A simple SDL RTS

We shall start by taking a closer look at the simplest solution where all the processes and procedures reside in the same address space[2] and when they actually execute in sequence.

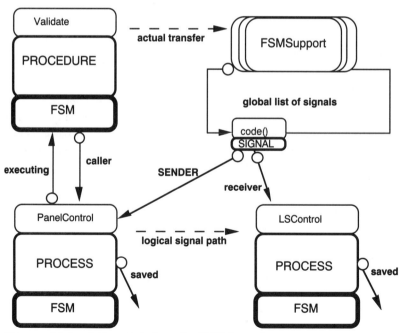

Figure 11.4   *A Snapshot of running FSM Support*

In such a situation, we can see the SDL processes merely as data objects which are handled by the SDL interpreter – the *FSMSupport* program. Furthermore, the signal instances are also data objects and they reside either in individual save-queues attached to the SDL processes or in an input queue of the *FSMSupport* which then represents the union of all input ports in the system.

Figure 11.4 shows a snapshot of a running SDL system. It is a snapshot of our *AccessControl* system in the situation where a *Panel* has received a *card* and a *PIN* and the *Validate* procedure has just sent the *Code* signal to *LSControl*[3]. Following our interpretation sketched in the introduction of this section there is only one software process in the system, namely the *FSMSupport*.

The SDL processes *PanelControl* and *LSControl* are data objects. Each of them consists of three parts originating from the fact that their types have inherited from the base classes *FSM* and *PROCESS*. The *Validate* object is also a data object with three parts originating from inheritance of *FSM* and *PROCEDURE* properties of the RTS. The *Validate* procedure forms one element in the execution stack of *PanelControl*. The execution stack is explicitly represented by the pointers *executing* (which points from the process base to the executing procedure) and *caller* (which points backward down the execution stack).

The signal instances (here only the *Code* instance) consist of two parts, one base part originating from the RTS concept *SIGNAL* and one application-specific part corresponding to the actual system type definition. The *SIGNAL* part contains two important pointers – one to the sender of the signal – and one to the receiver of the signal. Note that there are no signals in the save-queues of the two processes (denoted by '*saved*'). Note also that the signal instance refers to *PanelControl* as its sender and *LSControl* as its receiver. We have illustrated this by the arrow denoted by "logical signal path". On the other hand, it is actually the *Validate* SDL procedure that produces the signal (i.e. executes the *new*-operator) and the immediate receiver is the *FSMSupport's* global input port. We have depicted this by the arrow "actual transfer".

The SDL Machine

The *FSMSupport* represents the interpreter of SDL. The *FSMSupport* has two public operations: *execute()* and *terminate()*. The *execute()* function represents the running of the SDL system. The system will run until there are no signals in the global list of signals or the *terminate()* function has been called. Furthermore, the *FSMSupport* has some functions for the purpose of trace and observation. This will be covered in a later section.

The SDL concepts

Signal types in our application are classes derived from the base *SIGNAL*. *SIGNAL* is derived from *element* of a two-way list. Each signal type must also have a unique integer identification which is used when the proper transition is selected. The signal parameters are made parameters to the constructor[4] of the C++ class which corresponds to the signal type.

Process types and procedures are derived from the general *FSM* class which contains the bulk of the SDL primitives. PROCESS, PROCEDURE (and SERVICE) are derived classes from *FSM* and serve as bases for application process types and procedures (and service types). Central to the *FSM*s is the virtual function '*run*' which takes a signal type identification as argument. From its additional knowledge of current state it selects and runs one transition. Each application *FSM* class must redefine 'run'. States in an *FSM* are identified by a value of an enumeration type. The enumeration type is defined local to the application process class.

The class *PROCESS* is derived from *FSM* and contains the save queue.

In simple cases SDL blocks can be eliminated before the system is coded. This means that the blocks are expanded. Since we are talking about systems in one address space, the channels and signalroutes are eliminated, too. A simple SDL system, seen from this RTS, is a set of processes and a number of signal instances in save-queues and the input queue. When addressing is done implicitly or VIA channel/signalroute, this must be translated to a TO-clause when coding. Very often it is practical to have global PIds which point to each one of the processes. Later in the chapter we shall look at implementation of block types and of more elaborate addressing schemes.

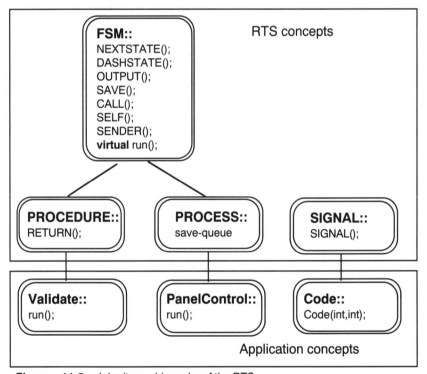

Figure   11.5   *Inheritance hierarchy of the RTS*

The SDL primitives

The class *FSM* contains the bulk of SDL primitives. There is a function corresponding to each SDL primitive. We have NEXTSTATE(), DASHSTATE() (corresponding to dash nextstate), OUTPUT(), SAVE(), CALL(), SELF(), SENDER(). Furthermore, one may add special support for continuous signals and enabling conditions. Decisions can be coded as signal sending where the answer signals will be handled with top priority or they can be coded as simple conditional statements.

As shown in Figure 11.5 the class *PROCEDURE* is derived from *FSM* and, in addition, contains the RETURN() function. Returning from a procedure (with states) is not quite straightforward when the coding is in standard C++. The *'run'* procedure should always return after either a CALL() or a NEXTSTATE(). When the procedure call returns through RETURN(), the remainder of the caller's transition shall be executed. This is handled by running a pseudo-transition which is selected by *'run'* through the current state having the value of a pseudo-state. The pseudo-state value is given in the generation of the call.

Example code (incomplete)

In the example below, we shall try to apply names consistently. Each SDL entity class has its own prefix in C++ class names: SDL procedures are prefixed by *PRC_* , processes by *PRO_* and signal types by *SIG_*. States have no prefix.

Our coding style is direct (see Section 10.4) which means that the algorithm to select the transition code is programmed entirely by the application. The RTS specifies that the transitions shall be found in a function called *'run'* which is virtual to class *FSM*. In our implementation we select the transition by means of nested switches. The alternative strategy suggested in Chapter 10, the table-driven approach can certainly be applied within the *run*-function, but this RTS offers no table-driving support. The reader should look at Figure 6.5 to see the SDL specification of PROCEDURE Validate.

```
// ACVALIDA.HXX
// Declaration of PROCEDURE Validate in PROCESS PanelControl Figure 6.5.

#ifndef D_ACVALIDA
#define D_ACVALIDA
// include the surrounding scope
#include "ACPACTRL.HXX"

class PRC_Validate : public PROCEDURE
{ private:
    /* local variable declarations */
    int cardid;  // IN parameter: card identification (read from card)
    int pin;     // IN parameter: personal identification number
    int trial_no; // number of erroneous trials
    /* state enumeration */
  protected:
```

```
enum Validate_states { Validate, AfterGetPIN };
public:
PRC_Validate
(FSM* callingFSM, int cardid_par, int pin_par);
// the constructor also contains start transition and parameter transfer
void run(int sign);        // runs one transition
};
#endif D_ACVALIDA
```

```
// ACVALIDA.CXX
// Definition of functions in PROCEDURE Validate of PROCESS PanelControl
// Normally the implementation resides in a different file than the
// declaration of the class⁵
#include "ACVALIDA.HXX"
```

```
/* The implementation of PRC_Validate. We start by implementing the "constructor"
which is automatically called when the PRC_Validate object is generated. It is used for
initialisation of local variables and for the start transition */
PRC_Validate::PRC_Validate
(FSM* callingFSM, int cardid_par, int pin_par)
/* The following is initialisation of local variables */
: PROCEDURE(callingFSM), cardid(cardid_par),
pin(pin_par), trial_no(0)
{ // Start Transition
  trial_no = 0;
  OUTPUT(new SIG_Code(cardid, pin),
   SELF()->GATE[GT_PanelControl_Co]);
  NEXTSTATE(Validate);
};
```

We note above that the address of the OUTPUT is given by "SELF()->GATE[GT_PanelControl_Co]". We have assigned gates to *PanelControl* even though it is a singular process. The gates correspond directly to the signalroutes connected to it. We must use "SELF()->" to reach the *PRO_PanelControl* object from the *PRC_Validate* object.

```
void PRC_Validate::run(int sign)
{ switch(cur_state)
  { case Validate:
    switch(sign)
    { case SIGID_OK:
        /* transition (Validate,OK) */
        OUTPUT(KEEPSIG(),
```

```
          SELF()->GATE[GT_PanelControl_D]);
          // NOTE: KEEPSIG() refers to the consumed signal directly
        OUTPUT(new SIG_ReleaseCard,
         SELF()->GATE[GT_PanelControl_CR]);
        RETURN();
     return;
     case SIGID_ERR:
       /* transition (Validate,ERR) */
        OUTPUT(KEEPSIG(),
         SELF()->GATE[GT_PanelControl_D]);
        OUTPUT(new SIG_ReleaseCard,
         SELF()->GATE[GT_PanelControl_CR]);
        RETURN();
     return;
     case SIGID_NOK:
        /* transition (Validate,NOK) */
        OUTPUT(KEEPSIG(),
         SELF()->GATE[GT_PanelControl_D]);
        trial_no = trial_no+1;
        if (trial_no < 4)
        { CALL(new PRC_GetPIN(this, &pin,
              ((PRO_PanelControl*)SELF())->no_dig),
              // accessing variable "no_dig" in process  PRO_PanelControl
               AfterGetPIN); // returning at AfterGetPIN
        }
        else
        { OUTPUT(new SIG_ERR,
           SELF()->GATE[GT_PanelControl_D]);
          OUTPUT(new SIG_ReleaseCard,
           SELF()->GATE[GT_PanelControl_CR]);
          RETURN();
        }
     return;
     case SIGID_Cid:
       /* transition (Validate,Cid) */
        OUTPUT(new SIG_ERR,
         SELF()->GATE[GT_PanelControl_D]);
        DASHSTATE();
     return;
     case SIGID_Digit:
       /* transition (Validate,Digit) */
        DASHSTATE();
     return;
     default:
```

```
      /* transition (Validate,*) */
      // only ignoring them
      DASHSTATE();
   return;
}

case AfterGetPIN:
   // pseudo-state after call to GetPIN
   OUTPUT(new SIG_Code(cardid, pin),
    SELF()->GATE[GT_PanelControl_Co]);
   NEXTSTATE(Validate);
return;

default:
   IERROR("Validate::run no such state");
return;
  }
}
```

The produced code can be read by machines as well as C++ programmers.

Note that the RTS takes care of the sequencing of the different *FSM*s. In case the procedure has states, the procedure must remain "alive" while other processes run and then resume execution later. There is a logical context switch, but standard C++ have no specific facilities for such context switching and we have to program such switching ourselves. The side-effects of our context switching is the occurrence of pseudo-states and pseudo-transitions. Unfortunately, this implies that the code of one logical SDL transition is split into several fragments scattered in the code.

The reader may worry about the frequent use of the operator 'new' which is the C++ operator for dynamic memory allocation. If the system is supplied with a good enough dynamic memory management system for C++, then there is no problem. Often when it comes to implementing real time systems, time and memory use is of the essence and the implementor wants to be in full control. When the implementation is in C++, we have the opportunity to implement 'new' for each class. The run-time system will provide an overloading of *new* on SIGNALs and very often the application should provide an overloading of *new* for those C++ classes representing procedures that are not recursive. All objects of that class may then be mapped directly to one static object.

11.2.2   Implementing blocks, block types and gates

Having shown a simple implementation of central parts of SDL systems, the FSM graphs, we shall go on to show an implementation of the most basic object-oriented concepts of SDL 92. The parts of the *AccessControl* system which are implemented are shown in Chapter 7. The reader may for his convenience assume that the whole system runs on one computer in one address space. Later we shall look into the situation more closely when this assumption does not hold.

We will in the following refer to file names of C++ files. The file names are not significant, but the distinction between *hxx* and *cxx* files is quite important. The *hxx* files are used to declare the concepts such that other compilation units can use them, while the *cxx* files are the actual definitions of the functions. We have tried to give file names which are close to the names found in the SDL description.

```
// File ACSYSTEM.HXX. Implementing Figure 7.9 and others
#ifndef D_ACSYSTEM
#define D_ACSYSTEM

#include "RTS.HXX"      // the run-time system
#include "ACENVIR.HXX"     // definition of the environment of AC

enum signals  // integer identifiers for all signal types
{ SIGID_EjectCard=1,SIGID_InputCard, SIGID_keys,
  SIGID_ReleaseCard, SIGID_Cid, SIGID_Digit,SIGID_Code,
  SIGID_OK, SIGID_NOK, SIGID_ERR,
  SIGID_Disable, SIGID_Enable,
  SIGID_open, SIGID_opened, SIGID_close, SIGID_closed
};

//////// The signal type declarations //// Figure 4.8 etc.
class SIG_EjectCard : public SIGNAL
{ public:
  SIG_EjectCard() {ident = SIGID_EjectCard;};
};

class SIG_Code : public SIGNAL
{ private:
  int Code_par_1 ;     // the value of the Card input
  int Code_par_2 ;     // the value of the keyboard PIN
  public:
  SIG_Code(int par_1, int par_2)
  : Code_par_1(par_1), Code_par_2(par_2)
  { ident = SIGID_Code; };
  void input(int& par_1, int& par_2)
  {par_1 = Code_par_1; par_2 = Code_par_2; };
};
```

The signal declarations are classes with *SIGNAL* as base class. The signal parameters are made member objects of the signal object and they are initialised through the constructor (the function which has the same name as the class itself). The function "input" is used when values are to be extracted from the signal object. The "input" function is not virtual, but there is always such a function in all signals. Its parameters are transferred "by reference" which means the actual parameters are being changed within the "input" function.

```
... and more signal declarations

// The system declaration
class SYS_AccessControl: public SYSTEM
{ BLOCKSET BLK_ls;
  BLOCKSET BLK_bls;
  PId PId_CentralUnit;  // In SDL: it is a trivial block
  public:
  void Initialize();
  void UpdateInGates();
  void UpdateOutGates();

  SYS_AccessControl():
    SYSTEM("AccessControl"),
    BLK_ls(this,"ls",10), BLK_bls(this,"bls",5){}
};
// define enumeration which defines the identifying numbers of the gates
// Similar to the situation with PanelControl we define gates for the system, too
enum AccessControl_gates
  {GT_AccessControl_CEi,GT_AccessControl_CEo,
   GT_AccessControl_CFi,GT_AccessControl_CFo};
#endif D_ACSYSTEM
```

The conditional compiling flag *D_ACSYSTEM* is set when this header file is included in the compilation. It ensures that the header file will not be included twice in one compilation. The basic principle for inclusion that we have used here is that we include from the header file the header file that represents the block (type) surrounding this. For the system, this means the environment, which is represented here by *ACENVIR.HXX*. The run-time system (here *RTS.HXX*) will be included by all compilations once.

As private members of the class we find the instances of the system. A BLOCKSET is an RTS concept describing a list of objects derived from BLOCK. The *CentralUnit* is defined directly as a process (represented by a pointer – a PId) since the block in SDL may trivially contain only a *CentralUnit* process[6].

Initialize() which is virtual in the RTS class BLOCK, will describe the initialisation of the system[7] and *UpdateInGates()* and *UpdateOutGates()* does the necessary updating of the GATE-array.

```
// File ACSYSTEM.CXX
#include "ACSYSTEM.HXX"     // the corresponding header file
// internal members
```

```
#include "ACLOCSTA.HXX"    // the def of LocalStation
#include "ACBLOSTA.HXX"    // the def of BlockingStation
#include "ACCENTRA.HXX"    // the def of CentralUnit

void SYS_AccessControl::Initialize()
{ /* PRECONDITION: GATE==0, member objects not initialized */
  // make GATE array (actually here they are channels to envir)
  // There is one gate for each direction on bidirectional gates (postfixed -i and -o)
  GATE = new PId[4]; // CEi, CEo, CFi, CFo
  // initialize (and possibly make) all internal structures
  BLOCK* lsrunner;
  // fill BLK_ls
  for (int i=1 ; i <= BLK_ls.Number(); i++)
  { lsrunner =new BLKTYP_LocalStation(this,i);
    BLK_ls.Append(lsrunner);
  }
  BLK_ls.Initialize();

  .... correspondingly for BLK_bls

  PId_CentralUnit = new PRO_CentralUnit(this);
  PId_CentralUnit->Initialize();
}


void SYS_AccessControl::UpdateInGates()
{ /* PRECONDITION: GATE generated, but empty, member objects existent */
  // update ingates of all member objects
  BLK_ls.UpdateInGates();
  BLK_bls.UpdateInGates();
  PId_CentralUnit->UpdateInGates();
  // update own ingates
  GATE[GT_AccessControl_CEi] =
    BLK_ls.GetGATE(GT_LocalStation_ei);
  GATE[GT_AccessControl_CFi] =
    BLK_bls.GetGATE(GT_LocalStation_ei);
  /* POSTCONDITION: ingates updated, all member objects' ingates updated */
}


void SYS_AccessControl::UpdateOutGates()
{ /* PRECONDITION:
      all ingates of the whole system (on all levels) updated,
      all outgates of outer levels updated,
      outgates of this block is updated (from outer levels) */
  // Update top system outgates
```

```
/* outgates of top system are trivially equal 'ENVIR' */
GATE[GT_AccessControl_CEo] = ENVIR;
GATE[GT_AccessControl_CFo] = ENVIR;
// update outgates of memberobjects
// Alternative 1: outgates to other member's ingate
BLK_ls.SetGATEs(GT_LocalStation_Co,
  PId_CentralUnit->GATE[GT_CentralUnit_Ci]);
BLK_bls.SetGATEs(GT_LocalStation_Co,
  PId_CentralUnit->GATE[GT_CentralUnit_CBi]);
PId_CentralUnit->GATE[GT_CentralUnit_Co]=
  BLK_ls.GetGATE(GT_LocalStation_Ci);
PId_CentralUnit->GATE[GT_CentralUnit_CBo]=
  BLK_bls.GetGATE(GT_LocalStation_Ci);
// Alternative 2: outgates from member to this blocks outgate
BLK_ls.SetGATEs
(GT_LocalStation_eo,GATE[GT_AccessControl_CEo]);
BLK_bls.SetGATEs
(GT_LocalStation_eo,GATE[GT_AccessControl_CFo]);
// Call recursively for all member objects
BLK_ls.UpdateOutGates();
BLK_bls.UpdateOutGates();
PId_CentralUnit->UpdateOutGates();
/* POSTCONDITION: All gates updated, from this level inwards */
}
```

First the block set is filled with generated blocks of the type *BLKTYP_LocalStation* (and *BLKTYP_BlockingStation*). Then the connections are set up. The BLOCKs and the PROCESSes each have a pointer GATE which contains the set of gates of the block type or the process type. The gates are actually PId values such that addressing VIA a gate is transformed to addressing TO a PId-expression. *GT_AccessControl_CEo* is an integer constant corresponding to the gate name. The gate identification definitions are given in enumerations.

The updating of GATEs is done recursively. Firstly, all the ingates are updated from the inside out. Bottom of the recursion is that the GATEs of a process instance are trivially pointing to the process instance itself. Then the outgates are updated from the outside inwards. On each level the outgates of the member objects are updated. The bottom of the recursion is that all outgates from the system go to a special environment process (called ENVIR).

Sometimes these gates represent a one-to-many relation and then this gate scheme selects one possible alternative arbitrarily similar to the SDL non-determinism scheme. The difference is, however, that our gate implementation scheme ignores information about the signallists on the gates, channels and signalroutes.

11.2.3 Implementing specialisation of block types and virtual processes

Having given the top level of our system which showed how the gates should be tackled, we go on to the definition of the two block types, *LocalStation* and *BlockingStations*, which form a generalisation hierarchy since *BlockingStation* is a specialisation of *LocalStation*. Furthermore, *LocalStation* contains the virtual process type *LSControl* which is redefined in *BlockingStation*.

```
// ACLOCSTA.HXX
// BLOCK TYPE LocalStation (Figure 7.11.)
#ifndef D_ACLOCSTA
#define D_ACLOCSTA

#include "ACSYSTEM.HXX"    // include surrounding system
// Signal type declarations inside LocalStation (omitted here in the textbook)
// Declaration of BLOCK TYPE LocalStation
class BLKTYP_LocalStation: public BLOCK
{ public:
    int id_no; // identification number
    protected:
    // 1. (references to) the internal structures
    BLOCKSET BLK_Panel; // rather than as 7.11. says: process with services
    PId PId_lsc; // pointer to (virtual) LSControl process
    PId PId_door; // pointer to Door process
    // 2. functions corresponding to (internal) virtual types
    virtual PId VIRPRO_LSControl();
    public:
    BLKTYP_LocalStation(BLOCK* surr, int identno)
    :BLOCK(surr),BLK_Panel(this,"Panel"),id_no(identno){}
    virtual void Initialize(); // set up the internal structure
    virtual void UpdateInGates(); // update ingates
    virtual void UpdateOutGates(); // update outgates
};

// define enumeration which defines the numbers of the gates
enum LocalStation_gates
    {GT_LocalStation_ei,GT_LocalStation_eo,
     GT_LocalStation_Ci,GT_LocalStation_Co};
#endif
```

The inclusion of "ACSYSTEM.HXX" ensures that the visible concepts of the enclosing scope are also visible here. This implements the general SDL scope rules.

We chose to implement *Panel* as a BLOCKSET (with one BLOCK only, containing three processes) rather than as a PROCESS with SERVICEs since we have not shown the implementation of services here. Mixing process and block definitions cannot be done in SDL, but in the implementation this restriction can be ignored.

The specifier "protected:" means that the concepts can be used by the derived classes, but not by users of variables of the class.

The BLOCK concept has one pointer to the surrounding scope object (sometimes in literature called "static link"). This pointer is initialised to "this" where the actual block is being generated.

```
// File ACLOCSTA.CXX
// Definitions of LocalStation functions
PId BLKTYP_LocalStation::VIRPRO_LSControl()
{ return (new PRO_LocalStation_LSControl(this)); }

void BLKTYP_LocalStation::Initialize()
{  /* PRECONDITION: GATE==0, member objects not initialized */
   // make GATE array
   GATE = new PId[4];  // eo, ei, Co, Ci
   // initialize (and possibly make) all internal structures
   BLK_Panel.Append(new BLKTYP_Panel(this));
   BLK_Panel.Initialize();
   PId_lsc = VIRPRO_LSControl(); PId_lsc->Initialize();
   PId_door = new PRO_Door(this);PId_door->Initialize();
}
... updating the gates is omitted here
```

The *lsc* instance is generated by using a virtual function. This means that in a class derived from *BLKTYP_LocalStation* (say *BLKTYP_BlockingStation.*) the generation can be redefined.

```
// ACBLOSTA.HXX
// BLOCK TYPE BlockingStation (Figure 7.10)
#ifndef D_ACBLOSTA
#define D_ACBLOSTA
#include "ACSYSTEM.HXX"      // include surrounding block
#include "ACLOCSTA.HXX"      // include supertype

class BLKTYP_BlockingStation
: public BLKTYP_LocalStation     // the supertype
{ protected:
    // 1. (references to) the internal structures
    /* There are no additional internal structures */
    // 2. functions corresponding to (internal) virtual types
    virtual PId VIRPRO_LSControl();      // redefinition
```

```
   public:
   BLKTYP_BlockingStation(BLOCK* surr, int identno)
   : BLKTYP_LocalStation(surr, identno) {}
   /* The virtual functions Initialize(), UpdateInGates() and UpdateOutGates()
   have no redefinition here i.e. it is sufficient to use those from LocalStation */
};

// define enumeration which defines the numbers of the gates
/* There are no additional gates */
#endif
```

// File ACBLOSTA.CXX
```
// Implementation of BlockingStation
#include "ACBLOSTA.HXX"
#include "ACLSCBLO.HXX"        // include all internal concepts

// implementation of redefined process
PId BLKTYP_BlockingStation::VIRPRO_LSControl()
{ return (new PRO_BlockingStation_LSControl(this) ); }
```

Just as Figure 7.10 specifies, not much is needed for this specialisation. The match of the virtual function *VIRPRO_LSControl()* ensures that the initialisation of instances of *BLKTYP_BlockingStation* will generate instances of the redefined *LSControl*.

Note also that we have utilised the inheritance mechanism of C++ for the inheritance of SDL block types.

11.2.4   Implementing specialisation of *FSM*s

We shall now turn to the implementation of *FSM*s and their specialisation. Inheritance of behaviour is not commonplace in computer languages and C++ cannot directly offer inheritance mechanisms for it, but the implementation is still not very difficult.

Let us first have a look at the basic *LSControl* process found in *LocalStation*.

// ACLSCONT.HXX
```
// Declaration of PROCESS TYPE LSControl of BLOCK TYPE LocalStation
// Figures 7.12. and 4.17.
#ifndef D_ACLSCONT
#define D_ACLSCONT
#include "ACLOCSTA.HXX"        // include surrounding block

class PRO_LocalStation_LSControl : public PROCESS
{ private:
   /* local variable declarations */
   PId cur_panel;   // current panel (whenever there will be more than one)
```

```
    int cid;  // card identification
    int pin;  // personal identification number
  protected:
  /* state enumeration */
  enum LocalStation_LSControl_states
  { Idle, Validation, Opening, Closing};
  public:
  PRO_LocalStation_LSControl(BLOCK* surr);
  // parameter: surrounding block, normally 'this'
  void run(int sign);        // runs one transition
  virtual void Initialize();     // make gate array
  virtual void UpdateInGates();      // update all ingates to 'this'
};

// Enumeration for the gates
enum LocalStation_LSControl_gates
{GT_LSControl_Pi,
GT_LSControl_Po,GT_LSControl_Di,GT_LSControl_Do,
GT_LSControl_Ui,GT_LSControl_Uo};
#endif D_ACLSCONT
```

We notice that the name of the *LSControl* process type includes the qualification of the surrounding block type (here: *LocalStation*). The implementation of the functions follows the same principles as described before and they will be omitted here, but we shall take a look at how the specialisation of it looks.

// ACLSCBLO.HXX
```
// Declaring PROCESS TYPE LSControl of BLOCK TYPE BlockingStation
// Figure 7.13.
#ifndef D_ACLSCBLO
#define D_ACLSCBLO
#include "ACBLOSTA.HXX"    // include surrounding block
#include "ACLSCONT.HXX"    // include supertype

class PRO_BlockingStation_LSControl
: public PRO_LocalStation_LSControl // the supertype
{ private:
  /* state enumeration */
  enum BlockingStation_LSControl_states
  { Blocked = Closing+1 };
      // notice that Blocked is in the same state space as the inherited
      // LSControl states. The number must be added to the last one
  public:
  PRO_BlockingStation_LSControl(BLOCK* surr);
```

```
      void run(int sign);        // runs one transition

   /*  The following functions are not redefined here, since there are
          no new gates, the gate array will be identical to the inherited one
          virtual void Initialize(); // make gate array
          virtual void UpdateInGates(); // update all ingates to 'this'
   */
};
#endif D_ACLSCBLO
```

// ACLSCBLO.CXX
// Implementing REDEFINED *LSControl* in *BlockingStation*

```
#include "ACLSCBLO.hxx"
PRO_BlockingStation_LSControl::
 PRO_BlockingStation_LSControl(BLOCK* surr)
 : PRO_LocalStation_LSControl(surr)
{ // Start Transition: There is no simple start transition in inherited processes } ;

void PRO_BlockingStation_LSControl::run(int sign)
{ /* transition (*, Disable) */
   if (sign==SIGID_Disable)
   { /* actually block the door */
     NEXTSTATE(Blocked);
     return;
   }

   // here (sign != SIGID_Disable)
   switch(cur_state)
   { case Blocked:
     switch(sign)
     { case SIGID_Enable:
          /* transition (Blocked,Enable) */
          NEXTSTATE(Idle);
       return;
       default:
          /* transition (Blocked,*) */
          SAVE();
       return;
     }

     default:
       // call the run of the supertype
       PRO_LocalStation_LSControl::run(sign);
```

```
        return;
    }
}
```

Much of the redefined *run*-function is trivial. The switches are used in order to select the correct transition. In those cases where the transition is found in the specialisation, it is executed directly and the run-function returns. When the subtype cannot offer the transition, then the run-function of the supertype must be run. This is simply done by qualifying the call by the name of the supertype.

11.2.5   Implementing other object-oriented features of SDL 92

We have by walking through the implementation of our *AccessControl* system come across a number of the most central mechanisms of SDL 92, but we have not covered all the important object-oriented facilities of SDL In this section we shall briefly comment upon some of the object-oriented mechanisms which have not been covered.

Virtual SDL procedures without states

Like procedures without states should be implemented as member functions, virtual procedures without states should be implemented as virtual member functions.

Virtual SDL procedures with states

We have in the preceding sections shown the implementation of virtual processes. The clue was to generate the instance within a virtual function. Exactly the same strategy should be used for virtual procedures with states.

Virtual transitions

Since the subtype's *run*-function is tried before the supertype's *run*-function, the specialised transitions will always be selected. Virtual transitions, thus, need no special attention.

Virtual save

The standard implementation of SAVE is to perform the single SAVE() operation of the RTS as a transition. This means that a SAVE is exactly like any ordinary transition and virtual save is exactly like virtual transitions in general.

Virtual start

In general, the start transition should be put in a separate function: *Start()*. This procedure should be called at the end of *Initialize()*. If the *Start()* function is virtual, a virtual start transition is implemented.

Package

SDL packages are simply collections of types. In C++ this can be implemented as header files which include other header files. The USE primitive is then simply implemented as an include of the header file representing the package.

Context parameters

C++ *templates* are perfectly suited for implementing context parameters.

11.2.6 Distributed systems

In the sections above we have made the assumption that the whole SDL system is implemented within one address space. Many of the systems specified by SDL are true distributed systems and the designers want to have full control of the distribution. By "distributed systems" we mean that there is more than one address space involved and there is communication between software of the different address spaces.

We may effectively use our notion of RTS in distributed environments as well as simpler environments. The only difference needed is the modification of the RTS itself. The application code should be unchanged from the one address space situation. We will in the following present two different ways to cope with SDL systems covering multiple address spaces[8].

Assume now that we distribute the *LSControl* and the *Panel* to two different processors with two different address spaces.

In order to communicate the *Code*-signal from the *Panel* process (actually the *Validate*-procedure) to the *LSControl* process across processor boundaries, the *Code*-object will have to be copied and communicated over a communication link shown here as "remote communication".

The remote communication may of course in itself be described with SDL and the remote communication will form a lower layer compared to our *AccessControl* system above. The simplest such model is a model where either end of the remote communication is a routing process which from the addresses knows whether the signal is to be sent out or kept locally (cf. Section 8.6).

PId in SDL is a data type which contains the values identifying all the processes in the system uniquely. It is the SDL concept for referencing or addressing. When we considered only one address space the PId may simply be a process pointer (i.e. of type "PROCESS*"). In more complex situations like the one sketched in Figure 11.6, the PId cannot consist merely of a pointer since we have more than one address space. In addition to the simple memory address, there must be some processor identifier (or "task" identifier if we work within an environment where there is more than one address space, but only one processor).

In our implementation PIds are used for two somewhat different purposes:

1. Denoting the destination of a signal instance;
2. Representing the gates (also the signalroutes and channels) which will be used when the destination is given not by a TO-clause, but by a VIA-clause in the SDL process graphs. (The assignment of the gates is a way to transform VIA-addressing into TO-addressing.)

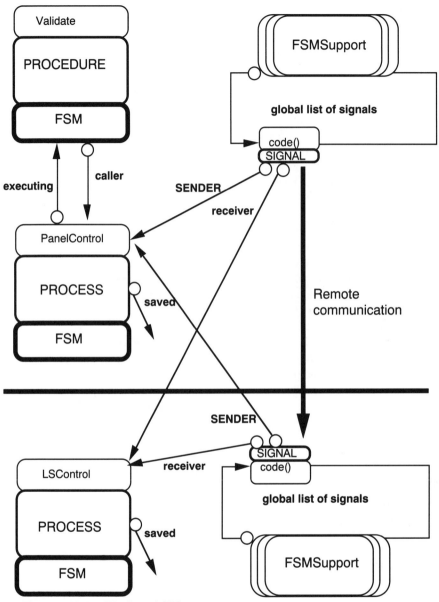

Figure 11.6   *Distributed SDL processes*

The routing process will serve as the representative for all processes on the outside of the processor and, thus, it should have all the gates to the outside as its own gates. In other words, when an external process is addressed, the local routing process will be addressed instead. In turn the routing process on a lower implementation level has special knowledge of the protocol to transmit the given signal to its final destination. On the other end of the remote communication the routing process will receive the remote signal and route it to the proper local SDL process according to the PId of its destination.

In C++ we can make the software in the distributed case be almost identical to the simple case of one address space by modifying the PId type. In the advanced case, the PId type can be a class where both local and remote addressing information is stored. The *operator->* (referencing) must be overloaded and then advanced addressing looks exactly like internal one address space addressing.

We shall go through some of the modifications needed in the example above and walk through in some detail how signal sending is performed.

```
// in file PID.HXX of SDL RTS  The definition of the PId type
extern PROCESS* routing ; // local pointer to gatekeeper
extern  int localnumber ; // number of local processor

class PId
{ int extrnl;    // external processor identification,
  PROCESS* intrnl;
    // internal address within local address space

  public:
  // overloaded reference operator
  PROCESS* operator-> ()
  { return (extrnl!=localnumber?routing:intrnl);
    // if external addressing go via gatekeeper
  }

  // constructor
  PId(PROCESS* pr): externl(localnumber), intrnl(pr) {}
};
```

The modified PId contains both external and internal addressing information keeping the invariant that a PId is unique in the whole system.

The overloaded *operator->* is used to give a local PROCESS* pointer even when the PId refers to an external address. The internal pointer given refers to the routing process. In this way the old use of the referencing operator will get a new and adequate meaning.

The constructor takes an internal *PROCESS** pointer and returns a *PId*. This can also be interpreted as converting from internal addresses to more general *PId*s where the external addressing information is the identification of this processor and the internal addressing information keeps the given pointer.

Now we shall have a closer look at the signal sending from the very conception of the signal:

```
// in file PANEL.CXX of application
// in run'of class PanelControl
OUTPUT(new SIG_code(cardid, PIN), PId_LSControl);
// PId_LSControl refers to a process of another computer
```

The *PId_LSControl* would correctly have been a gate reference, but we shall not go into those details now. We only assume that we have available a PId expression which uniquely points out the LSControl process which resides in another address space. The OUTPUT function will place the generated *SIGNAL* object into the common input port of the *FSMSupport*.

Let us now follow the signal in the *FSMSupport*.

```
// in file FSMSUP.CXX of SDL RTS The FSMSupport
// the RTS contains a monitor which starts the processes
PId current_process ;
SIGNAL* current_signal ;
...
current_signal = input_port.first();
input_port.Remove(current_signal);
current_prosess = current_signal->receiver;
current_prosess->run(current_signal->ident);
if (current_signal) delete current_signal;
// consumption completed
...
```

The question now is whose transition was run when the *SIG_code* object was consumed! Since *current_process* is a *PId*, the overloaded *operator->* would apply and it would in this case return a pointer to the routing process. Thus, it is a transition of the routing process which would run. That transition would then produce the adequate code for remote communication to the appropriate other processor.

In fact in order to optimise the routing, the signal sending to the routing process can often be optimised by using function calls instead of object moving. In this case that would mean that the OUTPUT-function of the *Panel* would be slightly modified. In C++ this is easily done by having OUTPUT as a virtual function and redefining it in *Panel*.

Let us now follow the remote signal sending to the other end, where another routing process decodes the remote signal and produces a local *SIG_code* object which is subsequently output to the PId given originally by *Panel*. Again the overloading of the *operator->* will ensure that this time the PId corresponds to an internal *PROCESS** pointer. The local *FSMSupport* will have no problem executing the proper transition from the *LSControl* process.

The problem of PId initialisation remains. SDL-wise, finding the PIds requires extensive signal sending in the start-up phase. In practice the implementor has a good knowledge of the unique identification of the processes. Such identification can serve as PIds which act as names, i.e. they are known before SDL interpretation time. These names are often not visible to each other through SDL scope rules, but for implementation this obstacle may be easily circumvented.

11.2.7 Optimisation through function calls

Above we have covered the case where the signal sending is implemented entirely by transferring signal objects into input ports. In many cases the signal sending overhead within one address space may be eliminated by using function calls instead of making signal objects.

The idea was presented in Section 10.3.2 and is simply that the receiver process defines a function with the same name (more or less) as the signal type. The function has parameters which correspond to the signal parameters. The function branches, e.g. through a case on which state the receiving process is in. The returning value of the function can be the returning signal value of some answering signal back to the sender.

The sender calls the "signal function" instead of making an OUTPUT through the RTS.

Since this implementation is not quite according to SDL semantics in the general case, care must be taken to ensure that the necessary requirements to use this optimisation are met. The requirements are listed in some detail in Chapter 10.

11.3 Interfacing to foreign code

Let us have a look again at the structure of an SDL implementation close to running the target program.

The implementor may have several different reasons for wanting to include foreign code into the system:

- The basic software system must be included.
- Some application parts are already written. The SDL system may be part of a larger software system.
- Some parts are better implemented in foreign code (programming) than through SDL. This may be true for numerical algorithms, some heavy data handling parts or low level drivers.

The foreign code can be included in our total system in a number of ways as indicated in Figure 11.7:

1. The foreign code is in the same programming language as the SDL implementation and the source code is available[9].
2. The relocatable object code is available and proper library information and documentation likewise. This holds normally for basic systems such as windowing systems and SDL RTS. The inclusion of the code will be at link-

time and assuming that the relocatable formats are compatible, an executable object code will be the result of the linking.

3. Additional executable code is available. This is re-entrant code which is used by a number of applications on the same machine. The additional executable code is not resident in specific processes, only the code is shared. This is the case for some basic systems such as MS-Windows and database systems. The inclusion of the foreign code is at load time. The foreign code is not loaded if it is already resident.

4. Our system cooperates with parallel systems. These systems may include operating systems, file servers, network servers, etc. They are real processes by themselves serving a number of parallel clients.

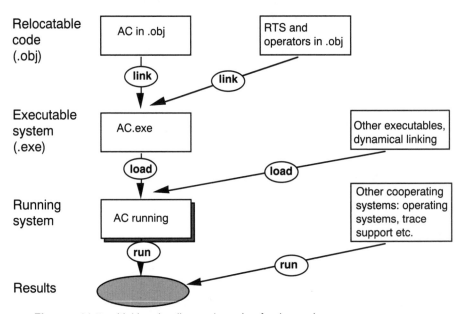

Figure 11.7   *Linking, loading and running foreign code*

For the implementor it is wise to keep the different ways of including foreign code apart, but from a programming point of view they normally look the same, namely as functions. Most basic systems offer a C-binding (i.e. a set of C function signatures) and this works well for C++, too.

11.4 Configuring SDL systems

11.4.1 Constants and numbers

One aspect of configuring SDL systems is determining a number of constants used in the specification and the implementation. There are different categories of configuration information:

- *Cardinality of block and process sets.* In SDL these things are normally specified by using external synonyms. In C or C++ such constants are specified by the const-specifier. If we have nested sets of sets then the configuration is a little more complicated in the case where within one block set, the number of processes in a process set will vary.
- *Length of buffers.* In SDL the length of the input port is infinite, but in any implementation there must be limits. The most dynamic solution is that each address space has one pool of dynamic objects (usually signal instances). The size of this must be configured. A more space-consuming strategy is to have one static input buffer for each process. Then the lengths must be individually configured. The size of the largest signal instance may also have to be configured if the storage allocation algorithm is to work as time-efficiently as possible.
- *Maximum number of dynamic processes.* The allocation of processes in one address space follows the same principles as for signal instances. When multiple address spaces are used within one operating system, there may be basic limits to the number of concurrent processes.

11.4.2 Dynamic configuration

The setting of constants and numbers is very static. Each installation of the system will have its own configuration, but it does not change dynamically. What if the configuration should change? We should distinguish between a set of different situations:

- *Dynamic processes and data structures.* This has been covered by the implementation itself. In C++ dynamic data structures are generated by using the *new*-operator which may also be overloaded by the application individually for each data type. Also, when a multitask environment is used, making processes dynamically is normally within the capabilities of the underlying system. This kind of dynamics is characterised by the fact that the definition of the objects does not change. The definition is normally re-entrant.
- *Dynamic inclusion of new objects of new types.* The most straightforward example of such dynamics is when we have a multitasking environment and new executing processes are started independently, but cooperating with, the already running processes. In principle this is no different from the first case. Each object is associated with one and only one stable definition. The objects

may share definitions if they are of the same type. This case will look more dynamic than the first because the new process may be a newer version of an old one and may in due time take over the work of the older one.

- *Dynamic substitution of definition when executing.* This is a much more serious step and often not desirable due to its dangers and limitations. The idea is to exchange all definitions of all the objects of a certain type in one big bang and afterwards the objects shall behave according to their new definition. Firstly, this requires that during the actual exchange of code, the executing system is halted with respect to the parts getting a new definition. Secondly, we must ascertain that the program pointer is at "the same point" in the new definition as it was in the old definition. This may be accomplished by halting the processes before they enter into a transition. Thirdly, the data of the objects must get a reasonable interpretation in the new definition. This may prove to be a strong limitation on the implementation of such upgrading.

- *Self-modifying and interpretative systems.* We go one step further and let the objects change definitions continuously. This is only possible in languages like LISP (the 'eval' function). There are both practical and theoretical difficulties. The practical limitation is that interpretation is slower than compiled code and, therefore, prohibitive in many real time applications. The theoretical difficulties centre around the fact that when the code is changed continuously you may have at some point in time a system that is not possibly described by the union of your definitions. The idea is good for experimentation, but not as attractive for time-critical and highly reliable systems.

11.4.3 Configuration management

Above we have given some insights into the problems associated with the introduction of new versions and variants into a running system. Even if we may take the whole system down before we reinstall a new one, there are still the administrative problems associated with the fact that different users have different versions and with somewhat different functionality. The administrative routines around such matters are called "configuration management". In this book we will not cover the subject in great detail, but we will try to highlight the differences between configuration management and developing the system itself.

Standard configuration management systems offer facilities to keep track of both software and hardware. One important piece of information which the configuration management must store is "who got what when?" – simply a customer base. This base does not include any software or hardware, but contains references to such items.

There is also a need for the storing of old and new pieces of software. Therefore, note the following extremely important distinction: the objects of a configuration management system are definitions (text, diagrams, etc.), while the objects of the real time system itself are hardware components and software data bytes. Relations between objects in the configuration management system are relations between pieces of description and they are, in principle, independent from any relations between objects of the target system.

SDL may be used to describe configuration management as it may be used to describe a number of problem areas other than telecommunication. That SDL is used to describe the target system does not necessarily mean we must use SDL to describe the configuration management (and vice versa).

Even though in principle the objects of the configuration management system are totally independent from the semantics of the objects of the target system, in practice there are strong correspondences. Types are good candidates to form code objects on configuration level.

In order to understand the relationship between the semantics of the target system and the organisation of the configuration, we distinguish between "versions" and "variants" in the configuration management system. A *version* is characterised by the fact that new users will be offered the latest one. New versions do everything an old version did and better. Sometimes versions are compatible and sometimes they are not. If two versions are compatible both ways then data generated by one can be used and manipulated by the other. Associated with each version there are a number of *variants*. Normally when a new version appears, there will be variants to the new version corresponding to the variants of the old version. The variants take into account specialities of the customer or they add special functionality not wanted by everybody. In object-oriented terms a variant can often be understood as a specialisation, while versions should not be considered having any inheritance relation. Sometimes the variants refer to the running of the system in specific environments.

11.5   Debugging

For the scope of this chapter we define "debugging" as the development activity which tracks down and corrects errors. It can be conceptually and factually distinguished from the test and verification phase which is concerned with establishing the existence of errors. In practice the two activities go hand in hand as finding an error often gives a strong clue to where the error lies.

There are two basic features of debuggers. Firstly, they must provide tracing facilities which visualise the execution. Secondly, they may add facilities to change the object data in order to modify the system execution. It may be questionable whether the second facility is a feature or a hazard as it becomes increasingly difficult to understand a system when the data has been "patched". This corresponds closely with some of the problems discussed under dynamic configuration above.

The close observation of a running system is without doubt the most valuable feature for debuggers. Our example run-time system provides a simple, but effective tracing mechanism. Combined with a good editor (browser) which can operate concurrently, the system can be scrutinised.

11.5.1   Simulation

Simulation is executing a system which is not exactly equivalent with the final target system, but where the differences should be well-understood and their consequences irrelevant.

The differences between the simulation system and the ultimate target system may be of several different categories:

- *The underlying hardware of the simulation is a "host" computer.* A host computer will normally offer other and better facilities than the final target hardware.
- *The stimuli of the simulation system are generated from statistical data.* The data or the statistics may not model the application faithfully.
- *The connected hardware is simulated by software* which may or may not capture the full definition of the hardware.
- *The simulation works in one address space*, while the target system may be distributed. Communication problems will thus disappear.
- *The simulation runs in simulated time.* Real time problems such as concurrent access problems may not occur in simulation. Time measurements are difficult.

11.5.2   Running on target

When the simulation returns correct results, the target execution code should be made. By "target" we mean the final system. The target execution code should preferably be as close to the simulation code as possible. We want the differences to be simple to overview and verify.

Unfortunately running on target offers a number of petty problems which should not occur, but which most certainly occur anyway. Some of the well-known transition problems when running on target after successful simulation are as follows:

- *Initialisation problems.* For example the RAM[10] of the simulation process was by accident different from what it was for the target. Possibly in the host computer the RAM area is scratched to all zeros, while no clearing is made on target (or the opposite) or variable alignment is different.
- *Interface problems with simulated hardware.* The hardware was not all correctly simulated or the interface routines did not quite work as expected.
- *Interface to foreign software.* Software which is specific to the target and which was simulated (or irrelevant) on the host, acts unexpectedly.
- *Capacity problems.* There is not enough RAM for the necessary data. The code exceeds the available ROM[11]. There are too few registers.
- *Speed problems.* The software is not fast enough. The context switching is not fast enough. The file access or RAM access is not fast enough.
- *Compiler problems.* The compiler used for the target is different from the compiler used for the host computer and they produce different results. Conditional compiling excludes from compilation on target things that should have been included.

11.6   Maintenance of the code

The code can be divided into three categories which should be kept separate since their maintenances differ.

Firstly, there is the code which is *automatically generated* from the SDL description. This code should be reprocessed when there are changes to the code generator. This may be changes in the commercial code generator or that the user defined compiler directives have been altered.

Secondly, there is the code which has been made *especially in programming language* in order to optimise or to implement such things as operator definitions described in SDL with axioms. This piece of code must be altered if the corresponding functional (SDL) description is changed. It may also be the case that the implementors have found more efficient or more robust implementation techniques.

Thirdly, there is the code which centres around *interfaces* to the system environment. When the environment changes, the interfaces must change accordingly. This may be protocols or external library interfaces etc.

Notes

[1] A compiler is called "native" when it produces relocatable code directly.

[2] By "address space" we mean the space spanned by simple C++ pointers. This will normally mean one software process or task under the operating system.

[3] The reader will remember that in Chapters 6 and 7 we let *Panel* be a single process consisting of three services. Since we will not show the implementation of services in this chapter, we show here an implementation where the three entities in *Panel* are described as separate processes. This means we see *Panel* was a block. The *PanelControl* process is the most central of the *Panel* processes.

[4] A C++ "constructor" is a special function with the same name as the class which is automatically run when an object of the class is generated. There can be several constructors of a class (called "overloading") if they are distinguishable by their parameter lists.

[5] Note the C++ syntax for qualification: "PRC_Validate::run" means "the 'run' of the class PRC_Validate"

[6] This implementation does not implement *CentralUnit* in detail as we did in Chapter 5. We assume a simpler solution with only one process *CentralUnit* which does the validation etc. on its own. The implementation is not shown here.

[7] Normally in C++ we use constructors for initialization, but there is an awkward restriction in C++ which makes it impractical to call virtual functions in a constructor. We need to call virtual functions in the initialization and to have the effect that the identitiy of the complete object determines which virtual match is chosen. Therefore, we use a separate function *Initialize()* which is called explicitly after the object has been created.

[8] The reader may wonder why we emphasize "address space" rather than "processor". From a software point of view the address space is the most important concept. Following our snapshot of a running SDL system in figure 11.4, we see that SDL processes are handled as data, and the sequencing is taken care of by the *FSMSupport*. One single *FSMSupport* is normally dependent upon the SDL processes being within one address space.

[9] This alternative is actually not including foreign code since the source code is included as if it were written by the application programmers themselves.

[10]RAM = Read Access Memory. Primary storage that can be written and read.

[11]ROM = Read Only Memory. Primary storage which cannot be written by the program. Often the program code is stored in ROM for real time systems.

CHAPTER 12

Verification and Validation

This chapter is concerned with more practical aspects of quality assurance; how to check that the system definitions produced at the various stages represent a system with the desired quality and the concrete system itself is a correct implementation. This involves reviews, formal analysis and testing.

12.1 What is verification and validation?

Quality systems are produced by a symbiotic interplay between two types of activity:

1. Constructing results (descriptions, documents, concrete systems).
2. Checking the quality of results.

Quality control correspondingly rests on two components that complement each other:

1. constructive methods that aim to generate the right results in the first place;
2. corrective methods that aim to detect and correct the errors that are made.

Constructive methods are necessary to build quality into the system! Constructive methods are therefore the main emphasis of this book, but given the limitations of human beings, errors will be made that have to be found and corrected. Validation and verification aims to detect such errors and other shortcomings.

Unfortunately the terms are used in the literature with varying definitions. We shall use a definition proposed by Boehm (Boehm, 1981):

Verification: to establish the truth of correspondence between a software product and its specification (from the Latin *veritas*, "truth").
Validation: to establish the fitness or worth of a software product for its operational mission (from the Latin *valere*, "to be worth").

Informally, these definintions translate to:

Verification: are we building the product right?
Validation: are we building the right product?"

By this definition, validation is directly related to the purpose of the system from the users and owners point of view, while verification is more of a means to achieve quality by ensuring correspondence between the descriptions developed at the various stages in the systems engineering process. This distinction is illustrated in Figure 1.7. The scope of validation is system quality (defined in Section 1.1.3), while the scope of verification is process quality (defined in Section 1.2.3).

Recall that the system quality depends on how well the system plays its roles in a given environment. Thus, a system can have good quality in one context and poor quality in another. It depends on the roles the environment expects the system to play. In Chapter 3 we emphasised system quality by urging you to focus on the needs of the environment. A critical issue is to find ways to describe roles such that system quality becomes measurable.

In Chapters 1 and 3 we explained how we use the requirement specification to express the needs as clearly as possible. Based on the requirement specification we develop a design and then an implementation. We have achieved process quality when the descriptions and the implementation we develop conforms with the requirement specification. Verification seeks to assure this conformance.

Process quality has the advantage of being precise and measurable. It is related to concrete documents and not to nebulous matters such as "needs" and "expectations". It is therefore the preferred definition among quality assurance people (see, for instance, Deutch and Willis, 1988).

It would be rather naive, however, to equal the concept of a specification with the real needs and expectations it is assumed to reflect. Therefore, it is essential to pay attention to the critical relation between the needs (in the real world) and the requirement specification (in the description world) and to involve the user and the owner actively in checking out this correspondence. This is the validation aspect illustrated in Figure 1.7.

The two definitions of quality are not in conflict with each other. Rather we must view process quality as a means to achieve system quality.

Verification and validation are corrective means for quality assurance.

12.2   Techniques

The two most used techniques for verification and validation today are manual reviews and testing.

Using a formal language like SDL to express the functional design enables us to explore two new techniques with a great potential:

1.   *Automatic program generation.* Automatic program generation helps to reduce the number of implementation errors and, therefore, it contributes to quality by construction. It also opens the way for "executable specifications" and "rapid prototyping" that may be used to validate the functionality at an early stage. In both techniques an operational system is generated that behaves like the real system and allows test cases to be carried out . In that way we may validate the functionality by animation before starting to design and implement the real system.

2.   *Formal analysis.* Syntactic and static semantic analysis is supported by most SDL tools available. Dynamic analysis, i.e. to analyse all possible courses of behaviour, checking that desirable properties are fulfilled and undesirable properties avoided, is far more difficult to achieve. The main reason is the computational complexity involved. But considerable progress has been made over the years and tools are gradually emerging that can be used to analyse realistic systems, at least partially.

In spite of the possibilities that are emerging, practical verification and validation will still have to rely on informal reasoning and review techniques for many years to come. It is therefore essential that the methods we use support human comprehension and reasoning.

Three techniques will be discussed in the remainder of this chapter:

1.   reviews;
2.   testing SDL systems;
3.   dynamic analysis of interfaces.

12.3   Reviews

Reviews may be performed on several levels in a project. As a minimum the quality of milestone results should be assessed. Otherwise it is impossible have any realistic measure of progress. If work continues on the basis of a milestone result with low quality, the cost of error corrections is likely to increase drastically as well.

Formal design reviews are used to check results at the milestones of a project. They may be organised in different ways, but should always be based on written descriptions and documents produced by the project, not on oral presentations. They must focus on concrete results and not on vague claims by members of the project team. Formal reviews serve two purposes:

1. to provide feedback to management on the status of the products under review;
2. to stimulate the development team towards producing quality results.

The formal review itself is performed after a product (here a description or a document) has been created and may result in the product being either accepted, partly accepted or rejected. It is not a constructive process that contributes directly to the product, but a check on the product that may lead to corrective actions. But the mere existence of formal reviews is a strong signal that quality is taken seriously and may therefore indirectly contribute to the results that are produced.

A more constructive form of reviews may be employed within the development team to provide more immediate feedback. A simple and very effective form is simply that team members read and comment about the work of each other. The author–reader commenting cycle is a practical way to organise this. It originates from SADT (Ross and Schoman, 1977) where it was formalised and combined with a system of archives that help to manage the document flow. The basic idea is very simple: put results on paper as early as possible and give them to other people to read and comment.

The members of a development team will alternate between being authors and being readers. When an author has something ready for commenting it is made into a document (called a reader kit in SADT) which is copied and distributed to the readers who will make written comment directly in their copy. The written comments are returned to the author who answers each comment before the copy is returned to the reader for filing. In this way each member of the team gets insight into the work of others and may contribute to it by giving constructive comments. The idea is to let authors and readers help each other, through constructive critique, to gradually build quality into the products. In addition, it helps to build a team with common goals and shared responsibility for the results.

Each member of the project may easily build files containing the results of the project and their own comments. Files representing the collective project results can also be built and maintained on the project level

The author–reader cycle does not provide the close interaction that sometimes is needed to solve a problem. It must therefore not be used as a substitute for informal interactions and meetings.

It is important that the readers are motivated to do the commenting. They should primarily try to verify and validate the technical content from their point of view. But they should also comment on the form to the extent that it can help to improve readability. Depending on the formalism used they may be able to perform some analysis and consistency checking. For SDL they may, for instance, perform a manual validation of interfaces in the way described in Section 12.5. They should also check that all the A-rules, S-rules and N-rules adopted by the project are adhered to and that project and company standards are followed.

It can be a hard job to read design descriptions and other documents so one needs motivation and time. Authors should not wait too long, but rather send out pieces of work as soon as possible. This will make the commenting job easier and help the authors to gradually build quality into their results based on the comments they receive during the course of their work.

Interaction with the user and owner may require special attention. Some users will be able to read and comment on specifications and descriptions in SDL quite well after a short course. More often they will prefer more intuitive descriptions like MSCs. In many cases it is necessary to use the formal descriptions as a basis for a meeting or walk-through, where they are explained and discussed with the users and owners.

12.4 Testing SDL systems

12.4.1 The purposes of testing

Our methodology emphasises that the functionality of the system is described separately in the functional design (the SDL description) and that the implementation is designed to be functionally equivalent to the functional design.

We may therefore identify two distinct aspects to test:

1. the functionality;
2. the implementation.

Up to a point the functionality can be tested by means of a simulation tool executing the functional design. Functionality testing does not depend on a particular implementation, but can be achieved with any implementation that is faithful to the functional design. The purposes of functionality testing are listed below:

1. verify the functional design against the functional requirements;
2. detect possible internal inconsistencies and errors in the functional design;
3. validate the functional design against the users and owners needs.

The scope of implementation testing is more limited. Its purposes are as follows:

1. verify the functionality of the implementation against the functional design;
2. verify the non-functional properties of the implementation against the non-functional requirements.

In many practical cases the functionality is executed for the first time in the implementation, so the functionality and the implementation are tested at the same time. Even so, the different purposes of testing call for different test strategies.

Verification of the functional design can be performed by the developers. For each functional requirement they should design a test to check that it is fulfilled. For each interface they should check that the signals and the protocols are as required. If an interface behaviour is described using an MSC, for instance, a similar MSC should be generated by a test.

Detecting possible inconsistencies and errors in the functional design is more difficult. To be sure that everything is found, all possible behaviours must be executed. Since this is unfeasible, one must try to design tests that focus on trouble spots in order to increase the probability that errors will be revealed. Test case design can be aided by analytic techniques such as the ones we shall discuss in Section 12.5.

Validating the functionality involves the users and the owners. In addition to verifying that the explicitly stated requirements are fulfilled, they must assess the way it is done against their real needs and expectations. This should, of course, be done as early in the development as possible, preferably by means of an executable functional design.

Implementation testing can be performed by the developers, firstly, by comparing the implementation with the functional design and then by testing the performance and other non-functional properties.

12.4.2   Test environment

Efficient and effective testing is best carried out by putting the units under test in a test environment where:

1.   inputs, including time-outs, may be generated and replayed;
2.   the responses can be traced;
3.   the execution controlled.

Since SDL processes are loosely coupled and communicate by means of signals it is relatively easy to design a general test environment that may simulate input signals and trace the responses in terms of output signals. The tester may then sit on a terminal and specify input signals, send them to the process under test and monitor the output signals that are generated in response. By storing the generated input signals and the responses on files, tests may be easily replayed and the results compared.

The signal interfaces of SDL hide the internal structures of blocks and processes from each other. Hence, there is no difference between the test environment and the real environment as seen from the processes under test. This means that the processes will work in exactly the same way when placed in the real environment. The only difference will be the arrival rate of inputs and the duration of time-outs. In the test environment, time-outs must be simulated because it is impossible for a human tester to generate inputs at the rates required. By simulating time-outs the test may be performed in a fully controlled and simulated time.

What kind of problems may remain after such a test in simulated time? They will be related to real time behaviour:

1.   The implementation may be too slow to handle the traffic load or to meet response time requirement.

2.   There may be time-dependent synchronisation problems with the real environment or with the real timers.

The first must be remedied by optimizing the execution speed or by adding computer resources. The second by correcting the synchronisation mechanisms. Normally, in a carefully designed system that uses a proven operating system, the second problem will be limited to the hardware–software interface.

SDL run-time support systems (Chapters 10 and 11) usually provide some testing support. There is often a well-instrumented version used for testing on the development computer or the host computer and a less instrumented version that will support the actual application on the target computer. Both versions look exactly the same to the application processes, but the host version normally provides more detailed trace and debug facilities. On the host one needs to look into the processes and to trace the states and transitions more closely than on the target. It should also be possible to force the processes into certain states by setting state and data values. On the target it may be sufficient to monitor the signal interfaces.

We recommend having some trace facilities in the real systems, even after they have been released. If messages are traced and placed on a ring buffer during normal operation, for instance, one may inspect the buffer after a fault has occurred to see the last few messages that were passed just before the fault occurred. Often this provides sufficient information to diagnose the fault.

12.4.3   Testing a single SDL process

A beautiful property of pure finite state machines is that the effort needed to test an implementation exhaustively is proportional to the number of transitions in the state transition diagram. Every possible behaviour is explicitly described by states and transitions. The state transition diagram itself may therefore serve as the test plan. Because there are no hidden data, it is sufficient to only test each transition once.

In an action-oriented description where the states are hidden in variables the situation is different. To test exhaustively it is not sufficient to only test each path in the description once. One must test each path for each possible state of the variables.

As we know the pure FSM is too limited and must be extended with data to serve most practical applications. This immediately sets the testability at peril. The guidelines of Chapter 8 aim to retain as much testability as possible. In particular one should:

1.   represent the control information as explicitly as possible using the finite state machine concepts, i.e. signals and states;
2.   use variables primarily for context knowledge and loop control, i.e. there should be few decisions;
3.   in each control state, assert the possible set of values that each variable and timer may have.

Such diagrams may serve as test plans in a manner similar to diagrams without data. What has to be done is to work through the diagram transition by transition and check that the specified outputs are generated that the next state is reached and that its assertion holds for the actual values. This must be done for some characteristic values. Values must be selected such that each branch of a decision is carefully tested. Moreover each asterisk transition and each save must be tested.

Of course, to test exhaustively, one must test every transition for every possible value. But practical experience indicates that when data are used primarily to hold context knowledge it is sufficient to test just a few characteristic values. Although this is not an exhaustive test, it seems to be sufficiently effective for practical purposes. In that way the implementation testing effort remains roughly proportional to the number of transitions.

It is our experience that testing can be carried out mainly on the SDL level. The test person will generate input signals and check the responses working through the SDL process graphs transition by transition. The code itself must be inspected only when errors are detected and need to be corrected. Since the SDL diagrams are useful during testing they also tend to be updated when errors are detected and corrected.

Normally there is no point in testing units smaller than an SDL process. Often it is practical to put several processes together, because they will generate signals to each other. Thus, a process that has been tested helps to drive the next one through its test and, at the same time, test the interface between them. This also extends the scope of the test to include a validation of the internal interfaces.

Testing an action-oriented SDL process graph is not as easy as testing a state-oriented one. Since the set of possible values may be very large and hard to determine one needs additional test plans aiming to uncover as many errors as possible with a limited effort.

12.4.4   Testing complete SDL systems

Most SDL systems consist of many processes operating concurrently and interacting with each other through a network of channels and signal routes. Implementation testing at this level means to test the implementation of concurrency support, synchronisation, signal transfer mechanisms and timers. This task is independent of the particular SDL application and only needs to be done once for each type of run-time support system.

On the system level we are more concerned with functionality testing than implementation testing. The challenge is not so much to test the implementation as to test if the cooperation between processes yields the desired functionality without undesirable side-effects or errors.

To verify that the functionality is right we need to compare the actual behaviour on the system interfaces with the required behaviour. In our *AccessControl* system we shall observe the same message sequences as those we specified in the requirement specification (Chapter 3). Thus, the MSCs in the requirement specification become useful testing aids. To simplify the comparison between the required and the actual behaviour it helps to present the test results in the form of MSCs.

Before SDL processes are integrated it is well worth the effort of inspecting the signal interfaces manually. Check that the signals produced by one process are the same signals as the receiver expects and vice versa. Also check that the signals are implemented the same way, i.e. that the signals are encoded in the same way.

System integration and integration testing has been a traumatic experience for many projects in the past. But it need not be so. One may test SDL processes separately, inspect the format of signals, signal by signal, to ascertain that they are consistent and bring the processes together without problems. It has happened, more than once, that processes developed by different people work together right away when they are integrated.

The most difficult task is to check that the system is internally consistent such that nothing may go wrong. It is not sufficient to test each SDL process alone and to check the static interfaces. There may still be dynamic problems in the combined behaviour. A deadlock may occur where two (or more) processes are unable to proceed because they wait endlessly for signals from each other. A livelock may also occur where processes cycle endlessly without making any useful progress. Such problems cannot be found by testing the processes separately. They may even be hard to find by inspecting the process graphs of the processes together.

In principle we must test all possible combinations of states and transitions in all the processes of the system. This means to drive the system through all states and transitions in the global behaviour product. Figure 8.2 illustrates what this means for two simple processes. For a complex system, this is a formidable task which is not practically feasible.

What can we do then? The first thing is to test that the system behaves as intended in normal situations. Run through all the requirements and verify that they are fulfilled. Be sure to exercise each state and transition in all the process types in the system at least once in the integrated system. The next thing is to cover all the exceptional situations. Try to provoke errors by giving inputs that are not specified and check that the exception handling is correct. Finally, try to reveal dynamic interworking problems by running input sequences concurrently on different interfaces. One way to do this is to generate random input on as many interfaces as possible, another is to design test cases that focus specifically on possible interworking problems. Such problems are often caused by conflicting initiatives, which occur when independent sources contend for the same service or resource (see Section 12.5). Therefore, one should look specifically for conflicting initiatives. In a process graph they are visible as states where the input signals may come from two or more sources independently of each other.

Since the total number of global states in even moderately sized systems is too high to allow exhaustive testing, interworking errors may survive in delivered systems. Therefore, it is important to have mechanisms for coping with them when they do occur. A symptom of such errors is unspecified input signals arriving in a state. Therefore, it is very useful to put a trace on all unspecified receptions, i.e. asterisk transitions in SDL. Quite often this is sufficient to detect and diagnose the error once a fault occurs.

When systems are designed the way we recommended in Chapters 9 and 10, such errors rarely have disastrous effects. The system as a whole will continue to operate, but some of its processes may be stuck.

To sum up:

1.   Always check the signal consistency before processes are integrated.

2. Try to use processes together as much as possible during the testing to increase the probability of reaching unforeseen combinations.
3. Try to deliberately provoke errors by generating abnormal input sequences.
4. Design specific test cases to exercise conflicting initiatives and other potential sources of interworking problems.

12.5   Validating interfaces

In this section we shall look more closely at the interworking problems and how we can analyse the dynamic behaviours looking for such problems. The focus will be on the interfaces between processes and how we can check that they are mutually consistent. We consider this as a validation problem because the interfaces are where the processes provide their services to each other.

12.5.1   The problem

The validation of interfaces has two aspects:

1. static checks on signals;
2. dynamic behaviour analysis.

Static signal checking is comparing the signal sets of each pair of processes that may cooperate. All signals that may be output from one of the processes in a pair should be specified as an input to the other. Otherwise unspecified reception may occur.

Static signal checks are not sufficient to guarantee that nothing will go wrong, however. To be sure it is necessary to check all possible interactions that may occur dynamically during actual behaviour. To this end we must analyse the behaviour of each process in relation to the other processes.

A general way to do this is to generate a global behaviour product, i.e. a graph representing the combined behaviour of the processes and the channels as if they were one process. This graph will represent all the possible ways that the behaviours of the processes may combine during actual behaviour. By inspecting the states and transitions of the global behaviour graph one may find errors. Deadlocks, for instance, will appear as states in the global graph without further transitions. This approach is generally known as reachability analysis.

The problem with reachability analysis is the computational complexity involved. Even for a moderately sized system such as our *AccessControl* system, the time and memory needed to generate the global graph, may be prohibitive. The global graph may even be infinite due to the possibly infinite queues and data objects. Therefore, some problems may not even be detectable by this kind of analysis.

Simplification is needed to make the analysis feasible in practice. Several approaches to reduced reachability analysis have been proposed in the literature (see, for instance, Lam and Shankar, 1984 and Kajiwara et al., 1985). In the following we shall briefly describe an approach that simplifies the problem by making projections (see Chapter 2) of the observable behaviour at interfaces before reachability analysis is performed.

It was clearly illustrated in Figure 8.2 that the global state graph grows very rapidly with the size of independent behaviours. To reduce the complexity one must therefore get rid of the independent parts and focus on the dependent parts of behaviour. This can be partially achieved by making projections where the interactions on other interfaces are hidden leaving only observable interactions on the interface under validation visible.

In order to validate all interfaces in a system, we need to know which processes are intended to cooperate with each other. It is not sufficient to look at the static picture of channels and signal routes in the SDL diagrams to see this. It is necessary to consider indirect connections, for instance, through several layers of protocol processes and dynamic associations too. When we know which processes are intended to communicate we are faced with two problems:

1. To decide that only the processes that are intended to communicate in reality will communicate. This problem is not trivial and will in the general case require that we perform a dynamic analysis tracing all the possible PId values that may be assigned to each PId variable. (Using special resource allocator processes as we recommended in Section 8.3.7 may help to reduce this problem.)
2. To validate the interfaces between those that communicate.

We will not discuss the first problem here, but have a closer look at the second. We shall present a practical way to validate interfaces between a pair of processes and, in addition, give some guidelines as to how process graphs should be made in order to ensure consistency.

12.5.2 Reachability analysis

Each process in an SDL system will normally communicate with several other processes. In order to simplify matters we will look at the interface between a pair of processes such as those represented informally in Figure 12.1. Even though it is a simple example, it serves to illustrate the approach.

We may note that this example contains conflicting initiatives. In state *1* of both processes the specified input signals come from two independent sources, either the environment or the other process. Does this lead to any problems in this case? As an exercise the reader should try to answer this question now before reading on.

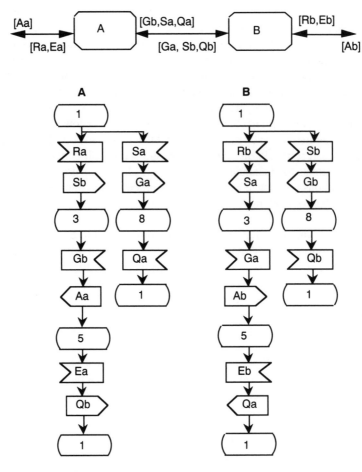

Figure 12.1   *Two SDL processes*

A full reachability analysis will expand the global behaviour product of the two
processes and the signal queues in their input ports. As a first step we transform the
process graphs into the transition charts shown in Figure 12.2, (transition charts were
introduced in Chapter 3).

In a transition chart each input is prefixed with a "?" and each output by a "!". Each
transition consists of one atomic action which is either an input or an output. Therefore,
there are more nodes in the transition charts than there are states in the corresponding
SDL process graphs. Otherwise the transition charts and the process graphs are
equivalent.

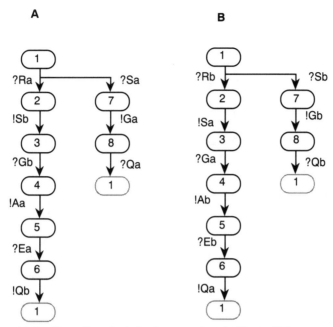

Figure 12.2 *Transition charts for the processes in Figure 12.1*

Figure 12.3 shows a partial global behaviour graph for the system. Each node represents a global state and each transition an atomic action, i.e. a signal reception or a signal sending. Note that a signal sending means that a signal is placed in the input port of another process. The signal reception occurs when the signal is consumed by the process. Thus, a signal transfer takes two distinct atomic actions. The same holds for signals to and from the environment. We have therefore included as the first actions the output actions *!Ra* and *!Rb* performed by the environment, which must precede the input actions *?Ra* and *?Rb*.

Figure 12.3 illustrates that the size of a global behaviour graph grows very quickly with the size of the processes. This growth, popularly called the "state explosion", is due to the following main reasons:

1. The signals from the environment arrive independently of each other. The global graph will contain all possible orderings of such independent signal receptions.
2. The states of the input queues are partly independent of the process graphs. The global graph contains all possible combinations of process states and queue states.
3. The atomic actions involved in sending, receiving and consuming signals in two directions between the processes may be ordered in many ways. The global graph will contain all such orderings.

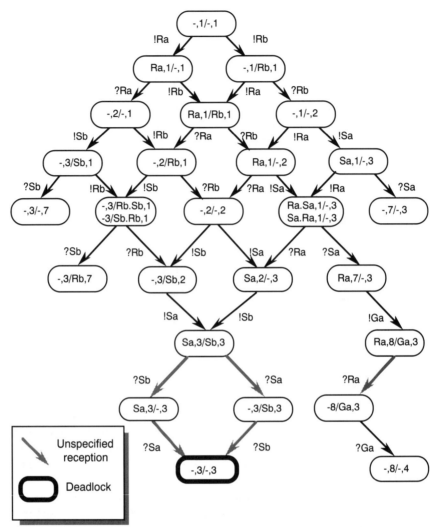

Figure 12.3   *A partial global behaviour graph for the example in Figure 12.2 (Each
global node is labelled with A-input, A-node/B-input, B-node.)*

From Figure 12.3 we see that conflicting initiatives may indeed cause trouble in this
example. The two initiatives are represented by the independent signals, *Ra* and *Rb*,
from the environment. If both signals are received before any internal signal, the system
will eventually end up in the deadlock state *(-,3/-,3)*. Before we reach that state, two
unspecified receptions will have occurred.

In this simple example a full reachability analysis is quite feasible. In more complex
cases it is necessary to simplify the job.

The first thing we will do is to reduce the independence between the behaviours. When we validate an interface between two processes it helps to make projections where all transitions that are not observable at that interface are hidden. We therefore try to derive the role behaviours the processes exhibit across the interface.

We have already seen an example of a role behaviour in Figure 3.19 where the observable behaviour of the *User* as seen from the *AccessControl* system was described. The user may do many different things, but only those that the system may observe are visible. We made that diagram in a constructive way, by putting ourselves in the position of the user. What we will do now is to derive role behaviours from the more detailed behaviours defined in SDL diagrams.

12.5.3 Deriving role behaviours

The procedure consists of the following main steps:

1. Transform the SDL process graph to a transition chart.
2. Mark invisible transitions by "τ".
3. For every node reachable by a visible transition, find the group of nodes that are reachable from it by following one or more invisible transitions. Such node groups are called node ambiguities (see below).
4. Replace each node ambiguity by a single node having all the visible transitions of the component nodes. The result is a possibly non-deterministic, role behaviour diagram.
4. Check that each ambiguity is formed according to given rules. If the rules are satisfied, the role behaviours will be faithful to the original behaviours. If not the original behaviour is internally inconsistent.

We shall illustrate the approach by means of the example in Figure 12.2. The first step, to transform the process graphs into transition charts, is already done.

The next step is to mark all transitions that are invisible in the roles (i.e. at the interface under study) with a special symbol, "τ", as illustrated in Figure 12.4.

In Figure 12.4 all transitions sending signals to and receiving signals from the environment have been marked by a "τ". All τ-transitions are unobservable at the interface. This means that process *B* is unable to know whether process *A* is in node *1* or *2*. We say that node *1* and *2* form a node ambiguity or, more specifically, the τ-ambiguity of node *1*.

Definition: node ambiguity
A set of nodes in a transition chart that cannot be distinguished from the outside is called a node ambiguity.

Definition: τ-ambiguity of a node

The set of nodes reachable from a given node by following one or more τ-transitions is the τ-ambiguity of that node.

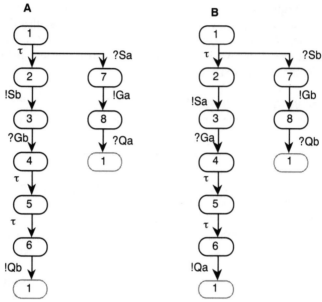

Figure 12.4 *Invisible transitions marked*

We form τ-ambiguities for all the nodes that are reachable by visible transitions. Our next step is to replace these τ-ambiguities by single nodes, as illustrated in Figure 12.5. The result is role behaviours where only the observable transitions are visible.

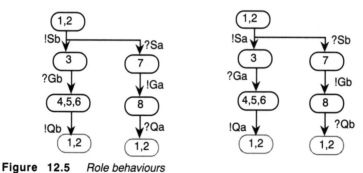

Figure 12.5 *Role behaviours*

We may now use reachability analysis to validate the role behaviours. Since all the independent external transitions have been removed, the global behaviour product of the role behaviours will be smaller than the product of the original behaviours (see Figure 12.6).

In Figure 12.6 the same deadlock appears as in Figure 12.3. Is that because we were lucky this time or will it always be the case that problems also show up in the role behaviours?

The answer depends on the properties of nodes that are merged in a node ambiguity. Consider for instance the τ-ambiguity formed by nodes *1* and *2*. Node *1* accepts an input whereas node *2* generates an output. This means that the merged nodes are not equivalent in terms of observable behaviour. But since one node is a pure input and the other is a pure output node, they may be merged in a consistent way. We can accept combining input nodes and output nodes, but we cannot accept combining input nodes with different input sets. The reason is that the environment is unable to distinguish between the nodes in the ambiguity and is therefore unable to adapt the set of outputs it may send to match the different input sets of the nodes. We therefore consider it as an inconsistency if input nodes in a node ambiguity have different input sets.

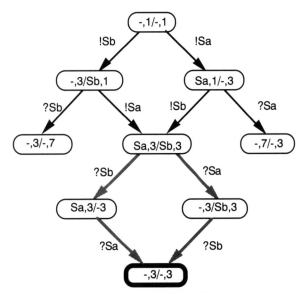

Figure 12.6 *The global graph generated from the role behaviours*

Definition: input consistent node ambiguity

A node ambiguity is input consistent if all its member nodes with (visible) input transitions accept the same set of (visible) inputs. Ambiguities with only output transitions are input consistent.

Definition: input consistent role behaviour
A role behaviour is input consistent if all its nodes are input consistent ambiguities.

An input consistent role behaviour will be faithful to the original behaviour in the sense that we can detect the same unspecified receptions and deadlocks by reachability analysis. The role behaviours in our example are input consistent and, therefore, they are faithful to the original behaviour.

If we take the input queues into account we may extend our ambiguities. Because of the input queue, process *B* will not know immediately when process *A* makes a transition from node 2 to node 3 sending signal *Sb*. In fact *B* may be doing a similar transition, sending *Sa* to *A* at the same time. Therefore, the nodes *1,2* and *3* form an output extended node ambiguity where node *3* and node *1* have different input sets. Hence, this output extended ambiguity is not input consistent.

This inconsistency was the underlying reason for the unspecified receptions preceding the deadlock in our simple example. We could easily have found this inconsistency by separately analysing the SDL process graphs in Figure 12.1 without performing any reachability analysis at all.

This is perhaps the most important result from role analysis. It helps us to analyse and detect inconsistencies in the behaviour of process types independently of any actual application context.

Definition: strongly input consistent role behaviour
A role behaviour is strongly input consistent if all ambiguities that can be formed by extending its nodes to include the nodes reachable by one or more output transitions, are input consistent.

The notion of input consistency can also be used constructively. Whenever we design a new process type we should ensure that it is strongly input consistent in all its role behaviours

S-rule: input consistent process
Design SDL processes such that all their role behaviours, i.e. the behaviour visible to processes in their environment, are strongly input consistent.

This rule can be checked during the construction of a process. For each state and role, find the output extended ambiguity and check that it is strongly input consistent. Do this for all states and roles as you construct the process graph. Whenever the rule is violated, additional inputs must be added in some states (or removed in other states). In this way it is possible to detect and correct potential problems in a process type before it is instantiated in a particular context. Reachability analysis on the other hand, requires a specific application context.

Conflicting initiatives are special trouble spots that should be checked carefully. An ambiguity containing both input nodes and output nodes represents a case of conflicting initiatives.

Definition: conflicting initiative node
A role node having both input and output transitions is a conflicting initiative node.

If a node with conflicting initiatives is not strongly input consistent it is likely to cause problems in any context. When two such nodes are combined as in our example, unspecified reception will occur and possibly a deadlock.

Part IV

Evolution

Chapter 13 deals with aspects of reuse and system evolution while Chapter 14 looks into maintenance.

Reuse Methodology

In this chapter we shall look at how software components can be reused.
Sometimes new needs similar to old solutions and sometimes the components
should initially be made for the explicit intent of reuse. We shall specify the
requirements for reuse and object-oriented techniques for acquiring reuse.

13.1 What is "reuse"?

Just like "recycling" is the dominant buzzword for showing environmental
awareness, "reuse" is becoming the buzzword for software engineering. Just like
recycling is sound and important for environmental reasons, reuse is sound and
desirable for software engineering. Actually "recycling" is a very concrete form of
"reuse" where the hardware is being captured, modified and applied again. The major
aim is to acquire the new application with less energy consumption than making it from
scratch. This is the major aim for software reuse, too.

In software, however, the copying is not energy-consuming, while for freezers, cars
and paper the copying (manufacturing) consumes large amounts of energy. In software
the energy is spent in designing it, so reuse is intended to minimise the effort spent in
designing software.

"Reuse" means "use again" or "use more than once" and we have already emphasised
the notion of "type" which is designed to be used more than once as the template, for

instance (or as base for other new types). In this chapter we shall have a look at how we may acquire reuse of components between systems as well as within systems.

We have considered earlier the development process as starting from scratch, but development never starts from scratch. There is always something that has triggered the development and often there are similar things available.

For the very early phases of the development it is important to know whether we are describing (partly) an existing system, made by ourselves or a competitor. To what degree can we actually observe the system? To what extent can we manipulate the existing system in order to observe specific aspects of it?

As we are beginning to produce descriptions, another set of questions should be answered. Is there documentation of a similar system already in existence? Have we available requirement specifications? Are we going to make it ourselves? Is the existing documentation written in any of the languages that we intend to use? There may only be programming code in an old-fashioned programming language (FORTRAN, C, etc.).

If we are really fortunate there may actually be SDL descriptions of similar systems and then the question arises: Has the SDL been properly and correctly used? If SDL 84 has been used, then it is not compatible with SDL 92, while if SDL 88 has been used it is compatible, but possibly not worth using directly without changing it into SDL 92 with object orientation.

Often we are not making the complete system, but merely a small part of it, such that the interface is given and it may or may not be well-suited for our methodology.

Every product needs some unique features to set it apart from other similar products. The reuse methodology addresses the very fundamental problem: how to make products that are essentially unique using, as much as possible, parts that are not unique.

This introduces three subproblems:

1. *Design for reuse.* How to achieve the generality needed in components from which many applications may be composed. What design criteria should be used to make components sufficiently general to be useful in many applications without making them too general or hard to use.
2. *Design with reuse.* How to use existing components to achieve the uniqueness desired in new systems (and new components) with minimum effort.
3. *Classification.* How to classify and store components so that they can be found and retrieved for reuse.
4. *Organisation.* How to organise the development process and how to reward reuse.

The main objective of the reuse methodology is to provide some answers to these questions. In this chapter we shall concentrate on the first two subproblems.

Reuse is not a new idea. Software engineers have been using their own and others' material for as long as software has existed. Some software is being reused without anybody thinking about it as reuse at all: operating system operations, mathematical functions (from libraries) and recently windowing systems. The productivity gained from using commercial windowing systems is so definite that very few even think of making their own windowing system, just like very few think about making their own operating system.

Some organisations have project management that promotes reuse. They make software available in libraries and there may even be a dedicated librarian. Such organisations have made reuse a part of their culture. In many organisations, however, the "not made by me" syndrome has been predominant, meaning that the developer has more faith in his own product than in something somebody else has made. This is often due to inadequate knowledge of what others have made. In some cases finding and adapting existing software takes more effort than making the software from scratch. The trend today is that software complexity increases and development time constraints decrease and then reuse is the only way to keep competitive.

Some software engineers have been reusing existing software by copy and paste. This kind of reuse is said to constitute the majority of software reuse today. The major problem with this kind of reuse is that there is no formal connection between the original piece of software and its descendants. In practice this means that original errors will proliferate while subsequent corrections on the original will not reach the descendants! Corrections within one of the descendants will not reach the original.

In this chapter we shall show that reuse is partly a technical problem, which can be handled well by object orientation and partly an organisational problem of the project and company management. Technical solutions do not suffice.

13.2 What can be reused from *AccessControl* ?

In principle we can reuse almost all parts on all levels of an existing system; the question is to what degree the existing components fit with the new application. In the *AccessControl* system case, we have designed it without the intent that it should be reused by some other application. It was not designed for reuse. This is the case for a lot of software. Often we believe it to be a singular system, but when we acquire better understanding, we improve it such that it gets a wider application domain. Figure 13.1 suggests what can be reused from the *AccessControl* system.

What are the characteristic features that a component should possess in order to be reusable? To some degree the answer depends on the nature of the component. Is it a physical thing such as an electronic device? Is it a piece of executable software such as an operating system? Or is it simply a piece of text such as a data declaration to be inserted in the source code?

For each application it must be more cost-effective to use the (existing) component than to develop a new one. For each component the sum of the productivity gains of all its applications should cover its development cost with some surplus. Reuse is more cost-effective the higher the abstraction level we can reuse. Our methodology aims at reuse on all levels with proper emphasis on the domain analysis. In Figure 13.1 we find the highest levels of reuse on top and the lowest on the bottom.

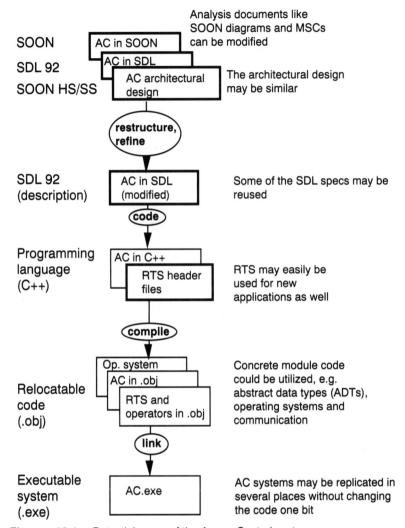

Figure 13.1   *Potential reuse of the AccessControl system*

Regardless of the nature of the component there seem to be at least six fundamental requirements:

1.   *It must be simpler to use than to build.* On the one hand a component must have a body of parts that take some effort to build, on the other hand the parts must be aggregated to form a unit that can be used as a whole. The *information hiding* principle must be employed yielding a clear distinction between the interface and the body. The interfaces of components should be considerably

simpler than their bodies. Pure data, such as a Pascal record, are not a suitable components because they have no separation between interface and body.

2. *It must be application-independent.* It must not be special to a specific application. It must be possible to define and to understand in its own terms independently from any particular application. Thus, it must be clearly isolated from its applications. In this respect the component should be general.

3. *It must be applicable.* It must be more than general. It must also provide something that is actually needed in applications and it must provide it in a way that is compatible with each particular application context. This may require some adaptations in each case. Thus, the applicability may depend on the *adaptability*. The functionality, the interface and the non-functional properties must suit (or be adaptable to) the needs of (many) applications.

4. *It must be competitive.* It must compare favourably with similar components in order to be the preferred choice. If, for instance, the performance is too low or the price too high it may not be competitive. It must not require more "glue" than its competitors.

5. *It must be controllable.* A part which is being reused should be prohibited from being used in contexts where it cannot perform according to its intentions.

6. *It must be separately maintainable.* Maintenance of the reused part should be kept independent from the use of it. The development of a component should not be affected by any specific use of it. Then it would lose its generality.

13.3   Example: bank

13.3.1   Why describe a bank?

In this book we have described an *AccessControl* system in great detail. We have applied reuse within the *AccessControl* system, for instance, by introducing the block type *LocalStation* with the specialisations *BlockingStation* and *LoggingStation*. We are now trying to find another overall application where we can reuse our software from the *AccessControl* system in order to explain reuse for our readers. This motivation for finding a *bank* as our reuse example may seem backward, but in fact it is not. Companies are always looking for products similar to what they have, but with another market. *Bank* systems are a different market from *AccessControl* systems.

We could also have presented the motivation the opposite way: we get the assignment to describe a *bank* from a communication perspective. We get this assignment because the requester knows that we are competent in describing complex real time systems. Since we have done several such jobs before, we have a number of descriptions which we may reuse. As a consequence of our methodology we find that the *AccessControl* system can offer a number of similar components to what we need.

13.3.2   Initial requirements

Our task is to describe a *bank* from a communication point of view. We choose without much argument to use SDL (cf. Chapters 4–8). Following our general methodology we will most probably use the SDL RTS which we have sketched in Chapters 10 and 11 as the base for the implementation. This implies that we will use C++ as the major implementation language (if at all possible).

These initial requirements must be seen as hypotheses, as further analysis may prove that other choices are preferable.

A-rule: initial requirements
State explicitly the requirements that are assumed to hold for the project. These requirements are often requirements to the tools and languages of the project.

We summarise these initial choices by a table (Figure 13.2).

Descriptions	**Initial requirements.**
Non-functional requirements	
Functional requirements	
Functional design	SDL shall be used
Implementation design	SDL RTS may be used
Implementation in C++	Basic C++ classes may be used
Product as such	

Figure   13.2   *Initial requirements*

In addition to the RTS being reused, there should be some general implementation classes in C++ that can be reused. These could be generic concepts like linked lists or more complex concepts like a graphic subsystem.

13.3.3   Partial analysis

Our first technique is to identify and understand the most important concepts of the subject area. At first we are less interested in the interrelationships than the pure concepts of the subject. We apply the rules given for domain analysis in Chapter 3 to develop a problem statement, a dictionary and possibly a conceptual model.

A *bank* is a place where *money* is handled. Money can be handled in many different ways, there is *cash* and there are *cheques*. Money can also be handled without any physical media denoting their value, e.g. by electronic means, internal transactions of the *accounts*. For our purpose we are mostly interested in the parts of the bank where physical representation of money is handled.

There are a number of *tellers* in the bank. Some of them have a *clerk*, while others have not. The ones having a clerk can be called *cashiers* and the automatic ones can be called an *automatic teller machines (ATMs)*.

Some of the *customers* prefer the automatic teller machine where they insert their *card* and *key* in their personal code in order to get access to their account and receive cash money. They may also get other services such as a *printout* of their account balance. The automatic teller machine is provided with a *display* which serves as the interaction sender to the customer.

Some of the customers prefer the manual cashiers which may be talked to and communicated with in a human fashion. The clerk, however, has his own data display and keyboard. The cashier can perform more services than the automatic teller machines.

Figure 13.3 *Problem statement of bank*

The problem statement gives us the first insight into what a bank is all about. It can be used to communicate with bank employees to improve our understanding.

Also, following the method in Section 3.2.2. we continue to make a structured dictionary containing definitions (in prose) of important words in the bank domain.

The bank could have the following initial dictionary (Figure 13.4).

Account	a computer representation of money associated with an owner
ATM	automatic teller machine
Bank	a place where money is handled
Branch	an office where the bank serves its customers
Card	personal identification means
Cash	physical representations of money guaranteed by the state
Cashier	manual teller (with clerk)
Cheque	representation of money with various guarantees
Customer	external processes signalling to and receiving from the bank
Display	screen to convey messages to customer or clerk
Key	part of keyboard
Money	the ultimate signals from a bank
Printout	written message on paper (signal to customer)
Teller	communication ports with the bank system

Figure 13.4 *Initial bank dictionary*

Producing a dictionary adds to the understanding of the subject being analysed. Furthermore, the system analysts will become even more able to communicate with *bank experts*. The concepts in the dictionary will often find their way into the SDL description as types. They may be signal types (such as *Money*) or they may be data types (such as *Account*) or block or process types (such as *Teller*).

We have now gained some insight into the *bank* domain, but the connection to the *AccessControl* system is not at all evident. We continue to make a simple sketch of what we believe is a typical *bank branch* instance (Figure 13.5).

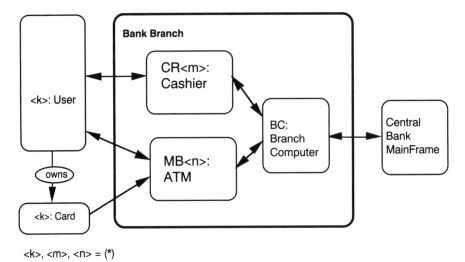

$\langle k\rangle, \langle m\rangle, \langle n\rangle = (*)$

Figure 13.5   *Structure of a specific bank branch instance*

In Figure 13.5 we see that the "consist-of" relation refers to one specific branch unit with a set of instances of tellers. You may want to make a more detailed sketch than that. For many purposes a realistic illustration of a typical instance supplied with labels will serve the purpose excellently. Sometimes photographs may even be used and the analysts themselves should use this informal sketch to make the first distinction between relevant and non-relevant objects.

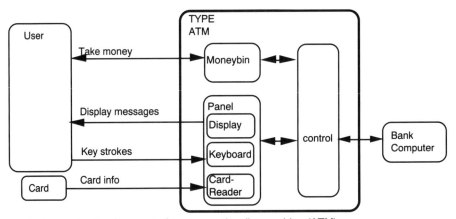

Figure 13.6   *Structure of an automatic teller machine (ATM)*

We will also take a look at the relationships between the bank and its immediate surroundings. Our *bank* may have a (incomplete) communication relation (Figure 13.7).

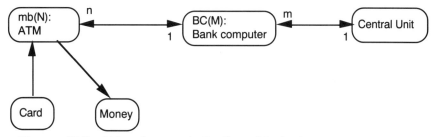

Figure 13.7 *External communication lines of the bank*

The similarities with the *AccessControl* system are becoming clearer, but we still want to improve our understanding by taking a closer look at the concept specialisation structures.

A bank has two kinds of *tellers*, either *automatic teller machines* or *cashiers*. This is also written down in the prose description. *Automatic teller machine* and *cashier* are specialisations of *teller* meaning that all *cashiers* and *automatic teller machines* are *tellers* and whatever general things can be said about *tellers* will be valid for both *automatic teller machines* and *cashiers*.

We obtain a specialisation hierarchy (Figure 13.8).

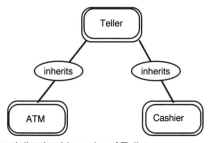

Figure 13.8 *Specialisation hierarchy of Teller*

We can also add specialisation hierarchies of *Display* and *CardReader,* etc. This leads to an even more complete understanding of the concept structure.

Having concentrated on static structure, we must also analyse the dynamics of the bank. According to the methodology, we can use MSCs (message sequence charts) to capture selected communication situations[1].

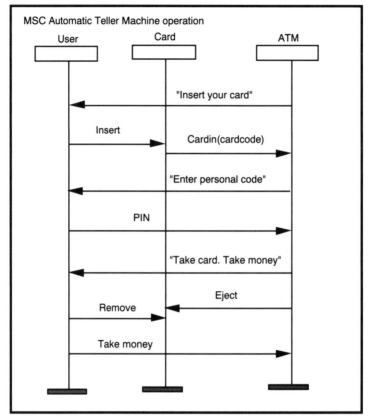

Figure 13.9   *Message sequence chart of an automatic teller machine*

The purpose of the partial analysis is to lay the foundation for finding existing components to match the components of the *bank* system. If we cannot find similar components in the library we will have to go on to make a detailed specification from scratch.

A-rule: partial analysis
Analyse the system such that it may be possible to recognise similarities with existing components. This should include both conceptual, structural and behavioural descriptions. Return to analysis if library search fails to produce the desired building blocks.

We summarise again using a table (Figure 13.10).

Descriptions	Initial requirements.	Partial analysis
Non-functional requirements		Problem statement dictionary
Functional requirements		SOON: specialisation hierarchies, system structure MSC: typical cases
Functional design	SDL shall be used	
Implementation design	SDL RTS may be used	
Implementation in C++	Basic C++ classes may be used	
Product as such		May be found

Figure 13.10 *Partial analysis*

During the partial analysis activity it should also be possible to see whether there are existing products that can fit into the system directly. In a bank the *AccessControl* system may be used as a subsystem of the *bank,* for example, to guard the security boxes in the safe.

13.3.4 Library search

Following our partial analysis of the bank, we want to see whether there are pieces residing in a library which may be used in the design of the *bank* system. We find that there are quite some similarities between the *AccessControl* system and the *Bank.* On an inner level a *LocalStation* is quite similar to a *Teller.*

How can we take advantage of the similarities between the *AccessControl* and the *Bank*? In the simplest case the application concept is a direct specialisation of the library concept.

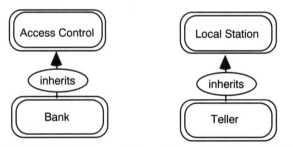

Figure 13.11 *Direct inheritance-relations between application and library*

If the inheritance-relation shown in Figure 13.11 is the case, then we are quite well off. We will inherit large parts of the description from the library and need only specify additional features. The potential problem is that even though the inheritance-relation is all right conceptually, adaptability is not planned. Typically, the library packages which were not designed with a *bank* in mind, have some internal structures that are not quite what we want for a *bank*. For instance, some internal types are not "virtual" and cannot be redefined. If we maintain both the supertype and the specialised type, we can easily modify the supertype to contain the necessary virtual specifications.

The second case is that we know that *AccessControl* and *Bank* are similar, but they are not directly inheritance-related. Being similar, but not directly inheritance-related means that they are both directly inheritance-related to a common, more general concept[2]:

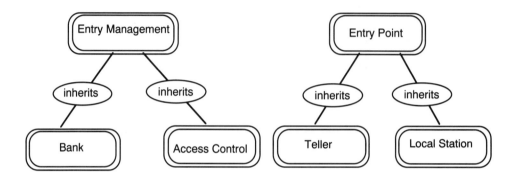

Figure 13.12 *Indirect inheritance-relations*

A-rule: library search
*See if there is a **Y** in a library which is similar to an **X** in your dictionary. When a similarity is found, either make **X** a direct specialisation of **Y** or restructure your library by making a **Z** which can be specialised to both **X** and **Y**.*

We find that this is the time when we want to use more formal SDL since we already have similar SDL diagrams in the library. Typically, we will find packages having parameterised types. Our application concepts will bind such parameters, redefine virtual types and specify additions.

The use of existing types within packages (libraries) is slightly different from (re)using types from your own specification. Let us now recapture the major principles behind reuse through object orientation and give a few structuring rules (S-rules) which will help the specifier in his quest for the best conceptual description.

Let us first take a look at the difference between traditional reuse of types (i.e. procedures of programming languages) and the corresponding object-oriented approach.

Traditional libraries are supplied with extra information for each element which is supposed to facilitate the library search. Since the technical structure is flat, the extra information is absolutely necessary. Furthermore, the individual elements cannot be used independently of each other. Information about the restrictions of use is only found in the documentation and is not directly reflected in the library structure. This is illustrated graphically in Figure 13.13.

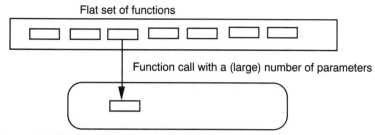

Figure **13.13** *Traditional function libraries*

When a type is specialised the general type is reused. The specialisation is still a type and may be specialised still further. The types are organised in a taxonomy which facilitates searching. There is not so much need for extra information to support the finding of the proper concept within the library (see Figure 13.14). Restrictions of use can be encapsulated in higher order objects.

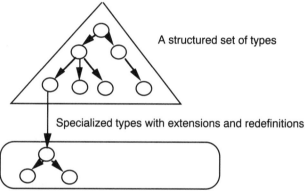

Figure **13.14** *Object-oriented libraries*

Virtual parts are redefined in specialisations. This means in effect that the general description is also being altered. This adds to the flexibility. A general type may be reused more easily when it includes redefinable parts. This is illustrated in Figure 13.15.

S-rule: generality separation
Organise your types in specialisation hierarchies such that the general concepts need no specific information about the different specialisations.

This rule emphasises the difference between the mechanism of specialisation and more traditional use of parameters. Using parameters the general level must know all possible specialisations. The object-oriented method states the contrary. This ensures separate maintainability meaning that the application may not even be known to the designer of the general concepts and the source code may not be available to the application level at all. Only a proper external specification is needed.

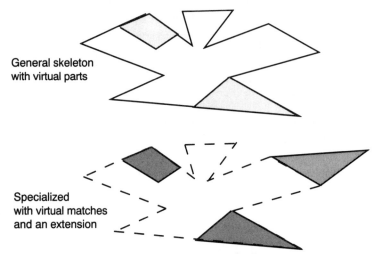

General skeleton
with virtual parts

Specialized
with virtual matches
and an extension

Figure   13.15 *The impact of virtual parts to reuse*

You will find that structuring the types in type hierarchies is not a trivial task. During the design phase it is common to move features from the special to the general levels and sometimes vice versa.

Flexibility is dangerous and should be kept under strict surveillance. It is much easier to loosen ties than tighten them. Loosening ties is backward compatible. The powers of languages such as SDL lie partly in the ability to check consistency at an early stage. Testing at run-time is much more expensive than checking the static description. The smaller the units that can be checked extensively, the better. The more you specify about the external interface of a type, the more can you check at specification time. In SDL, the virtual concept adds needed flexibility, but that does not mean that everything should be virtual.

S-rule: controllability and flexibility
If you are designing both the general and the special concepts, do not sacrifice the controllability of the general ones for flexibility of the specialised ones.

A common argument in favour of virtual types is that our world is changing rapidly, the software must be maintained extensively almost continuously and therefore maximum flexibility is needed. It is true that we see more rapid change in the software requirements now than we did before, but the demand for reliability has not been decreased. The reader should be aware that virtual types are not used in order to maintain the general concept. If the general concept needs maintenance as our *LocalStation* concept is made into *EntryPoint*, this cannot be done by matching virtual types only! We make a new version which should be handled by a configuration management system (see also Section 11.4.3) and we make a version that is backward compatible (preferably) and it is utterly important that the maintenance is controlled such that compatibility errors are caught immediately (most preferably by the SDL analyser program) and finalised types makes extensive analysis easier.

What virtual types really do is to facilitate the making of new "variants" or conceptual specialisations of a general concept. As we did with our original *AccessControl* system, we got new *LocalStation* variants (*BlockingStation* and *LoggingStation*) which could easily be described by additions and new virtual matches based on *LocalStation*. In this process of describing the new concepts (*BlockingStation* and *LoggingStation*) we had to introduce virtuality to types which we had finalised before. Thus, we actually created a new version (of *LocalStation*), as well as new variants (specialisations). However, as the new version is very close to the old, the increased flexibility can easily be identified and its consequences are finite.

The necessary generalisation may result in the parameterised type definition in SDL shown in Figure 13.16 (see also Figure 7.22).

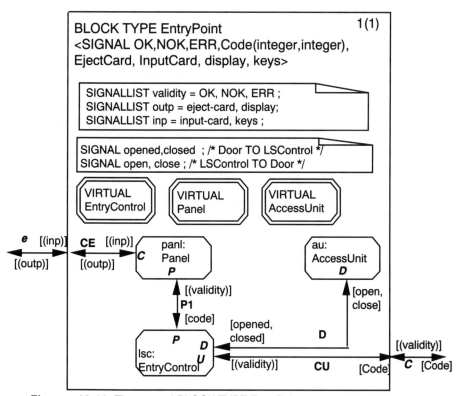

Figure 13.16 *The general BLOCK TYPE EntryPoint*

There are two dimensions over which we generalise. Firstly, we make the components adjustable, i.e. redefinable in specialisations. This is achieved by virtual types. Secondly, we assume that signals in a *bank* system are different from those of an *AccessControl* system. Thus, we generalise over signal names. This is achieved by using context signal parameters. Note that the type is parameterised and instances cannot be made directly from it.

We summarise our generalising activity in some S-rules:

S-rule: adaptable components
Achieve adaptable components by introducing virtual types. Ensure that such types get proper general names. Balance the adaptability of virtuals by using ATLEAST to limit the redefinability.

S-rule: context parameters
Achieve independence of signals and data types by introducing context parameters. Balance this independence by constraining the context parameters.

Again we illustrate this activity (see Figure 13.17).

Descriptions	Initial requirements	Partial analysis	Library search
Non-functional requirements		Problem statement dictionary	
Functional requirements		SOON: specialisation hierarchies, system structure MSC: typical cases	SOON: direct specialisation, generalising
Functional design	SDL shall be used		Types for direct specialisation or for generalisation
Implementation design	SDL RTS may be used		
Implementation in C++	Basic C++ classes may be used		Find applicable general classes
Product as such		May be found	

Figure   13.17 *Library search*

13.3.5   Adaptation

The necessary adaptation amounts to specialising the general types into the new application area.

The specialised version of the *EntryPoint* for the *bank* will be:

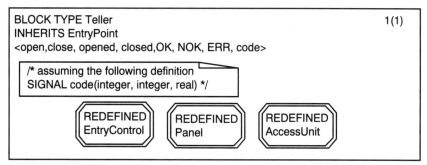

BLOCK TYPE Teller   1(1)
INHERITS EntryPoint
<open,close, opened, closed,OK, NOK, ERR, code>

/* assuming the following definition
SIGNAL code(integer, integer, real) */

REDEFINED EntryControl   REDEFINED Panel   REDEFINED AccessUnit

Figure **13.18** *Bank teller*

The activity will be to redefine virtual types and bind formal context parameters (see Figure 13.18 for both these mechanisms).

The subsequent phases of the methodology will also adapt to the new SDL descriptions. The hardware structure and software structure of the *AccessControl* system may or may not be adaptable to the *bank*. After some consideration we find that the same general design can be used for an *ATM* as we used for a *LocalStation* in the *AccessControl* system: this means that even though the SS type diagram of an *ATM* is new, most of its components belong to existing types.

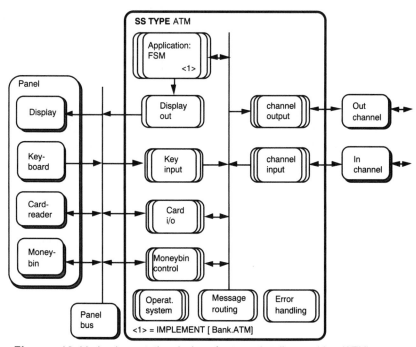

Figure **13.19** *Implementation design of automatic teller machine (ATM)*

Most gain of the restructuring will be achieved if it is possible to make a generalised implementation which matches the generalised SDL description.

Descriptions	Initial requirements	Partial analysis	Library search	Adaptation
Non-functional requirements		Problem statement dictionary		
Functional requirements		SOON: specialisation hierarchies, system structure MSC: typical cases	SOON: direct specialisation, generalising	MSC: validate the adaptation
Functional design	SDL shall be used		Types for direct specialisation or for generalisation	Specialise for new application
Implementation design	SDL RTS may be used			Apply corresponding HS and SS
Implementation in C++	Basic C++ classes may be used		Find applicable general classes	Implement generalised types
Product as such		May be found		

Figure   13.20 *Adaptation*

We have now in principle designed the *bank* system (suppressing the fact that we have not given all the SDL diagrams, the implementation design and C++ code here), but what about our original *AccessControl* system and what about the future reuse gains?

13.3.6   Clean up

Now there is a need to record the benefits and perform the clean up such that the development environment is ready to make the next reuse even easier.

By including the generalised types (such as *EntryPoint*) into the library, we have achieved the library becoming more general and, thus, more applicable to new applications other than *AccessControl* and *bank*.

Furthermore, the *AccessControl* is in effect identical to what it was before the restructuring. We are both forward and backward compatible[3]!

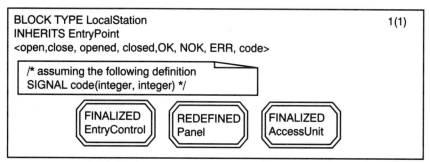

Figure 13.21 *Restructured LocalStation*

There are some effects of this library restructuring. We notice that the more general concepts are the more virtual types they will include[4]. Notice that the *Panel* and the *AccessUnit* are FINALIZED in order to restrict the flexibility and increase the analysability. Furthermore, this is done in this case to make the new *LocalStation* functionally compatible with the old one. We have not shown the system diagram here, but indicated that in the system diagram there is a signal definition of the actual context parameters. Consider the signal *Code* where the constraint indicates two integer parameters. This means that the actual signal type matching the context parameter *Code* must have at least two integer parameters, but it may have other auxiliary parameters.

N-rule: ATLEAST and FINALIZED
In specialising, take care to balance flexibility and analysability properly using ATLEAST and FINALIZED to constrain the virtual types.

Another very typical and very important effect of library search is that when realising the similarity between *AccessControl* and *bank*, we can find features of *AccessControl* which may be applied to *bank*, but which we had not thought of in the *bank* context. A possible example of this is the *LoggingStation* in *AccessControl*. A logging station for bank transactions may not be a bad idea!

The next clean up activity will be to adapt the implementation design and actual implementation of the *AccessControl* system to the new generalised scheme. In our case merely names are changed compared with the implementation structures of the *AccessControl* system.

The clean up activity whereby old products (here *AccessControl* system) are restructured according to a new scheme, may at first glance look futile: why restructure working software such that the user cannot know the difference?

- By restructuring old products, these will share maintenance with the new product. This implies that all corrections (and errors!) and improvements in the general parts are proliferated across all products.

Errors in the general parts will more easily be detected, since all products share that code. Thus, the *bank* system will take advantage of the extensive testing on installed *AccessControl* systems (updated with the new version).

This activity is summarised in Figure 13.22.

De-scriptions	Initial require-ments	Partial analysis	Library search	Adaptation	Clean up
Non-functional requirements		Problem statement dictionary			
Functional requirements		SOON: specialisation hierarchies, system structure MSC: typical cases	SOON: direct specialisation, generalising	MSC: validate the adaptation	
Functional design	SDL shall be used		Types for direct specialisation or for generalisation	Specialise for new application	Specialise for backward compatibility
Implementa-tion design	SDL RTS may be used			Apply corresponding HS and SS	Generalise HS and SS
Implementa-tion in C++	Basic C++ classes may be used		Find applicable general classes	Implement generalised types	Reimplement the old product
Product as such		May be found			

Figure 13.22 *Clean up*

We have now a more complete picture of the reuse activities. The organisational challenges of reuse are substantial. Clearly the effort needed to restructure the old product must be justified by future saving. But even if the future savings are substantial, it may be difficult to get the resources to do the job, because nobody sees it as their responsibility. Therefore, to reap the benefits of reuse organisations must be able to look beyond the immediate needs of each particular system development. It is important to make the developing organisation aware of the "anatomy" of effective reuse since the restructuring activities will especially require resources which may seem unproductive from a manager's point of view.

It is also a fact that organisational set-ups such as a sharp distinction between development and maintenance may hamper effective reuse. During a restructuring activity of old products, modern configuration management and project management are extremely important.

13.4   Modes of reuse

What to reuse	How to reuse	Tools to use	Problems
Instance as such (1)	Replicate directly	Production	Not always practical
Behavioural type: operator, procedure	Include library, call procedure (2)	Linker, pre-processor	Errors spread as well as corrections
Object type: class, blocktype etc.	Specialise, match virtuals (3)	Browser (4), (and as above)	(As above)
Parameterised type, template	Bind context parameters	(As above)	(As above)
Macro	Use and expand	Macro processor	Not analysable as a unit (5)
Text skeleton	Copy and edit	Editor	No feedback to origin of reuse (6)
Methodology (7)	Project managing	Methodology support tools (8)	
Competence	Moderate turn-over	Cooperative projects (9)	Inter- and intra-company competitiveness

Figure   13.23 *Modes of reuse*

The table in Figure 13.23 requires some supplementary explanation:

1.   "Instance as such" means an unmodified product, just replicated from the given description.
2.   Function libraries are the traditional way to reuse types. Libraries are included in the total execution by the linker and the function descriptions are technically brought to the attention of the compiler by inclusion.
3.   Object-oriented types (e.g. SDL types and C++ classes) can be most effectively reused by specialisation and redefinition of local virtual types.
4.   Browsers are used in order to search in the structure of types.
5.   Macros cannot be analysed as such, they must be analysed in the context in which they are called (expanded). This is because macros offer only syntactic substitution. (See Chapter 6 for more details.)

6. Text skeletons (or in general any syntactic pieces) can easily be copied and modified, but the reference back to its origin is normally lost (or it is utterly informal). Even when the reference back to the origin is known (e.g. by some configuration management system), maintenance of the origin does not automatically cause a change of the descendants. This may of course be an advantage sometimes.

7. Since we are mainly interested in the production of software of correct quality by using little energy, we cannot ignore the impact of a common methodology. If a number of development teams use the same methodology they can communicate more easily and change jobs within the company. The reuse of a methodology can be seen in this context as a "meta type" which describes the development. It can be adapted to each individual project and the reusing of a methodology may lead to more general methodology along the lines sketched in the sections above.

8. Methodology support tools include integrated chains of tools such as SDL-tools and program generation tools, run-time system, etc. In addition, we should have project management tools and configuration management tools.

9. In cooperative projects, competence may be reused to the benefit of all even when the methodologies differ. Experiences can be transferred and failures avoided.

13.5   Designing for reuse

In this chapter we have mainly concentrated on designing *with* reuse, i.e. the motivation for reuse has been the new application. In this final section we shall have a look at some of the problems that arise when an organisation wants to design *for* reuse, i.e. the motivation for design is not necessarily one new product, but a range of products where parts may be reused.

13.5.1   Granularity

The first types of software to be reused were small well-defined functions. They were documented by mathematics notation. Their problems were reasonably apparent as the theory behind them was known. The interface was a function interface and the adaptation amounted to supplying actual parameters. Such function libraries grew in size and we got operating systems and database management systems with a large number of interrelated functions.

In object orientation the most popular reused concepts are such basic concepts from computer science as lists, graphs and input/output.

In recent years, larger conceptual frameworks exemplified best by the industry standard windowing systems (Microsoft Windows®[5] and X) have become items for reuse. The new thing here is that the framework is not merely a set of advanced functions, but also a way of thinking including a set of "protocols" for how to use the individual functions in a consistent manner.

By using SDL 92, it is possible to define types on a variety of granularity levels. When context parameters are used to make the type self-contained, it can be used in a number of contexts. Through binding of the context parameters the types can be composed into types of higher complexity.

In organisations that will try to improve their reuse practice, there seems to be a natural maturation process from using small reusable components like mathematical functions to using larger frameworks like a windowing system or database system. Following this maturation process the organisation will improve their own production of components along the same lines.

13.5.2   Retrieval

When an organisation has promoted reuse, after a short time the number of available components may become fairly large. Furthermore, there will be a commercial market for components. We can see this already with such things as clip art libraries for artistic work and C++ class libraries. The problem arises: how to retrieve the best component from the library?

Firstly, the criteria for "best match" must be known and formalised. This is a problem well-known from classification theory. But even though the problem is well-known, the ultimate solution is not. The wanted component must be characterised according to a number of dimensions and a retrieval system must then obtain the closest components.

When some potential candidates have been isolated, the developer must study the detailed adaptation necessary. If the component is under the control of this organisation, it is feasible to work along the lines of the adaptation activity outlined above, but if the component is from an external library only direct specialisation or direct use is possible. Then the component may not be applicable after all!

13.5.3   Inclusion

The inverse problem of retrieval is the problem of inclusion into the library. When the number of components is small there may seem to be no real need for restricting the inclusion of components in the library, but the number may increase rapidly and then several problems have automatically been included as well.

Some of the problems are technical:

*   *Quality*. Are the included components of the same quality or has the quality been asserted (e.g. according to ISO 9000)?
*   *Diversity*. Are the included components sufficiently different from each other or is it desirable to have several similar components in the library?

Some other problems are organisational:

*   *Authorisation*. Who decides which components shall reside in the library?

- *Maintenance*. When a component is included in a library, who has the responsibility for maintaining it and are there resources available for such necessary maintenance?
- *Applicability*. Who decides which components are eligible for reuse in a specific project?

Such problems will always arise and must be taken into account by the software management of a company.

13.6   Conclusion

We have in this chapter touched upon the promises and challenges of software design. The ability of an organisation to apply reuse to its development and its product is essential for its technical success. Reuse of components through object orientation can give major new improvements with a minimum of effort and development time.

Most gain from reuse comes in organisations where designing for reuse is commonplace and where the emphasis is on the more abstract levels of descriptions. The successful organisations have resources for library clean up and for advanced component management.

Notes

[1] Compare the following message sequence chart with Figure 3.16 describing a message sequence chart of the *AccessControl* system.

[2] Even when there is no clear conceptual similarity between the two concepts, reuse may very well take place on components within them. Parts may be reused also when their enclosers have little in common.

[3] By "forward compatible" we mean that new versions to come will be compatible with this version. By "backward compatible" we mean that this version is compatible with older versions.

[4] This in turn lessens the analysis power, but not necessarily the descriptive power. of the enclosing description.

[5] Microsoft and Windows are registered trademarks of Microsoft Corporation, US Patent No. 4,974,159.

CHAPTER 14

Maintenance

In this final chapter we shall look at how to maintain systems after they have been developed the first time. The design-oriented descriptions shall be the starting point of the maintenance.

14.1 What is maintenance?

A common definition of the word "*maintain*" is: (1) to continue; carry on, (2) to preserve or retain, (3) to keep in repair, (4) to provide for; support, (5) to defend or sustain, (6) to assert or declare (American Heritage, 1979).

Most of these connotations fit well with what we understand by "maintenance" in software engineering. We shall, however, try to distinguish maintenance from other related matters, such as tailoring, adaptation and reuse. Furthermore, we shall look into the contents of the maintenance activity.

Definition: maintenance
Maintenance is the activity whereby a software product is modified to continue to fulfil its purpose (in relation to given users and markets).

By this definition we limit ourselves to software products. This means that if the software is not (a part of) a product, then we will not talk about "maintenance". This distinguishes "development" from "maintenance". We also require that maintenance is the preservation of the product's purpose, which technically may mean that the requirement specification will remain stable. This will distinguish maintenance from making another product.

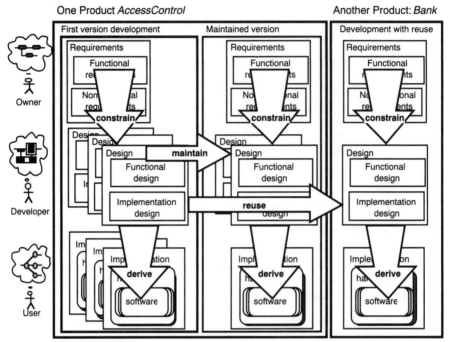

Figure 14.1   *Development, maintenance and making another product*

Let us classify some common causes that trigger maintenance.

14.1.1   Error correction

Error correction is the result of imperfect system development. Either there are logical errors in the functional design (SDL description) or there are errors in the transformation of the SDL descriptions onto target. For some products the error may even lie in the hardware. Our methodology tries to decrease the amount of errors which remain in the system at product delivery time, but errors will occur.

Error correction will normally have highest priority since a product with errors will have negative marketing effects.

14.1.2   Obvious changes

Obvious changes are those which will give substantial improvements with very little effort. Here we will also put deficiencies of the requirement specification which was not found until product delivery. Beta-releases[1] of software are well-suited to eliminate the need to do obvious changes on real product releases.

14.1.3 Simple enhancements

The users of a product will produce a number of good suggestions following the ability to experiment with the system. Most of these suggestions are hard to find in the development phases since the main focus is to then fulfil the requirements. Enhancements will extend the requirement specification without violating the overall purpose of the product.

14.1.4 Competition driven improvements

A product is seldom alone on the market and competitors find features other than our product has. From a market point of view some of the features of our competitors must be incorporated into our product in order not to lose market shares in the future.

14.1.5 Technology driven improvements

A product is always built on foundations which are not made by the product vendors themselves. Furthermore, the product may work in an environment where other parts are not made by the vendor of this product. Any changes in the product environment must be matched by the product.

Such changes may include operating system changes, hardware changes, network changes, basic software changes, etc.

Often the product vendors will suggest changes in the product environment themselves for either price or performance reasons.

Our *AccessControl* system could be improved by voice replies from the *LocalStation*. This technology has become more readily available at a moderate price.

14.2   Related activities

Let us have a look at activities which are related to maintenance, but which still have a different focus.

14.2.1 Configuring and adaptation

By "*configuring*" we mean the fitting together of a specific product for a customer which suits his/her needs exactly. The modifications are merely the selection of parts of existing types, typically to determine the various cardinalities of the system.

In our example *AccessControl* system, the number of *LocalStations* and number of *Panels* per *LocalStation* are such configuring information.

By "*adaptation*" we mean that the product is adapted to a different environment than it has worked in before. This is very close to technology-driven improvements which we classify as maintenance in Section 14.1.5, but adaptation is when the modifications are done to sell to new customers. Adaptations will rarely make the product better as such, but it will fit into more environments.

In our example *AccessControl* system, adaptations could for instance derive from the desire to use the already existing identity cards.

14.2.2 Tailoring

By "*tailoring*" we mean the modification of a product to suit the specific requirements of a customer. Tailoring will normally enhance the product to the needs of the specific customer.

Sometimes, but not always, tailoring may lead to general product improvements.

In our example systems, some of the enhancements of the *AccessControl* system such as *BlockingStation* and *LoggingStation* could have been tailored to a specific customer.

14.2.3 New product development with reuse

It is a matter of choice when to define that a version of an old product becomes a new product. The clue is when the purpose of the product has significantly changed. When does a word processor turn into a desktop publishing system?

On the other hand it may be simple to distinguish between products even though they are built with extensive reuse. The distinction between products is often a distinction between markets.

Our *bank* system is definitely a different product from our *AccessControl* system since their markets are different.

14.3   Organising maintenance

We have looked upon the reasons for maintenance and what modifications are to be done, but how do we do it?

14.3.1 Maintenance responsibility

Some companies find it purposeful to separate maintenance from development, not only by definition, but also by assigning different personnel to development and maintenance. One reason for this is that it secures a clear cut transition from development to maintenance synchronised with the first product release. Most probably this will encourage the developers to do their utmost before they leave the product. In some cases the effect may be the contrary as the developers want to get rid of a boring product to start an interesting new development.

A second reason for separating development and maintenance personnel is that it is believed that maintenance can be done by less qualified people than the initial development. When the modifications are beyond a certain complexity it will be defined as development and the development department will be involved again.

Thirdly, separation ensures that documentation must be good enough for communication between the development and maintenance departments. This will definitely decrease the degree of implicit knowledge which is resident in the development team, but not explicitly stated.

14.3.2 Design-oriented focus

The maintenance department will have several products to maintain and for each product there will be a number of maintenance requests of which some are due to inadequate use and some will lead to modifications of the product. When the maintenance team handles the requests they must have an adequate description of the product. The following are some requirements for such descriptions:

- It must be absolutely clear which descriptions describe the product of today and which descriptions are historic.
- There must be descriptions sufficiently precise to serve as a basis for reasoning about the system considering the maintenance request.
- The descriptions must be trusted, meaning there should be little need for extensive testing to verify the description at this stage.

Our methodology holds that the design-oriented descriptions (the functional design (SDL) and the implementation design (SS and HS notations)) are to be focused. These descriptions serve as a trustworthy starting point for the maintenance investigation. When there are alternative descriptions of the system (such as MSCs and programming code), the SDL description will be the definition of the functionality and the HS and SS diagrams will be the canonical description for the implementation. Deviations in other documents mean that they are either historic or that they are erroneous.

When modifications are made the design-oriented descriptions should be the first to be modified (possibly as a result of some new requirement specification) and the other documents should be derived from them.

This design-oriented focus ensures a common understanding of the framework for understanding the system and for changing it.

S-rule: maintenance with design-oriented focus

Start the maintenance investigation from the SDL description and the implementation design descriptions. Let maintenance modify these descriptions first and derive the other documentation and system descriptions from them.

14.4   Using the methodology

14.4.1   Effort needed in initial development

It is a common belief that the application of this methodology takes more resources and longer time than the traditional approach. This is not our experience. Data from actual projects indicate a normal productivity. Some projects have even had very high productivity.

The effort distribution as measured in actual projects, is approximately two-thirds on functional design and implementation design and one-third on implementation. In the measured projects a forerunner of this methodology, SOM[2] was used for functional design and implementation design, while various programming languages were used for implementation (Bræk et al., 1981). In all cases testing amounted to approximately half of the implementation effort, one-sixth of the total. This may be contrasted with the 50–60% commonly reported for implementation and testing in the literature (Boehm, 1981). There is no hard evidence that the projects were significantly more or significantly less expensive than they would have been with another methodology. The reliability and user satisfaction have, however, been good.

One interesting point is that no correlation was found between programming languages and effort distribution. This does not mean that no such correlation exists, simply that other factors were more dominant. One such factor is the clarity of the user's needs at the beginning of the project. If they are unclear, the effort spent on functional requirements and functional design increases drastically and changes the effort distribution correspondingly.

14.4.2 Effort needed in maintenance

One should note that functions tend to change more slowly than technology. A function definition that survives technology changes means that one-third of the cost can be saved. It is our experience that functional designs really survive changes in the implementation.

Independent measurements have indicated that the number of errors in software developed with the methodology is at least half the error density in software developed using a traditional approach. This is attributed to the clarity and precision of function definitions and to the reliability of the design approach.

Conclusively our methodology decreases the efforts needed for maintenance in two ways. Firstly, because there are fewer implementation errors in the initial implementation and, secondly, because functional descriptions are more stable than implementation-oriented descriptions.

14.5 Summary of the methodology

In Chapter 3 we showed different techniques to specify requirements. We used the notations MSC (message sequence charts) and SOON (SISU object-oriented notation).

In Chapters 4–7 we introduced the formal language SDL for functional design. In Chapter 8 we gave advice on how to use SDL in the most efficient way to achieve a proper functional design.

In Chapters 9 and 10 we looked at general principles for implementing SDL systems and how to express such designs in SOON-HS (hardware structure) and SOON-SS (software structure). We learned how to adapt the design to fit the non-functional as well as the functional requirements.

In Chapter 11 we had a closer look at an example implementation in C++. Code skeletons were given and the general implementation design principles shown.

In Chapter 12 we covered verification and validation and looked into expressing test scenarios and role behaviours with transition charts besides coming back to the MSCs produced in the requirement specification.

In Chapter 13 we looked at reuse and in this Chapter 14 we looked at maintenance.

Altogether the book constitutes a complete methodology for the engineering of real time systems.

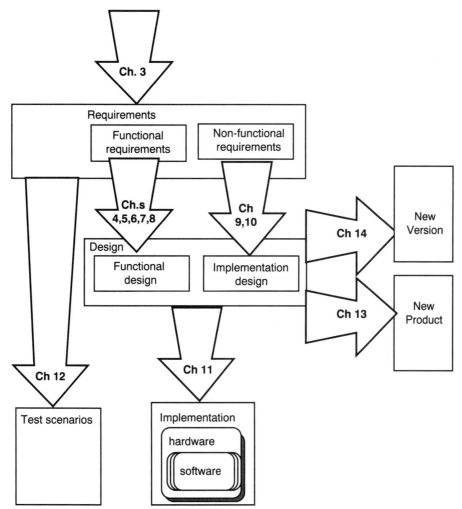

Figure 14.2 *Overview of our methodology*

Notes

[1]Beta-release means that a small number of good customers (or advanced customers) get a prerelease of the product with the explicit intention that they will report back immediately any changes that they want to have done.

[2] SDL-oriented methodology – a forerunner of the present SISU methodology.

Bibliography

American Heritage (1979) *American Heritage Dictionary of the English Language*
  Boston: American Heritage Publishing Co. Inc. and Houghton Mifflin Company.
ANSI (1973) 'Standard N45.2.10-973'
  New York: American National Standards Institute.
ANSI/IEEE (1984) *Software Engineering Standards.*
  IEEE and Wiley-Interscience.
ANSI/IEEE (1987) *Software Engineering Standards.*
  IEEE and Wiley-Interscience.
Belina, F., Hogrefe, D. and Sarma, A. (1991) *SDL with Applications from Protocol Specification.*
  Hemel Hempstead: Prentice Hall, BCS Practitioners Series.
Bennet, S. (1988) *Real-Time Computer Control: An Introduction.*
  Hemel Hempstead: Prentice Hall.
Birtwistle, G. M., Dahl, O-J., Myhrhaug, B.and Nygaard, K. (1975) *SIMULA BEGIN*
  New York : Petrocelli/Charter.
Boehm, B.W. (1981) *Software Engineering Economics.*
  Englewood Cliffs: Prentice Hall.
Boehm, B.W. (1986) 'A Spiral Model of Software Development and Enhancement'
  ACM SIGSOFT Software Engineering Notes, 11(4), August 1986.
Boehm, B.W. (1987) 'Improving Software productivity'
  IEEE Computer, September 1987.
Boehm, B.W. (1988) 'A spiral Model for Software Development and Enhancement'
  IEEE Computer, 21(5), May 1988.
Booch, G. (1991) *Object-Oriented Design with Applications.*
  Redwood City: Benjamin/Cummins.
Bræk, R., Helle, O. and Sandvik, F.(1981) 'SOM. A SDL compatible specification and design methodology. Experiences from 5 years of extensive use'

4th International Conference on Software Engineering for Telecommunication Switching Systems (SETSS), Coventry, July 1981. IEE conference publication no. 198.

Brectbuehl, M. (1991) 'Introduction of the SDL-methodology in a Company' SISU Report SISU-91001, ITUF Report R-27.
Forasekretariatet, Senter for Industriforskning, P.O. box 124 Blindern, N-0314, Oslo 3.

Brinch Hansen, P. (1973) *Operating System Principles.*
Englewood Cliffs: Prentice Hall.

Brooks, F. P. Jr. (1987) 'No silver Bullet. Essence and Accidents of Software Engineering'
IEEE Computer, April 1987.

CCITT Z.100 (1989) 'Specification and Description Language SDL'
Recommendation Z.100.
Geneva: ITU 1989.

CCITT Z.100 (1993) 'Specification and Description Language SDL'
Recommendation Z.100.
Geneva: ITU 1993.

CCITT Z.100-Z.104 (1985) 'Specification and Description Language SDL'
Recommendation Z.100 to Z.104.
Geneva: ITU 1985.

CCITT Z.120 (1993) 'Message Sequence Charts'
Recommendation Z120 ITU.
Geneva: ITU.

CCITT Z.200 (1993) 'CCITT High Level Language (CHILL)'
Recommendation Z200.
Geneva: ITU.

Chen, P. P. (1976) 'The Entity Relationship Model - Towards a Unified View of Data'
ACM Transactions on Database Systems, 1(1), 1976.

Christian, K. (1983) *The UNIX Operating System*
New York: John Wiley & Sons, Inc.

Coad, P., Yourdon, E. (1990) *Object-Oriented Analysis.*
Englewood Cliffs: Prentice Hall.

Cohen, B., Harwood, W.T. and Jackson, M.I. (1986) *The Specification of Complex Systems.*
Addison-Wesley.

Collins (1986) *The Collins Paperback English Dictionary.*
William Collins Sons & Co.

Dahl, O-J., Myrhaug, B. and Nygaard, K. (1968) 'The SIMULA Common Base Language'
Oslo: Report, The Norwegian Computing Centre.

DeMarco, T. (1979) *Structured Analysis and Systems Specification.*
Englewood Cliffs: Prentice Hall.

Deutsch, M.S. and Willis, R.R.(1988) *Software Quality Engineering. A Total Technical and Management Approach.*
Englewood Cliffs: Prentice Hall, Series in Software Engineering.

Dijkstra, E.W. (1968) 'Cooperating Sequential Processes'
In Genuys, F. (ed.), *Programming Languages.*
New York: Academic Press.

Dijkstra, E. W. (1972) 'Notes on Structured Programming'
In Dahl, O-J., Dijkstra, E. W. and Hoare, C. A. R (eds.) *Structured Programming.*
London and New York: Academic Press.

Ehrig, H., Frey, W. and Hansen, H.(1983) 'ACT ONE: An Algebraic Specification Language with Two Levels of Semantics'
Bericht Nr. 83-03, Technishe Universität Berlin.

Ellis, Stroustrup, B. (1990): *The Annotated C++ Reference Manual.*
Addison-Wesley.

Færgemand, O. and Marques M.M. (eds) (1989) *SDL ´89 The Language at Work.*
Proceedings of the Fourth SDL Forum, Lisbon, October 1989.
North Holland: Elsevier .

Færgemand, O. and Reed, R. (eds) (1991) *SDL ´91 Evolving Methods.*
Proceedings of the Fifth SDL Forum, Glasgow, October 1991.
North Holland: Elsevier .

Fagan, M.E. (1976) 'Design and Code Inspections to Reduce Errors In Program Development'
IBM Systems Journal, 15, 1976.

Flo, A., Kjærnes. M. and Skomedal, Å. (1992) 'A Bridge from Structured Analysis (SA/RT) to Specification and Description Language (SDL)'
Conference on Software Engineering for Telecommunication Switching Systems (SETSS), IEE, Florence 1992.

Gane, C. and Sarson, T. (1978) *Structured Systems Analysis: Tools and Techniques.*
Englewood Cliffs: Prentice-Hall.

Ghezzi, C., Jazayeri, M. and Mandrioli, D. (1991) *Fundamentals of Software Engineering.*
Englewood Cliffs: Prentice Hall.

Goldberg, A. and Robson, D. (1983) *SMALLTALK-80 The Language and its Implementation.*
Addison-Wesley, Series in Computer Science.

Hall, P.A.V. and Galal, G.H. (1989) 'Computer-aided Software Engineering'
Computer-aided Engineering Journal, 6(4), August 1989.

Hatley, D.J.and Pirbhai, I.A. (1987) *Strategies for Real-Time System Specification.*
New York: Dorset House Publishing.

Haugen, Ø. (1980) 'Hierarchies in Programming and System Description'
Master Thesis. University of Oslo 1980 (in Norwegian).

Hoare, C.A.R. (1978) 'Communicating Sequential Processes'
Communications of the ACM, 21(8), August 1978.

Hoare, C.A.R. (1985) *Communicating Sequential Processes.*
    Englewood Cliffs: Prentice Hall.
Holzmann, G.J. (1991) *Design and Validation of Computer Protocols.*
    Prentice Hall International.
IEEE 1076 (1987) 'VHDL Reference Manual'.
    IEEE standard 1076.
ISO 8807 'Information processing systems - Open System Interconnection – LOTOS–
    A Formal Description Technique Based on the Temporal Ordering of Observational
    Behaviour'.
    International Standard ISO 8807.
ISO 9000-3 'Guidelines for the Application of ISO 9001 to the Development of
    Software'.
    International Standard ISO 9000-3
ISO 9000 'Quality Management and Quality Assurance Standards. Guidelines for
    Selection and Use'.
    International Standard ISO 9000.
ISO 9001 'Quality Systems – Model of Quality Assurance in Design Development,
    Production, Installation and Servicing'.
    International Standard ISO 9001.
ISO 9074 'Information processing systems – Open System Interconnection –
    ESTELLE: A Formal Description Technique Based on an Extended State Transition
    Model'.
    International Standard ISO 9074.
Jacobson, I., Christerson, M., Jonsson, P. and Övergaard, G. (1992) *Object-Oriented
    Software Engineering A Use Case Driven Approach.*
    ACM Press Addison-Wesley.
Kajiwara, M., Ichikawa, H., Itoh, M. and Yoshida, Y. (1985) 'Specification and
    Verification of Switching Software'.
    IEEE Transactions on Communications, 33(3), March 1985.
Knudsen, J. L., Løfgren, M., Madsen, O. L. and Magnusson, B. (1992) *Object-
    oriented Software Development Environments. The Mjølner Approach.*
    (Preprint 1992, to be published by Prentice Hall International.)
Kristensen, B.B., Madsen, O.L., Møller-Pedersen, B. and Nygaard K. (1987)'The
    BETA Programming Language'.
    In Shriver, B. and Wegner, P. (eds), *Research Directions in Object-Oriented Lan-
    guages.*
    MIT Press.
Lam, S.S. and Shankar, A.U. (1984) 'Protocol Verification via Projections'.
    IEEE Transactions on Software Engineering SE10(4), July 1984.
Meyer, B. (1988) *Object-Oriented Software Constructions.*
    Hemel Hempstead: Prentice Hall, International Series in Computer Science.
Milner, R. (1980) *A Calculus of Communicating Systems.*
    Springer Verlag, Lecture Notes in Computer Science 92.

Milner, R. (1989) *Communication and Concurrency.*
  Hemel Hempstead: Prentice Hall.
Naur, P. and Randell, B. (1969) 'Software Engineering'.
  Report on a conference sponsored by the NATO Science Committee, Garmish
  1968. Scientific Affairs Division, NATO, Brussels 1969.
Ng, P.N. and Yeh, R.T. (1990) *Modern Software Engineering. Foundations and
  Current Perspectives.*
  New York: Van Nostrand Reinhold.
Nygaard, K. (1986) 'Basic Concepts in Object-oriented Programming'.
  Sigplan Notices, 21(10) October 1986.
Parnas, D.L (1971) 'On the Criteria to be Used in Decomposing Systems into Modules'
  Technical Report CMO-CS-71-101, AFOSR-TR-74-0095.
  Carnegie Mellon University, August 1971.
Parnas, D.L. (1972) 'On the Criteria to be Used in Decomposing Systems into
  Modules'.
  Communications of the ACM, 5(12), December 1972.
Pirsig, R.M. (1976) *Zen and the Art of Motorcycle Maintenance. An inquiry into
  Values.*
  Ealing: Transworld Publishers, Corgi Books.
Pressman, R.S. (1982) *Software Engineering: A Practitioner´s Approach.*
  McGraw-Hill, Series in Software Engineering and Technology.
Ross, D.T. (1977) 'Structured Analysis (SA). A Language for Communicating Ideas'.
  IEEE Transactions on Software Engineering SE-3(1), January 1977.
Ross, D.T. and Schoman, K. (1977) 'Structured Analysis for Requirements
  Definition'.
  IEEE Transactions on Software Engineering SE-3(1), January 1977.
Saracco, R., Smith, J.R.W. and Reed, R. (1989) *Telecommunications Systems
  Engineering using SDL.*
  North Holland: Elsevier.
Saracco, R.and Tilanus, P. eds (1987) *SDL´87 State of The Art and Future Trends.*
  Proccedings of the Third SDL Forum, The Hague, April 1987.
  North Holland: Elsevier.
Stroustrup, B. (1992) *The C++ Programming Language.* Second Edition.
  Addison-Wesley.
Walraet, B. (1991) *A Discipline of Software Engineering.*
  North Holland: Elsevier.
Ward, P.T. and Mellor, S.J. (1985) *Structured Development for Real Time Systems.*
  Englewood Cliffs: Prentice Hall.
Yeh, R.T. (1990) 'An Alternative Paradigm for Software Evolution'.
  In Ng, P.N. and Yeh, R.T. (1990) *Modern Software Engineering. Foundations
  and Current Perspectives.*
  New York: Van Nostrand Reinhold.
Yourdon, E. (1989) *Modern Structured Analysis*;
  Englewood Cliffs: Prentice Hall.

Yourdon, E.and Constantine, L. (1975) *Structured Design: Fundamentals of a Discipline of Computer Programs and System Design.* Englewood Cliffs: Prentice Hall.

Index

A-rule
  concept model 76
  context 80
  dictionary 75
  initial requirements 360
  library search 366
  message sequence charts 83
  partial analysis 364
  problem statement 74
  role behaviour 91
  sketch system structure 91
  specialisation hierarchies 79
A-rules 55, 74, 185
abstract data types 119, 132, 205
abstract system 218
abstraction 32
abstractions 12
AC-System 23
Access Control system 23
access point 74, 75
Access Points 24
access right 74
Access zone 75
access zones 74
AccessCode 139
action 28, 39
action-oriented 40, 188, 276
active 127
Active waiting 266
activities 17
actor 48, 190
actually interleave 264
Adaptation 372, 381

aggregate 34
aggregation 34
alarm clocks 127
analysis rules 185
answer 124
Application 256
application domain 74
architecture 235
Array 137
Arrow heads 98, 105
assignment 123
assignments 121
asterisk 109
asterisk input 111
asynchronous communication 232, 260, 293
Asynchronous medium 232, 233
Asynchronous operation 229
atleast 171, 177, 207, 370, 373
ATM 362
atomic 273
Authentication 75
Authorisation 75, 377
axiom 132
AXIOMS 133

bank 359
baseline 19
behaviour 28, 39, 103
behaviour product 192, 341, 342
behaviour role 195
Beta-releases 380
Block 98, 206, 210
block instances 99

block reference 98
block roles 209
block set 99
block structure 209
block substructure 112
block type 99
BLOCK TYPE EntryPoint 369
buffer overflow 233
buffers 261, 270

card 25, 75
card code 74, 75
Card-code 24
CardReader 120
CCITT 94
Central Station 24
centralised system 222
Channel 98, 228
channel substructure 112
Charstring 137
classes 44
Classification 356
clean up 372
cohesion 194, 288
comment symbol 111
communication 28, 260, 362
communication medium 265
composition 36
concatenation operator 152
conceptualizing 186
concrete 32
concrete system 218
Concurrency 229, 257, 260, 292
concurrent 30, 41, 191
concurrent processes 97, 191
conflicting initiatives 343
constructive 140
context knowledge 41, 190, 199
context signal parameters 370
continuous signals 143, 230, 273
control 118
control domain 188
control flow 124
control information 41
control states 188
controllable 359
coroutines 114
coupling 194, 288
create 145
Create symbol 146

dash 109
data 118, 198, 205
data domain 188
data flow 240, 284, 291
data flow diagrams 49, 54
DCL 121, 135
Deadlock 272, 341, 342
decision 188, 284
decision symbol 124
Definition
    behaviour 28
    conflicting initiative node 351
    input consistent node ambiguity 349
    input consistent role behaviour 350
    maintenance 379
    node ambiguity 347
    process quality 14
    real time system 31
    strongly input consistent role behaviour 350
    structure 30
    system 26
    system quality 6
    t-ambiguity 348
description 10, 39
design constraints 71, 72, 288
design reviews 335
design-oriented xiv, 16, 220
designation 76
Developer 6
dictionary 75, 361
direct code 289
distributed system 222
Documents 21
domain analysis 65
door 24, 74, 75
Duration 127

EFSM 54, 189, 276
EFSM) 96
embedded 31
enabling condition 142
encapsulation 42, 286
ENDNEWTYPE 133
engineering organisation 9
entities 25
entity classes 106
entity relationship 45
environment 5, 45, 66, 69, 80, 195, 334
ER descriptions 45
ER diagrams 45

ErrMessage 132
Error correction 380
Errors and noise 227
event 230
event detection 231, 232, 259, 289, 296
events 261, 265
executes 240
EXPORT/IMPORT 231
exported 143, 144, 161
extended finite state machine 54
extension 76

fail safe 32
fault tolerance 32
final destination 211
FINALIZED 174
Finite resources 229
finite state machine 51
first receiver 211
flowlines 108
frame 108
frame symbol 56, 240
free-pool 272
FSM 51, 189, 276
functional design 14
functional requirements 14, 64, 337
functionality 13
functionality testing 337

gate constraints 167
gate symbols 102
gates 102, 166, 207
GENERATOR 136
GetPIN 122, 157
Granularity 376
guidelines 55

hardware design 294
hardware structure 55, 237
hardware–software interface 219, 224, 227, 256
heading 108
hierarchical types 44
HS 55, 56

implement 240
implementation design 14, 218, 371
implementation design description 219
implementation testing 337
inactive 127
infix operator 137
informal text 121

information hiding 286
inheritance 36, 365
inheritance-relations 366
inherits 56, 169, 172
initialisation construct 124
inlet 152
input port 96, 109, 224, 229, 232
input symbol 109
Input–output 256
intention 76
interface behaviour 82
interface behaviours 87
interleave 267
interrupt 262
interrupts 261
is compiled 240
is loaded 240
is translated 240

layering 68, 196, 203, 209
layers 67
library restructuring 373
literals 132, 133
livelock 341
load 289, 296
load control 265, 272
Local Station 24
LocalStation 101
loop control data 190
LSControl 101, 129

macro 150
macrodefinition 152
macros 203
magnifying glass 105
maintain 379
maintenance 19
mapping 235
message communication 261
message sequence chart 82, 364
message sequence charts 55
method 10, 11, 54
methodology xiii, 10, 54
methodology, 10
milestone 19, 335
MSC 55, 56, 82, 340
multiplexing 230
mutual exclusion 233

N-rule
    ATLEAST and FINALIZED 373

names in macros 204
source and destination 205
State and Nextstate 205
state subdiagrams 204
N-rules 55, 185
needs 6
NEWTYPE 133
non-decisive data 190
non-functional properties 223, 235
non-functional requirements 14, 64, 71, 72, 221, 337
notation rules 185
note 100, 109
NOW 127, 263
Null 128

object 43, 53
Object orientation 43
object-oriented 31
objects 31
Obvious changes 380
OFFSPRING 128, 146
on-line system. 31
operating system 230, 239, 258, 261
Operator 75
OPERATORS 133
outlet 152
output symbol 110
Owner 6

packages 178, 365
page numbers 108
pages 205
Panel 119
PanelControl 121, 153
panels 24
paradigm 186
parallel 30, 191, 229
Parallel processes 191
parameterised types 136, 366
parameters 157
PARENT 128
partitioning 34
Passive waiting 267
Personal Identity Number 101
phases 19
Physical distribution 228, 296
PId 110, 128, 211, 274, 343
PIN 74, 75
play 5, 69, 78, 195, 334
Powerset 138

pre-emptive 267, 269, 271, 278, 289, 292
predefined types 121
priority 264, 267, 269, 271, 282, 289, 296
priority input 115
problem statement 74, 361
procedure 150, 153, 203
procedure (declaration) symbols 156
procedure call symbols 156
procedure calls 260, 269, 278, 289, 292
procedure diagram 157
procedure start symbol 157
process 102, 195, 210
Process Identifiers 211
process quality 334
Process requirements 64
process symbols 105
product 186
project system 9
projection 33, 88, 343
prose 74
purpose 27, 74

quality 5
quality assurance 15, 334
quality control 5
quasi-parallel 114, 229, 239
question 124
QuickBase 134, 139

reachability analysis 342
real time constraints 31, 248, 260, 264, 290
real time system 225
reality model 65
redefinable 370
REDEFINED 170
reference model 18
references 240
remote 144, 160, 161, 199, 211, 254, 321, 323, 324
requirement specification 334, 340
requirements 13, 14, 63
requirements specification 13, 64
RESET 127
resource allocation 201
resource allocator 201
resource pool 146
response time 227
response times 248, 296
return symbol 157
reuse 158
reviews 335

revision 19
role 5, 27, 34, 45, 48, 69, 78, 190, 195, 334
role behaviour 89, 347
role-play principle 69
routing process 131
RTS 55, 258, 284
run-time support 278
run-time support system 55, 302

S-rule
    abstract data types as software modules 286
    adaptable components 370
    block purposes 209
    communication-oriented design 265
    concurrency 191
    context parameters 370
    control flow 189
    control processes 210
    controllability and flexibility 368
    data 190
    data types 206
    decisions 189
    external signal priority 265
    free-pool limits 272
    generality 290
    generality separation 367
    golden rule of partitioning 194
    hardware similarity 252
    input consistent process 350
    input–output layering 268
    input–output processes 268
    interaction processes 195
    interconnections 196
    internal processing priority 265
    load control 265
    macros 204
    maintenance with design-oriented focus 383
    max waiting time 269
    mean peak load 248
    messages 291
    optimisation 290
    ownership of variables 291
    physical distribution 245
    PId variables 191
    procedures 203
    protocol layering 198
    resource allocation 202
    routing processes 211
    separate free-pools 273
    services 204
    shared data 200

shared variables 291
signal set 189
similar process instances 195
similarities within processes 203
state orientation 188
step 1, partition the environment behaviour 210
Step 2, identify behaviour roles 210
step 3, mirror the behaviour roles by actors in the system 210
step 4 , context knowledge 210
step 5, shared resources. 210
substance division 209
system and environment 207
S-rules 55, 185
sampling 232
save 131, 285, 340
scheduler 262, 264
scheduling 230, 259, 260, 270, 289
scope unit 152, 153
scope units 156
SDL 55, 56, 94
SDL bits 119
SDL description 223, 224
SDL procedures 277, 278, 285
SDL run-time support system 258
SDL signals 231
SDL specification 221, 224
SELF 128
semaphores 261
Semi-active waiting 266, 291
send 261
SENDER 128
sendint 263
separately maintainable 359
server 160
services 204
SET 127
shared resources 201, 232, 261
signal 103, 189, 274
signal constraint 181
signal definition 120
signal parameter 189
signal signature 181
signal types 189
signal units 230, 273
signallists 100
signalroutes 105
similarities 365
Similarity 35, 213
software engineering 3

software process 239, 261
software structure 238
software structures 55
SOON 25, 47, 55, 56, 76
sort 121
specialisation 36, 363
SS 55, 56
ST diagram 52
start 108
starttimer 263
state 28, 39, 108, 230
state explosion 192, 260, 345
state hiding 188
state transition 28
state transition diagram 52, 95, 278
state transition table 278
state-oriented 40, 53, 188, 276
Stop 148
stoptimer 263
storage 28
String 136
STRUCT 140
structure 27, 30
structured programming 41, 42
structuring rules 185
Subject 6
substance 30, 53, 194
substructure 112, 113, 208
support software 258
synchronisation 232, 259, 265, 267, 289, 296
synchronous communication 160, 232, 260,
        269, 289, 292
Synchronous medium 232, 233
Synchronous operation 229
system 96, 186
system quality 334
systems engineering 9
systems engineering methodology 10
systemware 5

table-driven code 289
table-driven implementation 279
tailoring 382
target 330
target systems 9
task symbol 121
tellers 360
testing 335
text extension symbol 130
text symbol 100
time-critical 296

Time-dependent synchronisation 232
Time-independent synchronisation 233
time-out 263
time-out message 263
TIMER 127, 263
TO-clause 110
trace 40
traffic load 227
transition 110
Transition Chart 56, 87, 344, 347
transition charts 55
type 36, 121, 150
type hierarchy 79

unique! 128
USE 179, 180, 320
User 6, 66, 75
User name 75

valid instance environment 48
validate 15
validation 69, 334
ValPool 148
value 28
Variable 121, 123
variables 28
verification 334
verify 15
VIA 274
VIA-clause 110
VIEW/REVEAL 231
VIRTUAL 170
virtual SDL machine 278
virtual types 370
virtuality constraint 171

wait 261
waitint 263
waterfall model 17, 18